Burne-Jones

What can I write to please you?
Season's Greetings, I know, look
so thoughtless and impersonal on
their own; and I would not have
you think me more thoughtless
than ~~the~~ I truly am, which is
thoughtless enough. Nor would I
have you think the giving of
this gift – nothing in itself – a
gesture devoid of any but common
place Christmas feeling. In view of
the pain I've caused you during
this and previous years, either
suspicion could easily be justified.
Still the right words do not come,
and for fear that in looking for them
I might lose my way completely, I'll
give up the search, such as it has
been. Take this book, my love, as an
emblem of those words unsaid: just
as the pictures reproduced in the following
pages are substitutes for the real ones in
an exhibition you may fail to see, so
what I've written here – poor negative
sentences – ~~////~~ is a second-rate offering
to you who deserve better. Can you, in
the dim light ~~of~~ a reflection, perceive the
shape of that which is reflected? I
hope it will be a shape to please you.
——— Good bless; Yours, with fondest love,
        Stephen.
                    1975.

        x x x x x x x .

Burne-Jones

Martin Harrison &
Bill Waters

Barrie & Jenkins
London

© 1973 Bill Waters and Martin Harrison.
Text by Bill Waters, with additional research
and sections on stained-glass by Martin
Harrison.

Published in 1973 by Barrie & Jenkins Ltd.,
24 Highbury Crescent, London N5 1RX
Reprinted, 1974

Designed by Michael Carter.

Printed and bound by Cox & Wyman Ltd.,
London, Fakenham and Reading.

Colour separations by Colour Workshop Ltd.,
Hertford.

ISBN 0 214 65376 5

Contents

List of Illustrations

ix

x

Acknowledgements

This book has inevitably been a corporate effort and we are deeply indebted to a great number of people for their co-operation and encouragement.

Our thanks are due to all of the Museums and Galleries that we have visited throughout the British Isles, and those we have corresponded with abroad. In addition, many private collections have been readily made available to us both for study and photography, frequently accompanied by generous acts of hospitality. We wish to acknowledge the owners of these collections and all of those whose help has proved invaluable in the compilation of the book:

Mrs Raymond Asquith
David Bailey
Mrs G. K. E. Barber
Mrs E. S. Bell
Miss Mary Bennett
Wilfred Blunt
Miss Susan Booth
Peter Cannon-Brookes
Lord Carlisle
John Christian
Frank Constantine
Miss Clare Crick
Albert and Eleanor Dawson
Maurice Dunphy
Lord Faringdon
Ralph Fastnedge
Alfred Fisher
Rodney and Barbara Gathercole
Mrs Dione Gibson
David Gould
Derrick Gray
Richard Green
Francis Greenacre
The late Mrs Mark Hambourg
Miss M. G. Hampshire
Julian Hartnoll
Lord Henley
Robert Hogg
Peter Howell
Peter Hughes
Paul Joyce

Lady Karminski
The Hon. Mrs George Lambton
The Marquess of Lansdowne
The Leathart Family
Jeremy Maas
The late Denis Mackail
Lady Rosalie Mander
Mrs Joanna Matthews
Charles Newton
Mrs Winifred Nicholson
The Earl of Oxford and Asquith
Linda Parry
Dennis Perriam
Godfrey Pilkington
Mrs Noel Rooke
Mrs Mary Ryde
Miss Sophia Ryde
Joseph Setton
Charles Sewter
Peyton Skipwith
Jon Swannell
René Taylor
Lance and Kate Thirkell
Clive Wainwright
Robert Walker
The Hon. Mrs Elizabeth Wansborough
Miss M. E. Weaver
Michael and Cynthia Wickham
Miss Glennys Wild
The Rev. Wilbur C. Woodhams
Mrs Anne Yorke

Introduction

Burne-Jones stands for a type of introspective analysis that is certainly pre-Freud yet is nothing like so gauche or superficial as that of many of his contemporary painters. He stumbled upon a method of visual metaphor and used it in a profound and integrated way. His imagery is that of the unconscious mind, and instead of making reference to the eternal sexual snakes or phallic forms, he strikes deeper than the psychology of mass advertising and reaches the vocabulary of the unconscious itself. Burne-Jones's introspection at almost any other period in history would have been self-indulgent, but at the time when he operated the age of Romantic self-confidence was over; having found the world of the imagination, the new generation of artists was tired of the grand affirmations of the earlier Romantics and wished to travel deep into the interior of the imagination to discover how it operated. The self-analysis of Burne-Jones was a manifestation of the second phase of romanticism of English painting, which came after the confirmation of Turneresque rhetoric that man had conquered his primeval fears.

Today we must recognise what Burne-Jones offered both to his contemporaries and to the world today. In understanding his subject matter we grow to know ourselves. Working in the final phase of figurative painting Burne-Jones took it to an extreme and used the natural forms as a springboard to leap into the abstract world of ideas; in doing so he began to point to total abstraction. Although stretching his figurative forms to their limit he portrayed, or at least made direct reference to, things as we see them. At the same time he made commentary upon them by conjuring them into life by means of abstract elements—line, design, colour, etc. His exploration of subjective response anticipated the Surrealists and the Expressionists but this is not why he should be remembered today. There exists in his output the evidence of one man's struggle for self-discovery; Burne-Jones was a great man and his life's work is the symbol of the common experience. As an artist he painted in miniature the larger struggle of man to free himself from ignorance. Burne-Jones experienced a struggle not only in the content of his pictures: his technical development was equally long and painfully sought. Emerging from a period of precocious talent he was encouraged to explore the possibilities offered by the medium through the agency of Rossetti. Thus followed a series of small-scale intimate pictures of themes of love which are more personal than universal, exquisite documents of a gentle, romantic nature but essentially esoteric and available only to a very sympathetic eye. Impatient with the scale of these works Burne-Jones sought to strike a deeper psychological level and began to design paintings which had greater universality. Their themes were the same, but he rejected the intimate level of communication and couched his archetypal motifs in a universal language. In this he took his painting out of a backwater of English minor art and placed it in the mainstream of European cultural development.

Finally, in later life, he returned to the intimacy of his earlier years and produced, alongside his monumental works, a series of virtuoso drawings astonishing in their skill.

They are remarkable for their economy of technique and precision of content.

The Pre-Raphaelite revolt in 1848 inaugurated the modern movement by rejecting neo-classical formulae and Romantic rhetoric and by introducing a new reality based upon experience of the natural world as it actually appeared to the senses. Rossetti and Burne-Jones went further than truth-to-appearance and sought a personal truth based upon their own interpretation of reality, so taking the Pre-Raphaelite ideal into the twentieth century. Today art is liberated from this type of subjective reality, our day-to-day experience takes if for granted, but it was the Pre-Raphaelites who first began to clarify the way we perceive ourselves and our environment.

Chapter One

Youth

Had he been able to, Edward Jones would not have chosen the 28th of August 1833 and the centre of Birmingham as the time and place of his birth. He would have preferred Florence of the fifteenth century with Botticelli as a companion. But the glories of the Medici patronage were not for him and, like it or not, he was faced with the problem of living in an age of expanding materialism; his life was spent either fighting it or withdrawing from it.

Misfortune dogged his childhood, beginning with the death of his mother six days after he was born. Consequently his father identified the child with his terrible loss, and he could not bring himself to touch his son until he was four years old. His father, a shy, pious, man, was at a loss to know how to treat the infant, employing one incompetent nurse after another until, finally, a relative sought a more reliable guardian in the form of a Miss Sampson. She was, in the words of Georgiana Burne-Jones, the artist's wife, '. . . passionately devoted to Edward, and it is pathetic to think how slight a clue she ever had to his nature. He loved her in the way that children often love parents from whom they greatly differ, seeming never to criticise her and never confide in her. She was uneducated, with strong feelings and instincts, and she must have suffered much in seeing him, as he grew up, for ever slipping away from her, gently though he treated her, and tightly as she clutched him to her heart.'

Edward Richard Jones grew to love his son in an undemonstrative way, but there was nothing in his gentle nature to induce strong admiration, to fulfil the role of hero for his small, impressionable son. Towards the end of his life Edward recalled these memories of his father in a letter to Mrs Gaskell:

> . . . he was a very poetical little fellow—& very tender hearted & touching—quite unfit for the world into which he was pitched. We had very, very few books, but they were poets all of them—and I remember when I was about twelve or so he used to read me little poems he had made himself—but as time went he grew shy of reading them to me—he used to read in a touching voice, melodious and pathetic, believing everything he read. I never heard such sympathetic reading and he believed all good things that were ever said of anyone and was altogether unworldly & pious. Like his countrymen he knew nothing at all of Art and couldn't understand what it was all about or why it should be—but Tennyson was like that & so was Carlyle—but for nature he had a passion & would seldom miss a sunset if it could be seen & would walk tired miles to see a cornfield & loved solitude & had no friends—for he was quickly offended & thinner skinned than his companions such as I remember them, but Art was always a great bewilderment to him & he couldn't have learnt, in a thousand years to discern one thing about it—but had so much poetry in his nature as to unfit him for this world, poor little fellow.

Each year on the anniversary of her death Mr Jones took the young child to his wife's

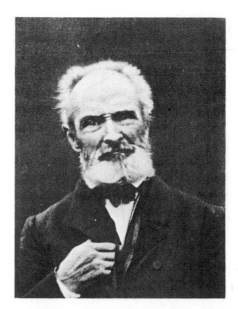

1. Edward Richard Jones, the artist's father, c. 1880
From the illustration in *Memorials*.

1

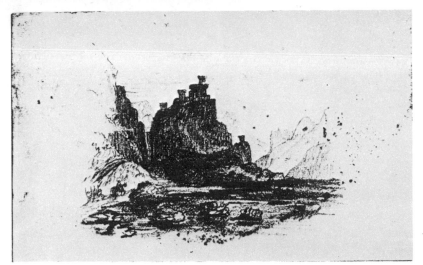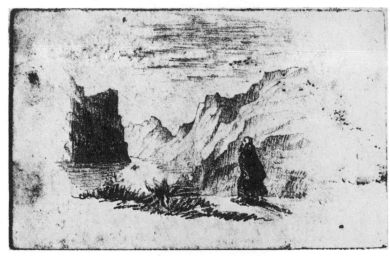

2–5. Four juvenile drawings; pencil, private collection

This is the type of drawing the artist had in mind when he said 'I was always drawing. Unmothered, with a sad papa, without sister or brother, always alone, I was never unhappy, because I was always drawing. . . . I couldn't draw people of course, but I never failed to draw mountains at the back of everything just as I do now [1890], though I'd never seen one.' The Gothic bridge is almost certainly a copy of an engraving.

grave and Edward would witness his father's tears. Insecure as a baby and growing increasingly aware of his isolation from those near to him, Edward developed a secret, inner life which he externalised in the form of drawings. When in later life an artist told him how, as a child, he never felt unhappy when alone, Burne-Jones replied:

'Ah, that was because you could draw. It was the same with me. I was always drawing. Unmothered, with a sad papa, without sister or brother, always alone, I was never unhappy, because I was always drawing. And when I think of what made the essence of a picture to me in those days it's wonderful how little I have stirred. I couldn't draw people, of course, but I never failed to draw mountains at the back of everything just as I do now, though I'd never seen one.'

There was a therapeutic necessity in his drawing, his insecurity led to restless nights with bad dreams, and in drawing the inventions of his vivid imagination he helped to release the tension resulting from his maladjustment. This is the subsequent role and character of the art of Burne-Jones; its singular autobiographical nature and passionate involvement indicate the part it played in his life.

Georgiana Burne-Jones recollects the alien quality of the interior of the Jones's household:

I recollect how destitute the house was of any visible thing that could appeal to imagination; chairs, carpets, tables and table furniture each duller and more commonplace than the other. The only objects that I saw within those walls that had a touch of humanity in them were some framed pieces of needlework that looked like windows into another world, because it seemed as if someone had been interested and amused in their making. Amongst them were two animals—one a lion with a face like a man, with a handsome aquiline nose—the other I believe, a tiger: also a smaller and finer piece of a girl mourning at a tomb, with a pendant which I forget. Over a mantlepiece and above a hard-featured clock was a picture of the church and churchyard of Snaith in Yorkshire which bristled with gravestones as if it had been a city cemetery. Miss Sampson told us that these were the tombs of her relatives, represented there as all together in order that the drawing might be kept within reasonable dimensions. Some pieces of old blue china, and the remnants of a Worcester dinner service copied from an Oriental pattern, together with a Sheffield-plated teapot and cream jug of elegant design were the only articles of household use that I remember as not actually ugly. Mr Jones himself seemed to care nothing for outside things unless they were connected in some way with his 'dear girl', as he named the wife who never grew old.

The Jones family was not wealthy, primarily because of Mr Jones's unwillingness to forgo the relaxed pace of his carving and gilding business. This did not upset the young Edward, as he later explained: 'Up to the time I was eighteen, I had only a penny a week for pocket money but that wasn't bad for me. There's not much talk of money among boys.'

When he was older, in order to buy the books he wanted, he raised money by making drawings of classical subjects and then auctioning them amongst his friends, or by selling

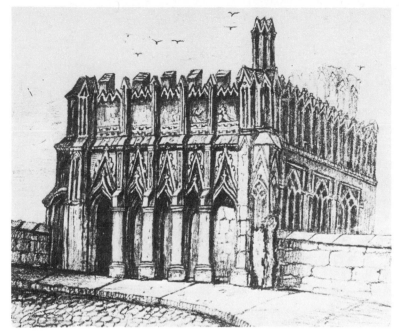
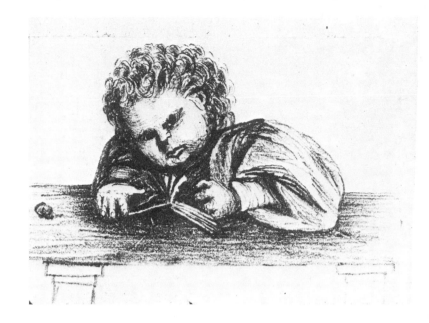

some books from his father's small collection.

In September 1844 at the age of eleven he began attending King Edward's School, Birmingham. At that time it was situated in New Street, not far from Bennett's Hill where he lived. Being a richly endowed school its students were not required to pay fees and, but for the cost of text-books, tuition was entirely free. That Edward was placed in the Commercial stream rather than the Classical indicates that at this point his father intended him for a career in Commerce. School, like his earlier childhood, had its traumas; he remembered them all his life and recalled them in the 1890s in conversation with his assistant, T. M. Rooke:

> There was a wretch of a boy who hated me horribly at school, he used to wait for me as I came out and, taking hold of my ankles, trundled me home on my hands, wheelbarrow fashion. He'd do this day after day until I could have killed him. I suppose he got tired of it at last. He called on me once here after I got known. I wouldn't see him, couldn't forgive the brute. He must have been always the same at heart. Now and then there used to be fights and I hated that. One day in school a very big boy sent me a message on a slip of paper that he'd fight me after school. How I got through the rest of the morning's work I don't know, for I was in an awful state of terror. When school was over and we were surrounded by the circle of boys I flew at him, and, to my astonishment down he went like a log—then I was sick as a dog.

Another incident made a strong impression:

'I was stabbed at school. . . the boy who did it was simply furious with me. It may have been my fault for anything I can remember—we hated each other I know.'

T. M. Rooke: 'Was it badly?'

'Yes rather, it was in the groin, which was in a dangerous place. It didn't hurt much, but I felt something warm from my leg and putting my hand there, I found it was blood. Then I was sick and afterwards I fainted and one of the masters went home with me in a cab. It had been during prayers and so was kept from the headmaster of course, I never told, boys never do, and when the doctor came to me he promised not to tell my father—I was home for over a week.'

These incidents occurred in the 1840s, within the context of Birmingham, an expanding industrial city. Bennett's Hill itself was respectable enough, but a short distance away there were densely populated slums. In the mid-1840s Birmingham had a population of approximately 220,000; nearly a quarter lived in two hundred undrained courts, many of which were unpaved. A statement published in 1842 declared:

'The streets are a scandal to the name—a nuisance in wet, and a greater nuisance in dry weather; the footpaths in the centre of the town would disgrace a rural village: both footway and horseway, in the remote streets and the outskirts, are but alternation of kennel

3

and mire; the lighting is little better than darkness visible.'

From 1843 onwards improvements were made as the city developed its civic pride, but the miseries of the poor were deeply imprinted on Jones's mind. He was to describe them vividly in a short story he wrote while at Oxford, in which a young man walking through a city at night stumbles upon the pathos of life among the poor:

'Oh! Richard—Dickey, doant—mercy! you'll hurt the child—oh!' God! the cry that went up shrieking to thy heaven—oh! didst Thou hear it? yet there came down no thunder nor fire, nor did the ground beneath open and consume. She had gone down before that fearful blow, her poor head striking, as it fell, against the projecting window frame—surely she is dead: three or four men came out of the tap room at the cry, for it was keen and piercing. I saw that they were drunk, all of them, like the monster who had done this evil deed he stood leaning against the wall, all unconscious uttering curses. I was kneeling upon the snow beside her now; it was a cruel sight beneath the glimmer of the lamp-light—her cheek and mouth were full of blood; as I raised her head it flowed over me; presently I think she would have choked in the swoon: her bonnet fell from her to the ground as I lifted her, and her hair, wet with trampled snow, was long and raven black. I took no heed to the inarticulate gabble round me; I knew the wretch had staggered towards me, making the air black with oaths, that his silly, half-witted comrades were doing their feeble best to lead him back, and once my arm received a kick meant for the helpless form it shielded. . . .

. . . the hand was very firmly clasping something—both hands; surely not a child?

'Wot's up 'ere, Sir?—a woman drunk I s'pose.'

'Oh policeman, look down here—look at this child.' He stopped and disengaged it tenderly enough for the man.

'Why it's dead, Sir, stone dead—but not yet cold; may be she killed it herself a-fallin.'

'No, no, no; the man's in there, in there her husband, who struck her down.' There was horror upon my face I know, and pride of experience in his voice as he answered; 'Why, bless yer, sir, these thing's 'appen plenty enough; every night pretty nigh.'

'See her looked to and sheltered for the night, and from the brute in there.' Then I left money with him and hurried away.'

There is no doubt that Jones is exaggerating in the cause of his story and that the subject and melodramatic atmosphere derive from his study of Dickens, Walter Scott, and Charlotte M. Yonge. It would, perhaps, be too much to deduce that Jones saw child-murders of this kind when he was a youth, but the story as a whole implies more than a literary acquaintance with these conditions.

But the time he spent at King Edward's School was by no means always gloomy. He developed a reputation for his humour; his practical jokes created a legend, and his habit of caricaturing his masters provided a source of amusement for his fellow pupils.

His circle of friends increased as did his intellectual ability; many, like him, were to progress to Oxford, among them Cormell Price, Richard Watson Dixon, George Macdonald, and William Fulford. By the time he was fifteen he had become an intelligent, quiet student with a wide knowledge of literature, fascinated by ancient and exotic cultures, and with a great sense of fun. At this time, on the recommendation of one of his teachers, he was transferred from the Commercial to the Classical stream. During the same year he began attending the Government School of Design for three evenings a week. His transference from the Commercial stream indicates that his father no longer wished to send him to Newcastle to train as an engineer as he had previously intended. Continuing to study at the School of Design after this change of direction demonstrates that drawing was no longer just an amusement for him, and that he began to take it more seriously and felt a need to apply greater discipline to his talent.

The curriculum was typical for an institution of this kind, insisting on basic exercises, minimalising the creative aspects. When opened, in 1842, the school provided the following:

4

Section I—Elementary Instruction.
1. Drawing, outline drawing, geometrical and freehand. Shadowing use of chalks, etc. Drawing from the round; drawing from nature, including anatomy, proportion and landscape.
2. Modelling from the antique and from nature.
3. Instruction in colours, water colours, including water body-colours and fixed oil-colours. Copies of coloured drawings, and colourings from nature.
4. Isometrical perspective.
Section II—Instruction.
1. History, principles and practice of ornamental art. This includes the antique styles, styles of the middle ages, and modern styles, with lectures.
Section III—Instruction in designs for manufactures, including study of the various processes of manufacture and practice of design for individual branches of industry.
Evidence of his having undertaken the first section at least is provided in Georgiana Burne-Jones's *Memorials*. She describes '. . . a neat little home-made note-book . . . containing carefully copied out lessons and exercises upon the principles of light and shade, together with diagrams of primary, secondary and tertiary colours. "Notes etc. on Water Colouring" it is called.'

From childhood Edward Jones suffered from frequent bouts of illness. He was handicapped by a weak chest for which he was sent yearly to country areas where he would

6. New Street, Birmingham in the 1840s. From a contemporary lithograph
On the left is King Edward's school, which was designed by Barry and Pugin, their first collaboration. Later they were responsible for the Houses of Parliament. Bennett's Hill is off to the right, a short distance up New Street.

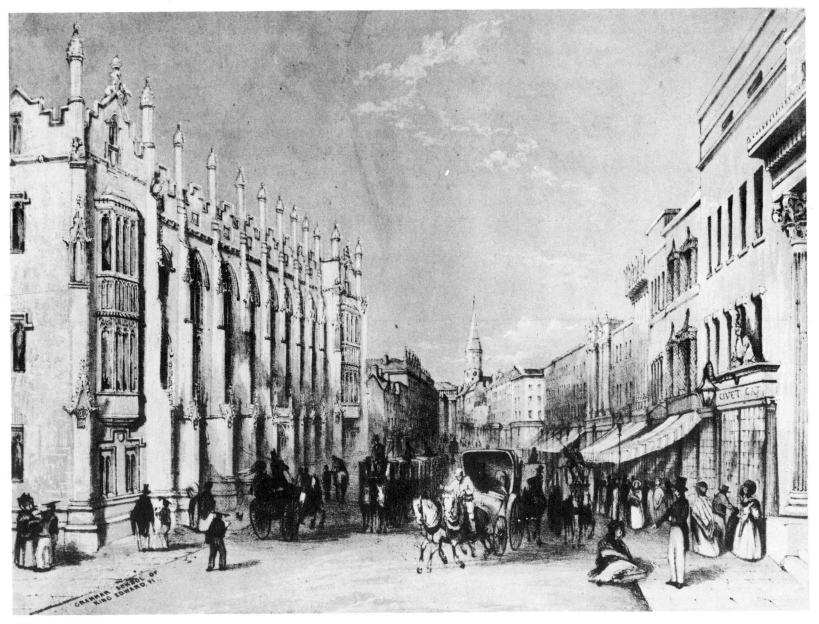

benefit from the cleaner air and out-of-doors activities. On one occasion, at Hereford, he met the newly ordained Rev. John Goss—an important event in his life; Goss introduced him to the spiritual mysteries of the Oxford Movement. In the setting of the ancient cathedral they appealed to his artistic imagination, especially after a recent dose of spartan ritual in Birmingham's evangelical churches. Begun in the 1830s by Keble, Froude, Newman, and Pusey, the Oxford Movement aimed at a new interpretation of the Thirty-Nine Articles. Its followers wished to purge the Church of the shame and errors they felt had accumulated from the time of Henry's reformation; to reinstate the dogma; and to remind Christians of the presence of the supernatural in everyday life. Above all, they sought to reintroduce the sacramental mysteries of the Mass. Mysticism of this type was calculated to fire the young artist. He began to study their writing, recognising in it an antidote to the materialism of his contemporaries. Writing many years later he described the nature of Newman's influence on him:

> In an age of sofas and cushions he taught me to be indifferent to comfort; and in an age of materialism he taught me to venture all on the unseen and this so early that it was well in me when life began, and I was equipped before I went to Oxford with a real good panoply.

A short time after this, on a holiday spent with his Aunt in the Leicestershire country-side, he visited Mount St Bernard, a Cistercian monastery newly built from Pugin's plan, in the Charnwood Forest. In this confined and secluded world of meditation he felt he had found his vocation. Leading a life of spiritual purpose amid beautiful surroundings, the monks glided silently before him; it was an image he retained all his life and the memory of it influenced much of his subsequent ideas (as late as 1894 he was writing 'And more and more my heart is pining for that monastery in Charnwood Forest.') Nothing seemed to have changed since the Middle Ages. The extent to which it captured his imagination is revealed in letters he wrote to his friend Lizzie Catherwood in 1850.

> To her most Celestial Highness, ye Ladye Annie Catherwood, May it please your ladyshippe, having been deputed by ye Ladye Catherwood, Countesse of Adding-toune, to advise you concerning sundrie articles of wearing apparelle, appertaining to Hornsie Universitie, your humble servante hath presumed to address this epistle. . . .

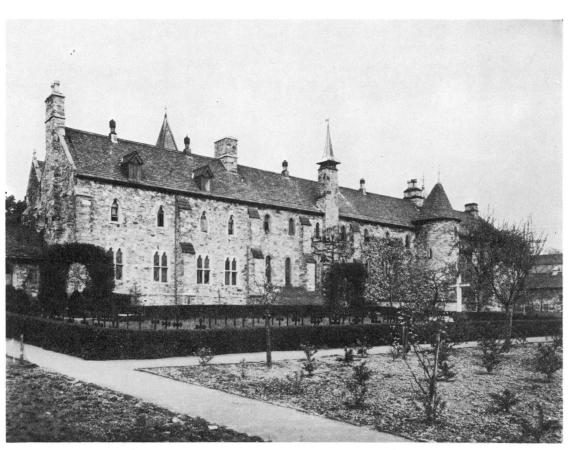

7. Mount St Bernard's Abbey. A monastery of the Cistercian order set in the Charnwood Forest, Leicestershire

At the age of eighteen Jones visited the site and was deeply impressed by the buildings, which had been designed by Pugin, and the authentic medieval atmosphere created by the monks, who were not allowed to talk except during strictly observed periods.

. . . Forasmuch as after diligent search made throughout our domains, and all thereunto appertainings, onlie two of the four articles of luxurie (whereof we were by you advised) have been discovered, it hath seemed good to our royalle person, at the instance of our secretarie Edouard, Cardinal de Byrmynghame, to send you timelie warnynge thereof to the ende that summarie measures be forthwith taken by you for the reclaiming of them. Given under our hand, at this place of Addington this 8th. day of June. A.S.H. 1850.

The letter, containing a postscript signed by 'Edouard Cardinal de Byrmyngham' himself, is written in red ink and imitates a medieval illuminated manuscript. Another letter of the same year from Hereford also conveys his exuberance:

Land of Caradoc,
Banks of the Wye.

Dear old Crom [Cormell Price]

You scamp not to write before; here I've been expecting a long, brilliant effusion of your scribbling powers, with a fine poetic description of your peregrinations, and you favour me with a 'skinny' affair lying before me—and now I'll be revenged . . .

The morning sun is just up as I emerge from the blankets, the hills of Wales mantled in snow lie beyond, and the meandering Wye flows between us. So soon as bound in cloth I wander by the banks of the lovely river, or round the Castle Green, get into a romantic fit, think how happy we should be together learning Welch, then bolt doors and bolt breakfast. This is about the third hour of the day; the next two hours are spent in sweet converse or reading (not Thucydides) and by this time it is Cathedral time, and for an hour I am in paradise. Oh that you could be with me then! From 12–3, I wander about the country, in the most romantic holes you can imagine, from 3–4 Cathedral, 4–8 occupied, I am sorry to say, in eating and taking dinner and tea. Then my reading hours commence, and I never think of going to bed before 1–2 or 3, or even later. Parties are horrible things. . . .

Already the legends of Wales were more than stories to him; as he walked among the hills and valleys they were transfigured by the force of his imagination into the land of faery. Intuitively, the Celt in him responded to the land of his forefathers. Under the same circumstances he first became aware of the sea and ships, 'I got all my strongest impressions of the beauty of ships and the sea from the Welsh coast.' Subsequently, he always saw them as partly magical things, carrying Norsemen off to strange lands or imprisoning sailors about to be destroyed by sirens.

He had, at this time, the wide interests which were to characterise the breadth of his learning in later years. In 1850 we find him visiting the British Museum to see the Nimroud Assyrian sculptures. Of these he wrote to his father:

I was quite surprised at the clearness and beauty of the sculpture. The bas-reliefs seem to be as perfect as when they emerged from the workman's shop, tho' not quite so clean. They seem to have had a very good idea of anatomy, in which they far out-strip the Egyptians; the feet and hands seem to have been their chief study and the muscles of the arms are finely portrayed.

The Ethnographical gallery gratified me, the Central Saloon pleased me. The Zoological gallery gratified me, the Mammalia Saloon delighted me, the Lycian, Nimroud, Phigalian, Elgin, Egyptian, Etruscan and above all the Fossil rooms put me into ecstacies. I spent a considerable time in the Egyptian rooms, which in point of antiquity excel even the Assyrian.

Price should have been with me to have seen the fossils—Marsilaceae, Equisetaceae, Lycopodaceae, Ashphodeleae, Euphorbiaceae, Ichthiosauri, Plesiosauri, etc., etc., etc.

Early in 1852 Edward first made a visit to the home of his friend Macdonald in Handsworth together with 'Crom', and through the eyes of Macdonald's sister, Georgiana, who later became Mrs Jones, we have the first recorded description of him:

Rather tall and very thin, though not especially slender, straightly built with wide shoulders. Extremely pale he was, with the paleness that belongs to fair people, and he looked delicate but not ill. His hair was perfectly straight, and of a colourless

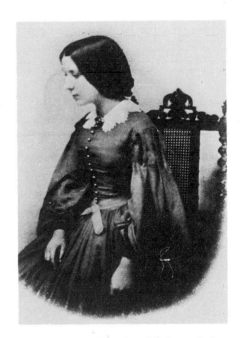

8. Georgiana Macdonald, the artist's future wife, aged sixteen.

Daughter of a methodist minister, she and her sisters married notable people. Louie married into the Baldwin family and Agnes married Edward J. Poynter, the painter. From *Memorials*.

kind. His eyes were light grey (if their colour could be described in words), and the space that their setting took up under his brow was extraordinary: the nose quite right in proportion, but very individual in outline, and a mouth large and well-moulded, the lips meeting with absolute sweetness and repose. The shape of his head was domed, and noticeable for its even balance; his forehead, wide and rather high, was smooth and calm, and the line of the brow over the eyes was a fine one. From the eyes themselves power simply radiated, and as he talked and listened, if anything moved him, not only his eyes but his whole face seemed lit up from within. I learned afterwards that he had an immovable conviction that he was hopelessly plain. His ordinary manner was shy, but not self-conscious, for it gave the impression that he noticed everything. At that time he sat as many men do who are not very strong, sunk down rather low in his chair with an appearance of the whole spine seeking for rest.

She continues by saying that he had a commanding way of speaking, that his voice was beautiful to hear but that he was obviously unused to young children. Georgie's description, although coloured by her fondness for Edward, is none the less consistent with later evidence.

Meanwhile his studies continued and, like his friends Price and Dixon, he had decided to go to Oxford University and to take Holy Orders. The Rev. Goss had recommended that he choose Exeter College. This he did, despite the tradition that men from King Edward's School should enter Pembroke. On June 1, 1852 he presented himself at Oxford for matriculation. His choice of Exeter College had, without him knowing it, great significance for him since it was also the choice of William Morris. The two actually sat next to one another in the examination, though having no friends in common at this time they did not make acquaintance. When the results of the examination were declared Jones found he had tied with a fellow student for a scholarship. Some time was spent deciding in whose favour the scholarship should be given and finally it was decided against him. Fortunately, however, his father was prepared to send him at his own expense. Even so, Jones became ill as a result of the tension, a reaction to stress which was to recur throughout his life. By January 1853, however, he had completely recovered and, in the middle of that month he went up to Oxford full of hope and excitement.

Chapter Two

Oxford

At first, Jones's new situation supplied the reality he sought: 'Oxford is a glorious place; godlike! at night I have walked round the colleges under the full moon, and thought it would be heaven to live and die here. The Dons are so terribly majestic, and the men are men, in spirit as well as name—they seem overflowing with generosity and good nature.'

The city that he found, like the monastery of St Bernard, impressed him as possessing the very spirit of the Middle Ages. Its ancient buildings 'set amidst winding streets full of the sound of many bells' filled him with delight. In his maturity he recalled:

> It was a different Oxford in those days from anything that a visitor would now dream of. On all sides, except where it touched the railway, the city ended abruptly, as if a wall had been about it, and you came suddenly upon the meadows. There was little brick in the city, it was either grey with stone or yellow with the wash of pebble-dash in the poorer streets. It was an endless delight to us to wander about the streets, where were still many old houses with wood-carvings and a little sculpture here and there. The Chapel of Merton College had lately been renovated by Butterfield, and Pollen, a former Fellow of Merton, had painted the roof of it. Many an afternoon we spent in that chapel. Indeed I think the buildings of Merton and the cloisters of New College were our chief shrines in Oxford.

Being freshmen together at Exeter College Jones and Morris became friends and quickly discovered the great deal they had in common. An intimate friendship sprang up between them and from this time on they were inseparable, walking together in the surrounding country or in their much-loved city.

Morris was born in 1834 into a wealthy middle-class family who lived on the outskirts of Epping Forest at Walthamstow. His background was different in every aspect from that of Jones; he was the eldest boy of a family of nine; they lived in a large Georgian house in a rural area. His childhood had been spent roaming the countryside on a pony. About the forest he said: 'I was born and bred in its neighbourhood and when I was a boy and a young man knew it yard by yard from Wanstead to the Theydons and from Hale End to the Fairlop Oak.' The creations of God were not his only interest, he was as absorbed by those of man; from an early age he knew intimately the old Essex churches with their monuments and brasses. At thirteen he entered Marlborough College, Wiltshire where his father had bought a place for him some time before he died. Although robust by nature, he despised, like the young Jones, the traditional field games and preferred to take his exercise rambling over the woods and surrounding hills. In 1852 he left Marlborough to study privately under a tutor prior to going to Oxford. Like Jones, he too had Welsh blood, and was passionately fond of Gothic buildings and Walter Scott. The College had a

9

strong High Church bias, and William Morris left school a 'pronounced Anglo-Catholic' like his new friend, and intending to enter the Church.

Morris and Jones realised soon that although the setting of the University was magnificent, the teaching was languid and indifferent. They were alienated by the pompous and boring style of the lecturers, and found no pleasure in the debauches of their fellow students. Little was left of the heated involvement in the Anglo-Catholic revival of ten years ago, when the debates in the union were almost wholly devoted to it. In contrast, most students were indifferent to such matters, and consequently the two friends were disillusioned by their discoveries at the university that had promised so much. The effect was to create a bond between them, together with the Birmingham men from Pembroke whom they frequently met. A group thus formed which found strength in common interests; under the leadership of Morris and Jones they gradually evolved a community of ideas which they had been unable to find in their formal studies. At this time, apart from Morris and Jones, the group consisted of Fulford, 'a hard and deep thinker with a perfectly magnetic influence over truth', Dixon, 'a most interesting man, as ladies would say, dark haired and pale faced with a beautiful brow, and deep melancholy voice', and Faulkner, not from Birmingham and not hitherto known by Jones. Faulkner's rooms provided the place for the group to meet. They were on a ground floor in a corner of the picturesque old quadrangle at Pembroke College. Here they discussed poetry, which they read to one another, and points of Church doctrine.

Letters written to Cormell Price, 'Crom', still at King Edward's, who was to join them the next year, outline the reading undertaken by the group. In these, Jones mentions Pope, Dryden, Moore, Alexander Smith, Keats, Shelley, Coleridge, and discusses at length Tennyson's 'Locksley Hall'. For the latter poet is reserved the highest praise, for he has

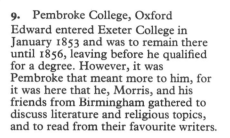

9. Pembroke College, Oxford
Edward entered Exeter College in January 1853 and was to remain there until 1856, leaving before he qualified for a degree. However, it was Pembroke that meant more to him, for it was here that he, Morris, and his friends from Birmingham gathered to discuss literature and religious topics, and to read from their favourite writers.

10. William Morris aged twenty-three, taken in 1857. From *Memorials*.

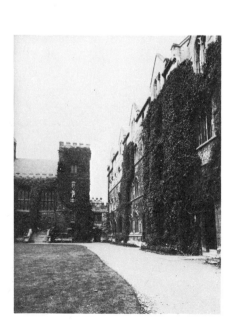

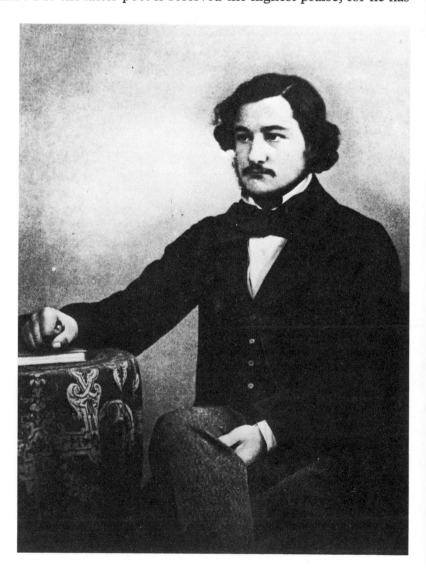

afforded Jones 'hours of unmitigated happiness', and is 'the only poet worth following far into dreamland.'

It is interesting to notice how this poem, and other literature they were reading, figures in Charlotte M. Yonge's book *The Heir of Redclyffe*, a favourite of theirs, which had been published in 1853. The novel was an instant success. Its author was a close friend of John Keble and an admirer of Hurrell Froude, so it is not surprising that her novel reflects their ideas. Guy Morville, the hero of the piece, was 'an absolute expression of the hero for the Oxford Movement, both in his life and in his death.' He is drawn as a hot-tempered, impetuous young man who struggles to transcend his limitations through rigorously applied self-discipline, and finally dies of a fever caught whilst nursing his enemy. The episode of the timely arrival at his deathbed of a priest to minister the last rites of the Church endeared the book to many Tractarians. Sir Guy was, in the 1850s, a popular hero; the group were certainly not alone in identifying with him. There are other aspects of the book, however, which influenced them. Throughout the story the characters make reference to Fouqué's 'Sintram', a romantic tale built around Dürer's engraving of 'Knight, Death and the Devil', and another of their highly esteemed books. There are parallels between the heroes of the two; Guy and Sintram each occupy a Gothic castle situated high amongst craggy rocks, and they both wrestle with their fate, assisted by the chastening influence of female companionship. It seems likely that the group was introduced to 'Sintram' through reading *The Heir*, but it also introduced them to another, even more important book. At one point, when the characters are playing a parlour game Guy, as a forefeit, declares his favourite character in fiction to be 'Sir Galahad—the knight of the Seige Perilous—who won the Saint Grael'; he mentions *Morte d'Arthur* and lists its merits: 'The depth, the mystery, the allegory—the beautiful characters of some of the knights.'

Malory's *Morte d'Arthur* was to become perhaps the greatest source of Burne-Jones's imagery, and he kept the book close by him throughout his life. He referred to Sir Galahad in the letters to 'Crom', and in one of these he first announces the idea of a brotherhood:

'Remember, I have set my heart on founding a Brotherhood. Learn Sir Galahad by heart. He is to be the patron of our order. I have enlisted *one* in the project up here heart and soul. You shall have a copy of the canons some day.

General of the Order of Sir Galahad.'

The 'Sir Galahad' he tells 'Crom' to learn is the poem by Tennyson, who had included in his collection of 1842 a version of the *Morte d'Arthur* story. Discovery and admiration of Malory is typical of the period, and is reflected in the success of *The Heir* in the 1850s and by the interest in Tennyson's earlier Arthurian poems.

The purpose of the Brotherhood was to make a 'Crusade and holy warfare against the age . . . the heartless coldness of the times.' It was based upon an idea in Hurrell Froude's *Project for the Revival of Religion in Great Towns*. He planned to create a conventual society of cleric and lay members who could pioneer Christianity in the poor areas of London. The group, especially Jones, was so fervent in its admiration of literary heroes that they hoped in this conventual brotherhood to emulate the knights who searched for the holy grail. As Tractarians they were also concerned with the mystical rites of the Mass as symbolised by the grail; though not pursuing it throughout the world, they were at least agitating for the return of sacramental mysteries into Christian daily life.

Jones first discovered a copy of *Morte d'Arthur* in a Birmingham bookshop and unhappily was unable to afford it; each day he returned, making some excuse to spend some time in the shop so that he could read it. Finally, when Morris was on a visit he secured the precious volume and they spent many hours reading it together, and to the rest of the Birmingham men.

Among contemporary writers their greatest admiration was for Ruskin. They eagerly read each of his volumes as it appeared, *Modern Painters*, *The Seven Lamps of Architecture*, and *Stones of Venice*. Ruskin gave them something definite to follow up the romantic images of 'Sintram' and *The Heir*; he gave them an intellectual justification for their love of the Middle Ages. But Ruskin was something more to them than an intellectual hero; he was able to show, particularly in his famous chapter 'On the Nature of Gothic' that there

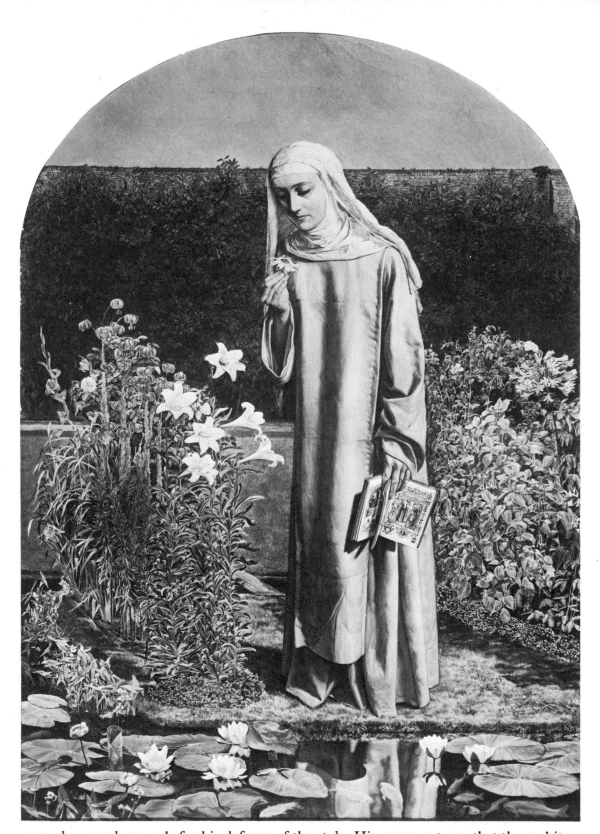

11. 'Convent Thoughts' by Charles Alston Collins, 1851, oil on canvas, $33\frac{1}{8} \times 23\frac{1}{4}$.* The Ashmolean Museum, Oxford

One of the first Pre-Raphaelite pictures that Edward Jones saw, he encountered it when he visited the collection of Thomas Combe in Oxford in 1855. Its influence can be seen in some of the drawings from the *Fairy Family*.

* Unless otherwise indicated, all measurements of works are given in inches.

were also moral grounds for his defence of the style. His argument was that the architectural styles that preceeded did not include opportunities for the individual craftsmen to express themselves. By reducing their decoration to simple patterns or highly stylised figurative adornments the Greek and Assyrian architects deliberately restricted their craftsmen to uncreative and automatic work. Ruskin argued that this was intolerable and that the Gothic style enabled each man to contribute his own particular decoration within the overall compass of the building. These arguments appealed to the group's social consciences, and for Morris in particular it was to affect considerably the course of his later thinking. Another aspect of Ruskin's theories was to influence Edward Jones at this time; in *Modern Painters* Ruskin stresses the importance of accurate observation of nature in all its forms, from rocks to clouds and from bird's feathers to leaf veins; he insisted that in drawing nature all detail must be respected. As a result, Edward began drawing in the woods and fields around Oxford, those same woods that Millais and Charles Alston Collins had been drawing in some two years before, under the same impetus. His enthusiasm for Ruskin is conveyed in a letter dated May 1853: '. . . he is the most profound investigator of the objective that I know of; the whole work [*Modern Painters*] is evidence of a painfully careful study of nature, universally and particularly; in aesthetics he is an authority.' And in another letter of November 8th the same year he wrote that Ruskin was '. . . in prose what Tennyson is in Poetry and what the Pre-Raphaelites are in painting, full of devotion and love for the subject.'

During the years after the first flourish of the Oxford Movement a number of philanthropic and educative schemes arose in an attempt to improve the social conditions of the poorer classes. As we have seen, the Birmingham group were stirred into these activities by Froude's writings, and they were quick to appreciate those of the Christian Socialists, Charles Kingsley and F. D. Maurice, and of a man sympathetic to them, Thomas Carlyle. Kingsley's *Alton Locke*, read at this time by the group, is a type of propaganda novel for the Christian Socialist Movement reflecting its bitterness against social evils:

Oh! Crossthwaite, are not children a blessing?
Would they be a blessing to me now? No, my lad. Let those bring slaves into the world who will! I will never beget children to swell the numbers of those who are trampling each other down in the struggle for daily bread, to minister in ever deepening poverty and misery to the rich man's luxury—perhaps his lust.'

Compare this with an extract from a letter Kingsley wrote to his wife in October 1849:

I was yesterday over the cholera districts of Bermondsey; and Oh God what I saw! people having no water to drink—hundreds of them—but the water of the common sewer which stagnated full of . . . dead fish, cats and dogs, under their windows. At the time the cholera was raging, Walsh saw them throwing untold horrors into the ditch, and then dipping out the water and drinking it. . . . Oh, that I had the tongue to tell what I saw myself, to stir up some rich men to go and rescue them from the tyranny of the small shopkeeping landlords, who get their rents out of the flesh of these men.

Similar bitterness and indignation was felt by Jones and his group, and they were anxious to do something about it. Primarily for this they founded *The Oxford and Cambridge Magazine* in 1855.

It would be erroneous however, to imply that the young men were pondorous or long-faced. They were able to combine in vigorous horseplay and practical jokes—amusing themselves by pouring water from Dixon's garret on to the crowd below and by ragging Morris, whose temper was quickly aroused. Much time was spent riding into the surrounding countryside, collecting brass rubbings, boating and fencing and boxing at Maclaren's gymnasium in Oriel Lane. Archibald Maclaren was an interesting and colourful personality, something of an intellect as well as an athlete; he became friendly with the young men and invited them out to his house in Summertown, just outside Oxford, where he encouraged them to discuss their interests. Visits to his house became a regular feature of each term and it was through them that he discovered that Jones could draw competently. He invited him to supply illustrations for a book he planned called *Fairy Family*, a collection of European fairy stories which, as initially conceived, was to have many illustrations. Edward began work upon them in 1854.

Meanwhile, he had encountered the work of the Pre-Raphaelite brothers; Millais and Collins, two years earlier, were working in Oxford, and Holman Hunt was also there painting in 1852. They were often discussed amongst the people who had known them; one of these, a printseller, had in turn become friendly with Edward Jones. He related stories of their activities to the ambitious young student who listened with enthusiasm and envy. Also known to the dealer, who actually displayed his work for sale, was a land-

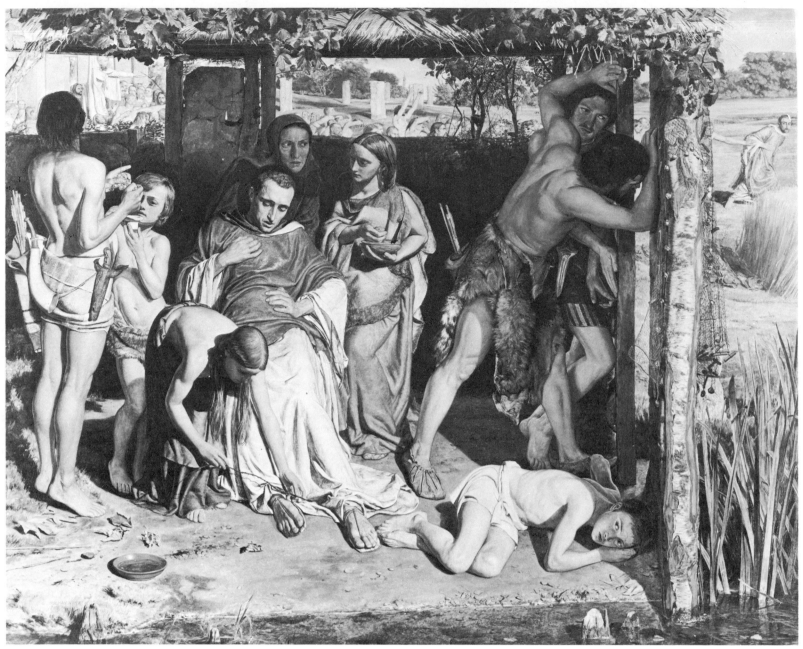

12. 'Early Britons Sheltering a Missionary From the Druids' by William Holman Hunt, 1850, oil on canvas, 43¾ × 52½. The Ashmolean Museum, Oxford

Like Collins's 'Convent Thoughts', this painting was seen by Jones in 1855 in the Combe collection.

scape painter, Alfred Hunt. Hunt, like Jones, had completed his education by a term at Oxford. Afterwards, he devoted himself entirely to his art, which must have especially impressed the embryonic artist in Jones.

In 1854, Ruskin's Edinburgh lectures, including discussion of the Pre-Raphaelites, were published and eagerly read by Jones. In the same year he saw Millais's 'Return of the Dove to the Ark' at Oxford. During the summer vacation on a visit to London, he attended the Royal Academy and saw Holman Hunt's 'Light of the World' and 'The Awakening Conscience'. Writing about the visit, he said, 'I saw the Preraphaelites had indeed come at a time when there was need for them and resolved after my little ability to depend and claim a patient hearing from them.'

Morris, during his vacation, made a tour of Belgium and Northern France, and returned full of enthusiasm for the cathedrals he saw, and full of praise for the Flemish painters Van Eyck and Memling. On this trip he discovered Dürer and brought back a collection of photographs of his work.

Having so much in common, and feeling the discoveries they had made were important not only for themselves but for the world at large, the group grew in strength; its members came to rely upon the stimulation of communal ideas to an extent that when isolated from it they felt deprived. We find Jones writing during the vacation that he 'longed to be back with Morris and his glorious company of martyrs.' He was still completely confident that

14

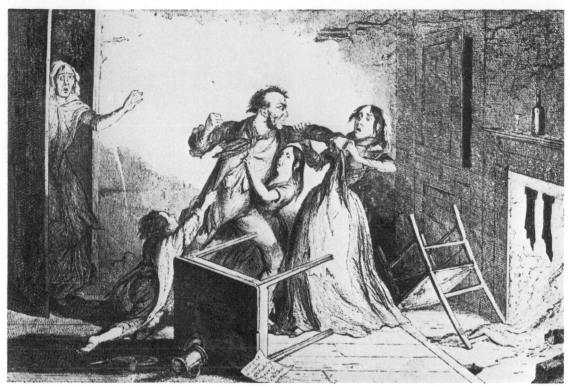

the celibate society in London would come into being: '. . . the monastery stands a fairer chance than ever of being founded, I know it will some day.' Autumn term that year, 1854, was spent discussing their recent discoveries. They visited the Bodleian Library to see the medieval illuminated manuscripts and to read ancient chronicles. They took to reading the Shakespeare plays aloud. Morris began writing verse which was Gothic in spirit and word. He called his first poem 'The Willow and the Red Cliff'. It is strongly influenced by *The Heir of Redclyffe* and the verse:

> One day when the wind moaned through that tree
> As it moans now through the willow
> On the cliffs sat a woman clasping her knee
> O'er the rise and fall of the billow.

echoes a passage from the novel:

> On he rushes, reckless whither he went, or what he did; driven forward by the wild impulse of passion, far over moor and hill, up and down, till at last exhausted at once by the tumult within, and by the violent bodily exertion, a stillness—a suspension of thought and sensation—ensued; and when this passed, he found himself seated on a rock which crowned the summit of one of the hills, his handkerchief loosened, his waistcoat open, his hat thrown off, his temples burning and throbbing with a feeling of distraction. . . .

Charlotte Yonge frequently uses the image of the sea overlooked from the vantage point of high, craggy cliffs as a symbol of wild passion. The similarities show how deep the novel had sunk into Morris's imagination; later we shall see how it had a similar effect upon Jones's drawing of this time.

Edward Jones was equally capable of a passionate response to something which stirred his Gothic sensitivity:

> I have just come in from my terminal pilgrimage to Godstowe ruins and the burial place of Fair Rosamund. The day has gone down magnificently; all by the river's side I came back in a delirium of joy the land was so enchanted with bright colours, blue and purple in the sky, shot over with a dust of golden shower, and in the water a

mirror'd counterpart, ruffled by a light west wind—and in my mind pictures of the old days, the abbey, and long processions of the faithful, banners of the cross, copes and crosiers, gay knights and ladies by the river bank, hawking-parties and all the pageantry of the golden age—it made me feel so wild and mad that I had to throw stones into the water to break the dream. I never remember having such an unutterable ecstasy, it was quite painful with intensity, as if my forehead would burst. I get frightened of indulging now in dreams, so vivid that they seem recollections rather than imaginations, but they seldom last more than half-an-hour; and the sound of earthly bells in the distance, and presently the wreathing of steam upon the trees where the railway runs, called me back to the years I cannot convince myself I am living in.

As well as making the illustrations for Maclaren, he was exercising his skill in other ways—his friend Macdonald had found him making designs for 'The Lady of Shalott'; yet the *Fairy Family* occupied most of his artistic effort. The sequence of fairy tales provided him with an opportunity to display his romantic imagination. They are finely wrought and betray a close study of contemporary illustration, the work of Birket Foster, 'Dicky' Doyle (who illustrated Ruskin's fairy tale 'The King of the Golden River', 1850), Cruikshank, and the illustrators of Dickens and Walter Scott. Minuteness of detail in their execution and the technique of cross-hatching to create shadow, reveal a considerable knowledge of the discipline of drawing for wood engraving. The subjects themselves show many influences at play, Walter Scott's paraphernalia of medieval battles, Charlotte Yonge's savage seas and solitary heroes, her large evocative setting suns and rising moons, and there is at least one Byronic prisoner. In short, the drawings at this stage were a brilliant interpretation of a typical early-Victorian fantasy. Throughout the series there are certain shortcomings in the draughtsmanship, but they do not interfere with the total success. Certain features are prophetic of the artist's later preoccupation with the illustrated books. The series is conceived as working closely with the text; each illustration is laid out so as to allow space for the printing and to incorporate it into the total impression of the page. This is not mere illustration of a story but an attempt to create a beautiful object in book form. As a consequence, the set comprises not only illustrations but decorative letters to head each chapter and a humourously illuminated title page; the latter features very much in the style of 'Dicky' Doyle and not far removed from those of 'The King of the Golden River'. The other influence which emerged in the drawings was, significantly, that of the Pre-Raphaelites. One can trace a movement away from the quaintness, towards refinement and a tighter psychological control derived from a greater familiarity with their painting and illustration. After his initial contact with their work at the Royal Academy he saw more of it in the collections of Thomas Combe at Oxford and G. B. Windus at Tottenham. Also during 1855 he read their magazine *The Germ*, and admired Rossetti's poem 'The Blessed Damozel' and Holman Hunt's illustrations. 1855 was a year of some significant changes in the ideas of the group at Oxford. In May we find Dixon writing, '[I] am afraid that our monastery will come to nought. Smith has changed his views to extreme latitudinarianism, Morris has gone questionable on doctrinal points. . . . [Ted was] too catholic to be ordained. He and Morris diverge more and more on views though not in friendship.'

At the same time Jones writes to his cousin:

Weary work this is—doubting, doubting, doubting—so anxious to do well, so unfortunate—friendly sympathy growing colder as the word broadens and deepens. I am offending everybody with my 'notions' and way of going on in general wreckless-ness in fact, yes I fear I have reached the summit of human audacity now, as to claim forebearance for thinking differently from the omnipotent many, and even of acting honestly by publishing my defection, I shall not grace my friends now by holding that highly *respectable* position of a clergyman—a sore point that, giving up so much respectability—going to be an artist too, probably poor and nameless and all because I can't think like my betters and conform myself to their teaching and read my bible.

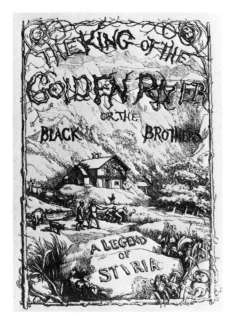

14. Frontispiece for Ruskin's story 'The King of the Golden River' by Richard Doyle. Written in 1841, the book was first published in 1850. Since Ruskin was so beloved by the young artist and the illustrations for *Fairy Family* are not far removed from Doyle's it is highly likely that Edward Jones was influenced by the book.

Both Morris and Jones had become disillusioned with their plan of entering the Church, as the above quotations show. Jones's tone is sardonic—understandably when one recalls his optimism when he first entered the University. Earlier in the same letter he writes that he would not like to be a parson for he had 'looked behind the veil, and grown sick of false hair and teeth and rouge'. Such a change of heart as this does not suddenly burst forth, as Jones outlined in this letter to his cousin:

> . . . this is quite the happiest time of my life, my first two years at college the newness of my friends now worn off, and an indissoluble friendship grown therefrom which will never be dissolved—quite the happiest time, the most bigoted and self satisfied I grant, but yet on the whole the best, for faith was very firm and constant and was strengthening every day—the time when all my plans were laid for future days— romantic and Utopian—but entirely meant and not impracticable if persevered with—a little brotherhood in the heart of London of cleric and lay members—the plan had gone far toward completion—I had six who promised to join and friends were not wanting; only we could not begin at once, not for two years more, because of ordination, and the delay broke up everything for meanwhile we went on reading and thinking, philosophy chiefly, both French and German, that presently shot up like lightning and sent all our hopes, for it shrivelled the belief of one and palsied mine, I fear for years, and so our poor little brotherhood fell through and did not even live to be born . . . .

Yet they were left with their consciences. The Christian Socialists appealed to them and under their influence, and following the example of the Pre-Raphaelites, they planned the magazine. At first it was to be for the educationally underprivileged with emphasis on drawings and illustration combined with a simple text which proved too ambitious, as a letter written by Macdonald indicated:

'It would be in fact to give up entirely the plan of putting their ideas within the reach of the poorer classes and to subordinate everything to the illustrations. At first—Morris was unwilling to do this and thought that Jones' illustrations could be far the most important part of the work but he has come round to the other plan whether he has changed his mind or not.'

Morris's reluctance to give up this idea is fascinating in the light of his subsequent Socialist involvement and it shows how basic it was to his nature, but his wish was over-ruled. The magazine became intellectual and critical without Jones's illustrations. As it finally appeared, *The Oxford and Cambridge Magazine* represents the fruition of ideas which had begun as High Church, moved to Christian Socialism, and had become modified by the artistic development of members of the group.

This development, and the eventual shape of the magazine, is best illuminated by recounting the events of the preceeding vacation. Morris, Jones, and Fulford made a tour of Northern France. It was a walking tour and they made a leisurely investigation of the churches and cathedrals they came across. While in Paris Jones visited the Louvre to see the Italian quattrocentist paintings. Coincidental with their visit was an exhibition of seven Pre-Raphaelite paintings—three by Hunt, three by Millais, and one by Charles Alston Collins—which they attended. From Paris they moved on to Normandy; Morris was enraptured by the architecture he saw:

'Crom, we have seen nine Cathedrals and let me see how many non-Cathedral churches; I must count them on my fingers; there, I think I have missed some but I have made out twenty-four, all splendid churches; some of them surpassing first-rate English Cathedrals.'

Jones was sketching as much as he could, indeed they all abandoned themselves to delight in the country, its churches and their works of art. Moved to ecstasy by High Mass in Beauvais, Sir Edward could recall the occasion many years afterward:

> I saw it and I remember it all—and the processions—and the trombones—and the ancient singing—more beautiful than anything I had ever heard and I think I have never heard the like since. And the great organ that made the air tremble—and the

15-22. Seven trial illustrations and a title page for Archibald MacLaren's *Fairy Family*. Private collection, London

Jones began designing the book in 1854 at the request of its author. He began by designing in a quaint style based upon contemporary illustrators such as Richard Doyle, John Leech, George Cruickshank, even Turner, whose engravings were used as frontispieces to Walter Scott's Waverley novels. Later, with the influx of Pre-Raphaelite ideas into the group his drawings became clearer and better structured, and finally Rossetti's influence can be traced. None of the designs here reproduced was included in the published book.

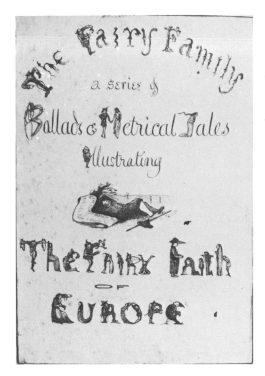

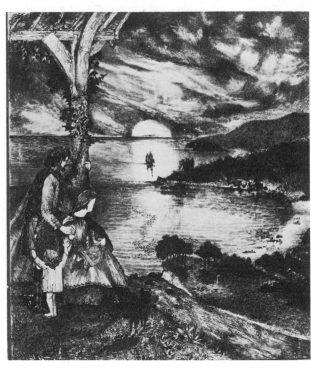

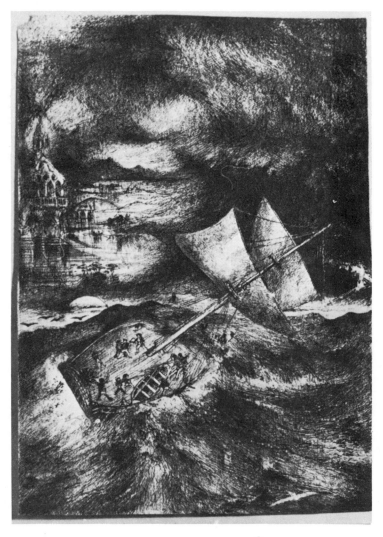

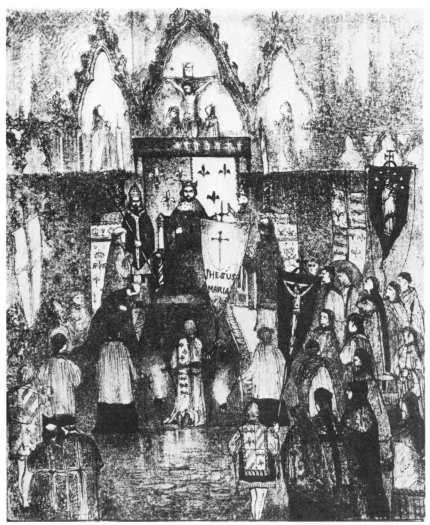

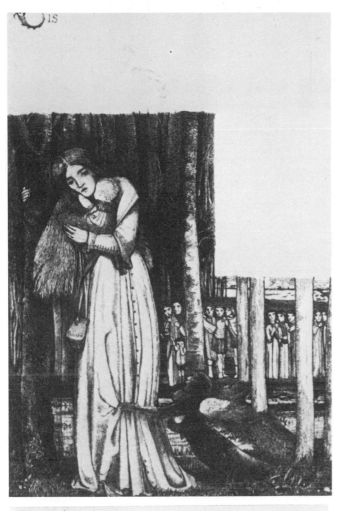

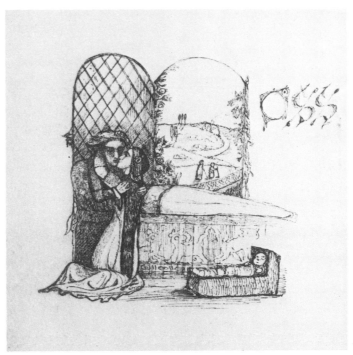

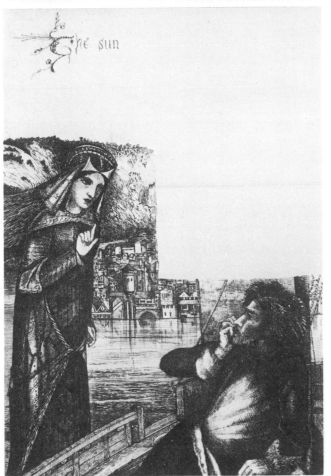

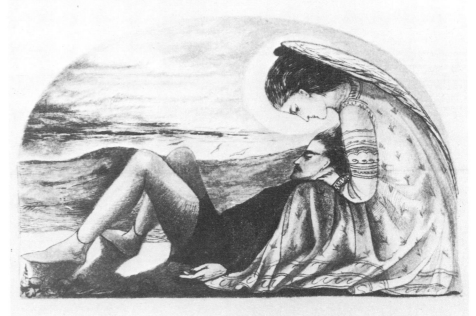

greater that pealed out suddenly, and I thought the Day of Judgement had come—and the roof and the long lights that are the most graceful things man has ever made. . . . What a day it was, and how alive I was, and young—and a blue dragon-fly stood still in the air so long that I could have painted him. Oh me, what fun it was to be young. Yes, if I took account of my life and the days in it that most went to make me, the Sunday at Beauvais would be the first day of creation.

These experiences carried them so far into happiness and fulfilment that they realised that it precipitated a decision about their future. On the quay at Havre, in the evening, Morris and Jones resolved to become artists—Jones a painter, Morris an architect. Morris's background would ensure that his decision made little difference to him financially, but for Jones it was a very brave step. His father was unable to support him, and his decision would be met with some hostility when he and Miss Sampson were informed.

On their return to Oxford they were quick to tell their friends the news. Macdonald, writing home, informs his parents of his friends' activities:

'Morris and Jones enjoyed their tour exceedingly, as well as Fulford did. It seems to have decided the first of them, the artistic Morris on becoming an architect. He intends to get himself articled to Street, an architect up here, and so to remain in Oxford for some time. Jones will probably stay here also and work at oil painting. If he can get a fellowship it will be delightful for him.'

Obviously Jones hoped to solve his financial problems by staying at the University.

On their return the group set about the task of the magazine. Having abandoned the idea of emphasis on illustration, they retained a notion of an engraving per issue, but this in turn was dropped, because of the expense involved. Morris financed the project and was to have been editor but he did not take to it, and so passed the position on to Fulford and paid him £100 a year. Production of the magazine cost Morris £500, of which he hoped to recover £300 from sales; it was to sell at one shilling a month. Articles were produced by Fulford, Jones, Morris, Dixon who had already written for *The London Quarterly*, Faulkner and Price. Macdonald, also on the staff, was really there to make up numbers and was to retire when Lushington joined. The two other members were recruits from Cambridge—Wilfred Heeley, a King Edward's man, and Vernon Lushington. They hoped to print 'reviews, tales, poems, political, historical and statistical articles'. An earnestness and evangelism in their approach recalls *The Germ*, and one is reminded of the Pre-Raphaelite brethren in a passage from a letter by Jones to his cousin: '. . . we have . . . banded ourselves into a brotherhood of seven.'

The Oxford and Cambridge Magazine ran for a year, twelve issues in all; this number because despite their declining enthusiasm they had committed themselves to produce it for a period of twelve months. Unhappily it was not a success, financially at least, but it did receive praise from Tennyson and Ruskin. Tennyson finding 'a truthfulness and earnestness very refreshing' to him. The later issues contained poems by Rossetti, 'The Burden of Nineveh' in August, 'The Blessed Damozel' in November, and 'The Staff and Scrip' in December. Jones contributed four pieces, comprising two stories 'The Cousins', 'A Story of the North', and two critical articles, 'An Essay on the Newcomes' and 'Mr Ruskin's New Volume', all of which occur in the issues of the first four months. After that Jones was busy as an artist and was reluctant to spend time writing articles.

The two stories (an extract from one of them has already been quoted in Chapter I) are rich in incident, colourful but derivative. Once again a debt is clearly owed to 'Sintram' and *The Heir*. 'The Story of the North' is set in an indefinite period of Scandinavia's distant past and is liberally strewn with Nordic characters who bear such exotic names as Engeltram and Irminhilda. Both stories lack maturity and show a tendency towards the melodramatic, unlike the more assured critical essays. Morris had bought a copy of Thackeray's *The Newcomes* when they were on holiday in France, growing to regard it as a masterpiece.

In his article on the book, Jones numbers its author amongst Tennyson, Holman Hunt,

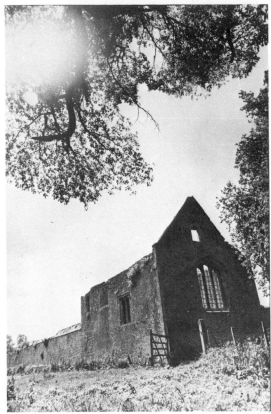

Ruskin, Carlyle and Kingsley as those 'who have led on this most godly crusade against falsehood, doubt and wretched fashion, against hypocrisy and mammon and lack of earnestness'. He continues by pointing out the central purpose of the book, which is to bring the reader's attention to 'the very core of social disease, unhappy wedded life'. He then proceeds to draw our attention to a character (in a situation curiously like his own), Clive, who wishes to become a painter but meets with opposition from his father, spending a considerable amount of space vindicating the aspiring artist. Finally, he analyses 'Dicky' Doyle's illustrations and the rise of contemporary illustration. The conclusions he draws are based upon 'looking over a vast majority of book engravings'. After indicating how much 'labour it necessitates to produce a slight engraving' he asks the reader to be less tolerant of bad examples, and then eulogises Holman Hunt's illustrations 'My Beautiful Lady' and 'Of my Lady in Death'—'an illustration indeed to a poem, but the latter having so little reference to it that it may well stand for an independent picture; truly a song without words.' Then follows the famous passage giving the highest praise to Rossetti's drawing 'The Maids of Elfenmere' in Allingham's 'Day and Night Songs': 'it is I think the most beautiful drawing for an illustration I have ever seen, the wierd faces of the maids of Elfenmere, the musical timed movement of their arms together as they sing, the face of the man, above all, are such as only a great artist could conceive'. Jones's other review is centred upon the fourth part of the third volume of Ruskin's *Modern Painters*, which is a splendid defence of the Pre-Raphaelite school. Ruskin sees the work of Watts and Rossetti as 'the dawn of a new era of art'. The reviewer is completely attuned with his subject, and displays his rapturous admiration for the paintings 'The Light of the World', 'The Huguenot', 'Mariana in the Moated Grange' and 'Ophelia'. His enthusiasm stimulates some beautiful writing:

> . . . the Ophelia—who does not remember that sorrowful picture? thinking that truly death was most terrible in youth, most fearful in the mocking light of day, and brightness of the Summer-time: for the banks were crowned with flowers, and the birds were out, the robin on the willow bough; and all lay in deep light and sunshine, but her eyes were glazed even now, and the inner light was closed for ever; and, upon the water lay fantastic garlands she had wrought of 'crowflowers, nettles, daisies and long purples'

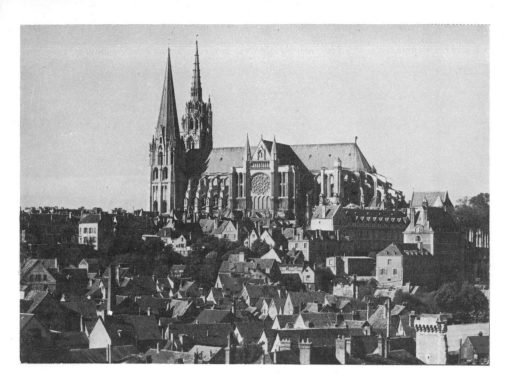

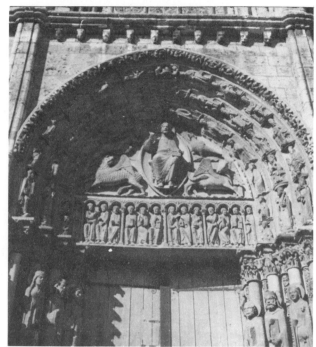

24 & 25. Chartres Cathedral. Morris and Jones visited Chartres during their tour of the Northern French cathedrals in 1855. Their admiration for this twelfth-century edifice was intense, and the sculpture had special significance for their subsequent designs.

'Her clothes spread wide;
And mermaid like a while they bore her up;
Which time she chaunted snatches of old tunes,
As one incapable of her own distress.'

Her brow looked very calm and quiet, but you might know how the fever burned under, for her hands rippled through the water in feverish playfulness, and so 'singing in her song she died'.

These two essays reveal the direction of the author's interest at the beginning of 1856, centred as it was upon the visual arts. They foreshadow his future in dwelling on the artists with whom he was to become on intimate terms very soon and who were to determine the direction of his art for some years to come.

Over the three years at Oxford he had grown more and more aware of the importance of the Pre-Raphaelites. Finally, on seeing 'The Maids of Elfinmere', he gave up the idea of continuing at the University and determined to go to London and seek out the artist who was capable of such a feat. In January 1856, during the Christmas recess, he went to the Working Men's College in Great Titchfield Street, hoping that Rossetti would be there, as he already knew that the artist was associated with it. In his own words:

[He] sat at a table and had thick bread and butter, but knowing no one. But good fellowship was the rule there, that was clear; and a man sitting opposite to me, spoke at once to me, introducing himself by the name of Furnivall. He reached across the table to a kindly-looking man, whom he introduced to me as Vernon Lushington, to whom I repeated my reason for coming, and begged him to tell me when Rossetti entered the room. It seemed that it was doubtful if he would appear at all, that he was constant in his work of teaching drawing at the College, but he had no great taste for the nights of addresses and speeches, and as I must have looked downcast in this, Lushington, with a kindness never to be forgotten by me, invited me to go to his rooms in Doctor's Commons a few nights afterwards, where Rossetti had promised to come. So I waited a good hour or two, listening to speeches . . . and then Lushington whispered to me that Rossetti had come in, and so I saw him for the first time, his face satisfying all my worship, and I listened to addresses no more, but had my fill of looking; only I would not be introduced.

Some nights later he went to Lushington's rooms and met the great man and saw that

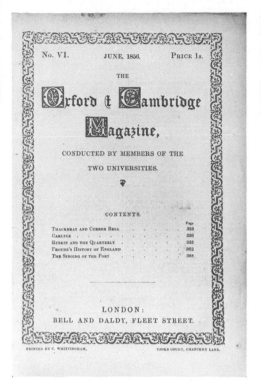

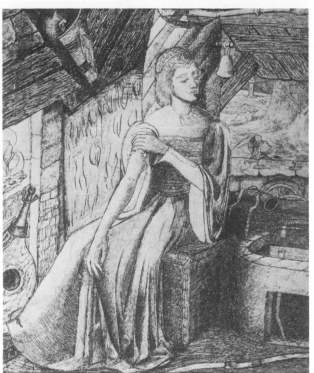

26. Front cover of *The Oxford and Cambridge Magazine* for June 1856
The magazine ran to twelve issues, one for each month of the year 1856.

27. An Arthurian incident, possibly the Lady of Shalott, *c.* 1856, pen and ink, $5\frac{1}{2} \times 4\frac{3}{4}$, William Morris Gallery, Walthamstow
It is possible that this drawing was made whilst Jones was still at Oxford —its numerous flaws indicate that it is transitional between the *Fairy Family* designs and the pen and ink drawings of subjects from medieval life of the late fifties.

'my hero could be a tyrant' when crossed in argument but that 'it sat finely upon him'. Rossetti spoke to him and invited him to his studio next day. It transpired that the painter had read some poems by Morris which he seemed to admire, asking many questions about them. There he allowed the young man to stay and watch him painting his watercolour 'Fra Pace'.

Returning to Oxford fully convinced that he was right in his decision to leave before he took his final examinations, he informed the others of his plans. He continued to read for the Final Schools during the Lent term but at Easter he went to London permanently, leaving College without taking his degree. Meanwhile, Morris had become articled to G. E. Street, a Gothic Revivalist architect who had his office in Oxford. Working in Street's office as senior clerk was a young man called Philip Webb; their ensuing friendship was founded upon a common interest in the applied arts, and the result of their co-operation over the next forty years had considerable influence on twentieth-century designers. Unlike Jones he took his finals, but it was hardly necessary as he had decided to become an architect and was now, after coming of age, receiving £900 a year.

With Edward Jones placing himself at Rossetti's feet, the two streams, the Pre-Raphaelite brethren and the Birmingham group, unite—an almost inevitable step since they were subject to much the same formative pressures. Each movement appeared in the aftermath of the soul-searching Oxford Movement, inheriting strong social awareness and a yearning for a more spiritual interpretation of man. The two groups recognised independently the fundamental importance of the writings of Ruskin, who added to social awareness and spiritual yearning a veneration for the visual aspects of natural phenomena. This quasi-scientific side of his writing, though carried out to the letter by Millais and Hunt, gradually became less important to Rossetti, and by the time he was joined by Jones it had almost disappeared. Consequently, detailed drawings from nature are infrequent in Jones's output and those made in the woods around Oxford are virtually unique. Like Rossetti, he was more concerned with the inner landscape of the mind and his use of the outer world was as a symbol of it. The senior artist must have recognised a common attitude while first talking with his young admirer, for he wrote a most perceptive comment after their meeting:

'a certain youthful Jones . . . one of the nicest young fellows in *Dreamland*.'

Chapter Three
Rossetti

I n Rossetti, Edward Jones found the hero that he was unable to find in his father. Until this point in his life he was unsure of the real direction of his ambition or career. He had outgrown his past interests, they had become inadequate because they only superficially expressed his spiritual yearnings. Under such a dominant personality as Rossetti he was able to reorganise the whole of his artistic activity into a way of life. His natural skills became the servant of his vision, and from this moment on he was able to channel his inner life into an external form through the visual arts.

After a short period spent with relatives in London, Edward decided to find rooms of his own, finally obtaining them in Sloane Street, Chelsea. Morris came up from Oxford at weekends. They spent the time in the company of Rossetti, whose taste began to supersede their own, visiting the theatre, walking about the London streets or talking until the early hours back at his studio overlooking the river in Cheyne Walk. The arts were ever in their conversation, the elder painter's ideas streaming out and becoming currency amongst them until the two young men thought them to be their own. They visited the Academy in the summer of 1856 where a glorious set of Pre-Raphaelite paintings met their eyes— five by Millais: 'The Random Shot', 'Peace Concluded', 'Autumn Leaves', 'The Blind Girl', and a portrait; Arthur Hughes's 'April Love' and 'The Eve of St Agnes'; Holman Hunt's 'The Scapegoat'; and 'Burd Helen' by the Liverpool painter W. L. Windus. Morris was so taken with Hughes's 'April Love' that he instructed his friend to go to the Academy and buy it for him.

In spite of Edward's having found a chosen career, having a master to guide and instruct him, there was still a problem. Unlike Morris he could not support himself; unless he found a way of earning a living he would not be able to follow his ambition. Here Rossetti was able to help. He first suggested that Edward should convert Windus's 'Burd Helen' into an engraving of the *Illustrated London News*, but when he saw some original work of Edward's (probably drawings from the *Fairy Family* series) he dropped the idea, because he was so stunned by their rich invention and profusion of images. Hitherto he had not appreciated the extent of the young man's capabilities; henceforward Rossetti consistently gave the highest praise to his pupil's work.

At the end of the summer, Street moved his office to London and, of course, his young apprentices moved with him. This proved a boon to Jones for he then shared rooms with Morris, which halved his rent and meant that he had a companion all the time. Their address was now Upper Gordon Street, Bloomsbury, a situation convenient for both of them, as it was close to Street's office in Montague Place, and it was also quite near to the drawing schools that Jones was attending. Although he was working in Rossetti's studio he still felt the need for continual practice and instruction. Consequently, he enrolled in Gandish's Schools in Newman Street and also in Cary's in Bloomsbury Place. In the evenings he attended night school; such was the fervour with which he threw himself into

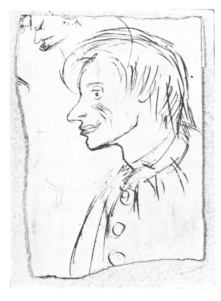

28. Humorous drawing of Edward Jones by Rossetti, 1857, pen and ink; private collection, England
One of the few drawings of Burne-Jones without a beard. The background figure is Val Prinsep.

his training. In these schools he had the opportunity of drawing from the model in the life class, gaining invaluable experience in draughtsmanship, which was not included in Rossetti's tuition. Rossetti preferred that he should plunge straight into imaginative composition, and in doing so, the rest would follow. Combining the two systems and possessing a high level of natural skill Edward Jones made rapid progress. After a very short time he was making designs of a high order. In fact, he thought his progress so great that any work done earlier was considered inferior. As a result he decided to abandon the *Fairy Family* project; not only was he embarrassed by his earlier work, but the drawings he was now making seemed incongruous with the ones he had done before, and because of this they would not combine with them into a single volume.

There is a marked difference between those drawings made at Oxford and those made in the Summer of 1856; the set as a whole demonstrates a progression. At the beginning, as mentioned before, the style derives from contemporary illustration of the Doyle type, slightly humorous, slightly grotesque; a little later the Pre-Raphaelite influence introduced its statuesque figures and simple outline. Finally, Rossetti's passion and densely-filled space invades; more dramatic, the figures play a more important role in the design and in the emotion of the works. In all, the young artist made approximately sixty designs. Perhaps there was justification in abandoning them, but one feels that there is considerable power in the set in spite of the changes in style, and that in combination with the fairy stories they are successful in intensifying the atmosphere. The book appeared in 1857 with a frontispiece, title page, and tail piece from drawings by Jones, but the text was completely unadorned.

Morris gradually succumbed to the spell that Rossetti cast over all those that knew him; we find him writing in July, whilst still at Oxford:

'Rossetti says I ought to paint, he says I shall be able; now as he is a very great man, and speaks with authority and not as the scribes, I *must* try. . . . So I am going to try, not giving up the architecture, but trying if it is possible to get six hours a day for drawing besides office work. . . . My work is the embodiment of dreams in one form or another. . . .'

It was characteristic of Rossetti to enlist Morris as a painter: he would encourage anyone who showed any artistic ability whatsoever to take up painting. After the same pattern, later in the year R. W. Dixon decided to become a painter, was given instruction by Rossetti, and went so far as to paint 'A Wedding scene from Chaucer'. That painting's flagrant violation of academic principles was characteristic of this singular artist. He inherited, from his days at the Royal Academy Schools, a bitterness which all the rebellious Pre-Raphaelites had felt. They recognised and grew to detest the formulae which passed for inspiration, the insipid subject matter of the 'professional' painter, the dry, sterile

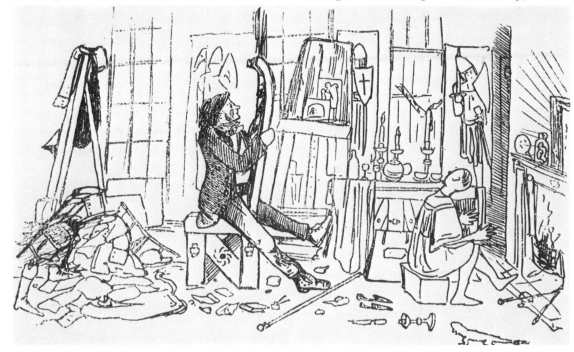

29. Edward Jones at work in his studio at 17, Red Lion Square

He appears to be painting the back of a large chair. Morris's interest in brass rubbing can be seen by the three examples at the back of the room. The two friends moved into these premises in November 1856. From *Memorials*.

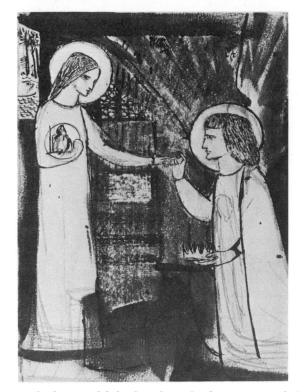

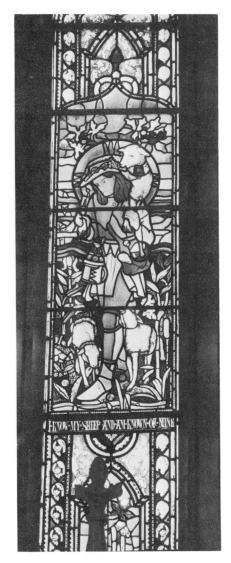

technique which developed after years of drawing from the antique. Rossetti's cult of what was virtually an amateur approach sprang from his firm belief in the values of sincerity, in the purity of inspiration which, when present in the artist, would manifest itself whatever his training. His aesthetic creed was his religion and was not to be treated as an empty display of virtuosity. Academies led to debasement; their training developed facility without vision. This was his motive in rejecting their methods when cultivating creativity in his young disciples. The high esteem in which he held the creative discovery accounts for his evangelism. Art was a religion and painting its most ideal manifestation, so all men should be painters. As we have seen, Edward Jones held much the same views; Rossetti was the perfect agent to give him confidence to develop his talents and to start him on his artistic career.

On the suggestion of Rossetti, Morris and Jones moved to Red Lion Square to take up the rooms that Rossetti had shared with the painter Deverell in the days of the Brotherhood. Since Jones was poor and the rent of Upper Gordon Street was expensive, and the rooms were too cramped for both of them, they decided to move. Their new accommodation consisted of three rooms on the first floor, one of which was large and faced North. Its windows had been enlarged up to the ceiling during the Rossetti tenancy, to adapt it as a studio. As the rooms were unfurnished and he considered shop-bought furniture objectionable, Morris began to design his own. These were massive, medievally inspired pieces, notable for their lack of ornament, in contrast to the decorative excesses practised by the contemporary commercial designers. They included a round table, chairs made famous by Rossetti's comment 'such as Barbarossa might have sat in', a large settle with three cupboards above it, and various others. A feature they all shared was having plain flat areas suitable for paintings, and upon these they set about making designs. Rossetti embellished the chairs with episodes from Morris's own poetry, one had Guendolen in the witch tower with the Prince below kissing her flowing locks, and another showed the arming of Sir Galahad. Upon the settle he made three more paintings—Dante meeting Beatrice in Florence and Dante meeting Beatrice in Paradise on either side of a figure of Love between emblems of the Sun and Moon. The paintings on the doors of the settle were removed later; in fact little of the furniture made in the Summer of 1856 still exists. However, there are in the collection at the Victoria and Albert Museum, four panels of thick deal which have obviously been taken from a piece of furniture. They bear paintings of four single figures of girls in medieval dress. As they exist today, the outer panels are by Rossetti, whilst the two in the centre are by Morris. Their style would date them at this time,

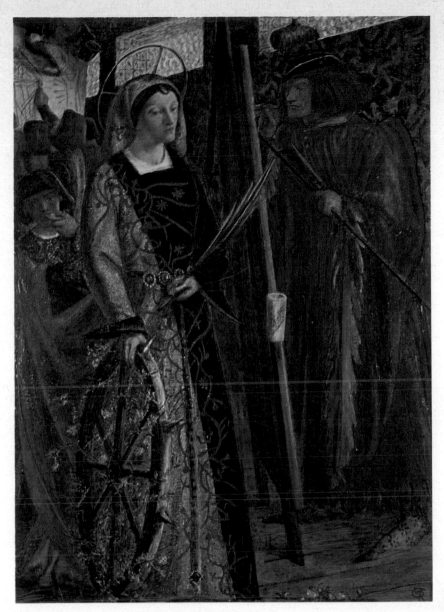

1. 'St Catherine' by Rossetti, 1857, oil on canvas, 13½×9½; Tate Gallery, London. The model for St Catherine was Elizabeth Siddal.

2. 'Wedding of Sir Tristram', one of a series of thirteen windows executed by Morris, Marshall, Faulkner & Co, 1862-63, for the music room at Harden Grange, Bingley, Yorkshire, home of Walter Dunlop, a Bradford merchant. Three others of the series were designed by Jones, four by Morris, two by Rossetti, and one each by Arthur Hughes, Madox Brown, and Val Prinsep. Corporation Art Gallery, Bradford, Cartwright Memorial Hall.

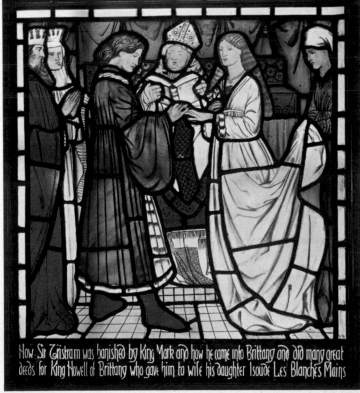

How Sir Tristram was banished by King Mark and how he came into Brittany and did many great deeds for King Howell of Brittany who gave him to wife his daughter Isoude Les Blanches Mains

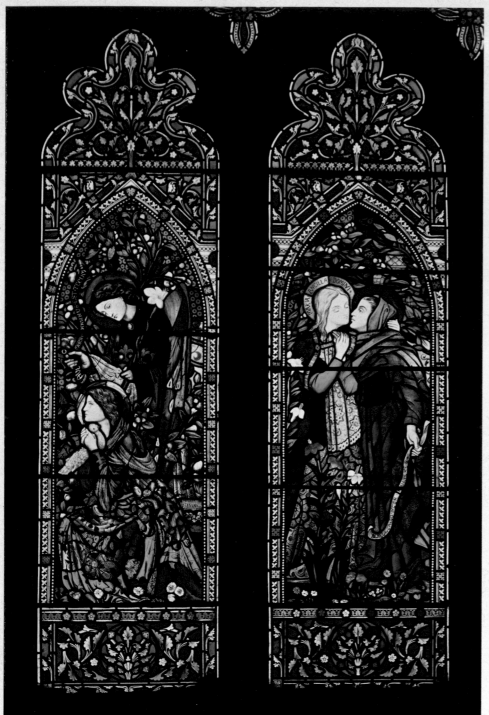

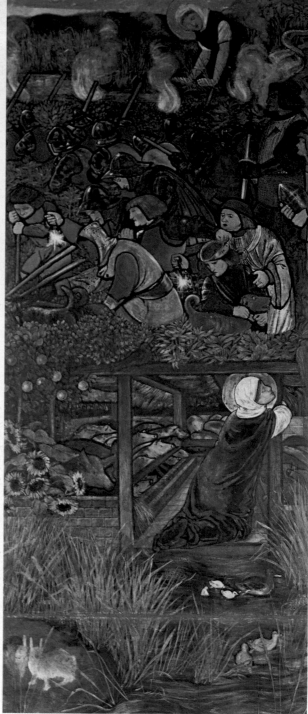

3. 'Annunciation', the left-hand and centre panels of a three-light window at St Columba's Church, Topcliffe, Yorkshire, 1860. The left-hand panel designed by Jones, the centre and right-hand by Michael Halliday. Executed by Lavers and Barraud. The cartoon for Jones's panel is at the Birmingham City Museum & Art Gallery. The 'Annunciation' was used subsequently at Cobham Church, Surrey (South aisle west window), and Christ Church, Surbiton Hill, Surrey (North aisle).

4. 'The Legend of St Frideswide', East Window of the Latin Chapel, Christ Church Cathedral, Oxford, 1859. Cheltenham Ladies College. Oil cartoon for the lower half of the centre-left panel approximately 60 × 36.

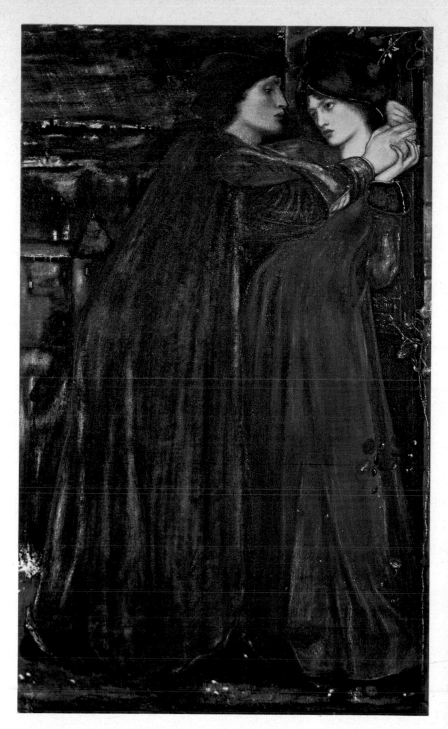

5. 'Clerk Saunders', 1861, gouache, $27\frac{1}{2} \times 16\frac{1}{2}$;
Tate Gallery, London. It is probable that Swinburne
and Burne-Jones discussed this theme, as Morris had
contemplated from 1858 the possibility of re-working
certain Border ballads.

6. 'Beatrice' by Simeon Solomon,
1860, watercolour, $17 \times 12\frac{1}{2}$; Hartnoll
& Eyre, London.

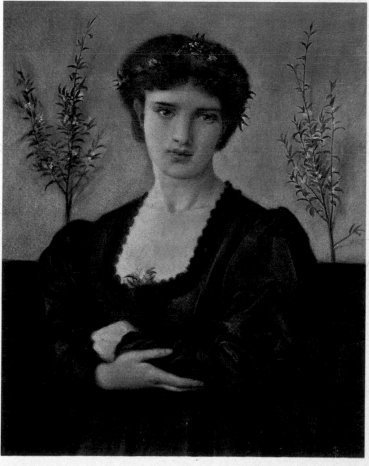

sharply in a colour called violet carmine. But I never saw him do any picture all the way through neither did I ever find I could do mine in the same way. The next time I came to him by appointment would be 3 or 4 days afterwards.'

Charles Fairfax Murray, who acted as studio assistant for both artists, noticed the similarities in technique between Jones's early work and Rossetti's. He observed that they both scraped the surfaces of their pen and ink drawings and watercolours and that 'Edward Burne-Jones in his early watercolours used considerable quantities of ox-gall, a practice he learnt from Rossetti who used it in still larger quantities probably, but this he denied. . . . I have an early picture of Eleanor and Fair Rosamund arrested at the first stage—it is drawn in with the pen with violent carmine, the heads being treated much like an etching. The background and draperies were put in with the same colour but with the brush. Then scraping set in until the whole of the surface of the paper was more or less destroyed for the purpose of painting into.

Another aspect of Rossetti's work can be traced in his young friend's output of this period. The scraping referred in the preceding passage indicates a concern for the surface of the painting. This went deeper than mere preparation. Rossetti's designs show an increasing interest in the spatial content and structure; they strive after a dense overall flatness that is so characteristic of Jones's painted wardrobe. Each one abounds in repeated forms or patterns that pass from side to side, the figures are treated frontally and there is an absence of intelligible perspective. There is little action, each figure he creates is absorbed within itself. The overall impression, therefore, is one of compact, richly filled surface, brilliantly described by James Smetham, the poet-painter (actually referring to the 'The Wedding of St George'): 'One of the grandest things, like a golden dim dream. Love credulous all gold; gold armour; a sense of secret enclosure in "palace chambers far apart"; but quaint chambers in quaint palaces, where angels creep in through sliding doors and stand behind rows of flowers, drumming on golden bells with wings crimson and green.'

They both considered painting as the creation of objects of beauty and this meant deliberately emphasising the synthetic nature of it and in no way attempting to recreate according to natural appearance.

The fact of Jones's borrowing Rossetti's type of model is self-evident, but actually he, Rossetti, and Morris shared almost the same iconography, Chaucer, Malory, and their own poetry being the most frequent sources. But Rossetti was not only their guide in aesthetic matters; he set about finding commissions and patronage. His delight in his follower's designs was obvious: 'Jones is doing designs . . . which quite put one to shame, so full are they of everything—Aurora Leighs of art.'

Two wealthy Northerners were found who were willing to buy work on his recommendation—T. E. Plint, a stockbroker of Leeds and James Leathart, a Newcastle industrialist. The former commissioned a £350 painting in the summer of 1857 based upon Rossetti's poem 'The Blessed Damozel', but Leathart did not receive a work until 1863. G. P. Boyce, the painter, also commissioned a painting of a girl in an orchard in 1859, but by that time Jones had made the acquaintance of Ruskin, who was either buying work or encouraging his friends to do so.

The most important contract to arise from Rossetti's efforts was with the firm of Powell's, the Whitefriars Glass Company. He had been approached by his architect friend, Benjamin Woodward, on behalf of the Company, who wished to make good-quality stained glass. Charles Winston was associated with the firm from the 1840s. During that time he had been researching into the history and techniques of stained-glass production. In 1847 he published his pioneer work in two volumes, *Hints on Glass Painting*, based upon experiments made at Whitefriars. The conclusions he drew were that the ancient stained glass was superior because it was based upon the mosaic system of glass painting. In the eighteenth century the direction had been away from that system, glass was then made in large pieces upon which the design was painted, in much the same way as easel painting. As late as 1851 the St Helen's Glass Company exhibited 'St Michael Casting Out the Great Red Dragon' which was 'painted upon one entire piece upwards of nine feet in height by nearly five in width.' This example takes the principle to extreme and it

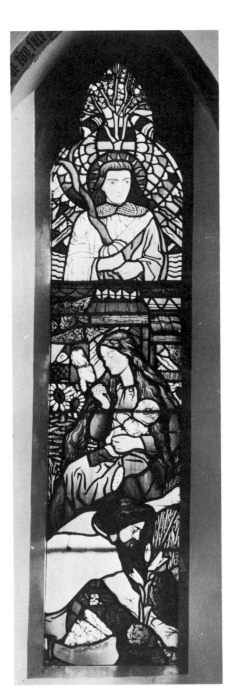

33. 'Adam and Eve': left-hand panel of a three-light window at Bradfield College, Berkshire, 1858
It is interesting to note the accessory sunflowers in the light of their subsequent adoption by the Aesthetic Movement. The lower half of this design has a strong affinity with an illustration made in the 1880s, 'When Adam delved . . .'. Cartoon: Victoria & Albert Museum, London.

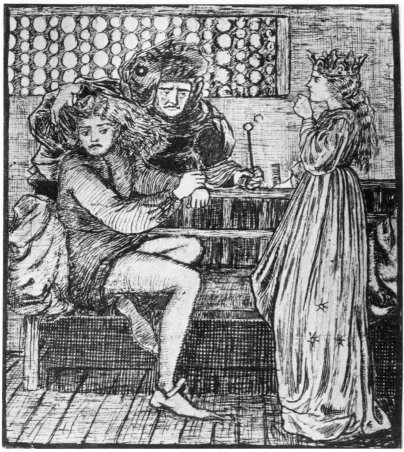

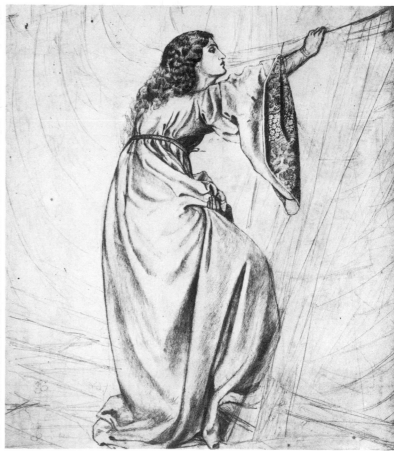

represents an opposite view to that put forward by Winston. He recognised the possibilities of small glass panes which intensify the colour since they have to be surrounded by the black leading; small panes are also much richer in total effect than large ones. He also advocated using a minimum of shading or modelling with dark enamels; the designer should 'paint' with the glass panels themselves, relying upon the contours of the lead lines and the glass to create the forms. Winston was a key figure in the history of stained glass in calling for a respect for the essential nature of the medium.

Edward Jones's first design, 'The Good Shepherd', though it was an experiment, turned out to be a great success. Rossetti wrote enthusiastically of it in a letter to Powell's:

'Jones has just been designing some stained glass which has driven Ruskin wild with joy: the subject is the Good Shepherd. Christ is here represented as a real shepherd, in such dress as is fit for walking the fields and hills. He carries the lost sheep on His shoulder, and it is chewing some vine leaves which are wound round his hat—a lovely idea is it not? A loaf and a bottle of wine, the Sacred Elements, hang at his girdle; and behind him is a wonderful piece of Gothic landscape. The colour of the whole is beyond description.'

The cartoons were painted in oil in some cases and opaque gouache in others. A series of six was made in 1857–58, the one here described by Rossetti (used at Maidstone, Kent), 'St Peter Receiving the Keys', 'St Paul' (no locality known), and the three which were executed for St Andrew's College, Bradfield, 'Adam and Eve', 'The Building of the Tower of Babel', and 'Solomon meeting the Queen of Sheba'. Wherever possible the colour of the cartoon was adhered to so that the final effect is more or less the responsibility of the artist. There still exists, in the factory, an early experimental window of this series—the 'St Peter'. It seems very likely that this was the first to be made as it contains an interesting variety of technique, ranging from modelling with opaque brown enamel to clear-coloured glass, from the naturalism of the faces to the stylisation of the fish, and also there is an unusual device of fusing the blue glass of the angel's eyes, without leading, into the pink area of the face. At one point a piece of lead-surrounded glass is so small that no light can possibly pass through it.

1859 produced the magnificent design for the St Frideswide window in Christ Church

34. Unknown subject, from a family scrapbook, pen and ink, *c.* 1860, by Georgiana Jones. Private collection, London

Once, Georgie and Rossetti's wife, Elizabeth, had decided to join in producing a book of illustrations, but nothing came of it. Georgie had attended the Government School of Design in Birmingham and had also taken lessons with Madox Brown, so that she was quite able to carry out the plan. In spite of this, the project was abandoned.

35. 'Iseult on the Ship' by William Morris, *c.* 1857. Pen and ink and pencil, $18\frac{1}{2} \times 15\frac{1}{2}$, William Morris Gallery, Walthamstow

Jane Burden, later the wife of Morris, was the model for Iseult. The ink-over-pencil technique used is similar to that of Jones.

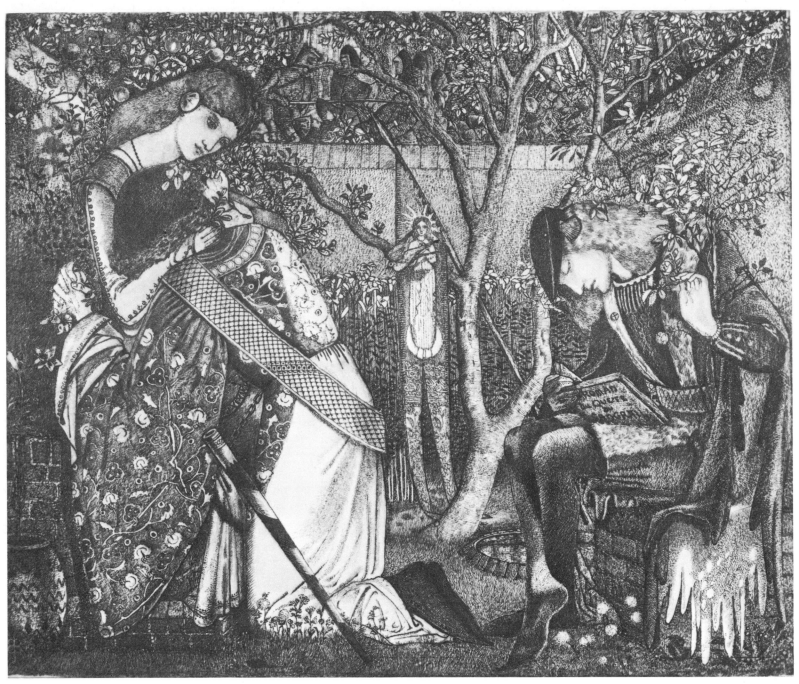

36. 'The Knight's Farewell', 1858, $6\frac{1}{4} \times 7\frac{1}{2}$, pen and ink on vellum. Private collection, England.

Cathedral, Oxford. It is in sixteen compartments spread across the four lights, which represent the life of the Saint. For sheer colour it must have been almost everything that Winston called for, its brilliance is evident over the whole window. Like all Jones's glass executed by Powell, at a distance the impact is one of deep majestic colour without association with images. As one approaches, the figurative elements emerge and one appreciates the twofold method of operation, distant and near. Above the lancets containing the story, the tracery lights are drawn on a slightly larger scale to accommodate for their further distance away from the congregation. A boat in full sail is entirely made up of streaky ruby glass which includes all the drawing, indicating how the firm held colour more important than detail, and how they understood it to be the first consideration in stained-glass manufacture. Originally, Swinburne was to have made verses to accompany each section, but he was slow in writing them, and anyway they had problems fitting all the scenes into the available space, leaving no room for legends. Woodward, the architect of the window, was growing forgetful at this time and gave Edward a wrong set of measurements, so that a Miss Oakham had to spend fifteen days reducing the cartoons to the correct size. In spite of this, the window remains true to Jones's designs. The cartoons themselves were made into a most impressive eight-partitioned screen, which he kept in his studio

30

until 1865 when Birket Foster, the artist-illustrator, purchased it for use in his studio.

William Burges was restoring Waltham Abbey in 1859–60 and commissioned Powell to make the glass for the east end. The designs and the resultant window are blue in overall effect compared with the reds and yellows of Christ Church, and the windows have a greater transparency. It represents the Tree of Jesse in three lights, and a rose window above contains 'Christ in Majesty' surrounded by seven circular 'Days of Creation'. Once again the artist was responsible for the colour of the glass. The 'Days of Creation' remind one of Samuel Palmer in their rich glowing colour and their mystical transfiguration of nature. Unlike the 'Frideswide' glass, the lancets are not divided horizontally into episodes, but the whole window is a complete design. The tiny figures are related to the size of the lancets by means of a vine whose tendrils encapsulate each scene to create a unity over the larger area. In the collection of the Birmingham Art Gallery is a small preliminary design for Waltham Abbey in pen and ink over pencil, which in style and technique relates quite closely to the pen and ink drawings of medieval subjects he was making concurrently. Conceived and executed in a similar way, it reveals how he first tackled large-scale work, and by keeping within the techniques to which he was accustomed he was able to adapt to stained-glass design. Only later were they converted into full scale by means of oil or gouache. In his treatment of the subject Jones was clearly following the inconography of the fourteenth-century prototypes, and may even have had in mind the 'Jesse Tree' window in the choir at Wells Cathedral. This example is unusual in having the Crucifixion in addition to the Virgin and Child which is the usual climax. Likewise Jones, in his preliminary drawing, included both Nativity and Crucifixion but eliminated the Nativity in his final designs. It is quite possible that he knew of the Wells example, as an acquaintance of his, J. R. Clayton, had made drawings of it in the mid-fifties.

William Burges, writing in the *Gentleman's Magazine* of July 1862 said of the Oxford windows:

'. . . the original paintings by Mr E. B. Jones for the stained glass lately fixed in Oxford Cathedral. Mr Jones is a colourist and consequently declines to trust the choice of the tones of his colours to the glass painter, he therefore makes a finished colour painting in oil, and the result is that the best modern stained glass windows are due to his design.' And of those at Waltham Abbey: '. . . . This window which in its place looks exceedingly rich and jewel-like, is here simply a mass of confusion.' (Referring to the cartoons).

William Butterfield had commissioned the stained-glass firm of Lavers and Barraud to supply a three-light design for the south chancel window in the parish church at Topcliffe in Yorkshire, which he was restoring. The firm employed Jones as designer, and he completed the first of the three lancets, an Annunciation. In it he demonstrates how complete was his mastery over all aspects of stained glass, the figures are exactly the right scale for the window, their grouping has just the right echo of its shape, quite a difficult task in such a tall, narrow window. He overcame it by having the Angel of Annunciation standing behind and bending over the kneeling Virgin, who clasps a dove to her bosom. These features, combined with its exquisite colour, make it as successful as anything that followed from the Morris workshop. Yet it angered the architect, so much so that he insisted that Jones should be withdrawn and another designer found. His reason was that the dove, as a symbol of the Holy Spirit, was used sacreligiously, in being clasped in what he thought an unduly sensuous manner. Jones was too stubborn to change the offending design as he described many years later:

'Once, in the ardour of youth, I tried an innovation. It was a mistake. I drew an Annunciation with Mary taking the Dove to her bosom; and when the architect who had commissioned me (he was a very good architect—Butterfield it was) objected, I wouldn't alter it. So he would never give me anything more to do, and he was quite right—and I lost a chance of a lot of work.'

Another designer, M. F. Halliday, an amateur painter who was a friend of Millais, completed the two other lights as best he could; his windows are competent, but they could never match Jones's. Because of this extraordinary state of affairs this single light is unique in being signed 'E. B. Jones'. At least three other versions were made however; William Burges ordered one for his rooms in 15 Buckingham Street, Strand;

a second can be seen in Cobham Parish Church, Surrey, and another at Christ Church, Surbiton Hill.

Such was the success of Rossetti on his pupil's behalf that his friend Macdonald was able to write a year after Edward had left for London:

'He [Edward's father] told me that he was now quite reconciled to Ted's pursuits, though it had cost him a great struggle at first, and then added how very fortunate Ted had been as he would have made about £300 in his first year. I was very glad to see him happy in his son's choice of profession at last, for if ever a man's bias was marked Ted's is.'

There is nothing like a good income to effect a paternal change of heart! It was not, however, entirely due to Rossetti's efforts that he improved his financial situation. From their first meeting in November 1856 Ruskin not only bought for himself but lost no time in carrying off Jones's works to potential purchasers and introducing him to anyone likely to be interested in them, and we find Jones, a month later, dining at Denmark Hill with the Ruskins, Sir William and Lady Trevelyan, and George and Thomas Richmond.

Early in the summer of 1857 Rossetti and Morris paid a visit to Oxford to meet Woodward, the architect friend of Rossetti who was engaged upon the building of the Oxford Union. It was being built in a mixture of Rhenish and Venetian Gothic styles. On being shown the debating hall, Rossetti was taken with the idea of painting murals on the areas of the wall above a narrow gallery that ran round the hall. Woodward, an ardent Gothicist, readily accepted the idea, recognising the suitability of painting the walls of a 'medieval' building.

Mural painting was a continual preoccupation with artists and architects during the first decades of the century. Benjamin Robert Haydon, inheriting the idea from Joshua Reynolds, repeatedly called for a revival of a grand form of decorative painting to grace our national buildings. When, in 1834, the old Houses of Parliament were burnt down an opportunity was presented for the creation of an edifice to impress the world. After a battle of styles won by the Gothicists, the Houses were designed by Sir Charles Barry, closely assisted by A. W. N. Pugin, in the symmetrical style of the Late Perpendicular. There followed, shortly after this, a call for its decoration. At last there were suitable vast spaces in a building of national pride. Prince Albert took a close interest in the scheme and

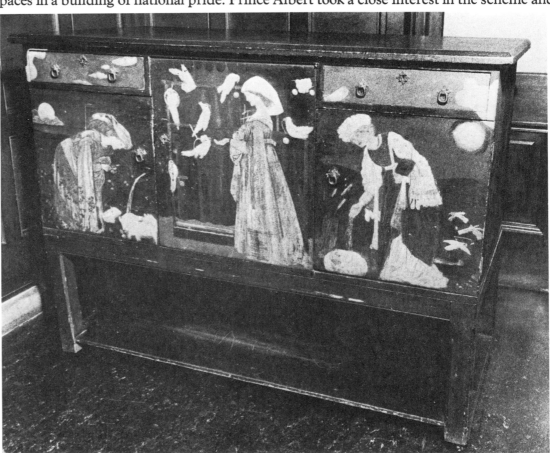

37. 'Good and Bad Animals' Cabinet, 1860, Victoria & Albert Museum, London
Like the piano, the cabinet was made to furnish the house of the newly wedded Edward and Georgie. Probably designed by Philip Webb.

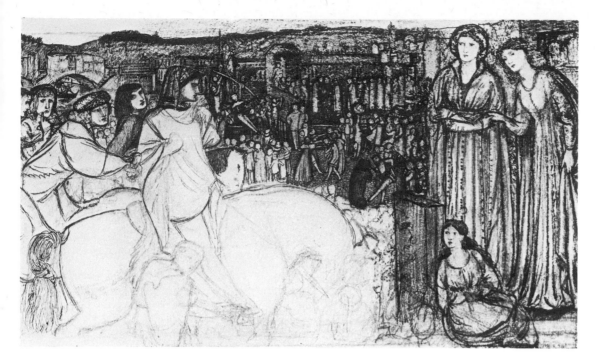

38. Subject from the story of the Guelphs and Ghibellines, *c.* 1859, pen and ink over pencil, $10\frac{3}{4} \times 7\frac{1}{2}$, unfinished. The Ashmolean Museum, Oxford

In its unfinished state the drawing displays the manner in which Jones developed a drawing. Not relying on separate studies, he first drew roughly in pencil and then clarified the lines by going over them again in ink. The technique is, of course, a far cry from his later one where he made hundreds of variant studies until he was convinced he was ready to finally commit himself.

39. 'Kings' Daughters', 1858–59, pen and ink on vellum, $6\frac{1}{4} \times 7\frac{1}{2}$. Private collection, England.

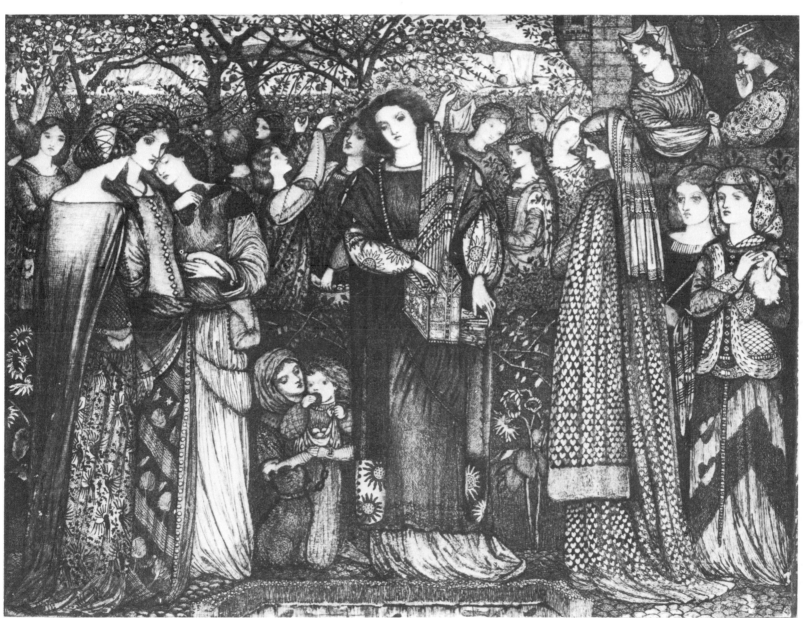

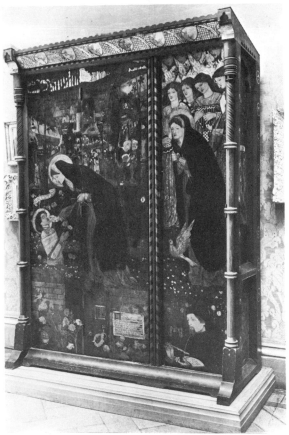

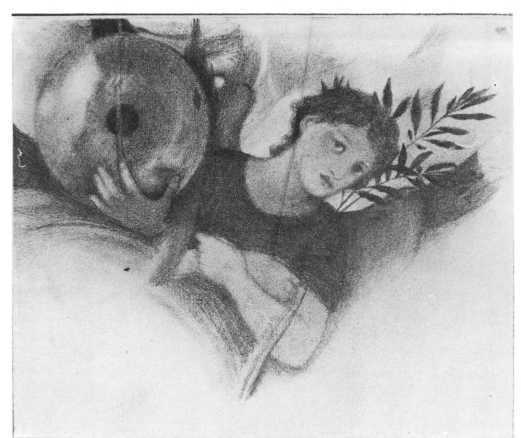

40. 'Prioress's Tale' Cabinet, 1860, designed by Philip Webb. Victoria & Albert Museum, London.

41. Copy after Tintoretto, 1859, pencil, 10¾ × 16⅜. The Ashmolean Museum, Oxford
Made for Ruskin on their visit to Italy. Although a copy, it has more of Jones in it than Tintoretto.

favoured the type of work made by the German Nazarene painters. But the British painters were outraged at any suggestion of a foreign interloper to execute them, and so, in April 1842, a competition was announced for the artists to decorate the building. Watts, Dyce, Horsley, and Armitage were among the winners and Ford Madox Brown was a competitor. All 140 entries were exhibited in May 1843 at the Westminster Hall. The exhibition was attended by Rossetti who, impressed by Madox Brown's entry, later sought him out and became his pupil for a short time. William Dyce received a commission to decorate the central space behind the throne in the House of Lords in 1844, choosing the Baptism of Ethelbert as his subject. The next year he visited Italy making notes on fresco painting, which appeared in the *Sixth Report of the Commission of the Fine Arts, 1846*. In 1847 he was asked by the Commissioners to decorate in fresco the Queen's Robing Room at the Palace of Westminster. The five pictures he made were scenes from the *Morte d'Arthur* which illustrate certain virtues, Faith—The Vision of Sir Galahad, Generosity—King Arthur spared by Sir Lancelot, Hospitality—The Admission of Sir Tristram to the Fellowship of the Round Table, etc. It is interesting that his subjects were taken from Malory—also the origin of the frescoes in the Oxford Union, but how different was the treatment! Dyce's stern and noble sentiments are exchanged for mystery and sensuality; his designs were formal and academic whilst those of Rossetti and his friends were innovatory and adventurous. Had they been as sure of the techniques of fresco as Dyce, there would have been more to witness their effort than there is today. Possibly Rossetti was also spurred on by his knowledge of Watts's vast mural in Lincoln's Inn, executed in 1854. He had paid visits to Little Holland House, and Watts had announced his desire for a national school of mural painters. Rossetti's decision to paint the murals, therefore, reflects a contemporary concern for this type of work and places his Oxford scheme within the stream of the Gothic revival.

On his return to London he set about mustering his friends into a band of painters; recalling the earlier Brotherhood he chose seven—Arthur Hughes, Val Prinsep, and Spencer Stanhope (associates of Watts at Little Holland House), J. Hungerford Pollen (a friend of Millais who had recently painted the ceiling of Merton College Chapel, much admired by his friends), Rossetti, Morris, and Jones. Alexander Munro accepted the invitation to carve a medallion, after Rossetti's design, over the door. Madox Brown, Holman Hunt, and William Bell Scott declined to accept the offer of a space, distrusting

Rossetti and the situation, realising that none had enough experience to take on such a project. Yet it went on. It was to have been complete after two months; the Union, on the advice of Woodward, had agreed to advance £500 to cover expenses only, the artists received no money at all but enough soda water to supply their needs, which were, it turned out, to drench each other during their amiable dogfights. In fact, this was the tone of the operation which later became known as 'the jovial campaign'; pots of paint were poured over each other, practical jokes were repeatedly played on the susceptible Morris, and the noise of their laughter often disturbed the students next door.

The subjects, all from the *Morte d'Arthur*, were as follows:

Pollen: 'King Arthur obtaining the sword Excalibur from the Damsel of the Lake'

Morris: 'Sir Palomides' jealousy of Sir Tristram'

Prinsep: 'Sir Peleas leaving the Lady Ettarde'

Stanhope: 'Sir Gawaine meeting three ladies at the well'

Rossetti: 'Sir Lancelot prevented by his sin from entering the Chapel of the San Graal' (this subject was actually executed). Another was to have been 'How Sir Galahad, Sir Bors and Sir Perceval were fed with the San Graal', but Rossetti never carried it out.

Hughes: 'Arthur and the weeping Queens'

Jones: 'Merlin imprisoned beneath a stone by the Damsel of the Lake'

Morris, the first to finish his mural, began making patterns on the roof, assisted by his friend Dixon, and then went off to a local blacksmith, who executed a suit of armour under his direction.

Jones found himself working next to Spencer Stanhope, and they rapidly became firm friends. When asked to comment on this stage in their friendship by Georgiana Burne-Jones, Stanhope replied:

'In spite of his high spirits and fun he devoted himself more thoroughly to his work than any of the others with the exception of Morris; he appeared unable to leave his picture as long as he thought he could improve it, and as I was behindhand with mine we had the place all to ourselves for some weeks after the rest had gone. Another thing I noted about him was that, in spite of his love of fun and frolic, he seemed absolutely indifferent to everything in the way of athletic games or exercises.'

No one, apart from a man who mixed their colours, was employed by the artists; when they required a model they sat for each other. In this way Jones was used as Sir Lancelot by Rossetti, and when Swinburne, a Balliol man, was introduced to the group by a fellow student, Birkbeck Hill, he was immediately requested to sit, again by Rossetti. On a visit to the theatre, in search of suitable female models Rossetti and Jones noticed a beautiful black-haired girl, tall-necked and graceful, sitting behind them, and immediately he asked her to sit for them. Eventually she did. This was Jane Burden, an ostler's daughter and was to become Morris's wife in 1859, and almost the only model in Rossetti's later work. To the group she became the absolute in 'stunners'; Guinevere, Isolde, Beatrice, La Belle Dame Sans Merçi, and the eternal femme fatale. Her features became for them the symbol of the soul's beauty, capable of expressing the refined and subtle nuances of the artist's malaise or ecstasy; henceforth she occupied a central position in Pre-Raphaelite imagery. Whether Rossetti was infatuated with her then as he was to become later it is difficult to determine, as he was prevented from expressing any such feeling by his entanglement with Elizabeth Siddal.

The two months passed. The murals showed no sign of completion. Because of Miss Siddal's ill-health Rossetti had to return to London, never to finish his picture. Hughes had to finish his part quickly owing to his poverty; the time taken was valuable, and could be better spent painting more remunerative easel pictures; Stanhope and Jones stayed on to terminate their work; Pollen and Prinsep had been able to finish theirs. Within a year, the folly of undertaking such a project without prior study of the medium became clear. The brickwork had not been damp-proofed, the uneven and unprepared surface caught the dust, the colour either became absorbed into the matrix or peeled off, and the unprotected gas flames of the lighting played havoc with the pigments. At that time the artists had whitewashed over the windows which pierced each mural to prevent the light from being over-bright (and they had drawn wombats on them) but today one is prevented from seeing what little remains of the murals by the direct light of the naked windows. In spite of Professor Tristram's restoration in the 1930s, what remains is disappointing.

For some time the Union committee had realised that the original plan of working would not accomplish the scheme, so they appointed, in June 1859, a Mr William Riviere to paint the three remaining bays. In so doing they alienated Rossetti, who refused to have anything more to do with the Union and its murals. As a consequence the whole scheme can be seen as a glorious failure due to the character of Rossetti, however fine his sincerity and enthusiasm. In this particular case the quasi-amateur approach was not sufficient, but it was symptomatic of the inability of British artists at this time who did not number mural techniques among their skills. Apart from Dyce, Watts, Maclise, and Leighton there were no painters capable of executing mural work until the latter part of the century.

The circle of artists around Rossetti was conscious of not having an exhibition space for its output and, not wishing to capitulate to the Academy, they felt the isolation. Like the earlier Pre-Raphaelite Brotherhood and the Oxford brotherhood, their group bonds were strengthened because of this. As a result, there arose a desire to form a community in which they could live and exchange ideas. As early as February 1857 Rossetti makes reference to the scheme in a letter to Madox Brown:

'Concerning the scheme of a college . . . on the night when Morris, Jones and I, came to you, & were discussing the scheme, I expressly said that I should be married by the time it came into operation & would require space accordingly in the building.'

Already their relationship was extremely close and often involved living together. Rossetti particularly encouraged his friends to stay, and naturally the idea emerged. In an unpublished manuscript written c. 1910 A. H. Mackmurdo, the architect, who in the 1880s was acquainted with many of the artists concerned with the project, wrote:

'In 1857, Linnell, Watts, Brown, Rossetti and Leighton were still refused admission into membership of the Academy. Brown feeling his isolation, suggested the establishment of a colony of artists to reside together with common room and general dining room. . . .'

Although the idea came to nothing, it was in part realised by the formation of the Hogarth Club, an exhibiting society made up of the artists around Rossetti. It was founded, through the communal wish for exhibition space and a gathering-place, in 1858. Much of the responsibility for it fell on Stanhope and Jones, who found the arrangements a chore:

'Stanhope and I thought it would be nice to have a club where we could chatter. But what a mistake I made. And then, to do him honour we elected Carlyle—and after that we sent him all the rules and reports and notices of meeting and adjournments of meetings

42. Copy of a detail from 'St George Fighting the Dragon' by Vittore Carpaccio, 1516, in the Church of San Giorgio Maggiore. Watercolour from a sketchbook, 1859, Fitzwilliam Museum, Cambridge

Carpaccio was one of Jones's first loves; in this he was ahead of his time, for Carpaccio was not extensively admired until later. It was Jones's practice to make many copies of the works he admired, using them subsequently as sources of ideas in new works.

43. 'Knight, Death and the Devil' by Albrecht Dürer, 1517, engraving

'Sir Galahad' is clearly based upon this work, Jones probably having it beside him while he worked upon it. He used the inscribed tablet, Dürer's method of signing his work, in many pictures up until 1870.

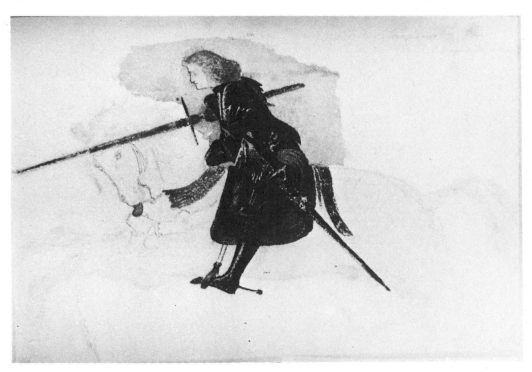

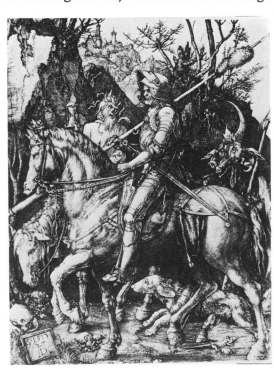

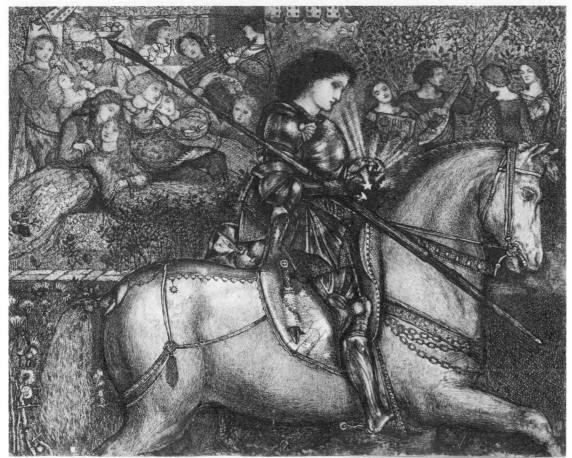

44. 'Sir Galahad', 1858, pen and ink on vellum, $6 \times 7\frac{1}{2}$, The Fogg Art Gallery, Cambridge, Massachusetts
The drawing was made at Little Holland House, while Jones was recuperating. It is interesting to realise that Tennyson made many visits while Jones was there. The horse's saturnine expression recalls that of the horse in Dürer's engraving 'Knight, Death and the Devil'.

and changes of meetings—till one day, talking to a friend of his who knew us, he said the communications of the Hogarth Club had become an afflictive phenomenon.'

A considerable number of artists eventually became members; the painters were G. P. Boyce, John Brett, Madox Brown, W. S. Burton, James Campbell, J. M. Carrick, J. R. Clayton, Eyre Crowe, William Davis, Alfred D. Fripp, Michael F. Halliday, Arthur Hughes, A. W. Hunt, Holman Hunt, J. W. Inchbold, Frederick, later Lord Leighton, R. B. Martineau, William Morris, T. Morten, J. W. Oakes, J. Hungerford Pollen, Val Prinsep, D. G. Rossetti, John Ruskin, W. Bell Scott, Spencer Stanhope, F. G. Stevens, J. L. Tupper, Henry Wallis, G. F. Watts, William Lindsay Windus. Thomas Woolner, the sculptor associated with the Pre-Raphaelites, was a member, as were certain architects: G. F. Bodley, G. E. Street, and Benjamin Woodward. In addition, there was an interesting list of honorary members; besides Carlyle there were David Cox, Francis Danby, Delacroix, William Dyce, William Hunt, J. F. Lewis and William Mulready. The last four of the honorary members had all anticipated the Pre-Raphaelite movement in some way, Cox and Danby were fine, romantic painters who naturally appealed to the group, but Delacroix is a surprising inclusion. One can detect the influence of Rossetti in the choice, for in 1855, when on a visit to Paris, he had seen some of Delacroix's work and he had written to Brown that he was 'the greatest painter of modern times'.

Exhibitions continued until 1861, providing an invaluable outlet for their paintings and drawings. The first, in 1859, contained a number of stained-glass designs by Jones hung along the corridor outside the room they had hired in the Dudley Gallery, Waterloo Place. Madox Brown withdrew his membership when the committee refused to allow him to exhibit his furniture designs as they, like all their contemporaries, considered them unworthy to hang next to 'High Art'. For the period that it lasted, the club fulfilled its function of providing a situation where patrons could view prospective purchases, where the artists could meet and exchange ideas. Periodically they hired a model. At one point, their sense of humour, rarely absent from any of their activities, carried them so far as to consider installing a billiard table in their meeting place! A decision that upset the sober Ruskin.

37

It is interesting to summarise the work that Edward Jones was making from the first moments with Rossetti. Apart from the stained-glass designs, the majority consisted of pen and ink drawings, strongly dependent upon Rossetti's example. The medium itself derives from his master who frequently made drawings of a detailed nature in pen and ink prior to making an oil or watercolour. Many, if not all, were based upon medieval themes which had their origins in Malory, medieval pageant, or, more rarely, contemporary poetry and the Bible. It would be unjust to Morris and Jones to interpret their medievalist imagery as stemming solely from Rossetti's influence. As we have seen, they were steeped in a detailed knowledge of the period whilst at Oxford, identifying with many of the stories. They had studied the illuminated manuscripts at Oxford and had discovered Malory independently of Rossetti. Many of the similarities are due to a community of interest which, once the friendship got under way, resulted in a common direction in all their works. Allowing for this, the maturity of Rossetti, his strength of character and magnetism ensured that he was the centre of interest and that he determined the direction that their art took. Morris was writing poetry which, when it was published in 1857, was entitled *The Defence of Guenevere*; many of the poems owed a great debt to Tennyson. As Alfred Noyes points out in his book on Morris, 'The august simplicity of [Tennyson] was now and always beyond the reach of Morris'. Their reading of that poet at Oxford no doubt helped form both the direction of the subject matter and mould of the younger man's verse. At the same time he could be critical of the poet, calling his Galahad 'a mild youth', and when comparing their two descriptions we can understand his meaning. In Tennyson's words he is:

> A maiden knight—to me is given
>   Such hope, I know not fear;
> I yearn to breathe the airs of heaven
>   That often meet me here.
> I muse on joy that will not cease,
>   Pure spaces clothed in living beams
> Pure lilies of eternal peace,
>   Whose odours haunt my dreams;
> And, stricken by an angel's hand,
>   This mortal armour that I wear,
> This weight and size, this heart and eyes,
>   Are touch'd, are turn'd to finest air.

How different from Morris's unwilling figure who stands alone:

> Night after night your horse treads down alone
>   The sere damp fern, night after night you sit
> Holding the bridle like a man of stone,
>   Dismal, unfriended, what thing comes of it.

And, after comparing his lot with that of more wordly knights he realises that:
> no maid will talk
> Of sitting on my tomb,

The power of Morris's poem lies in Galahad's knowledge of the world and its charm, which makes his act of faith more complex than that of Tennyson's knight, who is by nature saintly.

Jones, who knew both versions, made a pen and ink drawing of the knight in the years 1858–59 and chose to follow Morris's idea, as we see Galahad either riding by, or dreaming of his fellows at their sensual pleasures; at the same time the drawing can be interpreted on the lines of Tennyson, as the knight is so self-absorbed that he could be seen as 'virgin heart in work and will'.

Rossetti had, in fact, illustrated the poem in the *Illustrated Tennyson*, upon which he was working in 1856 when Jones first men him. Like Jones's, his Galahad is introspective,

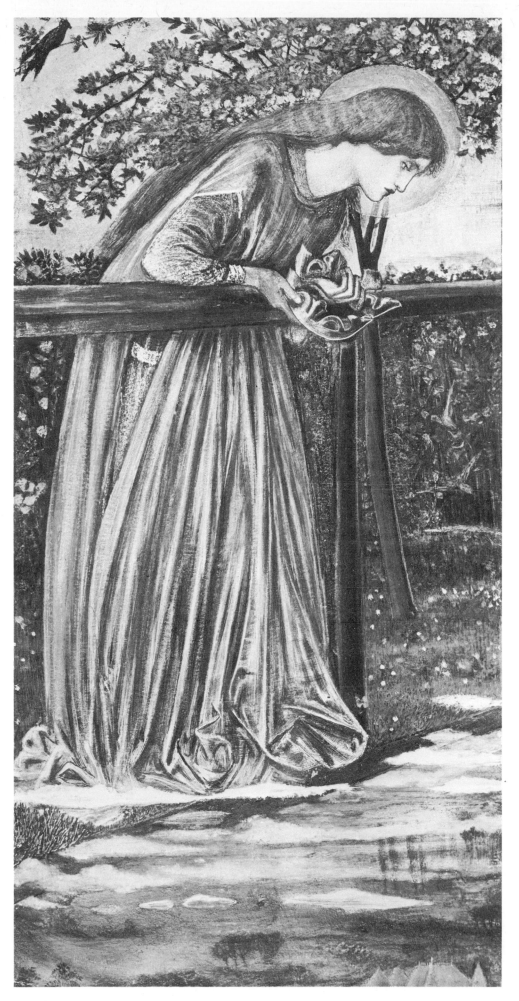

45. 'The Blessed Damozel', 1860, gouache, $15\frac{3}{4} \times 8$, The Fogg Art Gallery, Cambridge, Massachusetts

First conceived as a diptych, only one picture was finished; the one not completed was to have shown the lover on earth below. Rossetti's version of 1875–78 fulfils this intention. The picture was commissioned by T. E. Plint in 1857.

'The blessed damozel leaned out
From the gold bar of Heaven;
Her eyes were deeper than the depth
Of waters stilled or even.'

39

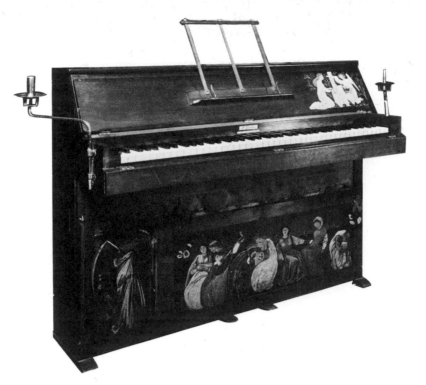

46. 'Piano' by F. Priestly, Victoria & Albert Museum, London
It was painted in 1860 with 'Ladies and Death' at the base, a somewhat macabre design based upon Orcagna's 'Triumph of Death' at the Campo Santo Pisa. The version of 'Chant d'Amour', above, was painted later, *c.* 1864.

but he is shown drinking from the stoop at the Chapel of the Holy Grail, at the point of fulfillment. He strikes a less desolate note.

At first Rossetti's pupil shares with him more than a common literary or historical source. Understandably, when the nature of the master's tuition is remembered, Jones borrowed ideas from his friend's methods of composition, his treatment of accessories and his iconography. His 'Wise and Foolish Virgins' design leans heavily on Rossetti's 'Mary Magdalen at the Door of Simon', for which Jones sat as the model of Christ. 'The Knight's Farewell' contains a decorative angel on the knight's banner which is almost a redrawing of Rossetti's figure in the centre of 'The Salutation of Beatrice'; St Cecilia attending the child Frideswide in the window at Oxford recalls the saint in Rossetti's illustration to Tennyson's 'Palace of Art' and he borrows many more Rossettian devices.

All three, Morris, Jones, and Rossetti were working in 1858 on a theme of the eve of a battle in medieval times, when maids bid their farewell, perhaps forever, to their lovers and attach some memento to their lances. Morris's poem on this theme was called 'The Eve of Crécy', and was written from the point of view of the hesitant lover who gathers courage at this portentous time. He dreams:

> Of Margaret sitting glorious there,
> In glory of gold and glory of hair,
> And glory of glorious face most fair;—
> Ah! qu'elle est belle La Marguerite.
>
> Likewise tonight I make good cheer,
> Because this battle draweth near
> For what have I to lose or fear?—
> Ah! qu'elle est belle La Marguerite.

Rossetti and Jones chose a moment when the knights are riding out; both contain an air of tragedy. Jones's drawing is minutely finished and has three maidens with long, flowing, hair, picking roses to throw to their lovers. Like the 'Prioress's Tale' cabinet, the background reveals Dürer's influence, which Rossetti, describing Jones's drawings, refers to in a letter: 'marvels in finish and imaginative detail, unequalled by anything except perhaps Albert Dürer's finest work.'

His drawing shows, like Rossetti's watercolour, 'Before the Battle', a development of the patterns of the girls' dresses into the structure of the picture. The significant flattening that results arises from a compressing of background and foreground into a single

40

plane, is also frequently found in Rossetti. It is prophetic of the concentration on two-dimensionality we find in Jones's later work. In 'Sir Galahad', the artist's most effective design to date, the organisation is completely successful; against the vertical figures of the girls the subsidiary horizontal lines of knights, castle ramparts and rose-hedge are in perfect poise. Diagonal movements are made by the patterns on their dresses and by the lances carried by the knights and, to prevent the structure from becoming obvious, final asymmetrical elements—the rose-bush, parrot, and spray of leaves held by one of the girls, are subtly placed. Rossetti's approach is basically the same, but all his subjects are condensed into the foreground and the impression is of an arrangement of shapes within a two-dimensional area. There is a similar emphasis on vertical and horizontal elements with the introduction of asymmetry for relief.

For the period 1856-59 much of Jones's activity centred around pen and ink work; these small drawings he could easily manipulate when he was ill, and it is also a convenient medium for experiment. Oil paints tended to make him unwell, which helps to explain the scarcity of early works in that medium. Life with Rossetti was bohemian and demanded great strength since it comprised irregular hours and meals:

'My first summer with Rossetti I worked with him entirely, and he would paint away without stopping to eat anything at all but such a thing as a huge dish of strawberries that he would share with me—and when it was dark he'd go out and wander about for a long time and sometimes wouldn't come home till very late, early morning even. Then begin again in good time for the next day, and that got to be too much for me, another season of it would have killed me off, for I wasn't strong then, so I had to give it up, couldn't go on any more.'

In his own words, he wasn't strong, in fact he became quite seriously ill. The result was that he was taken to Little Holland House, Kensington, to be nursed by Mrs Prinsep who already permanently housed G. F. Watts. Here she led an eccentric, sophisticated, social life where many cultured and fascinating people called; here she entertained such figures as Browning, Tennyson, Gladstone, George Howard, Thackeray, F. D. Maurice, Carlyle, Tom Hughes, and many of the Pre-Raphaelite circle. Rossetti had been a frequent visitor, and he introduced Morris and Jones, who were impressed and a little over-awed by the cosmopolitan style. It attracted Jones, but his friends had reservations. Never had he experienced such worldly company, such a breadth of experience, such maturity and self-possession. Acknowledging the importance of Mrs Prinsep's influence, Jones called her 'the nearest thing to a mother I ever knew'.

When Morris and Rossetti saw how comfortable he had become they immediately had fears that they might lose him altogether. What need had he of them?—for there was an artist of reputation willing to give him tuition which was of the kind that Jones could accept. Watts was grounded in the international academic style and readily preached the rules that Rossetti had hoped he had left behind. The situation precipitated a protestation of affection from Rossetti:

'There is nothing in the world that I care for more than your health dear old fellow—hardly anything nearly as much. I know I must be fonder of you than you can possibly be of me, for you describe it so much better. At any rate there is no man I love so well by half or who loves me so well. However this letter begins to read rather flatly.'

No doubt the letter was prompted in some respects by a feeling that the writer had caused the ill-health in the first place. Rossetti also refers to Plint, the Leeds stockbroker who had commissioned a painting, 'The Blessed Damozel', based on Rossetti's poem, and who had the habit of forwarding money in advance, telling Jones not to worry about owing Plint anything as it was an ingenious method of getting works at a reduced price whilst the artist was still unknown.

His friends did have something to fear for Watts had a considerable influence on the direction of Jones's art. Twenty years later he said that 'Watts compelled me to try and draw better,' meaning, in effect, that Watts made him realise the inadequacy of Rossetti's impromptu style and his own need for a sounder basis in his art. Spencer Stanhope was a pupil of Watts at the same time and described his procedure as a teacher in a letter to his father:

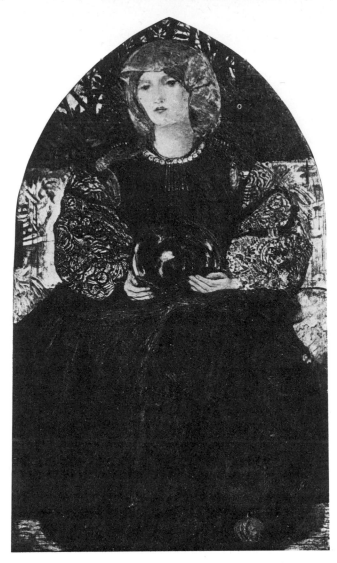

47. 'Art', panel on a cabinet designed by William Burges, 1860, oil on wood, Victoria & Albert Museum, London
Among other young artists who contributed panels were: Henry Holiday, T. S. Morten, E. J. Poynter, and N. H. J. Westlake.

I am undergoing what Watts terms the discipline of drawing, which I ought and should have done at first starting, had Bridges [his first teacher] impressed me with the importance. I am at work upon a towel scattered in a picturesque way upon the floor, and which Watts has enjoined me to draw with as hard a pencil as I can get, and shade with the finest lines possible, in order to study and imitate everything I see upon it, and even to the blacks. He says the first object is to acquire power and facility in representing any object whatsoever upon paper in black and white, and this is the greatest and quickest way of arriving at that facility. After that has been obtained the rest is comparatively easy, anatomy, study of form etc, being most necessary; and painting may follow close upon that. He recommends me to draw lots of outlines as well carefully and decidedly, and without rubbing out; but to avoid drawing even from the antiques indiscriminately, as he says it is a sure way of spoiling one's taste for form.

This method, close to that recommended at the Royal Academy, was able to keep its freshness under Watts as he himself had not studied there, but it was contrary to everything that Rossetti preached. Yet it is not so far removed from the technique described by Madox Brown in his article in *The Germ* of February 1855:

... the painter will have to combine three qualities, each subordinate to the other;— the intellectual, or clear development, dramatic truth and sentiment, of this incident;—the construction or deposition of his groups, the lines most conducive to clearness, effect and harmony;—and the chromatic, or arrangement of colours, light and shade, most suitable to impress and attract the beholder. ... study each separate figure in his composition, study his own acting or else that of any friend . . . not

42

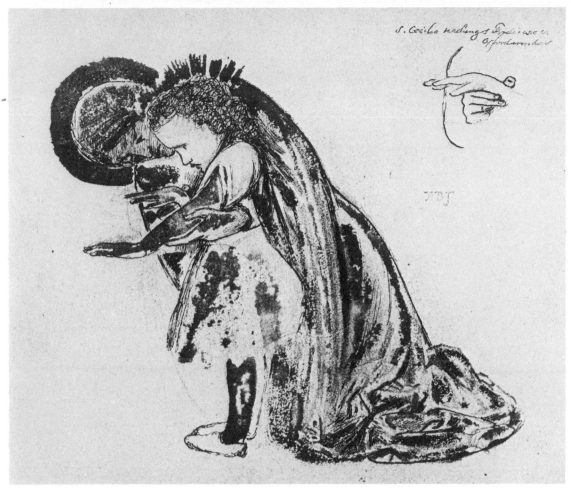

48. Study for 'The Education of
Frideswide': Christ Church Cathedral,
Oxford, Lady Chapel east window.
Birmingham City Museum & Art
Gallery
Left-hand light uppermost panel.
Executed 1860 by Powell's of
Whitefriars. Rossetti designed a
St Cecilia for Tennyson's 'Palace of
Art' in 1860 which obviously influenced
Jones in the preparation of this design.

employing . . . the ordinary paid models . . . they are stiff and feelingless. . . . tend to
curb the vivacity of a first conception . . . to enter into the character of each actor,
studying them one after the other, limb for limb, hand for hand, finger for finger
noting each inflection of joint or tension or sinew.

He then describes how the artist should make a series of sketches of the whole design
until he arrives at a full-scale cartoon. After that he can start on the final painting. Brown's
method is characteristically Pre-Raphaelite in detail, but there is, in common with Watts,
an insistence upon a thorough grounding. Edward Jones was in the fortunate position of
having both these methods and Rossetti's inspirational tuition in his training.

Watts's influence rapidly entered Jones's work. In the 1840s Watts had designed a
painting based upon the story of Buondelmonte 'who rode beneath a portico and looked
up towards a fair lady whose beauty brought about his murder'. At the time of going to
Little Holland House, Jones was working on the same story in pen and ink; it was an
elongated composition with a great many figures, rather unsatisfactory as a whole, but not
without charm. Whilst at the Prinseps's house he made another version closer to Watts's
design, much stronger in composition, choosing the same moment. Buondelmonte is
portrayed riding past the two beautiful girls. It is significant that at least three studies for
the design exist that display an increased sensitivity to the importance of structure and
clarity; because of these, as a whole it is a much more successful design. He had intended to
make a large painting from these studies, but this came to nothing.

In addition, Watts impressed upon him the importance of Italian art, having a great
reverence for it, which must have made the young artist feel the need of further study. Up
to this point he had seen work in the English collections and the Louvre, and of course he
had studied prints and engravings. Now, being less assured under Watts's supervision than
he had been under Rossetti's, he wanted to visit Italy to see for himself. So, in the summer
of 1859, under the watchful eye of Val Prinsep, who took a paternal interest in him, and in
company with Charles Faulkner, they set out on a tour of Northern Italy. They visited

Genoa, Pisa, Florence and Venice, studying and sketching all the time. Jones was making copious notes, assimilating as much as he could; a sketchbook filled during this visit includes figures taken from Botticelli, Ghirlandaio, Mantegna, Benozzo Gozzoli, Carpaccio, Signorelli, and Orcagna.

About Italy he was enthusiastic:

> There was never such a city [Venice] all built in the sea you know, with the houses and palaces in the water and gondolas for hansom cabs to take us everywhere: one comes every morning to take us from our hotel to breakfast in the great Square by the Ducal Palace and wonderful church—there everyone breakfasts in the open air, and girls bring flowers to lay on your plates, and music plays and everything is so bright and stunning. All day long we glide about the water streets in our boat, visiting palaces and churches—there are 100 islands all covered with churches and palaces, and all full of pictures. . . .

His taste for Italy may have been stirred by association with Watts, but behind it too was Ruskin, whose work he had studied from undergraduate days and whose recent friendship had encouraged him to look to Italian quattrocentist painters. Sketchbooks were filled with copies and details from paintings that contained some instruction for the emergent artist.

Meanwhile, before Jones embarked on his Italian tour, Morris had married Jane, and on his return he found plans for their house under way. It was in process of being designed by Philip Webb in a bluntly Gothic character in red brick, and without any fanciful decoration. Although a fine building, the Red House is not as revolutionary as is sometimes claimed. Butterfield's parsonages are of a similar pattern, and the earlier ones date from ten years before. Webb's building is uncompromising to any decorative fussiness and impresses its elemental nature on the beholder. Red bricks give a warmth and romance to this house set among the apple trees, that is central to the works which Jones, Morris and Rossetti, created there.

Inside, there were plenty of stretches of bare walls which provided Jones with an opportunity to paint the murals that he had been inspired to do by his recent Italian trip.

With Morris's marriage, the Red Lion Square days came to an end. Jones had become engaged to Georgiana Macdonald, sister of his friend from Birmingham and Oxford, daughter of a Methodist minister, and Rossetti planned to marry his ailing lover, Elizabeth Siddal. Inevitably marriage meant a reappraisal of their relationships, but for the time being at least there was no slackening in their friendship.

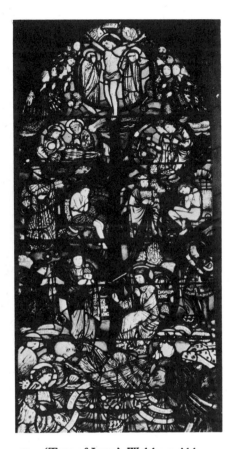

49. 'Tree of Jesse', Waltham Abbey, Essex. East window, 1860. Executed by Powell's of Whitefriars. Commissioned by Burges in 1860 as part of his restoration of the Abbey

The architect had originally engaged N. H. J. Westlake to design this window for Lavers & Barraud, stained-glass workers, but Westlake's scheme was rejected. Burges was a strong advocate of utilising the services of able young artists. He chose Edward J. Poynter to decorate the nave ceiling, which was based on that of Peterborough Cathedral, and Henry Holiday painted a 'blind' window, modelled on those in the Duomo in Florence. Powell's made a second version of the centre panel of this window and sent it to the International Exhibition in 1862. This is still owned by the Whitefriars Glass Co. The cartoons for 'Majesty' and the 'Third Day of Creation' are at the Victoria & Albert Museum, London.

Chapter Four

Foundation of the Firm

Philip Webb designed the 'Red House' in April 1859; it was ready for occupation towards the end of summer the following year. An important contribution to the atmosphere of the house was the orchard which existed on the site. The trees had been deliberately left intact during the building of the house, so that when the Morrises moved in it already had a mellow appearance. It was situated some few miles outside Bexley, Kent, surrounded by undulating country of woods and meadows. Amidst these rural surroundings Morris cultivated a garden to rival them. His knowledge of, and sympathy for, plant life was a fundamental part of his nature and his treatment of the garden was as medieval in spirit as Webb's building. When laying out beds of lilies, sunflowers and patches of bright summer flowers in gardens enclosed by rose trellises, he was remembering those of the illuminated manuscripts he had recently been studying in which the Madonna sat with her baby, or where scenes of Courtly Love were enacted. When the stately Jane moved along the grass paths reality and art became indistinguishable, especially when she wore the clothes Morris had designed for her to pose as La Belle Iseult or Guinevere. These dresses Jones also used for his models to wear in 'Clerk Sanders', 'King René', and the Tristram series, and is his 'Girl and Goldfish' where the dress, orchard and the red-bricked building gave an impression of the atmosphere of Morris's home in Kent, as he saw it. For them, medievalism was not just a style with which to decorate paintings or buildings (set among the Gothic revival their works are relatively sober), but a total way of life. Their paintings were genuine reflections of their contemporary life and mood. This was no playing at games or mere dressing up, but a desire to search out and return beauty to an age from which it seemed to have disappeared. Beauty was not monopolised by High Art. Neither was it exclusively medieval, but they felt that in the Middle Ages life and art were closer to nature and therefore less corrupt. For these reasons their work does not fall into superficial historicism but is intense and touched with visionary power. They believed in using medieval situations as an expression of their inner world, to fuse dream with reality and to combine their way of life with their art.

Such was their theory of art. It had been inherited from the Pre-Raphaelites who reintroduced earnestness in reaction against the art without high purpose with which they were faced at the Royal Academy. Rossetti particularly, was interested in the process of art and the relationship between the reality that the artist saw in the world around him and its subjective interpretation. Many of his drawings are centred on the artist and his model, who, in Rossetti's case, was his lover Elizabeth Siddal. He shows the artist struggling to create on his canvas that which appears before him. By including himself in the drawings he creates a paradox by making the question of the nature of art the content of art. In his masterpiece of this type, 'St Catherine' (1857), he portrays a medieval artist painting his model as the saint. But she is not treated as a model but as the saint herself. The work is conceived as though the artist has actually entered the painting to join the saint. As a pupil

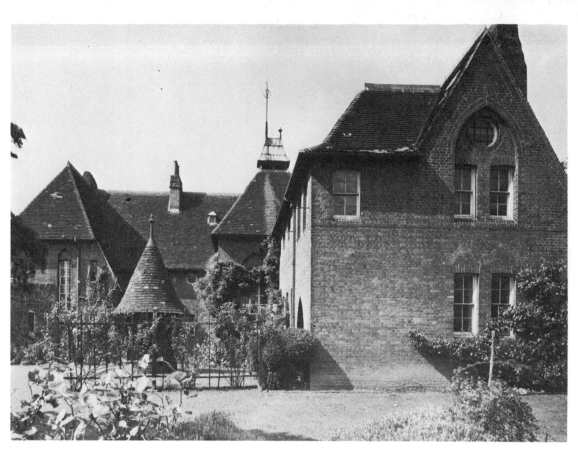

50. Red House, Bexley Heath, Kent, 1859. Philip Webb, architect.

of Rossetti, Jones inherited this concern for the definition of art with its various levels of operation and its relationship with life. It was to preoccupy him throughout his working years.

After the experience of furnishing the rooms in Red Lion Square, Morris was not prepared to rely on any existing designers to supply him with the contents for his new house. Any additions to the furniture moved from Red Lion Square either he or his friends designed. In fact 'the house that Top built' was created in the community spirit true to any of the Pre-Raphaelite enterprises. Morris designed hangings, embroidered by Jane, Jones designed hangings, stained glass, and murals which he painted on his visits. Much of the new furniture was designed by Philip Webb, who also contributed designs for fire-dogs, large copper candlesticks and table glass. Each weekend the friends collected there, contributing something to the beauty of the building until it became a 'palace of art'. The idea of a community of sympathetic artists still remained. Included in the plans was a scheme for extending the group of buildings into a square that surrounded a common courtyard. On its completion Jones was to have moved in, but because of his impecunious state he deferred, until in 1865 it proved no longer possible and the plan was dropped.

Jones's contribution to the decoration of the house was planned on a large scale; it was to have included the majority of the walls, upon which he was to have painted murals. Scenes from the Fall of Troy were conceived for the stairs; below them in the hall he designed a warship with rows of shields hung over the side. Unfortunately the scheme was never executed, and only a design of the ship was ever carried out, but in association with it, along a corridor, are two small stained-glass windows of 'Fortune' and 'Love' surrounded by quarries by Philip Webb and Morris. Later a set of paintings made in the early 1870s was based on the same story and included figures of 'Fortune' and 'Love', which would imply that although the decorative paintings came to nothing the ideas were important enough to stimulate later development. A belt of seven tempera paintings was to have run round the drawing room on the first floor, celebrating the marriage of Sir Degravaunt. Only three were executed, 'The Marriage', 'The Musicians', and 'The Wedding Feast', the latter containing portraits of Morris and Jane as the knight and his bride. Below the series was to have hung a continuous dado of painted hanging 'of bushy trees and parrots and labels on which he wrote Morris's motto "If I Can"'. One of the

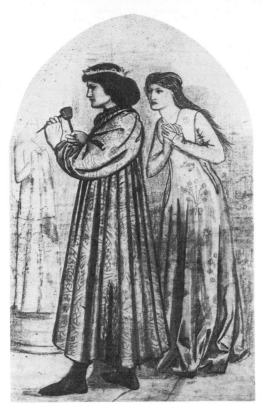

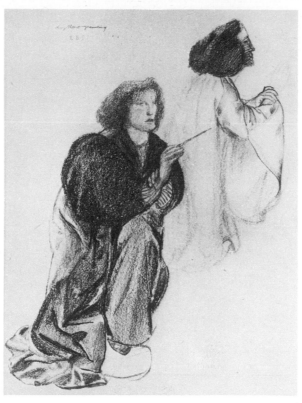

bedrooms contained Adam and Eve in the Garden of Eden but this was the only one to contain murals. Likewise unfinished were the paintings on a large cabinet built into the hall, which also contained a seat, drawers and a two-doored cabinet above. Upon these are two scenes from the *Niebelungen Lied*—one by Morris (for which the mis-named study 'Iseult on the Ship' is preparatory) and one by Jones.

Embroidered hangings were used liberally as wall-covering, no wall-paper being used in the house. The ceilings throughout the house had simple painted patterns which were pricked into the wet plaster to enable them to be repainted when required. Later they experimented in tile-making, at first with only partial success—as is shown by the inadequately fired tiles in a porch leading to the garden. Upon them is also inscribed Morris's motto. All this is evidence of their serious intention to live as their vision insisted; life had to be beautiful, but it could also be fun.

Stories of their larkings at Red House have become as famous as the house itself. They were able to indulge their *joie de vivre* because they were young and they had refused to accept the formalities of contemporary social conduct. Morris was usually the butt of their good-humoured jokes and generally sat for the villain if one was required in a drawing. Georgiana Burne-Jones tells in the following extract how the group could combine pranks with more constructive employment:

> Charles Faulkner came down a couple of days after we did, and helped to paint patterns on walls and ceilings, and played bowls in the alley, and in intervals between work joined in triangular bear fights in the drawing room. Once, in the middle of a scrimmage that had surged up the steps into the 'Minstrel's Gallery', he suddenly leapt clear over the parapet into the middle of the floor with an astounding noise; another time he stored windfallen apples in the gallery and defended himself against all comers until a too well delivered apple gave Morris a black eye.

The 'Minstrel's Gallery' referred to was a parapet on top of the Red Lion Square settle, which had been installed in the drawing room and from which the group intended to sing carols at Christmas.

Out of the necessity of furnishing Red House the wider issue of decoration for others emerged. The friends realised that between them they had considerable experience in designing a variety of objects. Morris was wealthy enough to cover the initial period of the

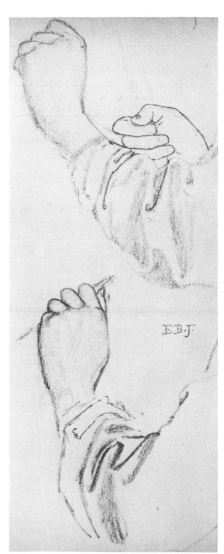

formation of a firm, and to the others it represented a very possible means of earning an income. After much discussion they decided to create a company which was registered as Morris, Marshall, Faulkner and Company. The other members were Rossetti, Philip Webb, Edward Jones, and Ford Madox Brown. Arthur Hughes was invited to join but declined, although he actually designed one of a series of stained-glass panels in 1862. The firm came into being on April 11, 1861 and published a circular giving details of its scope and intention:

> The growth of decorative art in this country, owing to the efforts of English Architects, has now reached a point at which it seems desirable that Artists of reputation should devote their time to it. . . . It is anticipated that by such co-operation, the largest amount of what is essentially the artist's work, along with his constant supervision, will be secured at the smallest possible expense, while the work done must necessarily be of a much more complete order, than if any single artist were incidentally employed in the usual manner.

Then followed a list of the fields in which the firm was to operate:

I Mural Decoration, either in Pictures or in Pattern Work, or merely in the arrangement of colours, as applied to dwelling-houses, churches, or public buildings.
II Carving generally as applied to Architecture.
III Stained Glass, especially with reference to Mural Decoration.
IV Metal Work in all its branches, including Jewellery.
V Furniture, either for its beauty on its own design, on the application of materials hitherto overlooked, or on its conjunction with Figure and Pattern Painting. Under this head is included Embroidery of all kinds, Stamped Leather, and ornamental work in such other materials, besides every article necessary for domestic use.

Premises were taken at 8 Red Lion Square not far from Morris's and Jones's old quarters. On the first floor, over a jeweller's, were office and showrooms, the workshops were on the third floor and part of the basement together with a kiln for firing glass and tiles. This establishment consisted of twelve boys taken from a Home in the Euston Road, and two men, both with experience in the production of stained glass—George Campfield who had been employed by Heaton, Butler and Bayne, and C. E. Holloway from Powell's Stained Glass Company of Whitefriars.

What the circular said of the growth of decorative art in the early part of the nineteenth century was true. With the increase in church-building following the population explosion and the religious revival came a need for decorators. Many churches built in the 1850s came under the influence of either the Oxford Movement or the Cambridge University Camden Society. They demanded an architecture which could accommodate the High Church ritual, a focal position for the altar at the chancel end, nave, two aisles at the sides, and a transept. Any decoration that aided the service and intensified the devotion of the worshippers was also encouraged. There was also another influence at work: in 1849 Ruskin's *Seven Lamps of Architecture* appeared, which extolled the materials used in Gothic architecture, particularly the use of constructional polychromy, a theme which Ruskin followed up in 1851 in his *Stones of Venice*. Consequently, churches were being built in red, yellow, and blue brick, with interiors using polychromatic encaustic tiles, mixtures of coloured marbles and painted roofs. Decoration in the form of mosaic, mural, and stained glass obviously suited such architecture, and from the 1830s they became more and more an important part of the building. Charles Winston was an early investigator of the new stained glass, and the firm with which he was associated also developed mosaic as part of its business. A. W. N. Pugin was also a pioneer in the decorative arts from the 1830s, designing chalices, stained glass, and other accessories. Together with William Butterfield, who made a modern style by combining the use of contemporary materials in a frank way with a Gothic imagery, he set the scene for the firms of decorators such as Morris and Co., Clayton and Bell, Gibbs and Howard, etc. At

48

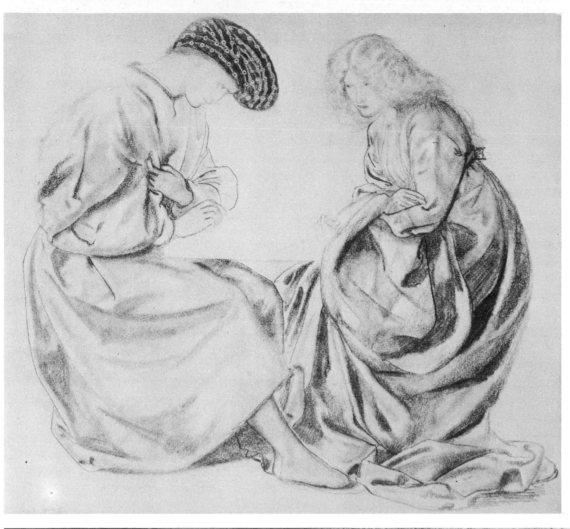

54. 'The Backgammon Players', 1861, pencil, $11\frac{1}{2} \times 12\frac{3}{4}$, private collection

This is a study for the painting at the Birmingham City Museum & Art Gallery; a very finished pencil version is at the Fitzwilliam Museum, Cambridge, and a cabinet in the Museum of Modern Art in New York has a version on its doors.

55. 'An Idyllic Scene', *c.* 1861, pencil, $7\frac{1}{2} \times 12$, Tate Gallery, London

Possibly an early idea for the painting 'Chant d'Amour'. An idyllic pastoral atmosphere pervades the drawing, which may derive from Giorgione.

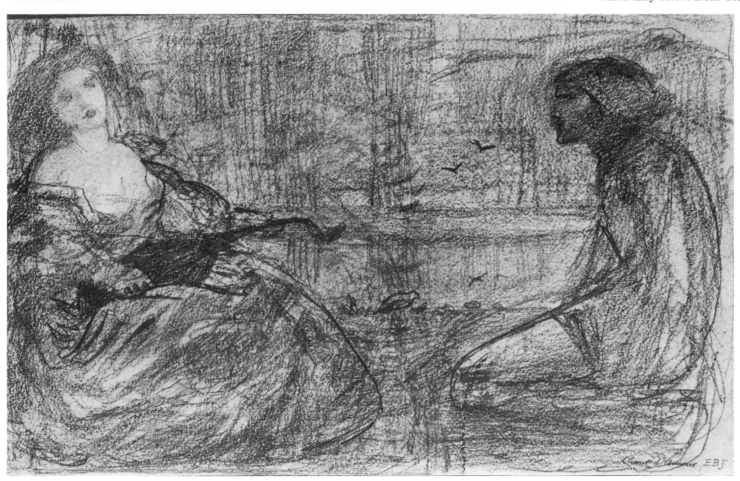

the time of their appearance Morris and Co. were certainly not innovators, but their style of decoration was different from that of their fellows. This was due to their being painters, which enabled them to make fresh appraisals of the disciplines of the various crafts. As painters they were more original and less dependent on archaeological accuracy; the art they created, like Butterfield's, was genuinely nineteenth-century in essence, however much it took from earlier styles.

The success of the company can be attributed to one primary factor; Morris's and Philip Webb's association with architects, a number of whom were important figures. G. F. Bodley had met them while they were working in Street's office in the 1850s; J. P. Seddon they knew and they also worked for Butterfield. Through the Pre-Raphaelite circle William Burges had become known to most of the firm's members; Jones designed the Waltham Abbey window for Powells to his commission and he had contributed a panel to a cabinet Burges designed in 1860.

More of an innovation was their inclusion of secular areas of design. Decorative furniture is almost by its nature singular and difficult to produce. Hitherto, furniture of the kind the firm was now offering had only been available as special commissions, often as part of a larger plan. Also on offer were smaller, more functional pieces designed by Madox Brown, but the famous Sussex chair was a later addition to their lists. Besides the furniture, there were tiles, embroideries, and stained glass available to the average customer, which were of a stock design. They were also suppliers of smaller domestic pieces, table-glass and beaten metal-ware. Philip Webb was the designer of most of the material as well as the jewellery, which was made by the jeweller on the ground floor. The company was thus among the first to attempt to raise the standard of commercial design after the 1851 exhibition, and as a co-operation of artists combining to improve standards they set an example which was followed by similar ventures (Century Guild, Guild of Handicraft, etc) which eventually revolutionised design-consciousness.

However, church-decoration was their most important activity during the early years of the firm. Their first commission was to supply stained glass for Bodley's church, All Saints, Selsley, Gloucestershire. It called for a large number of designs. Of these, six were contributed by Rossetti, five by Morris, two by Madox Brown, four by Philip Webb, and four by Peter Marshall. Jones designed Christ in Majesty, Resurrection, three panels of Christ Blessing the Children, and Adam and Eve. The large Creation rose window was a joint effort. Their inexperience is shown in the carrying out of this first commission; the colour is duller and less effective than later productions, their drawing with enamels is clumsy and obvious, and the designs are poorly related to the framing windows. The faults arose not from inadequate cartoons, these are well handled by each individual artist, but during the workshop stage of production, and in the overall planning by Philip Webb. A significant difference is apparent when the glass at Selsley is compared with that made by Powell's to Jones's designs. Winston's influence is felt in the small pieces of glass; the emphasis is on simple drawing with the lead and bright colours which, at a distance, lose their narrative quality to become pure colour. The Whitefriars glass draws with colour but never to a degree that obscures the biblical scene it portrays, the chief figures are isolated from the surround by a subtle use of colour and the abstract mosaic effect at a distance is much less pronounced. During the first years of the firm's existence Morris purchased coloured glass panes from Powell and Company, yet, in spite of this, their use of colour appears idiosyncratic. As in its drawing, Morris and Co. preferred to follow naturalism in colour, choosing more earth colours and less red.

Morris himself was responsible for the selection of the glass from Powell's, and he also chose the colour for each window. All the designers had to supply were the cartoons, which were quite often bold drawings without indication of lead lines. These Morris drew over, indicating the extent of each piece of glass. At other times the designer only supplied a small drawing, which was then re-drawn on a large scale by Campfield to the size of the window. This was the case with the Adam and Eve at Selsley, and would account for the fact that the finished window hardly looks like Jones's work.

A composite scheme of glass required an overall continuity; with Morris supervising the designs from the various artists a homogeneous style was assured. Philip Webb had the

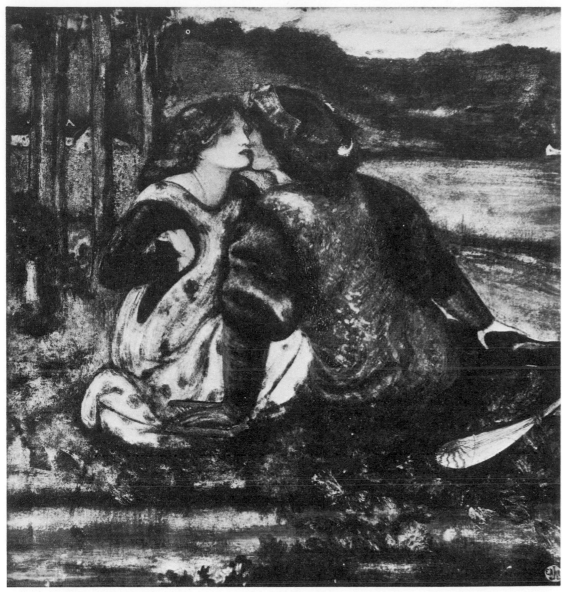

56. 'An Idyll', 1862, gouache and gum, 12 × 11, Birmingham City Museum & Art Gallery
This love-scene owes something to Giorgione in subject and colour; it has the mood of a *fête champêtre* and is similar in some respects to a Giorgionesque drawing in the collection at Christ Church, Oxford.

responsibility of designing the setting of each window, designing canopies and patterning to fill any traceries not included in other artists' designs. Both he and Morris contributed quarry designs where necessary.

Over the next few commissions their command of the techniques improved as did the quality of design. The glass supplied to St Michael's, Brighton, another Bodley church, is more assured in its use of enamels and leading to create form, and the colour is much stronger. Edward Jones's contribution is not uniformly successful. A series of angels playing bells is weak because the tiny angels are lost amid the large traceries, yet a two-light window at the east end (the Flight into Egypt) shows the mastery to which we are accustomed in his later glass. After a few hesitant designs when the firm first began he exhibits a striking command of the medium and is able to distribute the masses in perfect harmony with the shape and size of each window. The examples at Lyndhurst (1862–63) and Darley Dale (1861) are the finest of his early work for the firm but the latter is marred by deterioration of the enamels—another indication of inexperience. Especially successful is the panel 'Peter being delivered from Prison' in the north transept at Lyndhurst (1863), in which the construction is based upon a series of diagonals that lead from the sleeping knights at the base to the angel leading Peter at the top. Particularly attractive is the glass that makes up the angel's wing—Morris has made use of the accidental streakiness to suggest its texture. He must have noticed Powell's use of glass of that kind in Jones's Frideswide window at Christ Church Cathedral, Oxford, where it is used over the sails of the boat in the centre tracery light. An unusual feature of the Darley Dale window is that a panel of five girls playing instruments is used twice. As it is not part

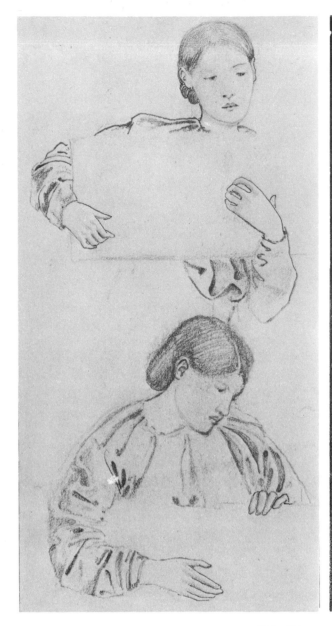

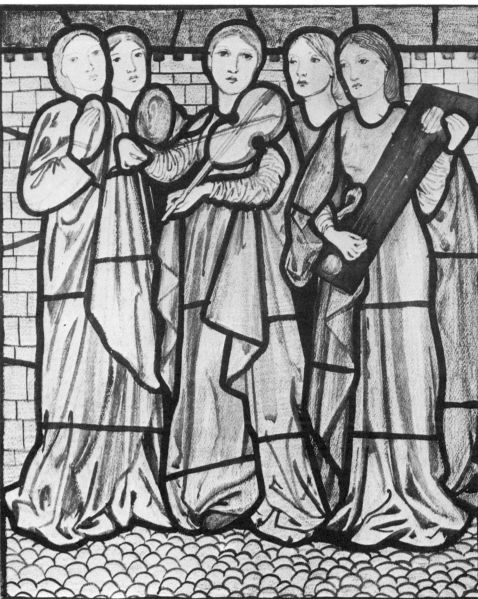

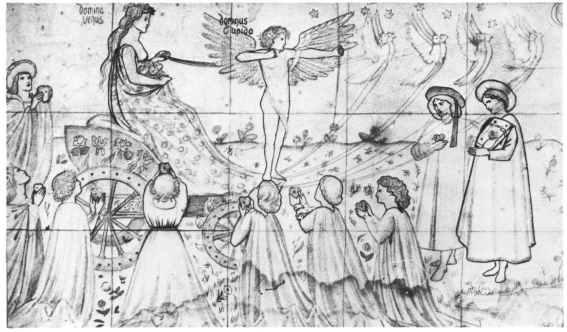

57. Two studies of Georgiana, 1861, pencil, $9\frac{3}{4} \times 5$, private collection
The drawings were preparatory for a cartoon of an angel, used in a tracery light of the 'Song of Solomon' window at St Helen's Church, Darley Dale, Derbyshire.

58. 'Girl Musicians', cartoon for 'Song of Solomon' window, St Helen's Church, Darley Dale, Derbyshire, 1861. Coloured chalks, $23\frac{1}{2} \times 18\frac{1}{2}$. Birmingham City Museum & Art Gallery.

59. 'The Passing of Venus', 1861, pencil, crayon and ink, $14\frac{1}{4} \times 24\frac{3}{8}$; collection of Joanna Matthews
A design for tiles, this is the earliest version of the subject, which later appeared as the background of 'Laus Veneris', as a tapestry, and as a large, unfinished oil painting (in the Tate Gallery, London).

52

of a pattern, it suggests that its use a second time was to fill the window for which there was one cartoon short—another example which shows the firm had not yet reached complete fluency in production. Yet they soon overcame their short-comings and were receiving many commissions from this time on. One reason for their success was the 1862 International Exhibition in London; they took two stalls exhibiting tiles, painted furniture, embroideries and stained glass. £150 worth of goods were sold and they received two gold medals in spite of being accused of exhibiting actual medieval glass.

To a lesser extent the firm executed mural decoration; amongst the first were Butterfield's Church, St Albans, Holborn (1862), now sadly mostly destroyed; Lyndhurst Parish Church (by William White 1862), for which Jones designed angels that were painted by Hungerford Pollen (these have been restored recently), and St Martin's, Scarborough (by G. F. Bodley 1862). This last is the most important, a magnum opus measured against the early commissions lasting for a number of years.

The windows at Scarborough were designed by Rossetti, Jones, Morris, Marshall and Webb; Spencer Stanhope designed figures for the organ case. Rossetti's, Madox Brown's and Morris's designs were executed by Campfield on the pulpit, and Jones and Morris designed murals which, unfortunately, are now faded. (Jones's were adapted from his stained-glass 'Adoration of the Magi' (Amington, 1864). Rossetti's glass series 'The Parable of the Vineyard' (designed 1861) is of considerable interest since it contains portraits of many of the circle, but most noticeable is his choice of Morris as the villain and Jones as the saintly son of the owner of the vineyard. (Rossetti's portrait appears in the upper-left corner of 'The Battle of Beth Horon' by Jones at Lyndhurst.)

In 1864 the firm supplied a triptych reredos for Cheddleton Parish Church and decorated the organ at Beddington Parish Church; the figures, designed by Morris and executed by Campfield, are welded into an elaborate scheme of murals at the apsidal end which are strongly influenced by William Burges. They demonstrate how two different companies could combine successfully during this period of the revival of church decoration and how Morris, Faulkner and Co. were a typical part of it. A similar combination was to be found at St Peter's, Hinton Road, Bournemouth (restored by G. E. Street), where sets of tiles designed by Jones were set amidst contemporary murals behind the altar. They are now replaced by mosaics put there in the 1890s after the tiles had deteriorated.

Secular commissions came in at the outset of the firm, which was a logical step from their experiments in the production of domestic material. During the first year, Jones painted panels for three cabinets which were designed by Philip Webb. They were simple Gothic structures with expanses of flat areas to cater for the decorative panels. Upon each cabinet Jones painted a single picture. His painting 'The Backgammon Players' first appeared on one of these, and on the other two he painted 'Ladies in a Wood' ('Green Summer') and 'Cophetua and the Beggar Maid'. As decorations the paintings are not as effective as the cabinet the artist painted for himself in 1860. Upon this is a series of girls attending to, or being frightened by, various animals. Unlike the firm's productions the decoration runs continuously around, including the whole area at the front and sides, which integrates the painting with the form of the piece of furniture. This does not occur in 'The Backgammon Players' cabinet because the decoration is restricted to the doors which are positioned in the centre and are dwarfed by the size of the whole. Consequently, the paintings remain what they are—mounted easel paintings. Morris painted the 'St George' cabinet, designed by Webb at the same time, which, like Jones's girls and animals piece, is painted throughout, being specially made for the 1862 exhibition. J. P. Seddon, the architect, commissioned Morris's company, in 1862, to decorate a bureau he had designed with a series of paintings from the imaginary incidents from the honeymoon of King René of Anjou, as related in Walter Scott's *Anna von Geierstein*. Another collective enterprise resulted. King René was described by Scott as having made excursions into the various arts; the artists made this an excuse to portray the king at Architecture (Madox Brown), Music (Rossetti), Painting (Jones), and Sculpture (Jones). A smaller set of panels at the top show Gardening (Rossetti), Glass Blowing (Prinsep), Metalwork (Prinsep), and Sewing (Jones). Seddon became diocesan architect for Llandaff for ten years from 1852 and was responsible for the commissions for the stained glass and Rossetti's triptych in the cathedral, and also the three-light window designed by Marshal at Coity Parish Church, Glamorgan.

Seddon's bureau was also exhibited at the 1862 International Exhibition. It gave the press an opportunity to comment, generally unfavourably. 'The colouring is particularly crude and unpleasing while the design is laboriously grotesque', was the opinion of the *Ecclesiologist*, and *The Builder* thought it 'unnecessarily crude and ugly'. Obviously their view was not shared by an important minority, who re-commissioned the designs in various other forms.

By the late 1860s furniture of this type was superseded by more utilitarian examples for two reasons, firstly because their products were becoming less obviously Gothic and, secondly, each artist was more involved with his personal work and could not afford to spend precious time painting furniture for small return.

Tiles were included in an addition the company made to its circular in 1862; 'Paper Hangings and Painted Earthenware including wall Tiles with pictured subjects, figures or patterns'. In fact Jones had already designed a 'Triumph of Love' set of tiles in 1861, and from that date until 1863, he designed many more, including sets of the fairy tales Cinderella (1862–63), Sleeping Beauty (1863), and Beauty and the Beast (1863). His designs for tiles are singular, quaint, and slightly comic; they are delightfully apposite for their decorative use in the drawing or dining room. Often they were incorporated into a larger commission. In Birket Foster's house at Witley, Surrey, they were used in the bedroom fireplaces and on the chimney breasts. The Dining Hall of Queen's College, Cambridge has tiles from the hands of many members of the firm; once again they cover the chimney breast and represent the seasons, the sun, moon, and two Queens. After 1866 tile production came to an end as a major part of their output; figure tiles disappeared completely, but pattern tiles remained as decorative accessories. For the whole time that the firm included them in their production none were made, all were bought in and then painted and fired on the premises. The painting was done from small cartoons the size of the tiles by members of the workshop, Faulkner or his sister or 'Georgie' Jones. Later, any large tile commissions were performed by William de Morgan, working in conjunction with Morris and Co.

Although much less evident, secular stained glass of this period also stimulated a number of important designs from the members of the firm. A commission in 1862 from a Mr Walter Dunlop of Bradford produced a series based upon the story of Sir Tristram from Malory. Rossetti made two designs, Arthur Hughes one, Val Prinsep one, and four were

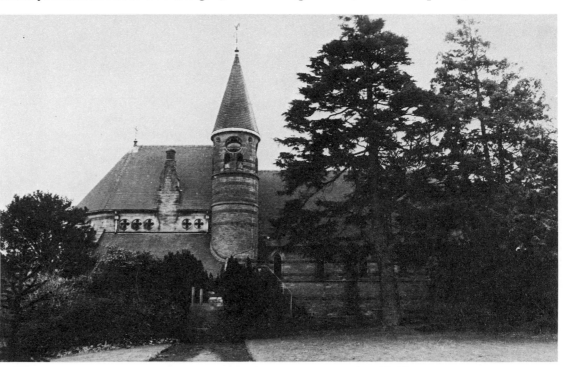

60. All Saints Church, Denstone, Staffordshire, 1860–62, G. E. Street, architect

This church has a particularly fine series of stained-glass windows by Clayton & Bell, commissioned by Street.

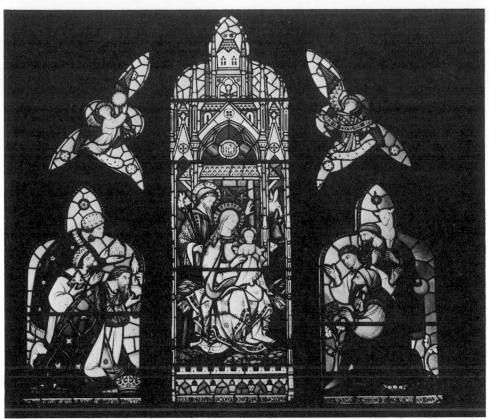

61. 'Nativity' window by Clayton & Bell in the south chancel of Lapworth Church, Warwickshire, 1861
Commissioned by G. E. Street. Although this is a very fine window, it is far more authentically based on medieval examples than contemporary work by the Morris firm, whose artists had a more romantic view of the period.

62. All Saints Church, Selsley, Gloucestershire, 1861–62, G. F. Bodley, architect
Bodley was the most important architect-patron of the Morris firm during the 1860s and, generally, shared the responsibility for the character of the glass.

63. Architectural plan of south nave westernmost window at All Saints Church, Selsley, Gloucestershire by Philip Webb. Figure panels by Burne-Jones. Executed to slightly altered designs by Morris, Marshall, Faulkner & Co., 1861. Birmingham City Museum & Art Gallery.

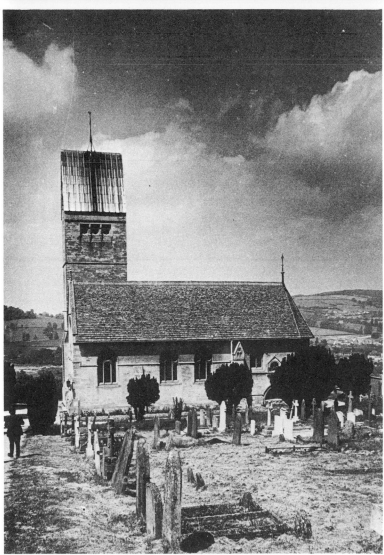

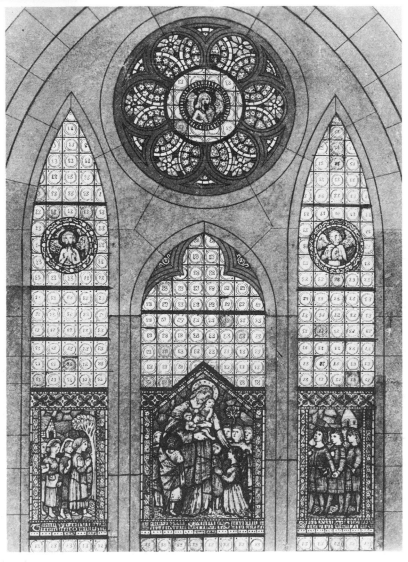

made by Morris, one by Madox Brown, and four by Edward Jones—'The Wedding', 'The Madness . . .' and 'The Burial of Tristram', and 'King Mark preventing Isoude from slaying herself'. Arthurian, too, are two three-quarter-length figures of a youthful prince and maiden that Jones designed in 1861, although they derive from the Beauty and the Beast fairy tale.

The formation of the company which involved so much of his time was of seminal importance in directing the course of Jones's art. It came during a period when he had completed a type of apprenticeship and yet was not fully formed as an artist. Rossetti, Watts, and Ruskin had each influenced him, and he gradually felt more confident and inspired to develop by his recent acquaintance with Italian art at first hand. Morris turned more towards Gothic prototypes; he had, during his period at university, visited the low countries twice and his designs for glass, embroidery, and furniture decoration, show a Flemish treatment of drapery and posture which can also be traced in his friend's art. Jones was aware of these influences at work and was able at this early date to fuse them into a distinguishable style. But he was continuously dogged by doubts and insecurity which were increased by contact with fellow artists who had had the benefit of an academic training. He hated the formulae that passed for inspiration, but at the same time was reminded that they possessed a technique which he envied. As a result he studied the old masters in much greater depth than usually recommended even by an academy, and persisted in evolving a technique until he possessed an unrivalled virtuosity—but he never overcame his fear of academies.

Designing for Morris and Company meant that he worked fast producing a great corpus of work; he was unable to dwell long on each composition. Consequently he drew upon all the resources that were available and experimented with them. The influence of Rossetti persisted in the stained-glass designs some time after it had passed from his paintings, which were created at a much more leisurely pace. The influence of quattrocentist Italian and Flemish painting and illuminated manuscripts of the same period is traceable. But his designs are no mere art-historical pastiche, they are imbued with his personal vision which overlays a borrowed construction. Both he and Morris chose a Flemish prototype for their 'Annunciation' in which the kneeling Virgin turns from her prayers to greet the angel Gabriel, who stands behind her. Jones's 'Resurrection' at Selsley is clearly based upon a tradition that included Memling's in the Louvre, and the same tradition inspired his several 'Christ in Majesty' versions, which are so frequent amongst the early glass. Other designs are Italianate in origin, revealing a knowledge of Giotto, Fra Angelica, Piero della Francesca, and Giovanni da Matteo. Many of these masters he knew from the paintings themselves; he spent a great deal of time in the British Museum, the newly opened South Kensington Museum, and the National Gallery, but he also relied upon the recently published prints and books of reproductions. Sketchbooks from this period bear witness to his consulting numerous sources to widen his knowledge and increase his technique; they include drawings taken from *Costumes of the Ancients* by Thomas Hope (1809), *Dresses and Decorations of the Middle Ages* by Henry Shaw (1843), sketches from works by Luca della Robbia, ('The Labours of the Months') by Andrea della Robia, ('The Assumption of the Virgin') and from Lucas Cranach, Van Eyck, Lucas van Leyden, and many others. The list could even include Attic vase-paintings.

However, the impression of his designs when seen collectively is not that he took from each individual work but that he studied widely and was conscious of working within a tradition which had begun with the Renaissance and sometimes earlier. At this stage in his development he reflects the contemporary taste among artists and designers for the early Renaissance painters, and he was only exceptional in the depth of his knowledge. Ruskin was the chief mentor and Jones, being close to the critic, naturally shared some of his enthusiasms. After his 1862 visit and subsequent trips to Italy he was able to decide for himself about Italian painting, and from that time there developed significant differences of opinion between the artist and the critic over Carpaccio, Signorelli, and Pollaiuolo, whom Jones championed. Dürer's influence is more obvious in the pen and ink drawings of the late 1850s than in his work of a few years later. Jones's study of fifteenth-century manuscripts is revealed in the following entry from G. P. Boyce's diary for April 12, 1860:

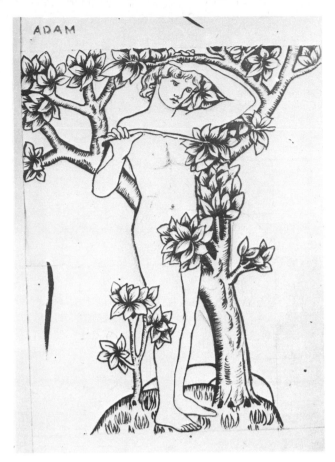

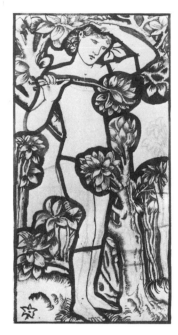

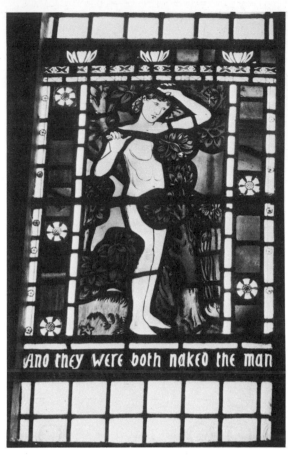

'Met Jones and H. Wells & Joanna at B. M. Jones having promised to show us some of the most beautiful manuscripts in the collection. First the Roman de la Rose. . . .'

May 15, 1862 saw Jones, his wife, and John Ruskin bound for Paris en route for Northern Italy. At this point he was as near being a pupil of the critic as he ever was. It was Ruskin who impressed upon him the necessity of drinking from the fountain of Italian painting. As we have seen, he was a willing visitor and was still in search of a style. Whilst in Paris they visited the Louvre where, one can assume, they saw Fra Angelico's 'Coronation of the Virgin' and Giorgione's 'Concert Champêtre', since these had attracted earlier Pre-Raphaelite visitors. From France they moved on to Milan, where they visited the Cathedral and San Ambrogio, where Ruskin had treasures brought out from behind the altar. Next, they studied the examples of Correggio's art to be seen in Parma and thence returned to Milan. There the Jones's parted from Ruskin to visit Verona, Padua, and Venice. While they were at Padua they went to the Arena Chapel where Edward made drawings from the Virtues and Vices by Giotto. Finally they reached Venice in the middle of June. Ruskin had him copy two Christs by Luini in Milan, and in Venice he instructed him to copy from 'St Sebastian', and the high priest in 'The Circumcision' by Tintoretto, the Scuola di San Rocco, and a head of Bacchus also from Tintoretto, a head from Veronese's 'Triumph' at the Ducal Palace, a head from his 'Marriage at Cana', and a St Catherine, possibly from his 'Marriage of St Catherine', in the Church of St Cattarina. These were the works Ruskin had singled out in the Venetian Index of his *Stones of Venice*. Of the St Sebastian he wrote:

> This . . . is one of the finest things in the whole room, and assuredly the most majestic St Sebastian in existence, as far as mere humanity can be majestic, for there is no effort at any expression of angelic or saintly resignation. The effort is simply to realise the fact of the martydom, and it seems to me that this is done to an extent not even attempted by any other painter.

Similarly Ruskin eulogised the head of the high priest in Tintoretto's 'Circumcision'.:

> Tintoret has taken immense pains with the head of the high priest. I know not any

64. 'Adam'. Original design by Burne-Jones for tower west window of All Saints Church, Selsley, Gloucestershire, 1862. Sepia drawing, William Morris Gallery, Walthamstow.

65. 'Adam' workshop cartoon, 1862, india ink and sepia, $22\frac{1}{2} \times 11\frac{1}{2}$, Birmingham City Museum & Art Gallery.

66. 'Adam' window. All Saints Church, Selsley, Gloucestershire, 1862
It will be seen that a design becomes altered through the inevitable copying that is involved in stained-glass production, which would account for some of the flaws in the firm's early glass. Later these were to be eliminated by greater fluency in production.

existing old man's head so exquisitely tender, or so noble in its lines. . . . Next to the 'Adoration of the Magi' this picture is the most laboriously finished of the Scuola di San Rocco, and is unquestionably the highest existing type of the sublimity which may be thrown into the treatment of accessories of dress and decoration.

No doubt Edward Jones would not have used quite so high a form of praise as this. His copying these specific works was done as a favour to his friend and in return for payment. It enabled him to make the trip which he otherwise would not have been able to. High Venetian art was never foremost in his taste for the Italian School, and except for 'An Idyll' of 1862, where Giorgione's influence can be felt, there is little direct reference to it in his oeuvre. Venetian rhetoric was out of character for him, the pageantry and clarity of light found in the Bellini's, however, he appreciated, and at some time during his visit he studied Carpaccio's cycle of paintings on the life of St Ursula in the Scuola di Sant Orsola and his 'Legend of St George' in the Scuola di San Giorgio degli Schiavoni.

A letter written from Venice to Ruskin gives some idea of his reaction to the great Italian city and its treasures:

> The look of the pictures has done me good: I feel that I could paint so much better already. I never knew quite what a memorial of old St Mark's that picture of Gentile Bellini's is. We followed it carefully bit by bit today, and it is as exact down to the least item as it can be. . . . I hung quite affectionately about that Bellini and thought how soon it might be the only record of that seventh heaven.

Ruskin was more than generous to those artists in whom he took an avuncular interest, and without him the early years of Jones's career would have been much leaner. Not only did he purchase or commission works himself but he introduced his friend's drawings and paintings to potential patrons and used his influence, which was considerable, to persuade them to buy from him. He himself bought a number of works, among them a pen and ink drawing of 'Childe Rolande' and an early version of 'Danae'. His father bought, unprompted by his son, a watercolour of Fair Rosamond standing against a rose trellis, which delighted him.

But fits of depression harassed the author of the *Stones of Venice*. He had left the Joneses

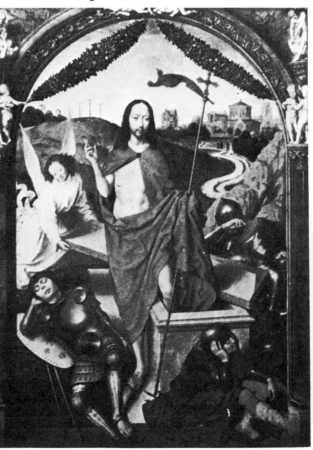 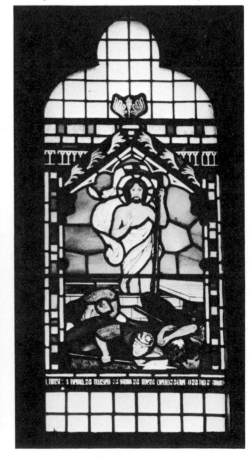

67. 'The Resurrection' by Hans Memling, *c.* 1490, oil on panel, 24 × 17
Jones admired Memling in the early 1860s, and although the design of this painting is archetypal, it is probable that he based his stained-glass design upon it.

68. 'Resurrection', 1861, one of a series of windows, the others by Rossetti, Madox Brown, and Morris, in the apse of All Saints Church, Selsley, Gloucestershire. Cartoon in Birmingham City Museum & Art Gallery.

58

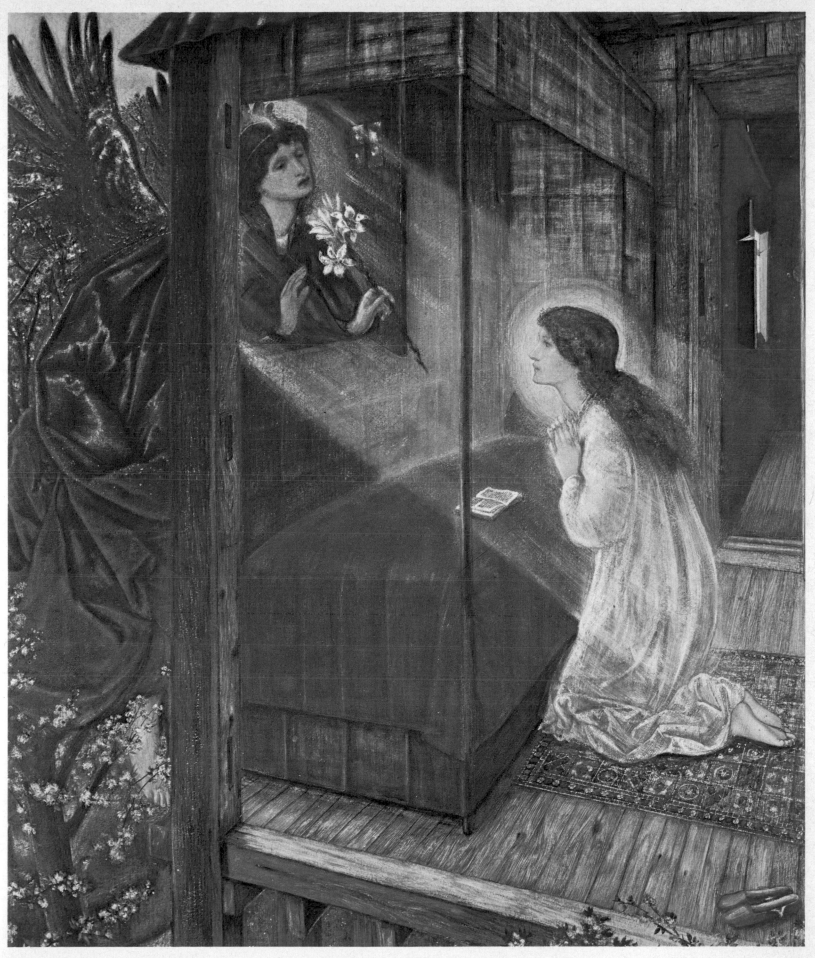

_10._ 'The Annunciation, The Flower of God', 1862, gouache, 24 × 21; private collection, London. Jones based his design upon the illuminated manuscripts of the fifteenth century which he had studied in the British Museum. The very Italianate later conception of 1876-79 shows how far the artist had moved away from his medievalism, yet it was derived in the first instance from this version.

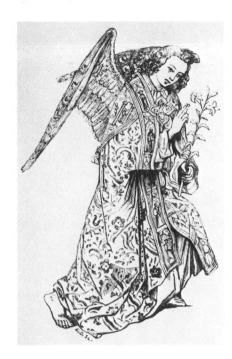

71. 'Annunciating Angel', based upon Van Eyck from Mrs Jamieson's *Sacred and Legendary Art*, London, 1848.

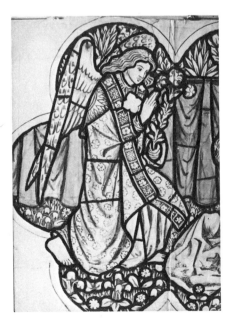

72. 'Annunciating Angel' from a cartoon for stained glass by William Morris, 1861.

in Milan after one such bout, and another particularly severe one resulted in his desire to leave England for good and build a house amid his beloved Swiss Alps. Jones's concern over this was deeply felt, and he set about reversing the decision. To try and dissuade Ruskin from taking such extreme action the young artist suggested that he should commission a house in the Wye valley. With this in mind he suggested that he should make a set of designs for embroidery of the story of the *Legend of Good Women* from Chaucer, based upon an existing set of designs for figure tiles but much altered and enlarged. They were prepared during the summer of 1863. Correspondence between them shows how it proceeded: Jones to Ruskin, Autumn 1863:

> . . . it is such a comfort to begin the tapestry, already I have schemed it all out, assigned the figures and ordered the embroidery frames (i.e. Miss Bell ordered them) and the holland for working upon and the wools for working with—and now Winnington is full of excitement about it, and you are to have the sweetest and costliest room in all the world. But dear, please never again say about the little mountain spot you may want some day or night, because that really breaks babes' hearts. . . . As far as I can calculate it will take nearly a year to get all the figures ready. They are about fourteen or fifteen in number; but only half the work; for scrolls, roses, daisies and birds will more than double it—the design I think you will like. . . . All pictures seem small matters till I can get the designs finished. . . . The ground thereof will be green cloth or serge, and the fence of roses will run along behind the figures about half way up them: these roses to be cabbage and dog red and white. All the ground will be powdered with daisies—only where Dido, Hypsiphile and Medea and Ariadne come there will be sea instead of grass and shells instead of daisies. First will come Chaucer looking very frightened according to the poem, and inditing the poem with a thrush on his shoulder—then comes Love a little angry, bringing Alcestis. Chaucer in black, Love in red and white and Alcestis in green—then a tree, and a vision of ladies begins, all to have scrolls with their name and life and death written above their heads. The ladies are to be in uniforms of blue and white and red and white alternately, and at the end of all—to come by your fireplace, will be Edward the third and Philippa sitting and looking on. So on one side of your fireplace will be Chaucer beginning the subject, and on the other side of it the king and queen.

Ruskin to Jones, April 29, 1864:

> I couldn't tell you how beautiful I thought the Medea and Thisbe—the Philomela is exquisite in her expression also—Cleopatra I have seen—Chaucer is nice—but wasted time here—you might have done him at home—and put some more princesses in—I was disappointed at Dido and you might have made a beautiful one (for) Annie as well as Aggie—but it is all well.

Annie and Aggie were girls at Winnington's girls' school who were to embroider the series. Ruskin had a singular interest in the school, giving financial and intellectual support; in return he enjoyed the company of the bright-faced young girls, helping him to forget his passionate malaise over Rose La Touche. Annie happened to be embroidering the only male figure, of Chaucer. Like so many other ventures the embroideries remained incomplete, all that remain are the large cartoons and sketches of the general layout, but it succeeded in creating a divertissement for the depressed writer.

That the artist's affection for the critic was sincere is evident from the foregoing extracts. Ruskin received something more from Jones's friendship than his usual relationships with artists offered. He indicated this when answering a letter of goodwill from Rossetti:

> I am grateful for your love but yet I do not want love. I have had boundless love from many people during my life. And in more than one case that love has been my

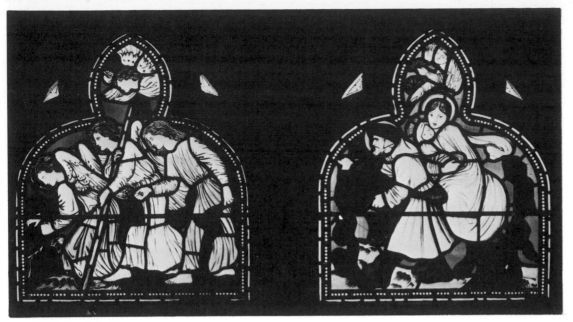

greatest calamity—I have boundlessly *suffered* from it. But the thing in any helpful degree I have never been able to get, except from two women . . . and from Edward Jones is 'understanding'.

Friendship with Ruskin had its drawbacks, as Rossetti, Millais and John Brett had found in the 1850s. Jones was more sympathetic to his advice because of his gentle nature and feeling of inadequacy as an artist. As his self-assurance grew, however, he took less advice and acted independently of his friend. The critic still persisted in passing advice, which must have been tiresome to an artist as accomplished and as sensitive as Edward Jones, especially on the subject of colour in which he excelled; Ruskin wrote:

. . . it seems to me rather an occasion for you to practise every now and then—painting with fewer colours than you usually allow yourself. I should say for instance— put black out of the box & the browns & the indigo blues or perhaps it might be shorter to shake everything out of the box and then put in vermillion & the violet carmine & the cobalt and malt and chinese white—and perhaps the emerald green or so and try what you can do with those—on gold ground—so as not to have any nasty black and brown things to make me look at.

(Letter to Jones, March 1865)

If Ruskin could be something of a burden, Jones had enough compensation from the milieu in which he found himself at this time. Rossetti's influence on his painting was on the decline, but he and Morris were still very much part of the circle. Many weekends were spent at Red House, where he was stimulated to draw and paint in the mellow atmosphere. Something of it is conveyed in the watercolour 'Girl and Goldfish' and the drawing 'Childe Rolande' which were made there. He spent time with Spencer Stanhope at his house in Cobham, Surrey, which Philip Webb had designed soon after Red House. It was there that he painted landscape studies for his 'Merciful Knight'. Henry Wallis lived in Russell Square near the Jones's Russell Place home and was a frequent caller to his studio, as were Henry Holiday and Simeon Solomon. Aesthetic problems were discussed and exchanged among this group of artists whose youthful ambitions made them feel discontented with the Royal Academy. They pooled their ideas, and for a short time their work had much in common.

Albert Moore was introduced into the group through Henry Holiday and Solomon, who were studying at the Academy Schools with him. Through this connection Moore, Solomon, and William de Morgan, another student at the Academy, were commissioned by Morris's Company, during the period 1861–66, to design stained-glass cartoons. 1862 was the year Whistler became a friend, with Rossetti, bringing George du Maurier and

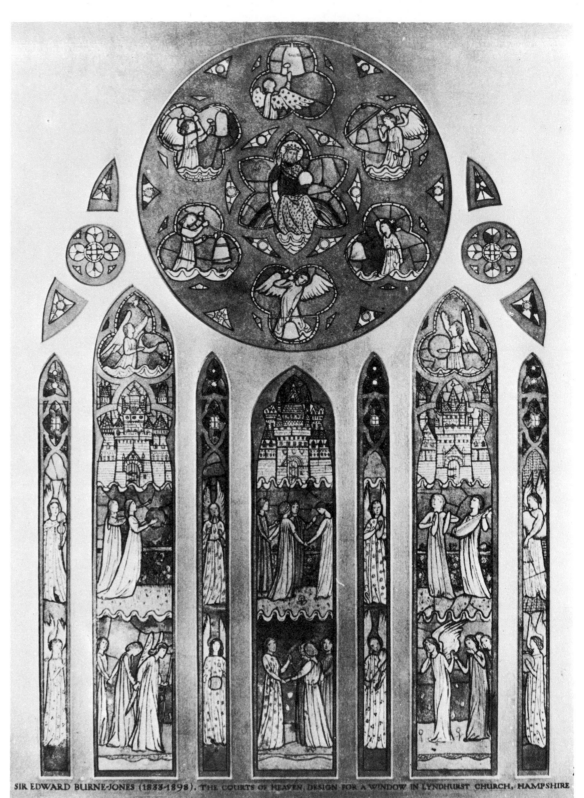

SIR EDWARD BURNE-JONES (1833-1898). THE COURTS OF HEAVEN, DESIGN FOR A WINDOW IN LYNDHURST CHURCH, HAMPSHIRE.

74. 'Courts of Heaven', preliminary design, watercolour. The series of 'Angels Playing Bells' in the tracery lights were first used early in 1862 at Bodley's Church of St Michael, Brighton, Sussex. Fitzwilliam Museum, Cambridge.

75. Chancel east window, Lyndhurst, St Michael's Church, Hampshire. Executed by Morris, Marshall, Faulkner & Co., 1862. The top panel of the centre light, 'The Four Marys' was adapted as a painting in the early 1860s. The canopy work is by Philip Webb. Cartoons are at Birmingham City Museum & Art Gallery, Fitzwilliam Museum, Cambridge, and the William Morris Gallery, Walthamstow.

Edward Poynter into the circle. They had trained in the ateliers of Paris and brought with them an international attitude and breadth of thought that opened out the claustrophobic, medieval enclosure of the Pre-Raphaelite clique. It had the result of loosening the Gothic tightness of their line and took away the emphasis from the esoteric narrative of their paintings, replacing it with more decorative considerations. The general direction of painting at this time was away from the tight, accurately observed drawing of the 1850s towards the more aesthetic concerns of 'Art for Art's Sake', as will be seen in the next chapter. Jones remained devoted to medieval culture all his life but was moving away from literal medievalism in his art during this period. Whistler began his first 'Symphony in White' in 1861, the same year Jones painted a harmony in blue for Ruskin and a harmony in red. 'The Annunciation' followed for the engravers, the Dalziel brothers. In Jones's work the

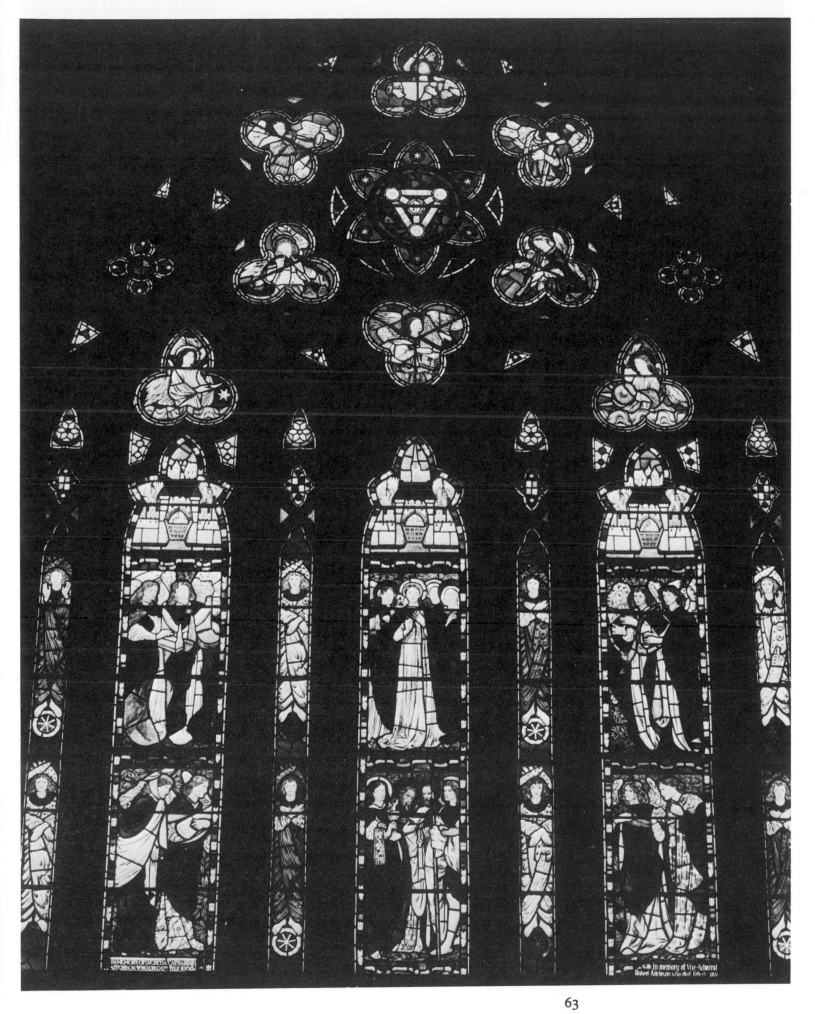

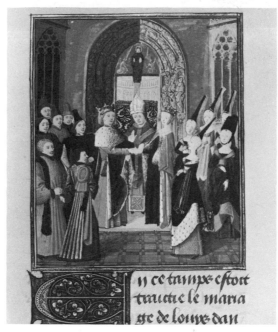

76. 'The Marriage of King Louis of Naples and Sicily to Princess Yolande of Aragon', an illustration from Froissart's *Chronicles*, a French late-fifteenth-century manuscript which Jones had in mind when designing his 'Marriage of Sir Tristram'. The British Museum, London.

transition from narrative to decorative treatment came naturally to him because, from Rossetti he had inherited a flat, decorative construction and his designs were coming more and more to consist of a simple arrangement of figures. Whistler and his friends had the effect of dissolving away the accessory detail which accompanied Rossetti's type of design. That is not to say that Jones began to paint works on the lines of Whistler's symphonies, but that his, and later Albert Moore's, influence invaded his work to the extent of causing a re-direction. As a result, the paintings conceived during and immediately after the period of contact with these two artists, tell no story and operate on an emphatically visual level. 'The Lament' (1866) and 'Venus's Mirror' (1866–67) are arrangements of figures, aiming at a maximum decorative effect. Colour and the expression of the figures are the elements which create mood and atmosphere. Narrative was thus reduced as much as possible in a figurative painting. Work of this type is firstly decorative with an almost abstract role, but it was secondly a communion of artist with viewer, conveying something of the artist's spiritual tension. In clarifying the images into simple decorative units, the artists hoped to make a more direct communication.

A comparison between 'The Knight's Farewell' (1858) and 'The Lament' will make clear his shift of direction. Their essential difference lies, not so much in the detailed medievalism of the former, the indefinite, almost classical, setting of the latter, nor in the heavy symbolism of the accessories in 'The Knight's Farewell', but in the relaxed mood and clarity of the composition. Unlike the enigmatic details of lilies, fruit trees, walled garden, knights, and opened book that piece together the 'story' in 'The Knight's Farewell', the images used in 'The Lament' can be quickly assimilated at a glance; the 'story' aspect is completely missing. It was the artist's intention to create a response in the viewer by instilling the painting with a single mood generated by the two figures and not to have to tarry, attempting to unravel a story from his visual clues. Complex narrative paintings still played an important part in his work, but their treatment became modified by considerations other than the narrative itself.

Swinburne, Simeon Solomon, and Edward Jones formed themselves into rather an unlikely trio. Swinburne was an excitable hedonist, who proclaimed aloud the theory of 'Art for Art's Sake', and who led the susceptible Solomon into subterranean depths from which he was never able to find his way out. The gifted poet admired Whistler, who had just the cosmopolitan sophistication that he wished to see in a friend. Like Whistler, he admired contemporary French poetry, particularly Baudelaire, and unlike his Pre-Raphaelite friends, did not find Whistlers' paintings' lack of 'finish' upsetting. Solomon's palette and texture became modified through his contact with Jones in the early 1860s, whilst his friendship with Swinburne inspired a set of illustrations to his novel *Lesbia Brandon* and to the poem 'The Flogging Block'. Swinburne wrote two poems based upon drawings by

64

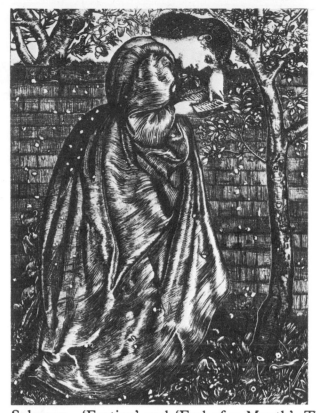 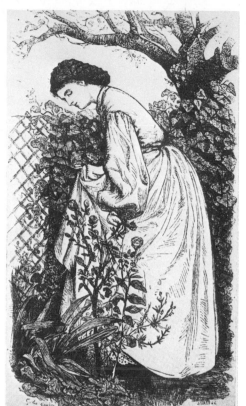 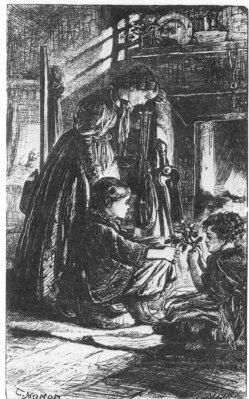

Solomon—'Erotion' and 'End of a Month'. The former was published in *Poems and Ballads* of 1866, which bore the inscription: 'To my friend Edward Burne Jones these poems are affectionately and admiringly dedicated.' More complex, because less involved, was the effect the poet had upon Jones's art. They first met while Jones was engaged upon the Oxford Union murals in 1857. Immediately a friendship sprang up between them. Through Rossetti, Morris and Jones, Swinburne came to know *Morte d'Arthur*, Meinhold and Froissart, books from which they drew inspiration for their work. So too, Swinburne became infected with medieval romance, writing in 1858 what he intended to be his masterpiece, *Tristram and Lyonesse*. A verse play, *Rosamond*, was published privately in 1860. This was a treatment of the legend of the Fair Rosamond, the mistress of Henry II and how she was put to death by his jealous wife, Queen Eleanor. Rossetti's oil painting of the same title is dated 1861, and Jones's four versions of the story were painted between 1860 and 1863. Godstow, the burial place of Rosamond, is situated a few miles from Oxford and had been a place of pilgrimage for Jones in 1854, the year Arthur Hughes exhibited his treatment of the subject at the Royal Academy. Some five years later Jones and a group of friends, including Swinburne, took a boat up river to visit her purported grave amongst the ruins. In their interpretation of the legend, poet and painter alike treat Rosamond sympathetically as the victim of natural passion who reaps the inevitable doom of illicit love.

> Ay, and love
> That makes the daily flesh an altar cup
> To carry tears and rarest blood within
> And touch pained lips with feast of sacrament
> So sweet it is, God made it sweet!

Rossetti's interpretation is the more sensual of the two painters' treatments; his heroine, loose-haired, with bare, voluptuous neck and shoulders, waits for her lover to come. Jones chooses, in three of his versions, the poignant moment of the two women meeting, before the Queen despatches Rosamond. There is an air of sadness; no hint of sensuality reminds us of the reason for Eleanor's presence in Rosamond's bower. To heighten the tension, Jones included a circular mirror with a set of smaller mirrors about its circumference. Each reflected the Queen's face to amplify the sense of persecution. The artist has not

77. 'Summer Snow', 1863, engraving, private collection
Accompanying the illustration in the 1863 *Good Words* was the poem of the same name. A watercolour version of the subject is in the William Morris Gallery, Walthamstow.

> 'Soft falls the summer snow,
> On the springing grass drops light,
> Not like that which long ago,
> Fell so deadly cold and white;
> This wears the Rose's flush,
> Faint, ere bloom hath quite foregone her,
> Soft as maiden's timid blush,
> With the looks she loves upon her.'

78. 'Non Satis', 1860, engraving by George du Maurier
Jones may well have had in mind the engraving from the 1860 *Once a Week* when he designed it.

79. 'An Orphan's Family Christmas', 1863, engraving by T. S. Morten. Private collection
Included in the same volume of *Good Words* as 'Summer Snow', this engraving bears a strong similarity to Jones's in the pose of the standing girl.

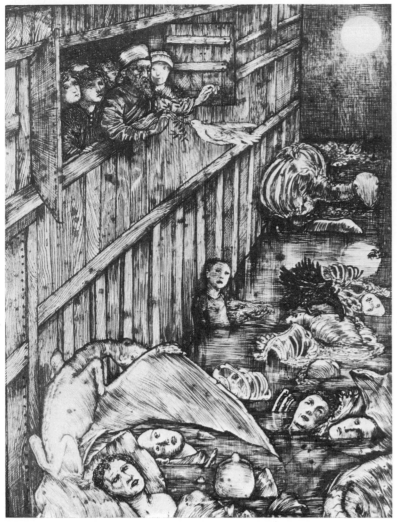

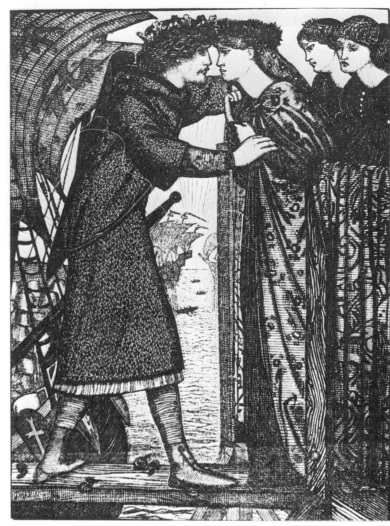

80. 'The Return of the Dove to the Ark', *c.* 1863, pen and ink, 4 × 3½ approx., Victoria & Albert Museum, London

A rejected design for Dalziel's illustrated Bible, which, when it finally appeared in 1880 had a single illustration by Jones: 'Ezekiel and the Boiling Pot'. The animals were designed by Philip Webb.

81. 'King Sigurd', 1862, engraving, private collection

The illustration appeared in the 1862 *Good Words* and was engraved by the Dalziel brothers.

'Through smiles and tears, and
  loving cheers,
And trumpet notes of fame,
Came King Sigurd, the Crusader—
Like a conqueror he came.

There stood the noblest of the land,
The pride of many a hall,
But the lovely lady Hinda's hand
He kissed before them all.'

succeeded in his intention for two reasons. Firstly, the mirror he painted from was inadequate, his father had not been able to construct it according to his design, and secondly, the mirror, which is too small within the picture space, is not an integral part of it. His intention to intensify the drama by creating three emotional centres—the two women's faces with the mirror between reflecting them, is rendered ineffectual by the insignificant size of the mirrors. Yet the idea does point to the importance of facial expression for Jones. At this time, like Rossetti, he used it as a means to convey the essence of the painting. Each of the faces is the pivotal point of the design in relation to the rest of the picture space. To both Jones and Rossetti the image of a beautiful woman was used as a symbol of the artist's mental life and spirit. 'Fair Rosamond and Queen Eleanor' is not a narrative of an historical event, but its situation parallels a psychological state in the artist's mind. This is equally true of the other version Jones painted in 1863. Rosamond is here shown alone in her rose bower about to pluck a rose. Like the version discussed above, it is a rich textural composition that centres on her face. Detail of the kind found in the early Pre-Raphaelites plays no part in these works. Facial expression and texture together are the factors through which the painting operates to reveal the artist's soul.

Swinburne was at work on *Poems and Ballads* from 1860, the period of most intimacy with Jones; Georgiana records how he would often rush into their house in Russell Place bringing fresh poems to recite. There is a community of subject and atmosphere between the collection of poems and Jones's work concurrently produced. Lines from 'In the Orchard' capture something of the mood found in a Jones idyll such as 'Green Summer', 'An Idyll', or 'Chant d'Amour':

The grass is thick and cool, it lets us lie.
Kissed upon either cheek and either eye,

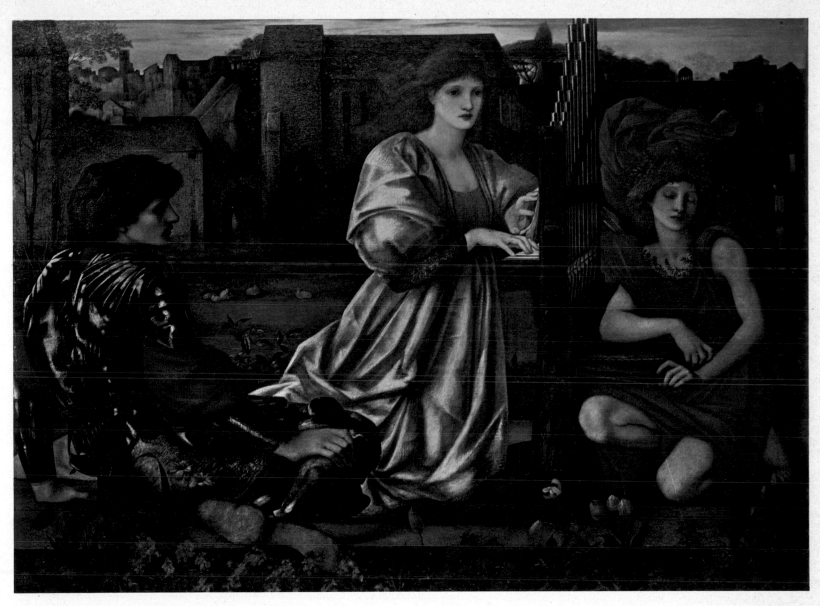

15. 'Chant d'Amour', 1868-73, oil on canvas,
44 × 60; The Metropolitan Museum of Art, New
York. A small watercolour version (1865) is at the
Boston Art Gallery in Massachusetts. This version
was exhibited at the Grosvenor Gallery in 1878, and
then passed into the collection of William Graham.

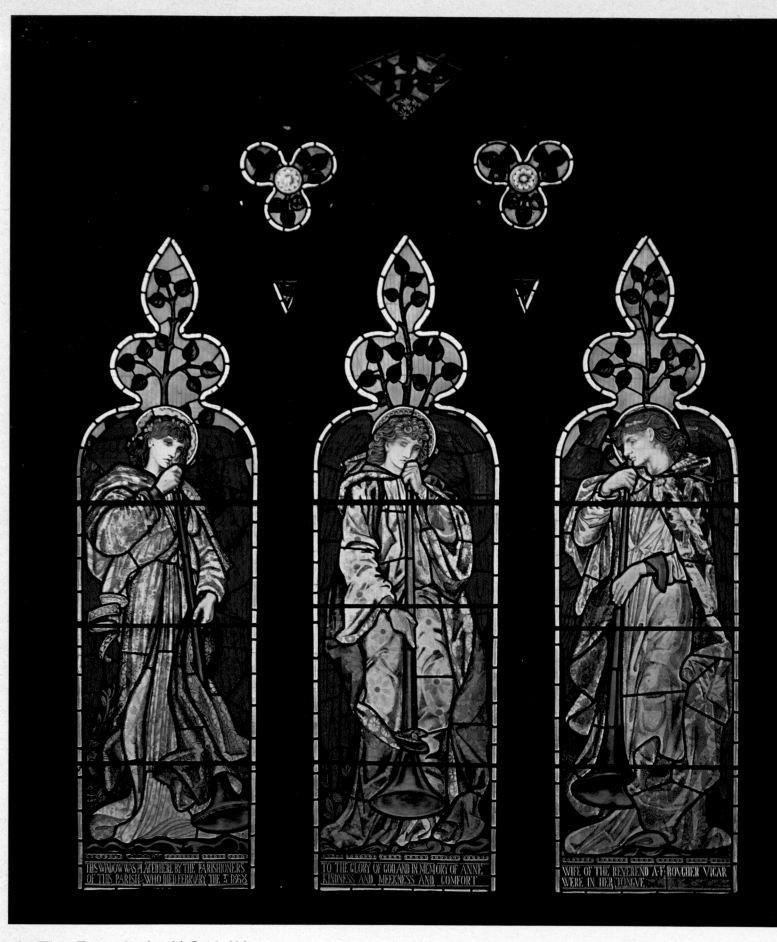

16. 'Three Trumpeting Angels', South Aisle
window St Edward the Confessor Church,
Cheddleton, Staffordshire, 1869; executed by
Morris, Marshall, Faulkner & Co.

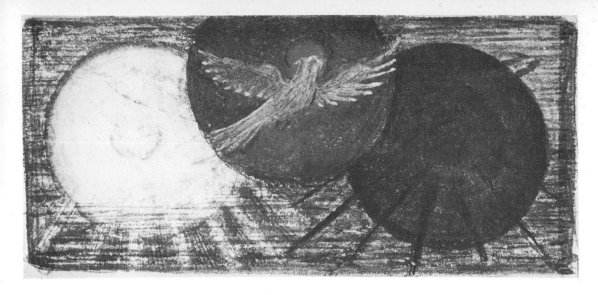

82. 'The Fifth Day of Creation', 1862–63, gouache heightened with gold, $2\frac{1}{4} \times 5\frac{1}{8}$, Birmingham City Museum & Art Gallery
One of a set of seven Days of Creation made for Dalziel's Bible.

> I turned to thee as some green afternoon
> Turns toward sunset, and is loth to die;

A watercolour version of 'Laus Veneris' was painted in 1861 which, although not an illustration of Swinburne's poem of the same name, is very close to it in subject. 'St Theophilus and the Angel' occupied the artist during the years 1863–67, which means that it was painted at the same time as Swinburne was composing his 'St Dorothy', a narrative poem of some 550 lines. Each of these is a treatment of the legend of St Dorothy who was martyred for refusing to worship the goddess Venus. Theophilus, a Roman, taunts the saint and asks her when she gets to paradise to send him some flowers. This she does miraculously by sending an agent with them:

> There came a child before Theophilus
> Bearing a basket, and said suddenly:
> Fair Sir, this is my mistress Dorothy
> That sends you gifts;

Swinburne adopted a Chaucerian style in recounting the tale, which with its combination of Pagan and Christian references would have pleased that poet. Likewise, Morris was attracted by the legend. He wrote a version, later discarded, which he intended to include in his *The Earthly Paradise*. The story is similar to the one included in *The Prioress's Tale* in *Canterbury Tales*, and Jones's treatment of it resembles his rendering of that story on the cabinet in 1858. In both cases he uses simultaneous representation of different parts of the story. Dorothy is seen on the right being borne away on her bier at the same time as on the left portion Theophilus is about to receive the flowers from paradise. On the cabinet, the foreground figure of the Virgin is placing the ear of corn in the boy's mouth while behind her are the preceding events of the story. This was one way Jones overcame the problem of visual narration. Later he developed the alternative method of creating a series of pictures in which part of the story is revealed in each.

It has already been said that Swinburne was to have supplied verses for the St Frideswide window in 1859; he also wrote a set of Latin verses for Jones's decorative series of panels 'The Seasons' in 1864. Friendship with Swinburne lasted for a good many years after the middle of the sixties but, like that with Rossetti, it ceased to have the moulding influence which it had had up to that time. As each artist grew older, he evolved his own distinctive style. It was inevitable that under the influence of Solomon and Swinburne, another element entered Jones's work, that of hermaphroditism. This was to become a permanent feature of his art, yet not in the same form as it first appeared. This ambiguous interpretation of the sexes is not present in any form in the art of Rossetti, nor was it in Jones's work until his intimacy with Solomon and Swinburne. At first, Jones's

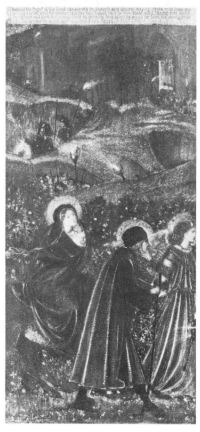
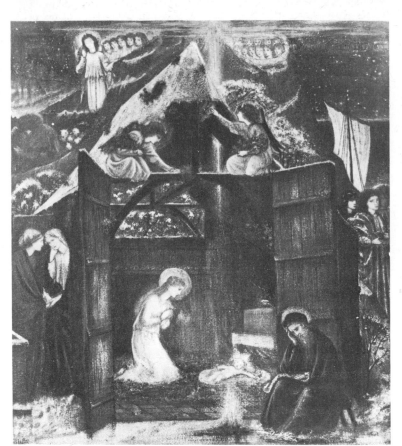
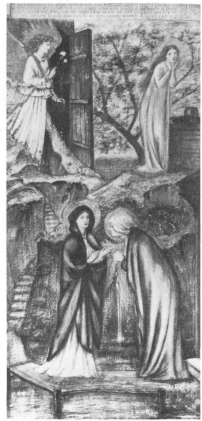

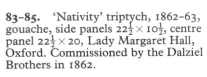

83–85. 'Nativity' triptych, 1862–63, gouache, side panels $22\frac{1}{2} \times 10\frac{1}{2}$, centre panel $22\frac{1}{2} \times 20$, Lady Margaret Hall, Oxford. Commissioned by the Dalziel Brothers in 1862.

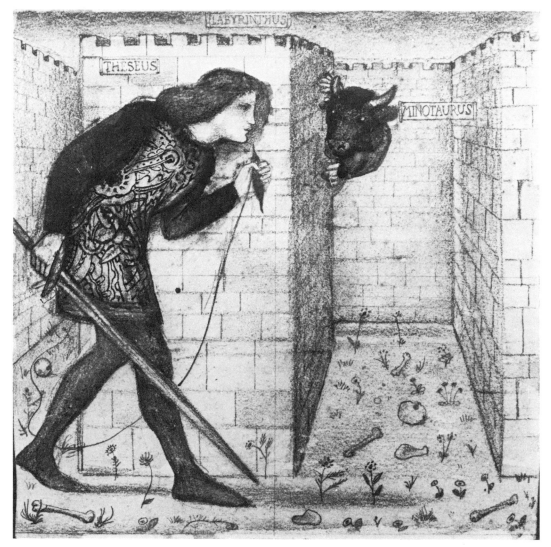

86. 'Theseus in the Labyrinth', designs for a tile, 1862, Birmingham City Museum & Art Gallery.

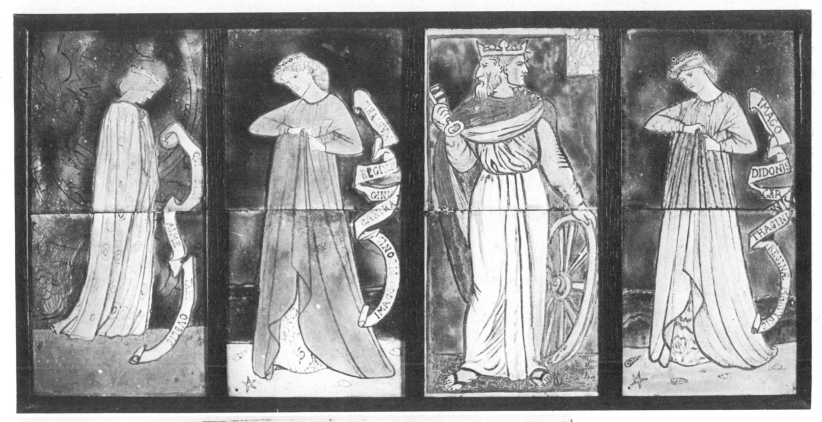

87. Four tiles, 1861, each 12 × 6, The Ashmolean Museum, Oxford

From left to right: 'A Queen', 'Dido', 'January', 'Dido'. 'Dido' was part of a series of heroines from Chaucer's 'Dream of Good Women', 'January' was part of a set of twelve months used at Queen's College, Cambridge in the Dining Hall, and 'A Queen' was one of a pair, a King and Queen. These particular examples are experimental and were never part of any decorative scheme.

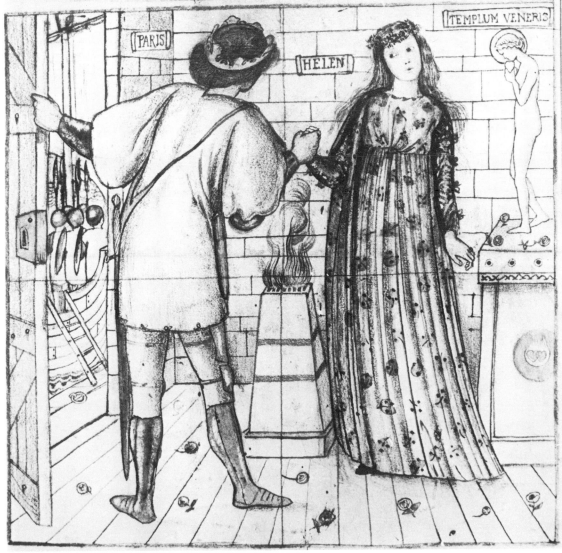

88. 'Paris and Helen', design for a tile, 1862, Fitzwilliam Museum, Cambridge.

and Solomon's work show many similarities, but by the late 1860s Jones had developed his own, more individual use of the androgyne, which had become less overtly sensual, more refined and removed from physical reality.

Swinburne was obviously the motivating force behind the initial interest, the preoccupation with it being a fundamental part of his nature. In 1863 he addressed a poem to 'Hermaphroditus', a Greek sculpture in the Louvre:

> Choose of two loves and cleave unto the best;
> Two loves at either blossom of thy breast
> Strive until one be under and one above
> Their breath is fire upon the amorous air,
> Fire in thine eyes and where thy lips suspire:
> And whosoever hath seen thee being so fair,
> Two things turn all his life and blood to fire;
> A strong desire begot a great despair,
> A great despair cast out by a strong desire
>
> Yet by no sunset and by no moonrise
> Shall make thee man and ease a woman's sighs,
> Or make thee woman for a man's delight.

Such a heightened appreciation of hermaphroditism as Swinburne's was not part of Jones's nature, neither was he interested in Solomon's variety of hedonism, and so the influence subsided to become integrated into the intricate framework of his later style.

Although Morris, Marshal, Faulkner and Co. provided him with a small but reliable income, Jones had to rely upon other sources. As a painter he was known only to a few patrons, and though he was held in high regard by other painters, his work was bought by few people. After Ruskin and Rossetti's help he was able to sell fairly successfully each work as it appeared. Gradually his patrons increased. Until 1861 they included the painters G. P. Boyce, H. T. Wells—Boyce's brother-in-law, Spencer Stanhope and Major Gillum—a wealthy amateur. T. E. Plint, as we have seen, was one of the first industrialists to buy from him, but unfortunately, to the embarrassment of many of Rossetti's circle, he died in 1861, having paid large advance sums to them without receiving anything in return. Consequently, they had to produce work for his executors. Gambart, a dealer, acted as their agent and became much disliked, Rossetti taking his revenge by representing him as Judas or some other villain in his cartoons. Plint's collection included: 'The Waxen Image' (1856), 'Wise and Foolish Virgins' (1859), pen and ink drawings, the watercolours 'Blessed Damozel' (1860), a small version of 'Sidonia von Bork' (1860) and 'Rosamond and Queen Eleanor' (1861). His collection also included an oil triptych of 'The Adoration of the Magi', the side-panels representing the Annunciation. It had been designed for the altar of St Paul's, Brighton, but Jones had been unsatisfied with the scale and painted a second version, giving the first to Plint's executors as his return for the advances. James Leathart, the Newcastle industrialist, had six early watercolours, 'Fair Rosamond and Queen Eleanor' (1861), 'Sidonia and Clara von Bork' (1860), 'Merlin and Nimue' (1861), 'The Merciful Knight' (1863), and 'Valentine's Morning' (1863). 'Fair Rosamond' and the pen and ink 'Buondelmonte's Wedding' he bought from Plint's estate. 1861 was the year William Miller, a Liverpool counterpart of Leathart, began buying with a watercolour of 'Belle et Blonde et Colorée'.

With the firm well-established the number of his patrons increased, but still his reputation remained within a small group of cognoscenti until the late 1870s.

By selling directly to his industrialist patrons, Jones was following a pattern set by Rossetti and the Pre-Raphaelite Brothers. A personal rapport grew up between artist and patron which invalidated the need for public display. It was a convenient arrangement, true to the best traditions of patronage, based upon respect for one another. After long hours spent on accounts or within earshot of the machine, on returning to their homes they were confronted with highly imaginative and colourful pictures that set them free from the tyranny of commerce. These self-made men were aware of their need for

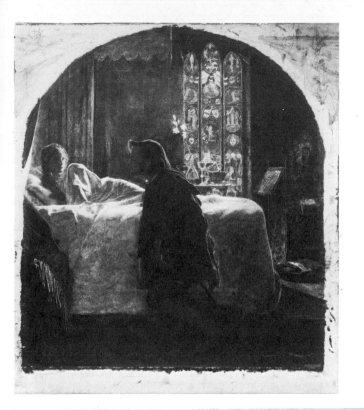

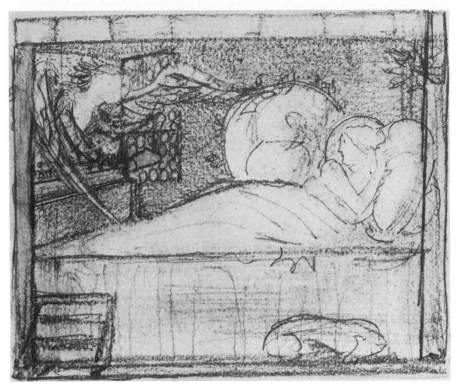

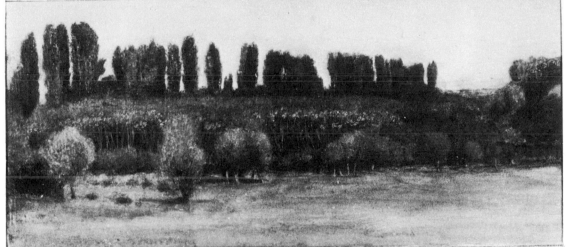

contemporary painting; they had not been schooled in the classics, they were embarrassed by the 'chocolate coated' old masters that appealed to the cultured classes. They needed an art that arose from their own time that was immediate in its appeal, an art that offered escape from 'six counties overhung with smoke, the snorting steam and piston stroke' and this they found in Jones's painting. Without fully understanding the visionary qualities, they were attracted by the tense or dreamy sensuality and the exotic subjects. Paradoxically the vision arose from an impulse similar to the patrons' need to escape: the artists' revulsion against materialism. Another reason why the industrialists found it convenient to deal with this group of artists was the fact that they were not associated with the Royal Academy, they did not have pompous or pretentious ideas about art, but knew very well that genuine art rose directly from the fabric of life itself. They did not nullify its vitality by drawing an academic or intellectual veil across their inspiration. Their patrons could understand the sincerity of their ideals and were prepared to accept bohemianism as an accompaniment to art.

A further small, but useful, income came from the designs Jones made to be executed on wood for the illustrated books and magazines of the Dalziel brothers. During the 1850s book illustration had undergone something of a revolution through the combined effort of the Dalziel brothers and the Pre-Raphaelites who drew for them. A decorated edition of Tennyson's poems appeared in 1857 with illustrations that differed from others of the time in being firmly drawn, prominently linear, and in using texture and blacks only sparingly with dramatic effect. A number of artists contributed to the collection but the most innovatory designs were those by Millais, Hunt, and Rossetti. Under the direction of the Dalziels and later Swain, book illustration in the 1860s reached a peak of success.

Holman Hunt introduced Jones to the engravers at the end of 1861, with these words: 'He is perhaps the most remarkable of all the younger men of the profession for talent, and will undeniably, in a few years fill the high position in general public favour which at present he holds in the professional world. He has yet, I think, made but few drawings on wood, but he has had much practice in working with the point both with pencil and pen-and-ink on paper, and so would have no difficulty with the material.'

As a result the brothers paid him a visit, were so impressed by what they saw that they not only commissioned him to work for them but asked for a painting 'A Harmony in Red' (an Annunciation finished in 1862) and another later in the year. At that time the Dalziels were keen to collect together a series of specially commissioned Bible illustrations by different artists, and Jones made drawings of 'Ezekiel and the Boiling Pot', 'The Eve of the Deluge', 'Return of the Dove to the Ark', 'Christ in the Garden', and seven small vignettes of the Days of Creation. Only the Ezekiel subject was used when Dalziel's *Bible Gallery* was published in 1880. Three other designs complete the list of those made for them: 'The Deliverer', a nativity for Mrs Gatty's *Parables from Nature*, and 'Summer Snow' and 'King Sigurd', accompanying verses in the 1862 and 1863 editions of the magazine *Good Words*. This periodical's most important feature was the high standard of the

92. Study for 'The Merciful Knight', 1863, pencil, 10 × 6, Tate Gallery, London.

93. 'I Have Trod the Winepress Alone' by Spencer Stanhope, *c.* 1864, oil on canvas, 37 × 26½, Tate Gallery, London
The construction of the boxed-in space is similar to that of 'The Merciful Knight', upon which Jones was working at the same time as Stanhope was at work on this painting. Jones painted the background of his picture from the countryside round Cobham, Surrey, whilst staying there with Stanhope.

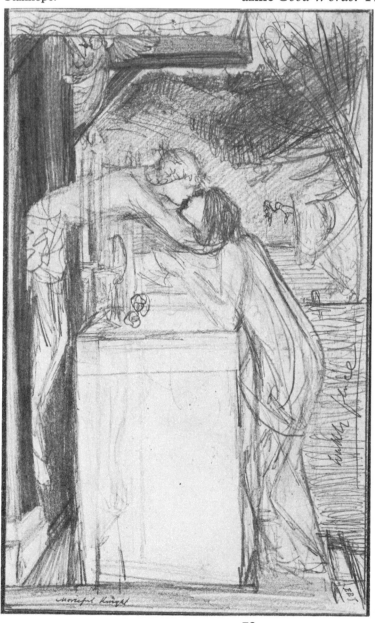

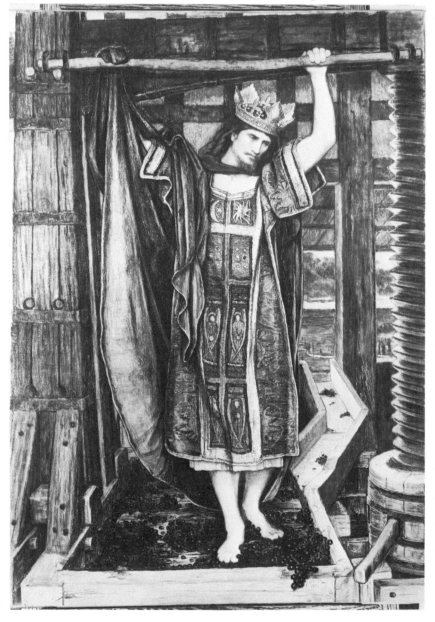

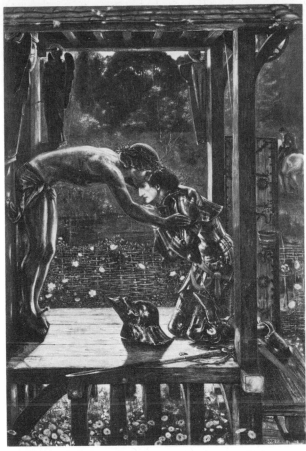

94. 'The Merciful Knight', 1863, gouache, $39\frac{1}{2} \times 27$, Middlemore Loan, Birmingham City Museum & Art Gallery
The subject was taken from the story of San Giovanni Guilberto, an eleventh-century knight who was miraculously comforted by Christ in a wayside shrine for an act of forgiveness.

illustrations; they included designs from Millais, Arthur Hughes, Simeon Solomon, Holman Hunt, Matthew Lawless, Fred Walker, Frederick Sandys, T. Morten, Charles Keene, and many others—in fact, a significant number of the members of the Hogarth Club.

Beside those of his fellow contributors Jones's designs are less accurately observed and more stylised in draughtmanship, but much less dependent upon the text for their success, being complete in themselves. His handling of the form is dense with strong black outlines on white paper, so that the viewer is presented with a boldly contrasting black and white image. In doing this he avoids the fault of many of the designers of the old school—that of using too fine a line and an ineffectual grey shading.

A short time before her marriage to Edward Jones, Georgiana had studied with Madox Brown. She did not enter his studio as a complete novice as she had attended the Government School of Design when she lived at Birmingham. Thus, she was not without experience when she decided to work from her husband's drawings to convert them into engravings by cutting them on to the woodblock. An outcome of her decision was that she, working with Rossetti's wife, should make a book illustrated from her husband's designs. George du Maurier's wife, Emma, went to Georgie for instruction. On hearing of the ladies' activities Ruskin was delighted at this symbol of 'woman's mission':

I'm delighted [he wrote to Georgie] to hear of the woodcutting. It will not, I believe interfere with any motherly care or duty and is far more useful noble work than any other of which feminine thought and nature are capable. I cant imagine anything prettier or more wifely than cutting one's husband's drawings on the wood block— there is just the proper quality of echo in it . . .

Georgie's little sister took to wood engraving and this elicited some advice from Jones, which reveals how conscious the artist was in the development of his genius and how soundly he thought of the fundamental criteria of his art:

I see that for the engraving I want, the most perfect design and beautiful drawing is

73

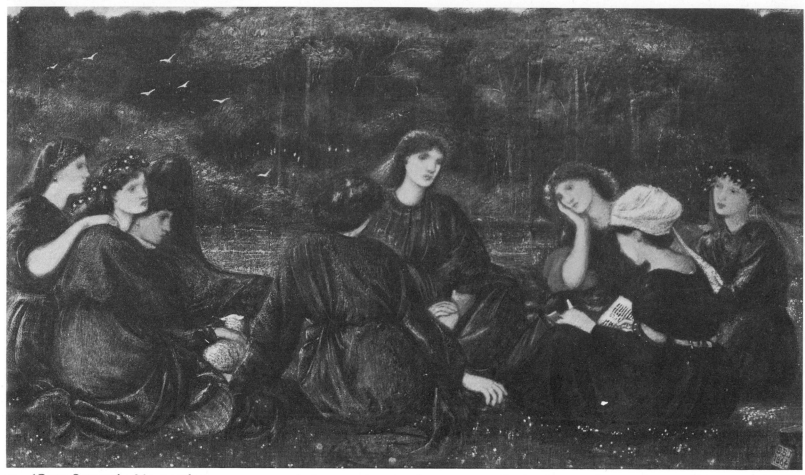

95. 'Green Summer', 1864, gouache,
11 × 19, private collection, New
Zealand
Essentially a 'harmony in green', this
painting is another of the idylls
derived from Giorgione.

needed, more than in pictures even, for in them so many other qualities come in and
have their say. . . . But in engraving every faculty is needed,—simplicity, the hardest
of all things to learn—restraint in leaving out every idea that is not wanted—perfect
outline, as correct as can be without effort, and still more essentially, neat—and a due
amount of quaintness. . . . As to scribbly work. . . . Nearly all book illustration is full
of it—drawings . . . that have wild work in all the corners, stupid senseless rot that
takes an artist half a minute to sketch and an engraver half a week to engrave. . . .

He continues, after giving sixteenth-century wood engravings as an example of the
most perfect ancient type, with the advice to engrave:

> . . . Very simply, with little or no cross-hatching, and no useless cleverness, and no
> attempt whatever to do anything that copper or steel would do a thousand times
> better. . . . Of course people generally will prefer Birket Foster illustrations to
> anything else. They have all the sole qualities that are cared for—delicacy, smoothness
> or rather wooliness and prettiness.

Then follows a most impressive and articulate description of the artist's technique:

> . . . In drawing the mouth, you need to know, for instance what part of the lips may
> be expressed in drawing and what not—the cleft of course must always be a little and
> the strongest line. The whole of the upper lip may be perfectly expressed in drawing,
> because although the lip itself is really only another tint in colour from the flesh, still
> the ridge is so sharp that it makes the strongest shadow. But in the under lip, the
> blending of lip colour and chin colour is so soft and indefinite that only paint can
> express it, and drawing has to be contended with the deep shadowed little pit right
> in the centre.

'The room was crowded with works of various kinds, in every sort of method, all

74

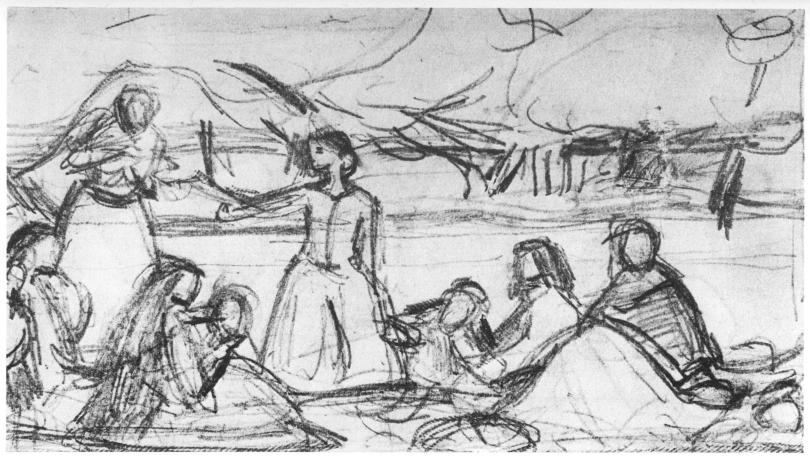

showing wonderful power of design, vivid imagination and richness of colour.' So wrote Mr Dalziel on visiting Jones's studio towards the end of 1862. Watercolour was the medium he used most from 1860 to 1870, but he used it for the smaller scale it offered rather than for reasons of transparency. With it he achieved a whole range of effects, by working on madder, gold, or white grounds, by mixing the medium with oxgall or gum, a technique derived from Blake through Rossetti, by scratching the surface of the paper, and by sponging and blotting the wet colour. In this way, using it as a versatile opaque medium it became a perfect vehicle for his imagination. There is a sense of exploration in some of the earlier examples. 'The Annunciation', begun in 1857, is patchy and rather flat, the design rather clumsy, 'The Forge of Cupid', completed in 1861, is awkward in the whole composition, although the figure of the girl is beautiful, Cupid is stiffly drawn. Jones was quick, however, in overcoming his problems, and beginning with the two von Borks (1860), he embarked upon the magnificent sequence of beautiful girls: 'Viridis of Milan' (1861), 'Girl and Goldfish' (1861), 'Rosamond' (1863), 'Cinderella' (1863). Jones was primarily a colourist, and the works of the period are pre-eminently colour pieces; any of his paintings could have been called 'a harmony' not just 'Viridis of Milan'—a harmony in blue, or 'The Annunciation'—a harmony in red, but 'Clerk Sanders' (1861) could be called a harmony in brown or 'Green Summer' a harmony in green.

Being a designer for the firm had repercussions on him as a fine artist, particularly in his later work. The time spent at his applied designs affected his pictures by continually reminding him that art was primarily decorated surface. Some of his paintings in the early 1860s have their origin in decorative schemes; 'The Backgammon Players', 'Green Summer' and 'King Cophetua and the Beggar Maid' (all 1861) had their origin in painted cabinets as did the two scenes from 'King René's Honeymoon' (1861). From the stained-glass designs came 'The Madness of Sir Tristram', 'The Marriage of Sir Tristram', and 'King Marc and Iseult' (all of 1862); 'Cinderella' began as a tile design and 'Morgan le Fay' was originally designed as an embroidery.

Like the watercolours, the drawings of the period show an acute sensitivity to abstract elements. Typical of this time are the red-chalk drawings in which the form emerges from textural variations; only an artist who had had considerable experience in drawing could model with such assurance, allowing his subject-matter to dissolve into the overall texture. Preliminary drawings for larger works were fewer in number than in the later

96. Study for 'Apple Blossoms', c. 1856, pencil, 6×9, The Stone Gallery, Newcastle upon Tyne

Millais was at work upon his painting 'Apple Blossoms' from 1856 to 1859, during which period Jones would certainly have had a lot of contact with the artist. The ideas of 'Apple Blossoms' and 'Green Summer' are basically the same, but the different techniques used stress how far Jones was from the Pre-Raphaelite ideal of verisimilitude to nature.

75

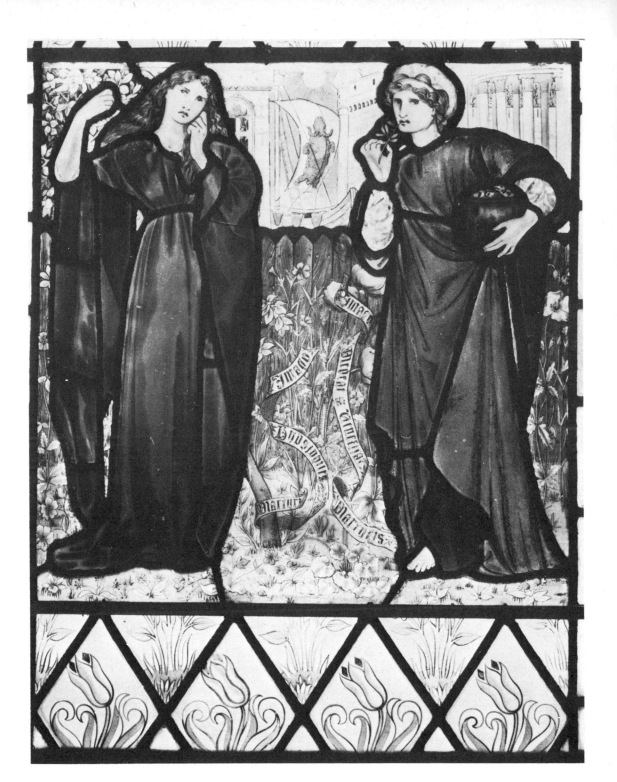

97. 'Hypsiphile and Medea': stained-glass panel, Combination Room, Peterhouse College, Cambridge. Designed in 1864, and executed by Morris, Marshall, Faulkner & Co. a few years later

One of a series of six such panels at Peterhouse. A 'sleeping Chaucer' which completes it is at the Victoria & Albert Museum, London. The series derives from the embroidery panels made for Ruskin in 1863. Cartoons for the windows are at Birmingham City Museum & Art Gallery. The figure of 'Medea' is a repetition of the watercolour 'Morgan Le Fay' (Fulham Library, London) of 1862.

period as he was content to make studies without isolating each part of the figure, hands, feet, and drapery etc. These do exist but are rare because emphasis was not laid on details but on a general impression; detail was subordinate to textural or chromatic considerations.

Jones's public debut was made in 1864, when he exhibited four of his pictures at the Royal Water-Colour Society. They were the second version of 'Fair Rosamond', 'The Merciful Knight', 'Cinderella' and 'The Annunciation'. They were badly received by members of the Society and the press; the *Spectator* critic damned him and the *Athenaeum* ridiculed him. An altogether depressing start, especially when he attended the show to see his four works 'skied'. Many years later, recalling the episode, he commented: '[It] left an impression that didn't wear off, and was always being added to by a sense of continual opposition and even covert insult every now and again. . . .'

He continued to exhibit there each year until his differences with the Society came to a

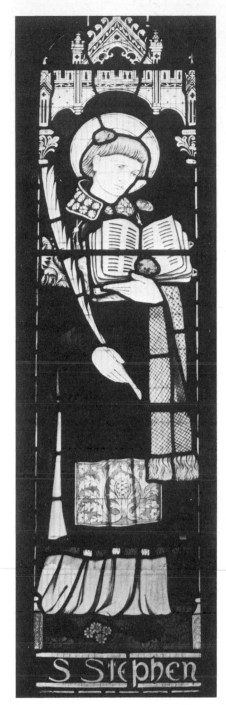 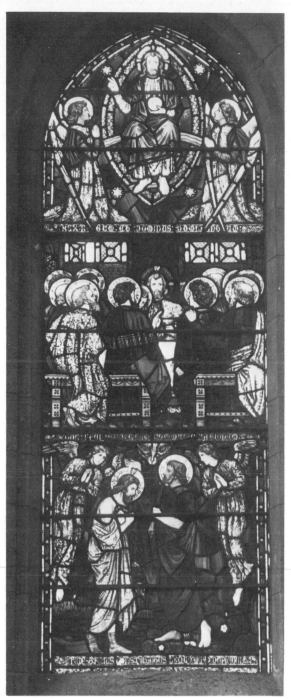

98. 'Christ in Majesty; The Last Supper; The Baptism', window in the east wall of Waltham Abbey, Essex; designed by Henry Holiday, 1864 and executed by Powell's. On the advice of Albert Moore, Holiday took over Burne-Jones's post as chief designer to Powell's in 1863.

99. 'St Stephen'. Window of 1865 for the Chancel, south side, in Gilbert Scott's church at Langton Green, Kent. Canopy by Philip Webb. A preliminary sketch for this window is at the Fitzwilliam Museum, Cambridge.

confrontation when they accused him of creating an indecent picture, 'Phyllis and Demophöon', in 1870. He immediately resigned his membership. The Society, a conservative body, were unable to take an individual art which blended medieval manuscript with Whistlerian colour-theory, that drew on Carpaccio, Giorgione, and the symbolism of Rossetti.

1864 was altogether a bad year for Edward Jones. An excerpt from du Maurier's letter written on Christmas Day 1864 succinctly describes his depressed situation:

> Jones poor fellow has given up all idea of building his house [i.e. at Red House]; he has had lots of troubles and not done a stroke of work for four months—his wife's confinement and scarlet fever and his own horrible funk about it have quite knocked him up. He's looking out for a house in Kensington, and Poynter is going to take his rooms . . . Jones's studies for decoration in red chalk have been raved about.

Chapter Five

Towards the Aesthetic Movement

The epic narrative poems which Morris was engaged upon in the early sixties were developed over a period of six years into *The Earthly Paradise* and *Jason*. In this complex of stories he moved from the terse dramatic verses of *The Defence of Guenevere* to a quietly flowing, relaxed story-telling style, in which the length of the story was a fundamental part of its existence. Morris wished the reader to enter his world and escape from contemporary problems and to be soothed by diverting tales of romance and adventure. The length of the poem enabled him to become totally absorbed in it. Quite early, almost from its inception, Morris conceived the projected volume as a sumptuous presentation with profuse illustrations from designs by Jones.

Structured like Chaucer's *Canterbury Tales* and Boccaccio's *Decameron*, *The Earthly Paradise* consists of a series of tales, each related by a member of a group to entertain his fellows. The conjectural time is somewhere at the beginning of the Middle Ages, as the classical era draws to a close, a background which enabled Morris to combine stories from Greek, Scandinavian, Celtic and, in one case, Arabian sources.

The Earthly Paradise consists of twenty-four stories with a dramatic prologue that links, with introductory passages, to each story. Unlike its model, the *Canterbury Tales*, there is no change of atmosphere from story to story, but a single mood runs through each section. Its effect is a hypnotic stagnation, remote from reality, which beguiles the reader and leaves him with a sense of tranquillity. Between the first draft and the final published version is a significant suppression of dramatic action and a development of the qualities of sweetness and restraint, 'Like an old dream, dreamed in another dream'. Morris is unashamed of the function of his epic:

> The heavy trouble, the bewildering care
> That weighs us down who live and earn our bread,
> These idle verses have no power to bear;

Again, at the beginning of the prologue we are instructed to:

> Forget six counties overhung by smoke,
> Forget the snorting steam and piston stroke,
> Forget the spreading of the hideous town;

The Earthly Paradise marks a departure from the intense situations of his earlier verse, in which there is a forceful identification with medieval figures. Morris has become more passively self-absorbed, less passionate, and the verses contain less of the autobiographical 'angst' than his preceding poetry. But there is a greater concern for the design of the piece;

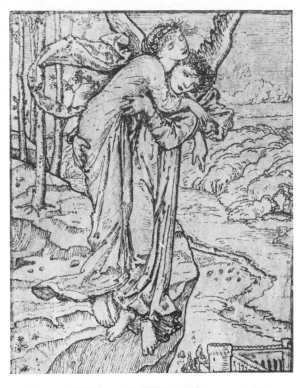

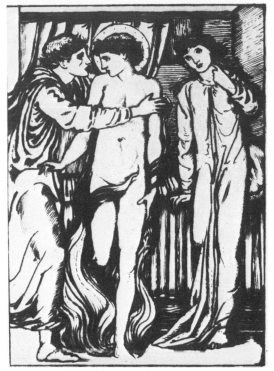

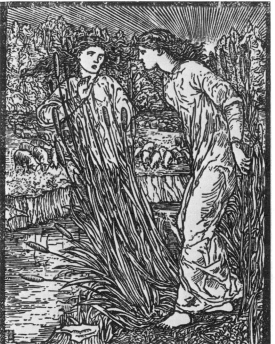

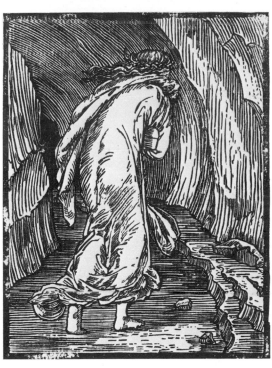

100–3. Four illustrations from *The Earthly Paradise*:

100. 'Zephyrus and Psyche', 1864, ink over pencil, $4\frac{1}{4} \times 3\frac{3}{8}$, The Ashmolean Museum, Oxford.

101. 'Laurence prevented by Venus from joining his Bride', 1865, metal engraving, $4\frac{1}{2} \times 6\frac{1}{2}$. William Morris Gallery, Walthamstow
This illustration is one of the only two metal engravings Jones ever made; both were for the story 'The Ring Given to Venus'. The relationship between Laurence and Venus contains the germ of the design used in 'Phyllis and Demophöon'.

102. 'The Talking Reed', 1865, wood engraving, $4\frac{1}{2} \times 6\frac{1}{2}$. William Morris Gallery, Walthamstow.

103. 'Psyche Entering Hades', 1865, wood engraving, $4\frac{1}{2} \times 6\frac{1}{2}$, William Morris Gallery, Walthamstow
The design is based upon Mantegna's 'Christ's Descent into Limbo'.

in suppressing the action and dealing with nuances, the poet has to develop more subtle variants in style, rhythm, and metre. In fact, there is a more sophisticated and mature understanding of poetry as art. Less concerned with reality, it has to create an existence of its own. Description is paramount throughout, diluting the narrative, at times bringing it to a standstill.

A parallel situation appears in the work of Jones, and the works which date from the mid- to the late sixties show a similar moving away from the earlier Rossetti-inspired paintings; the designs made to accompany *The Earthly Paradise* show the transition. In the early sixties most of his compositions showed one or two figures who were victims of the eternal 'maladie d'amour'. Jones's work, too, shows the slackening in tension combined with a reappraisal of the role and anatomy of a work of art. Poet and painter were both leaving the overdominant influence of Rossetti to look for a more personal expression. Since neither

79

of them had an academic training they were free to investigate completely uninhibited the art of the past, and to arrive at a conclusion which was influential in deciding what direction their own art should take. This search for a style inaugurated a period of discontent for Jones which lasted intermittently until his maturity in the late 1870s, when he finally accepted that he had achieved a personal style in which all the formatory influences had been fully integrated.

Jones's work on the book introduced a new idea to his painting, the concept of a series of pictures. Obviously, to illustrate a text, this is a fundamental requirement. A story must either be made very apparent in a single picture, a method likely to produce a poor visual effect, or told in a series of pictures. The second method involves the isolation of a single episode to enable the artist to treat it in the most successful way possible in terms of design. A chain of designs, each with a minimum of story-telling, links up to reveal the narrative. Jones chose this form, and used it with great artistry, not creating banalities for the sake of telling a story, but producing a great many designs which were later developed into striking, independent pictures. *The Earthly Paradise* project supplied enough material to engage his attention intermittently from its initial creation to the time of his death; in all, about thirty-five paintings had their origin in the book.

All the stories were to have been illustrated, but only a selection of designs appeared before the scheme was abandoned, and an unillustrated text was published in 1868. The most complete designs were for the story of Cupid and Psyche and were the first to be executed. This was the only series to go so far as to be cut into wood. When asked much later to comment on a set of wood engravings, George Wardle, the company's manager at that time, described the process from drawing to block:

These designs were made by E. Burne-Jones for *The Earthly Paradise*, the greater number being for the Cupid and Psyche, the first poem taken up for illustration. They

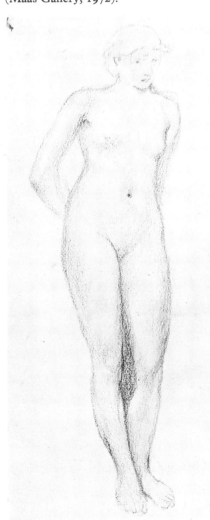

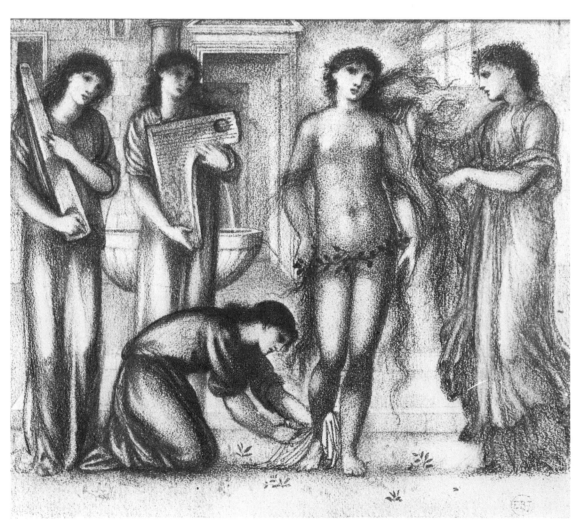

were all put on the block by me from B-J's rather rough drawings on tracing paper. Before the plan of publishing was abandoned the blocks here printed had been cut. A few were given at first to the trade to be cut but the result was so unsatisfactory that Morris tried to get the cutting done by unprofessional hands. G. F. Campfield, then a foreman of painters to the firm, and Miss Lucy Faulkner, sister of Charles Faulkner, each made a trial. I also was asked and I began cutting the block of 'Psyche passing by the Speaking Tower'. I then cut 'The Despair of Psyche'. After this I cut no more. Morris himself, seeing that wood engravings of this kind did not require an apprenticeship, took up the work and he liked it so much that he cut all the remaining blocks. The greater number are therefore by him.

It was typical of Morris to reject the technique offered by the trade as unsatisfactory and to do it himself; Swain, the firm to whom he took the designs, had been responsible for many high-quality Pre-Raphaelite illustrations, such as Frederick Sandys's Düreresque 'Rosamond, Queen of the Lombards'. But Morris had a more primitive Italianate style in mind and consequently was impatient with Swain's product; originality was fundamental to his nature and he had to be wholly responsible for all that he did. For the reasons that he created a new type of poem he was equally unwilling to follow in the wake of the Pre-Raphaelite illustrators. Thus he changed the course of book illustration. Although his volume never reached the printing stage its implications reached fruition in the Kelmscott Press, and through this had considerable influence on subsequent book presentation.

Jones concentrated much of his effort into the scheme from 1864 until 1868 and it had the result of implanting a new style which spread throughout his paintings and designs in other media. Feeling the need to benefit by earlier book illustrators' experience, he consulted works of the fifteenth century that he and Morris admired. These included the

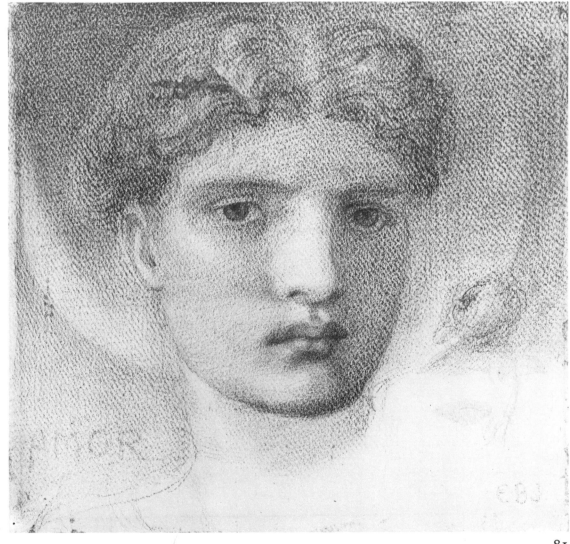

106. 'Amor', c. 1865, red crayon, $8\frac{1}{2} \times 8\frac{1}{2}$, Henri Dorra collection, California.

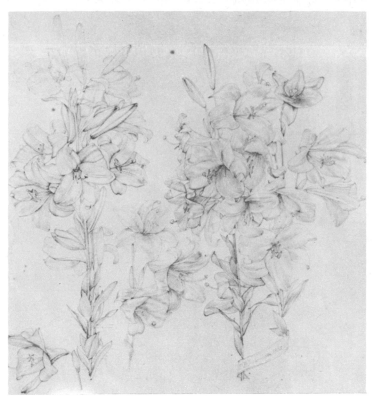

107. 'Lilies', 1865, pencil on brown paper, 11½×11, The Philadelphia Museum of Art, Pennsylvania.

Hypnerotomachia Poliphili, *Quadri Reggia*, and the Ulm edition of Boccaccio's *De Claris Mulieribus*. How closely he followed these precursors is indicated by an entry in William Allingham's diary for Saturday, August 18, 1866:

> Ned only makes a few pencil sketches. He occupies himself, when in the mood, with designs for the Big Book of Stories in verse by Morris, and has done several from Cupid and Psyche, also pilgrims going to Rome (i.e. The Hill of Venus) & others. He founds his style in these on old woodcuts, especially those in Hypnerotomachia, of which he has a fine copy.

The *Hypnerotomachia* is no surprising choice as it closely parallels *The Earthly Paradise* in many ways, as an extract from Sir Anthony Blunt's description of the book shows:

> The same mixture of medieval and classical elements (as in Mantegna's paintings) appears in the Hypnerotomachia. In form it is a Gothic romance, of the type of *Roman de la Rose*, but taken more directly from the *Amorose Visione* of Boccaccio. The wanderings of the unhappy lover, Poliphilus, in search of his Polia are accompanied by all the adventures and allegories traditional in the romances of the Middle Ages. But the author has used this medieval form to express above all his over-whelming passion for antiquity. Every episode, every allegory is dressed up in classical phraseology. The language and names are a bastard mixture of Italian, Latin and Greek; the buildings described are in the ancient manner; the monuments are covered with Latin or Greek inscriptions, or with hieroglyphs which the author painstakingly transcribes and explains; every ceremony is dedicated to a classical god or goddess.

A transparent linear type of drawing characterises the illustrations, shading is reduced to a minimum and is created by means of fine lines. Jones's designs show similar emphasis on line and economy of shading; his architectural settings are very close to those of the *Hypnerotomachia*, and he took from it the high-waisted, loose fitting garment for some of his figures, together with the stance of many of the girls. Most obviously, he borrowed the figure of a girl seen from behind with one backwardly directed flexed leg—it occurs many times in *The Earthly Paradise* illustrations and subsequent work ('Hesperides', 'The Garland', etc.).

82

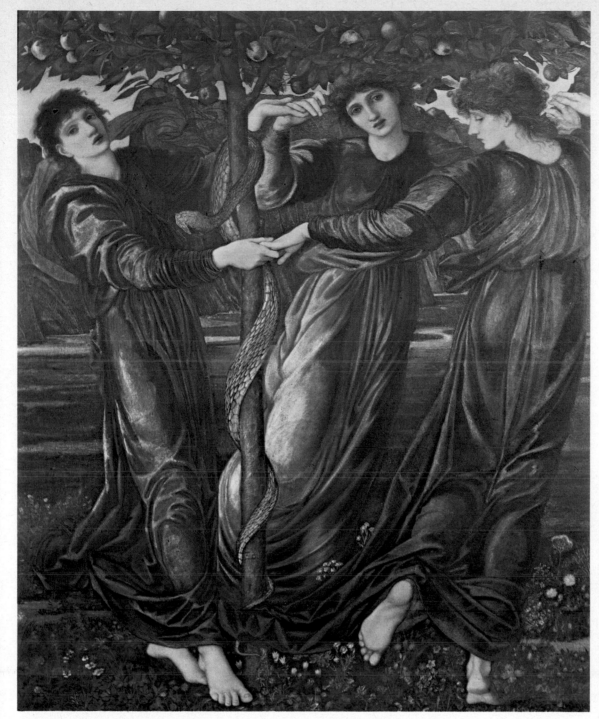

17. 'The Garden of the Hesperides', 1870-73,
gouache, 47×38½; private collection. The theme of
this picture is taken from the story of Jason, which
was treated by Morris concurrently.

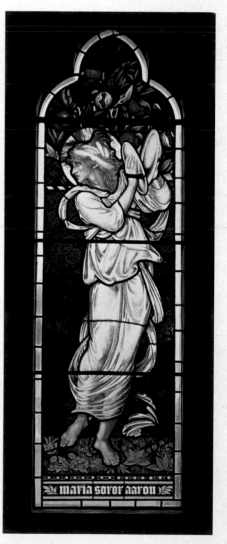

18. 'Miriam', Chancel South
Window, St Michael and All Angels
Church, Waterford, Hertfordshire,
1872, executed by Morris, Marshall,
Faulkner & Co. This commission,
from the architect Henry Woodyer,
produced a number of fine windows
by the firm, notable for the careful
selection of glass.

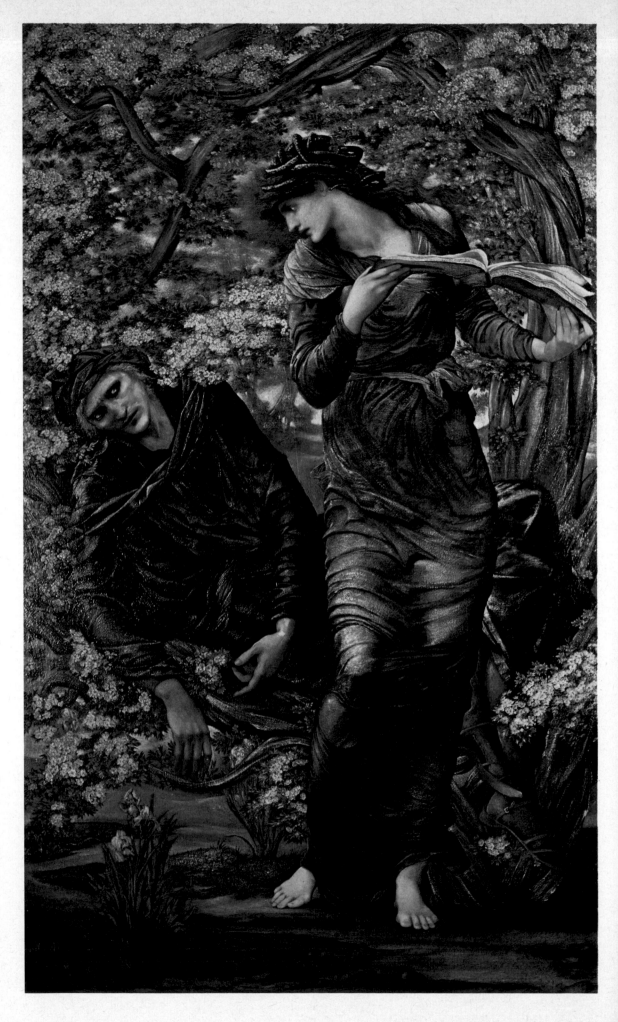

19.   'Merlin and Vivien', 1870-74,
oil, 72 ×43; Lady Lever Art Gallery,
Port Sunlight, Cheshire.

The technique that he employed to evolve an illustration began first, as did all of his ideas, with a rough, loose sketch, often in soft black pencil. At this exploratory stage he constructed the basic design, then by means of tracing paper he refined the drawing until it was in linear form, ready for cutting. The particular benefit gained from this was that a number of identical drawings were available for each of the cutters. There is no doubt that the enterprise was by way of an experiment for all those who participated in it; Morris had had no previous experience in cutting, neither had the others, and as we have seen, the style was entirely new. Jones, in connection with the project, made what are his only two metal engravings, for the story of *The Ring Given to Venus*. But, finally, their inexperience

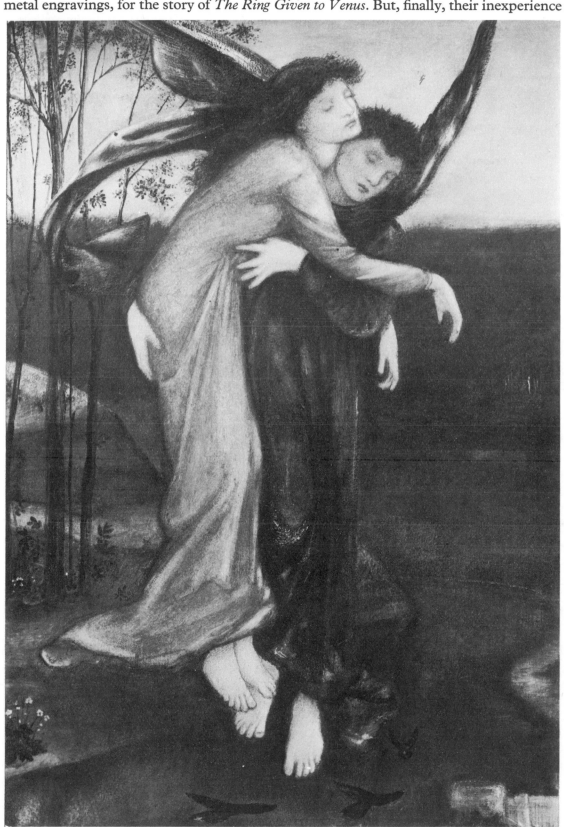

108. 'Zephyrus and Psyche', 1865, gouache, $15 \times 10\frac{1}{4}$. Robert Walker Collection, Paris

Morris's *The Earthly Paradise* is once again the inspiration for a painting, and this was originally designed as an illustration for it. At Cupid's command, Zephyrus is bearing the unconscious Psyche to a mansion below, for instead of destroying her as Venus had instructed him, Cupid wished to keep her for himself.

proved too much, and the scheme came to an end in 1868 when Morris published without the illustrations. A single wood engraving of three musical maidens appeared on the title page—a silent reminder of what might have been.

The importance of these illustrations in the œuvre of Burne-Jones could never be overstressed. At a time when he was leaving his old interests and emerging as a mature artist they had a deep effect on his subsequent ideas. For four years they were at the forefront of his thoughts. Yet only one set, the Cupid and Psyche series, ever approached completion, fifty-two reaching the final stage of the block. A number of drawings were made, however, to other stories, at least twelve for 'Pygmalion', twelve for 'The Hill of Venus', twenty-eight for 'The Doom of King Acrisius', eight for 'A Man Born to be King', eight for 'Atlanta's Race', about twelve for the 'Story of Orpheus', and there were probably others which have not yet come to light. In spite of their being abandoned, the designs reappeared in different guises at later dates. The Cupid and Psyche series was modified into a mural frieze for George Howard at 1 Palace Green, Kensington (1872–81). Two sets of four paintings derive from the 'Pygmalion' (1868–70, 1869–79). From 'The Doom of Acrisius' arose a mural scheme for A. J. Balfour's house in Carlton Gardens (1875–98, unfinished) along with various paintings. Drawings for the Orpheus story were made into decorations for William Graham's piano (1873–79). 'Danae and the Tower of Brass' was developed into four separate paintings, (c. 1866, 1869, 1872 and 1876–88) from a design in the Acrisius series, 'The Wedding of Psyche' became a painting in 1894–95; both the 'Bath of Venus' (1873–88) and the two versions of 'The Mirror of Venus' (1866–77 and 1873–75) arise from the Cupid and Psyche story; and so do the many versions of 'Cupid delivering Psyche' and 'Cupid's first sight of Psyche'. Quite clearly, the whole project was responsible for much of the character of Jones's work after the 1860s.

During the period from 1864–68 the few paintings that he made were almost all derived from his designs from *The Earthly Paradise*, or in some way associated with them. Thus 'Zephyrus and Psyche', 'Cupid delivering Psyche', and 'Cupid's first sight of Psyche' date from 1865, and he was engaged upon 'The Mirror of Venus', 'The Court of Venus', and 'Theophilus and the Angel' (the story was used by Morris in *The Earthly Paradise* as well as by Swinburne) during this time.

He exhibited five works in the Old Water-Colour Society in the summer of 1865 which were reviewed patronisingly by the *Art Journal*. A long passage devoted to him would not have helped to lift any misgivings he may have had:

> . . . but there can, at all events, be little doubt that upon him has fallen to an eminent degree the common lot of being loved by the initiate few and laughed at by the profligate many. The fate which has come upon this artist, we are bound to say, he heartily deserves. At the outset we confess ourselves one of the uninitiate multitude who are wholly unworthy of the rare revelation of which Mr Jones is the favoured recipient. We certainly admit most readily that this artist possesses some gifts which move to sympathy. Even his confirmed medievalism is not without winning charm. Its quaintness, bordering on the grotesque, and even touching the impossible, is far removed at least from the modern modes of commonplace, lies close upon the marvellous, and constitutes, as it were, a species of pictorial miracle. For a manifestation so unusual, either in daily life or within the circuit of our exhibitions, as exemplified, for instance, in pictures such as 'Astrologia' (18), 'The Enchantments of Nimue . . .' (230) and 'Cupid and Delight' from Chaucer's *Assembly of Fowls* (97), we cannot but render to Mr Jones our best thanks . . . for it cannot be denied that some of the works by this painter have in colour a subdued and shadowed lustre; that they possess in their subjects, seen for example in the pretty conceit called 'Blind Love' (89), originality of thought; and that in sentiment as manifest by the composition 'Green Summer' (105), they are not devoid of poetry . . . we would inquire why it is that he overlooks usual anatomical proportions and the acknowledged bases on which the human body is constructed? Again, we would wish to know how it is that he does not put draperies upon his figures with some express relation to the forms they clothe, and why he does not cast these draperies into folds and masses which by the well-

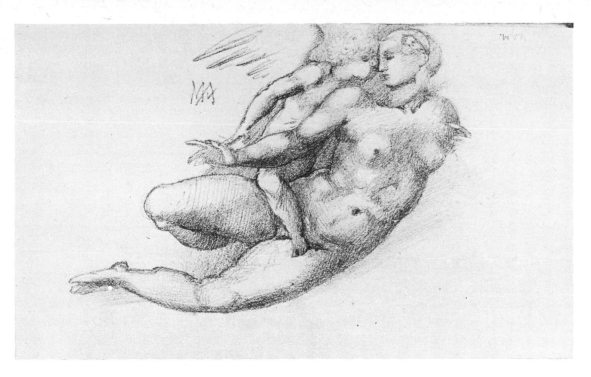

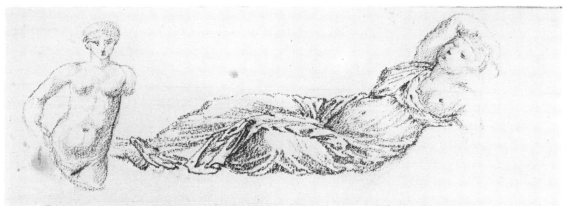

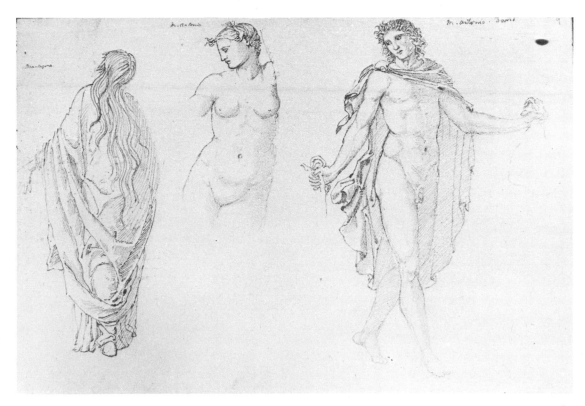

109-11. Three drawings from a sketchbook, after (a) Michelangelo, (b) a classical relief, (c) Mantegna and Marcantonio Raimondi; 1866–67; pencil and red chalk; Victoria & Albert Museum, London.

85

ascertained laws of gravity they are bound to assume? Once more, we would query of Mr Jones as a colourist, how it is that in the Boccaccio composition, 'Green Summer', he has made his 'in verdure clad', why it is that he has woven the robes of the picnic party of the green grass whereon they sit, thus bidding defiance to known laws of chromatic art, which are now established with the certainty of scientific axioms?

Then follows their advice to go to nature to prevent him from going 'from bad to worse'.

His contemporaries were not able to understand his art which obeyed its own rules and did not follow nature. It was not his concern to present natural colour or the correct fall of draperies but to construct an aesthetic vitality; 'Green Summer' was a 'harmony in green', not a photographic reconstruction of an actual event. However indifferent his development was to their recommended course, it is interesting to note that in the same year Jones was making a careful study of lilies in an almost academic method of drawing.

Not all the world was against him, the 'initiate few' grew slowly larger in number and new patrons encouraged him. Two in particular, William Graham, M.P. for Glasgow, and F. R. Leyland of Liverpool, eagerly purchased his works almost before they were dry. Relations with these men were more than as painter to purchaser; it was a complex situation in which the patron directed the flow of the artist's inspiration by selecting certain works, ignoring others; and by entering into the artist's world he was able to offer objective advice as to the success or failure of each particular piece. Graham had an insatiable appetite for Jones's work, continually enquiring whether there was anything new. Georgiana Burne-Jones describes him:

When Mr Graham came to the studio he was a man of forty-eight and Edward was

112. Study for 'The Lament', *c*. 1866, red chalk slightly touched with pencil, $13\frac{7}{8} \times 12$, Birmingham City Museum & Art Gallery
The mood and form of the drawing bring to mind Rossetti's 'Beata Beatrix', which was worked upon after a time of neglect in 1864 and finished later.

113. Part of the decoration of the Green Dining Room at the Victoria & Albert Museum, London
The Commission was received in 1866. Jones, Morris, and Philip Webb worked in conjunction: Jones designed the figure panels, Morris the leafy patterning, and Webb the frieze at the top. Webb was responsible for the overall plan. At first the firm's employees painted the figure panels, but these were so poor that Morris called in the artist to reconsider the scheme. Jones then asked his assistant, Fairfax Murray, to repaint them. The figures represented the signs of the zodiac, the cartoons for them are at Kelmscott Manor, Lechlade, Oxfordshire.

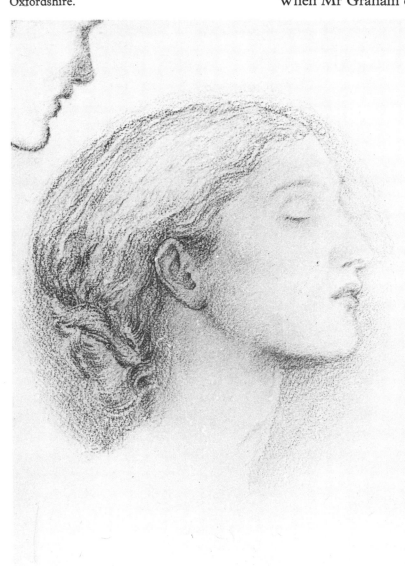

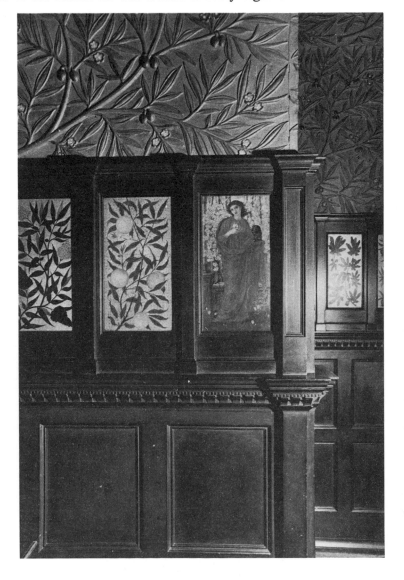

86

some fifteen years younger. Their friendship lasted for nearly twenty years without a cloud, and then was only ended by Graham's death. Keen man of business though he was, simplicity and devotion of soul were as evident in him as in a cloistered monk. His face was that of a saint, and at times like one transfigured. He had an inborn instinct for old pictures that was marvellous. He liked to come and look on while Edward painted, appearing and disappearing very swiftly, but bringing no sense of disturbance with him. I believe Edward cared for his sympathy about his pictures next to that of Gabriel and missed it almost as much when it was gone.

Writing in August 1869, Graham reveals his passionate interest:

I want to have the 'Love is Passing' very much and I am to have the little jew boy— you showed me yesterday—then the 'Spring' and 'Venus Mirror' and the sleeping Princess' knights enchanted. And a fellow to the Pygmalion I saw yesterday, and the Psyche and Pan—and if your busy brain produces something more beautiful than any of them *I am to have it*—is this not right?

William Graham's collection was not confined to works by Rossetti, Hunt, Millais, Burne-Jones, J. W. North and the many other contemporary painters, but his far-ranging taste led him to include early Renaissance Sienese, Florentine, and Venetian paintings, works by Leonardo, Luini, the Mannerists; and his aesthetic curiosity took this highly cultured man to Roman sculpture, Persian fabrics, even Byzantine icons. Neither was his collection restricted to painting and sculpture alone, but incorporated all manner of decorative art. Graham therefore was something more than a generous patron, he was responsible, by making this treasure house of art available to Jones, for at least a small part of his aesthetic outlook. Should the Graham collection be reassembled it would, no doubt, prove to be not only revealing on the subject of Burne-Jones's art but on the Pre-Raphaelite movement as a whole.

The new patronage meant that with the increase in income came additional pressures of having to get things done. Already there existed the demand for decorative designs from the firm and so, in November 1866, Fairfax Murray joined his studio as an assistant, to

114. 'The Marriage Feast at Cana', 1866, pencil heightened with green chalk, $10\frac{1}{2} \times 10\frac{1}{2}$, Birmingham City Museum & Art Gallery
A design for tiles in the chancel of St Peter's Church, Bournemouth, rebuilt by G. E. Street. These deteriorated so badly that they were removed in 1890.

115. 'Two Flying Girls', *c.* 1869, white chalk on brown paper, Birmingham City Museum & Art Gallery
A number of paintings including flying girls were made around 1870, and presumably these figures are associated with one of these.

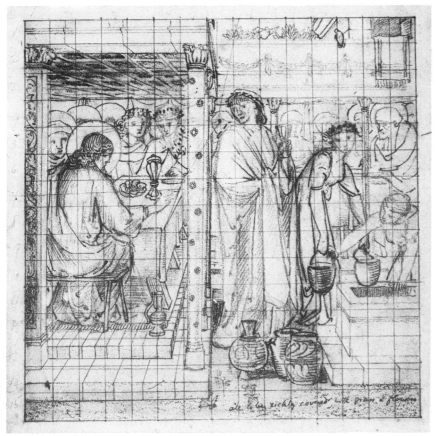

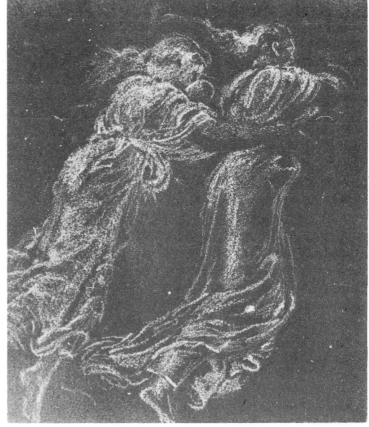

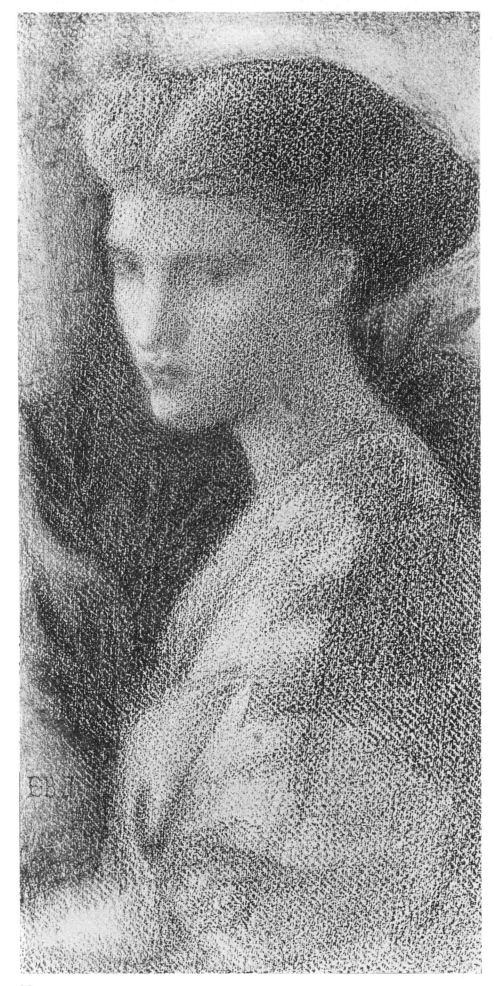

116. 'Portrait of a Girl', *c.* 1866, red
crayon, $7\frac{1}{2} \times 5\frac{3}{4}$, The Ashmolean
Museum, Oxford
Swinburne was the original owner of
this drawing.

copy existing paintings, to transfer designs from preliminary drawings on to canvas and to help with work associated with the firm. He began by painting the third of the St George series which Jones was preparing for Birket Foster's house in Surrey, working from the elaborately finished pencil design. Birket Foster commissioned the series when Jones had accompanied Morris on a visit during the time that the company was decorating the house. The conversation had turned to Morris's and Rossetti's recent versions of the St George legend, and Birket Foster then asked Jones to paint one for him. That was in 1864, and by 1866 Foster was becoming impatient. With Murray's help the series was finished in that year. Compared with the original pencil designs from which Murray worked, they betray themselves to be workshop productions. Many of the figures are pedestrian copies, having none of the grace or fluency of the originals; in transferring them on to the canvas Murray misjudged their distribution, causing obvious gaps to appear in the design which had to be filled with additional faces or draperies; he also failed to give them any anatomical solidarity or the decorative vitality to the draperies that characterises the work of his master. The most apparent flaw is Murray's inability to recreate the texture of the originals, and his paint is clumsily applied by an inexperienced hand.

The St George paintings shed more light on the origin of the idea of a series of pictures. The legend of St George is the subject of the murals by Carpaccio in the Scuola di San Giorgio in Venice, which Jones visited in 1862. Carpaccio had been a long-standing favourite of Jones, and it was natural that when he was commissioned for the mural scheme based upon the legend he should have thought of that artist when preparing them. Stylistically, the drawings he made preparatory to his St George are very close to the Psyche drawings; Sabra, the ill-fated princess, and the hapless Psyche are almost interchangeable in the story and so are they in his paintings. Carpaccio also executed a series of murals on the life of St Ursula, known to Jones from his visit to them in the Venice Academy in the same year. Evidence of his familiarity with them is contained in the painting 'Theophilus and the Angel' (1863–67), since the subject-matter, treatment of space, distribution of figures, and the situation of the body of the dead saint all recall 'The Martyrdom and Funeral of St Ursula'. Hence Jones's admiration for this early Venetian artist combined with his experience as an illustrator to lead him to develop a similar technique in his own art. 'Theophilus' is, for all that, an unsatisfactory whole. Although the background groups are welded together well enough, Theophilus and his attendant angel are presented as though independent of them, and the two foreground girls, painted from Georgie's two sisters, are even more unrelated. Although they are supposed to be drawing water from the frozen well, they rather unconvincingly gaze into an indefinite space that is not part of the painting; it is likely that they were added as an afterthought. The assurance over complex designs that was to be so evident in his later work is absent, his practice of isolating each part during the evolution of a painting being here all too evident, but since this is almost the first work to have a large number of studies associated with it, its shortcomings are hardly surprising.

In 1867, an improving financial state enabled Jones to move to 'The Grange', North End Road, Fulham, once the home of the eighteenth-century novelist, Samuel Richardson. Unable to afford such a large house—it was actually two houses joined together—he and Wilfred Heeley, a friend from University days, took a joint tenancy. 'The Grange' so suited him that it remained his London home for the rest of his life. Its almost country surroundings and fine walled garden provided a retreat in which he could develop the right atmosphere for his work. A short time after the family moved in they gave a house-warming, described by Madox Brown in a letter to George Rae (another Pre-Raphaelite patron, who lived at Birkenhead):

'As to the news, I will give you what I have. Jones; having moved to his new house, gave a dance, a very swell affair, the house being newly decorated in the "firm" taste, looked charming; the women looked lovely, the singing unrivalled.'

Warrington Taylor joined the firm as its manager in 1865, taking over the responsibility from Morris, who had been a careless administrator. Taylor immediately set about organising the members into systematic workmanship, insisting on an efficient approach, in contrast to Morris's deliberately amateur, good-natured policy. Bringing the members

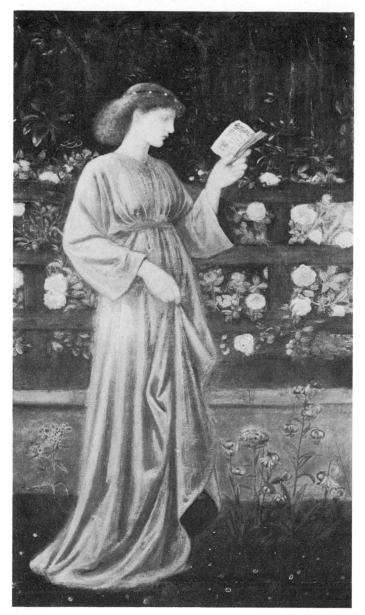

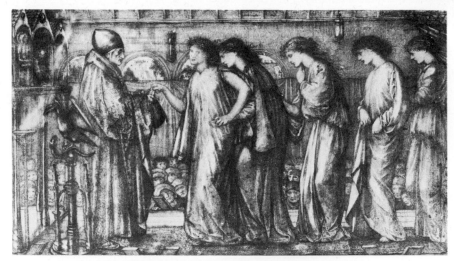

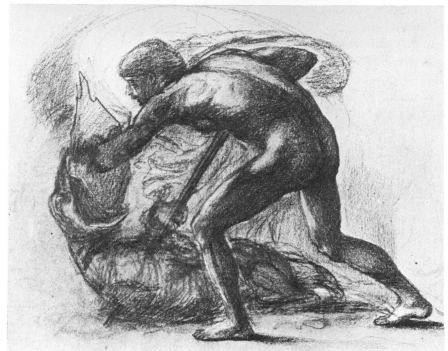

117. 'The King's Daughter', 1865–66, gouache, 42 × 24, Musée National d'Art Moderne, Paris

The first of the St George series. The model was Augusta Jones, who was also used in 'Cinderella', 1863 and 'Astrologia', 1865.

118. 'Moritura—The Princess Draws the Lot', *c.* 1865, pencil, $13\frac{7}{8} \times 23\frac{1}{2}$. The British Museum, London

A highly finished preparatory drawing for one of Birket Foster's decorative series of paintings, based on the story of St George. The drawing was once owned by Sir Edward Poynter.

119. Study for 'St George Fighting the Dragon', *c.* 1865, pencil, $13\frac{7}{8} \times 17$, Birmingham City Museum & Art Gallery

This is the sixth in the series; the finished painting is in the Art Gallery of New South Wales, Sydney, Australia, and a 1868 variant is in the William Morris Gallery, Walthamstow.

down to realities, Taylor pressed them to produce designs punctually and to deal with one thing at a time. In fact, he saved the firm from total disintegration. He was shocked at the deteriorating quality of some of their recent work, notably the tiles at St Peter's Church, Bournemouth, which he thought a disgrace. An example of the type of influence he had is given in a letter to Philip Webb about 1867, explaining that they would be unable to accept commissions for murals. A year earlier Morris's firm had undertaken to decorate the dining room in the South Kensington Museum. Philip Webb was responsible for the plan and decorative scheme, whilst Jones was assigned a set of twelve panels of the months, and the stained glass. The panels executed by the firm's workmen proved so poor that Jones instructed Murray to repaint all except one. After the experience Taylor realised that they could not undertake such a commission again:

1. It would be impossible to give any idea how long it would take to paint in oil 16 feet square from a cartoon by Ned.

2. We have no experience in oil painting.

3. How much ought to be done over and over again.

4. Oil painting cannot be looked upon at all as a mechanical work like painting in one colour on glass.

5. If people want oil paintings they ought to go to proper painters for them . . .

8. If people want east end altarpieces let them pay Rossetti or Jones for proper paintings—things really proper and fit.

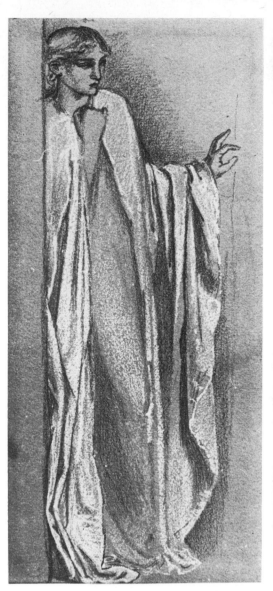

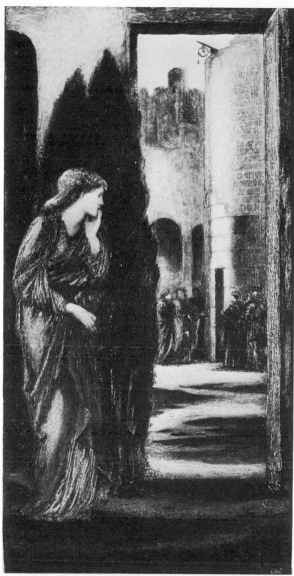

120. Study for 'Danae' (?), *c.* 1867, black and white chalks on brown paper, $13\frac{3}{8} \times 5\frac{5}{8}$, The Ashmolean Museum, Oxford.

121. 'Danae' by Charles Fairfax Murray, after Burne-Jones, *c.* 1869, oil on panel, 38×19, The Ashmolean Museum, Oxford

The earliest version of the subject was said to have been destroyed at the framers by fire, another version made at the same time in in The Fogg Art Gallery, Cambridge, Massachusetts; but by far the largest is the version of 1888 bought from the artist by the Glasgow Art Gallery.

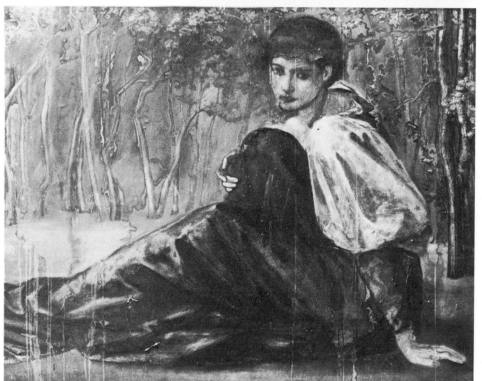

122. 'Hermia', *c.* 1869, watercolour, 36×45 approx., private collection, England

A large watercolour which is transitional from the small, intimately scaled works of the early 1860s and the grander, more massive paintings of the period after 1870. Although large, it is created by a technique that was used in much smaller work; that is, a thinly applied paint which takes the texture from the paper. The later technique completely obscures the paper by building up dense layers of paint.

91

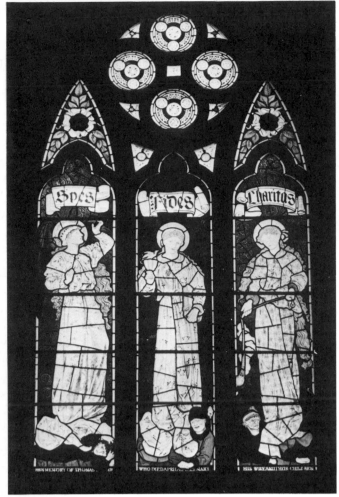

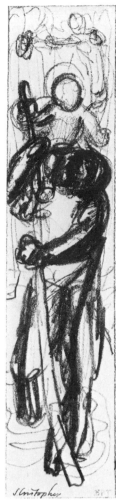

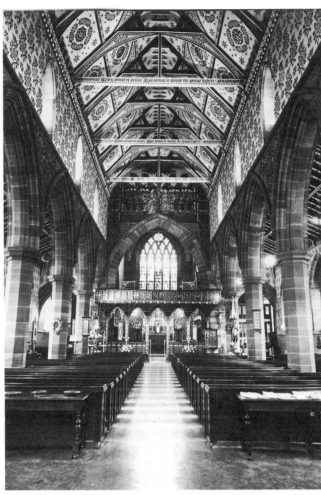

123. 'Faith; Hope; Charity', east window in the south side of St Edburg Church, Bicester, Oxfordshire, executed by Morris, Marshall, Faulkner & Co, 1866
Jones's conception of the Virtues standing on impersonations of the vices derives from thirteenth-century Gothic sculpture.

124. Sketch for St Christopher window, 1868, pencil, $8 \times 1\frac{3}{4}$. Collection: Albert Dawson, Carlisle
St Christopher was first used in 1868 in the centre light of a south aisle window in All Saints Church, Wigan, Lancashire, flanked by two pairs of Morris Angels.

125. The interior of St John's Church, Tue Brook, Liverpool, looking east. Church of 1868 by G. F. Bodley; the decoration is by C. E. Kempe
The Morris firm is represented in this church by two windows, co-eval with the church, which are now sadly deteriorated.

9. If you want to be jack-of-all-trades you must have separate staffs.

10. We have no means of making an estimate for oil-painting—we know nothing about the cost of the work.

11. You cannot manage more than one class of work (glass) with one establishment. If you can make that pay it as much as you can do.

Needless to say Taylor found no place for 'Ned's' jocular method of going about his work and there was a respectful but reserved distance between them.

The year 1865 was the most productive in the field of stained-glass designs. Jones was able to direct his attention to this because he was not occupied with any major paintings, just the book illustrations. The figure he created as Psyche, who wears a loose garment which falls from the neck, whose hair flows down her back, and whose face is a personal variation of the Rossetti type, frequently occurs in the windows of this time. At Bicester we find her as Charity; at Brighton, Chapel of the Annunciation, she is both angel and Virgin; at St John's, Torquay, she is portrayed as Virgin holding the Child (the small preliminary design for the latter at the Victoria and Albert Museum is so like the book-illustration designs that for some time it was catalogued as one), and at Cheddleton she occurs as an angel pouring water.

Rossetti's influence persists in the stained-glass window designs until the late 1860s, but a new style, more lyrical and less formal than the earlier Gothic style, emerged around 1865. In search of a greater expression in his glass, he developed a graceful but animated line, became less planar and more complex in his utilisation of the space. The draperies no longer fall in simple folds but fly up on themselves and develop intricate patterns. As in his work in other media, naturalism is eschewed in favour of more aesthetic considerations. Morris's colour also underwent a similar change, passing from the rich, dark hues of the early glass to sweeter, lighter and more delicate colour. Particularly prominent is the introduction of pale-coloured and white glass used in the draperies with most telling

92

effect, especially when juxtaposed with a dark blue or green scroll-work background.

The withdrawal from the Gothic to a more consciously decorative manner can be accounted for by the influence of painters trained in the Paris ateliers. As we have noted, Whistler's ideas on the role of the painter had a profound effect upon Jones, and the white figures in stained glass are one feature of the new decorative art that resulted. Other artists of the period became interested in a curious decorative inertia which in fact heralded the Aesthetic Movement based upon the maxim 'Art for Art's Sake'. It was a reaction against the Gothic revival and narrative painting. Painting, they cried, has no business to tell stories but must deal with the figures themselves, that is its only function. So to rid them of any suspicion of a story the models were painted either languishing or sleeping in decorative attitudes complimentary to each other, or standing wholly engrossed within themselves. Albert Moore is the most characteristic of these artists; his works are painterly arrangements of models in harmonious colours and design. The antithesis of naturalism, each item is carefully selected before it is included in a painting, a far cry from the early Pre-Raphaelites who went to nature 'selecting nothing, rejecting nothing'. Albert Moore was perhaps the most extreme but many in the circle of Jones's friends used this mode of artistic expression—Henry Holiday, Simeon Solomon, Walter Crane, Thomas Armstrong and Frederick Leighton.

Although influenced to the extent of painting a few works according to the 'Aesthetic'

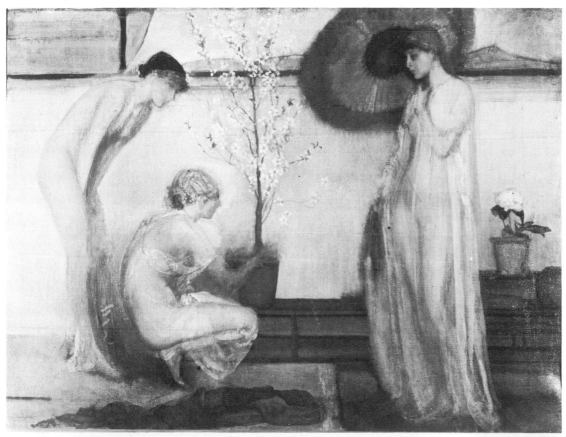

126. 'Three Figures: Pink and Grey' by James Abbot McNeill Whistler, 1867–68, oil on canvas, $54\frac{3}{4} \times 73$, Tate Gallery, London
Jones was working on 'The Mirror of Venus' at this date, and the two pictures are abstract arrangements of female figures.

127. 'Apples' by Albert Moore, 1875, oil on canvas, $11\frac{1}{2} \times 20$; private collection, England
This type of picture emerged in the mid-1860s through the agency of Moore, Whistler, Rossetti, and Jones. By 1880 it had become identified with the Aesthetic Movement.

128. 'The Sleeping Beauty', 1871, gouache, $10\frac{5}{8} \times 14\frac{7}{8}$, Manchester City Art Gallery
Murray Marks commissioned this picture, which is on vellum; it is the first portrayal of a favourite subject.

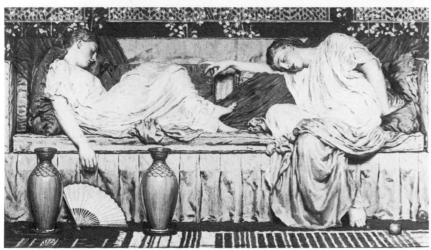

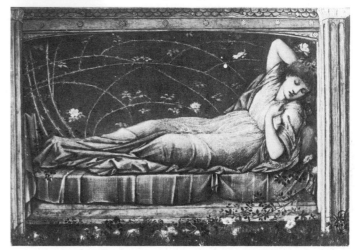

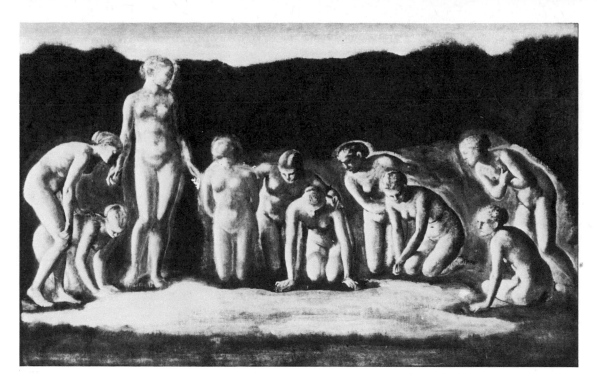

principle, Jones never became wholly a convert, to the exclusion of his esoteric narrative. Its main effect was to make him conscious of the importance of the abstract components of a painting, colour, line, etc. Ironically, his painting became identified, in the eyes of the public, with the Aesthetic Movement, when it was at its height. An important part of the Movement was its love of Japanese and Chinese objects, especially blue and white porcelain; Rossetti, Whistler, and Charles Augustus Howell vied with each other to see who could collect the finest pieces. Towards the end of the 1860s they became fashionable items to collect and a scheme arose to form a business dealing in these and other objets d'art. Murray Marks proposed to start a fine art company with Alexander Ionides, a wealthy Greek merchant, who was to advance £2000 to £3000, and Rossetti, Jones and Morris were to have advanced an equivalent amount. The aim was to deal in pictures, prints, blue and white ware, and other decorative products; secondly they were to have the exclusive right to sell Watts's, Jones's, and Rossetti's paintings and Whistler's etchings, and perhaps later his paintings too. Considering that such volatile personalities were involved, it was predictable that the scheme should come to nothing.

From 1865 the number of studies that Jones produced for a particular painting increased; the characteristic details of hands, facial expressions, draperies began to appear. The first works to have these types of studies were 'Theophilus' and 'The Wine of Circe', but there is, in fact, a gradual transition from the preparatory studies made for earlier works. The studies of the early 1860s have a slightly different function; they were made of necessity, to practice the hand before committing the image to the canvas. The later studies are distillations of Jones's vision; each attempts to materialise the perfect image that is in the artist's mind, each is perfect in itself, yet a fragment of the final painting. This change in practice is part of the fundamental redirection of his outlook which we have noted and marks a greater awareness of his individual contribution as an artist.

At the end of the 1860s Jones's work was becoming more Italianate, and he began working on a much larger scale. Until this time he had mostly chosen small or intimate levels upon which to operate; now, becoming more confident in his own ability he wished to enter the spheres of 'High Art', whose predominant characteristic was large size. Occasionally, as a stained-glass designer, he had been obliged to work on a large scale, but the majority of the works before the late 1860s were small. New considerations arose with the increased dimensions, a large area needed careful thought since proportionately there was much more space to fill. Smaller work could be conceived and structured as a whole, but each separate part of the composition became important in itself when working on a large scale. Whatever the size, Jones always first developed a composition by means of

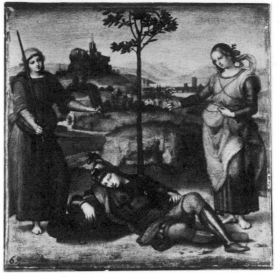

a small rough sketch. As it crystallised in his mind he prepared a larger drawing approximating the design of the final work. With the overall plan finally settled he set about making detailed preparatory studies of each part, draperies, nude studies, details of faces, hands, feet, and accessories. In the course of its development a painting underwent every conceivable variation until exactly the image he desired appeared on the canvas before him. This continual reappraisal was not restricted to details, compositional variants arose at all stages; colour studies and cartoons, often finished as independent versions later, contribute to the immense body of his work.

The transfer from drawing to a vast canvas entailed considerable work which was not particularly creative and could be carried out by a studio assistant. For this Jones employed T. M. Rooke from this time until his death. Rooke was a watercolourist and oil painter of some talent, and perfect as an assistant, being of a mild nature prone to hero-worship. His work, which he exhibited independently, often reveals the strong influence of his master, but there is always a character of its own. Scenes from the Old Testament, often in series, were the interest for which he may be remembered today, but he was a competent portraitist and also executed many watercolours of French cathedrals for Ruskin, who sent him abroad each summer.

Old friendships with Rossetti and Ruskin, though not severed, were on the decline. After a period of very close relations with Ruskin, their mutually unsympathetic views caused them to become more distant; a projected portrait of the critic remained as a few drawings made at a single sitting. Ruskin was becoming more eccentric with the years, eventually reaching total madness in later life. The drug chloral was responsible for a change in Rossetti's character. Much to the sadness of Jones, his friend had no wish to resume close acquaintance, but there was still, in 1869, some communication and affection between them, as a letter Rossetti wrote to William Allingham in March 1870 shows:

> P.S. I copy on the spare leaf a sonnet I have just written on Burne-Jones's Circe, which I know you saw at the water-colour gallery. I wanted to have some record of his work in my book. I have tried in the first lines to give some notion of the colour, and, in the last some impression of the scope of the work—taking the transformed beasts as images of ruined passion—the torn seaweed of the sea of pleasure!

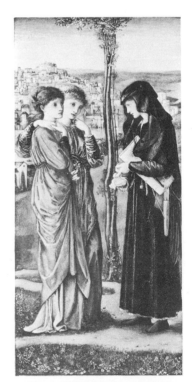

> Dusk-haired and gold-robed o'er golden wine
> She stoops, wherein, distilled of death and shame,
> Sink the black drops; while lit with fragrant flame,
> Round her head board the golden sunflowers shine.
> Doth Nelios here with Hecate combine
> (O Circe, thou their votaress?) to proclaim
> For these thy guests all rapture in Love's name,
> Till pitiless Night give Day the countersign?

95

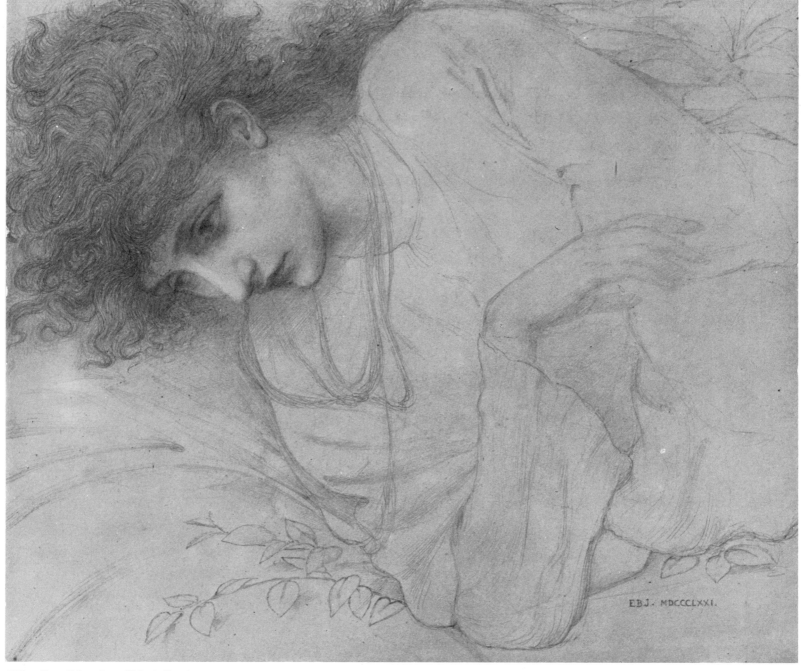

132. Pencil drawing of Maria Zambaco,
13 × 14½, private collection, London.

133. 'Venus Epithalamia', 1871,
gouache touched with gold, 14½ × 10¼,
The Fogg Art Gallery, Cambridge,
Massachusetts
The model for Venus was Maria
Zambaco; the picture was painted for
Marie Spartali. Fairfax Murray made a
copy in the same year.

Lord of their hour, they come. And by her knee
Those cowering beasts, their equals heretofore,
Wait; who with them in new equality
Tonight shall echo back the sea's dull roar
With a vain wail from passion's tide-strown shore
Where the dishevelled seaweed hates the sea.

Rossetti was the amused observer when Jones became entangled with a beautiful
Greek sculptress, Maria T. Zambaco. She was a daughter of Mrs E. Casavetti, one of the
Greek colony in London who were friends of the Rossetti circle and who purchased the
Pre-Raphaelite's paintings. The women were wealthy, talented, and beautiful, and Maria
was no exception. She posed for Rossetti, who portrayed her as a dusky maid, sharp
featured with soft gentle eyes. That Jones saw her as much more than a model can be
deduced from the extraordinary series of pencil drawings he made of her. They are almost
unique in his work. Finely drawn, they are tender and intimate; very feminine, they
stress the intensity of his relationship with her. His involvement with her lasted from 1868
until 1871 and during that time she inspired a number of significant works. She figures

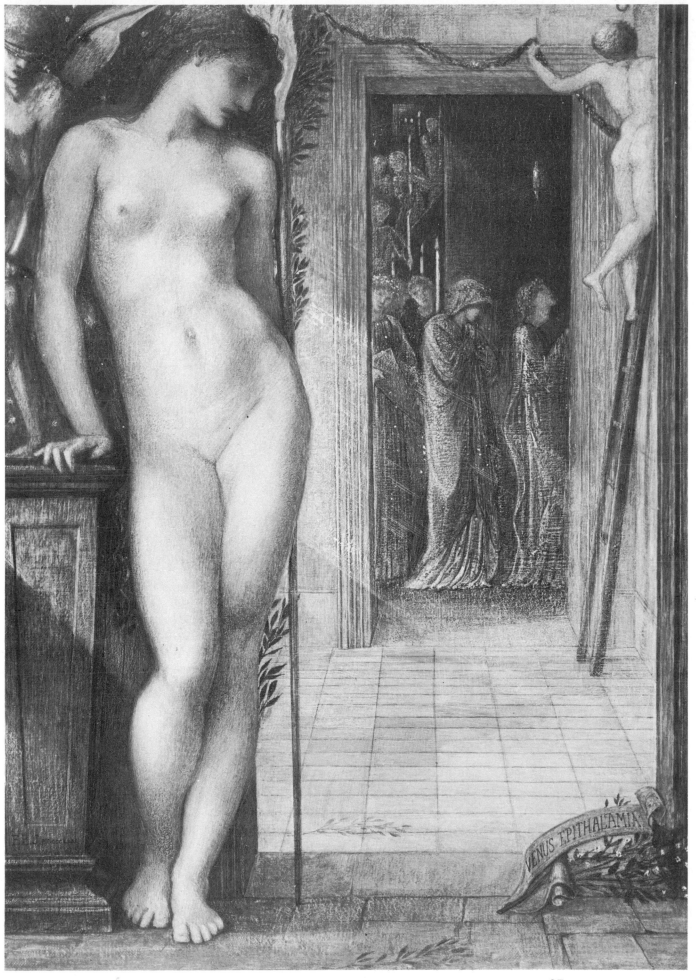

VENVS EPITHALAMIA

97

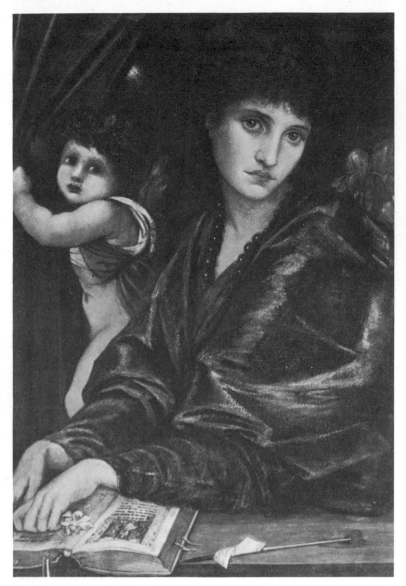

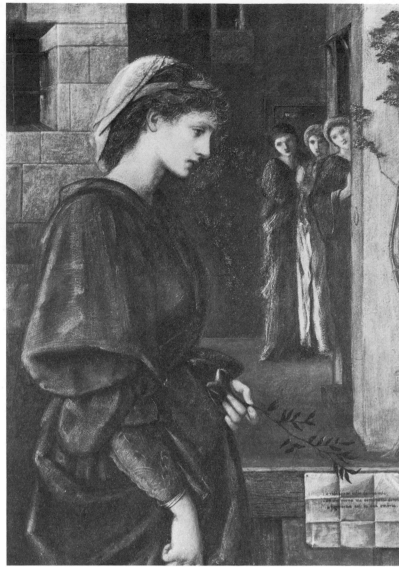

134. Portrait of Maria Zambaco, 1870, gouache; private collection, England
There is little attempt to disguise the affection the artist felt for his model in this picture: the arrow with his name on it, Cupid drawing a curtain (an ancient device for portraying Venus), and the book which opens on an illustration of his own 'Chant d'Amour'.

135. 'Beatrice', 1870, gouache, $26\frac{1}{4} \times 19\frac{1}{4}$; private collection, London.

20-23. The Pygmalion Series, 1868-70, oil on canvas, each 26 × 20; Joseph Setton collection Paris. Painted for Mrs Cassavetti, the series is a development of the illustrations to the story in *The Earthly Paradise*. The more famous series in Birmingham City Art Gallery was finished in 1878. The titles are, respectively, 'The Heart Desires', 'The Hand Refrains', 'The Godhead Fires', 'The Soul Attains'.

as 'Summer', one of the four decorative panels painted for Leyland during 1869-70, as the dancing girls in the first version of 'Hesperides' (1869-72), as Phyllis in 'Phyllis and Demophoön' (1870), and perhaps the most revealing as 'Beatrice' (1870). In the light of Rossetti's sequence of Beatrices, in which the women who obsessed him in life became the symbol of ideal love in his paintings, it is not without significance that in Jones's only painting of the subject Maria appears as the divine Beatrice. What is more, the painting contains part of a sonnet by Guido Cavalcanti in Italian which reads:

'Io vidi donne con la donna mia
Non che niuna me sembrasse donna,
Ma figuravan sol la sua ombria.'

Rossetti had published a translation of the verse in 1861:

'With other women I beheld my love:—
Not that the rest were women to mine eyes,
Who only as her shadow seemed to move.'

Their relationship, however, did not run smoothly, and in 1869 we find Rossetti writing to Madox Brown:

'Poor old Ned's affairs have come to a smash together, and he and Topsy (Morris), after the most dreadful to do, started for Rome suddenly, leaving the Greek damsel beating up the quarters of all his friends for him and howling like Cassandra, Georgie staying behind. I hear today however that Top and Ned got no further than Dover, Ned

98

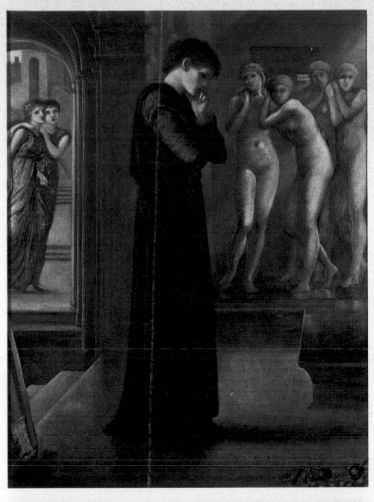

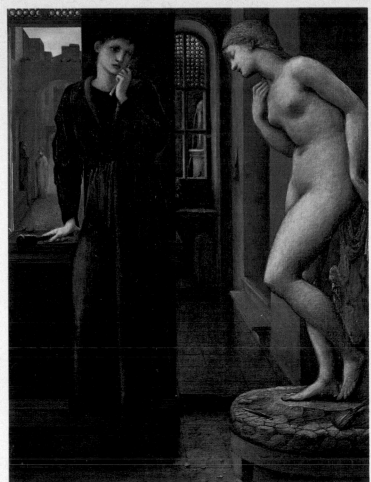

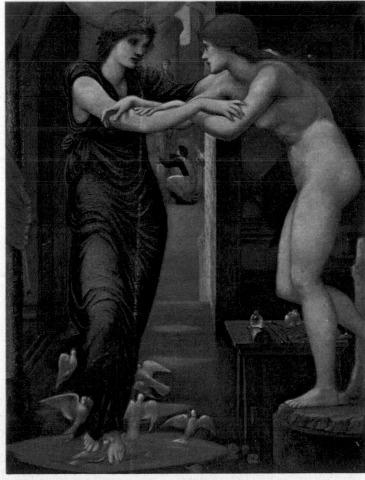

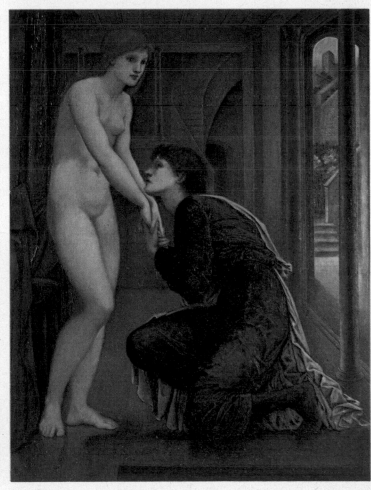

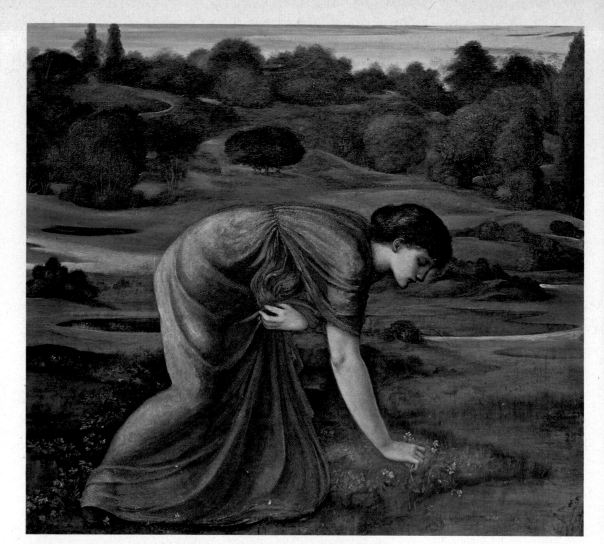

24. 'The March Marigold', c. 1870, oil on canvas, 28¼ × 30½; The Piccadilly Gallery, London. The figure was used again in a painting of Hero gathering firewood of 1875. It could be that this subject too originates from the Cupid and Psyche story. The figure is very similar to Jones's conception of Psyche, and the incident of 'The March Marigold' may well have been inspired by the tale of Psyche, who is left in a meadow by Zephyrus and then wanders about gathering flowers.

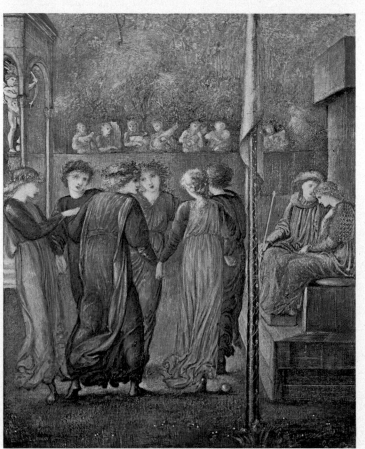

25. 'King's Wedding', 1870, gouache on vellum, 12¾ × 10½; private collection, England.

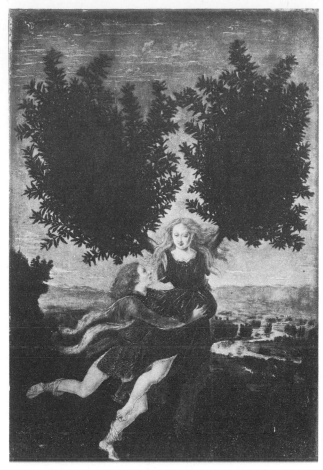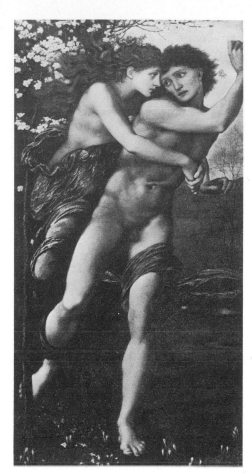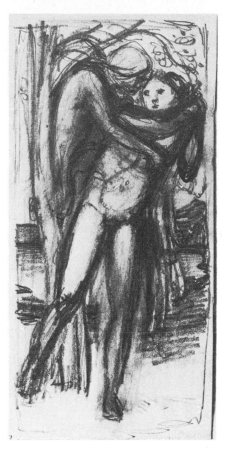

being so dreadfully ill that they will probably have to return to London.'

With this episode in mind 'Phyllis and Demophoön', whether consciously or not, has a certain biographical relevance. Demophoön is shown struggling with Phyllis who has reverted to human form while he passes by. She, loving and forgiving, wishes to enfold him in her arms but he, fearful, struggles to be free; a situation it seems, not far from reality.

136. 'Apollo and Daphne' by Antonio Pollaiuolo, mid-fifteenth century, oil, $11\frac{1}{4} \times 7\frac{1}{2}$, The National Gallery, London

Jones was familiar with this painting at The National Gallery which shows a reversal of the situation in his 'Phyllis and Demophoön'.

137. 'Phyllis and Demophoön', 1870, gouache, 36×18, Birmingham City Museum & Art Gallery

The story, taken from Ovid, recounts how Phyllis, metamorphosed into an almond tree, embraces her lover on his return.

138. Study for 'Phyllis and Demophoön', c. 1868, pencil, $3\frac{1}{4} \times 1\frac{1}{2}$, William Morris Gallery, Walthamstow.

Chapter Six

Italy

A controversy arose over 'Phyllis and Demophoön' when it was exhibited at the Water-Colour Society in 1870. An anonymous letter was °ent to the Society complaining of the nudity of the male figure, which did not have the usual discreet covering of old drapery. Disturbed by the complaint, the Society requested that the offending picture should be removed. Burne-Jones complied with the request and returned it to his studio. At the close of the exhibition in July, he sent a formal resignation of his membership, refusing to withdraw it even when asked by the Society itself. Frederick Burton, incensed at the slight to his friend, resigned at the same time.

Burne-Jones's victimisation heralded a series of blows to the group of artists associated with Rossetti's circle. A year later, in the autumn of 1871, Robert Buchanan's famous article 'The Fleshly School of Poetry' attacked Rossetti and Swinburne, among others, for the undue prominence of sensuality in their work. The article did irreparable damage to Rossetti's morale, and from then on he had a conviction that there was a conspiracy against him, a feeling induced and exaggerated by his addiction to the drug chloral. Following this, in 1873, Simeon Solomon came up for trial on charges of homosexuality and was sentenced to a short term of imprisonment. It has been suggested that the reasons for these attacks on the licence of artists was that society was becoming more restrictive because of the disturbances across the channel. Shocked at the horrors of the Paris Commune, the Establishment in England saw the more liberal artists as a possible threat to themselves and wanted to bring them to heel.

After his withdrawal from the Water-Colour Society, Burne-Jones did not exhibit in public for seven years, with a single exception however, in 1873, when he exhibited the second version of 'The Hesperides' and 'Love among the Ruins' at the Dudley Gallery. No real hardship resulted, for he was still able to sell direct from his studio to an increasing number of patrons.

Watts painted Morris's and Burne-Jones's portraits in 1870, the latter being exhibited at the Royal Academy the same year. Close contact with Watts at this moment was important for him since Watts was as enthusiastic about Italian art as ever.

As we have seen, Burne-Jones was gradually evolving away from his early 'medieval', intimately-scaled works towards larger, Italianate, compositions. From Dürer and the Flemish and Italian quattrocentist painters he transferred his interest to Mantegna, Michaelangelo, Raphael, Botticelli, and Leonardo. These were the artists who were the chief exemplars for his later work. At the end of the 1860s he was beginning to feel in need of a fresh look at Italian painting. In spite of frequent visits to the National Gallery and the South Kensington Museum, which proved fertile sources, he felt handicapped at not knowing more of the paintings at first hand. He began to feel uncertain, starting many new paintings but was unable to decide how to continue them; a nervous line invades his work

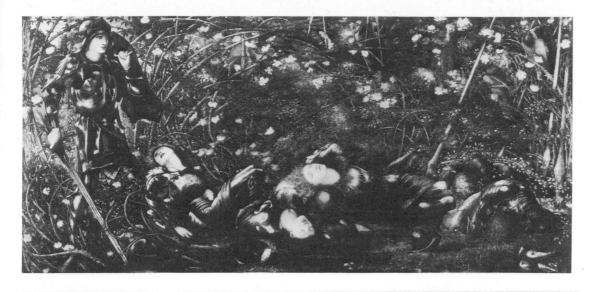

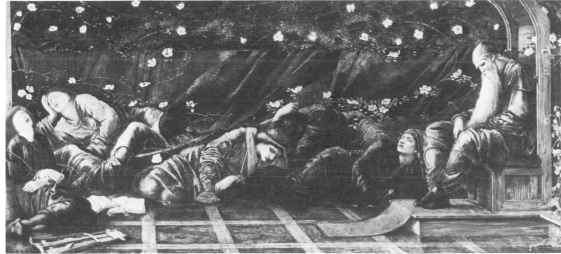

139-41.   The first 'Briar Rose' series, 1870-73, Museo de Arte, Ponce, Puerto Rico:
139.   'The Prince Enters the Wood', oil, 24 × 51.
140.   'The King and his Court', oil, 24 × 53.
141.   'The Sleeping Beauty', oil, 24 × 46.

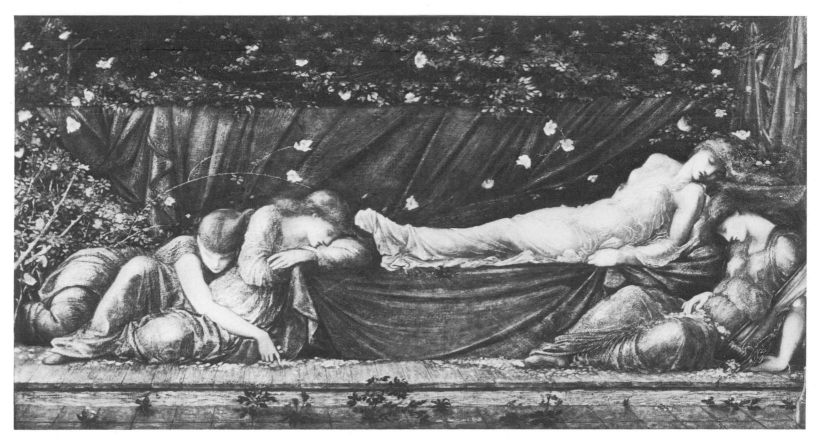

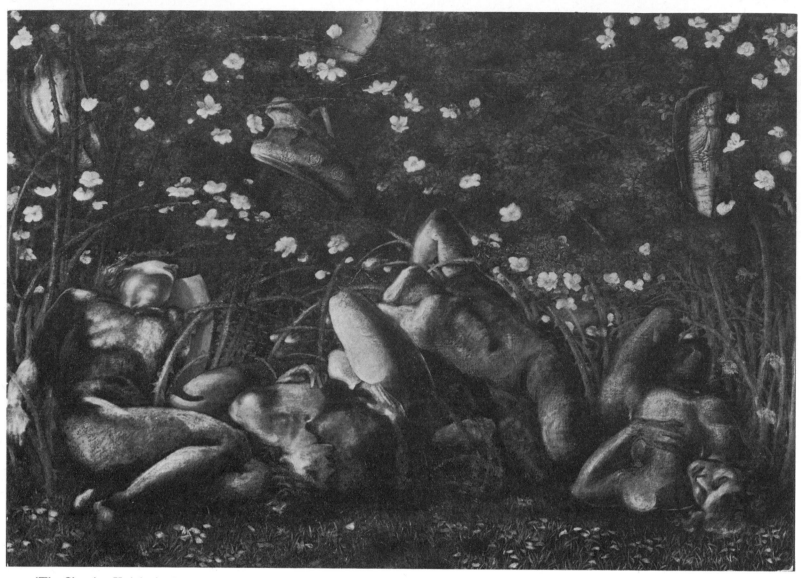

142. 'The Sleeping Knights', 1871,
oil, $23\frac{1}{4} \times 32\frac{1}{2}$, The Walker Art Gallery,
Liverpool
A study for the first of the 'Briar Rose'
series without the figure of the prince.

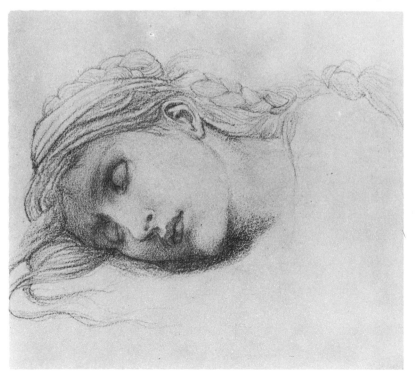

143. Study for one of the princess's
attendants, *c.* 1878, crayon, $8\frac{1}{4} \times 9\frac{1}{4}$;
private collection.

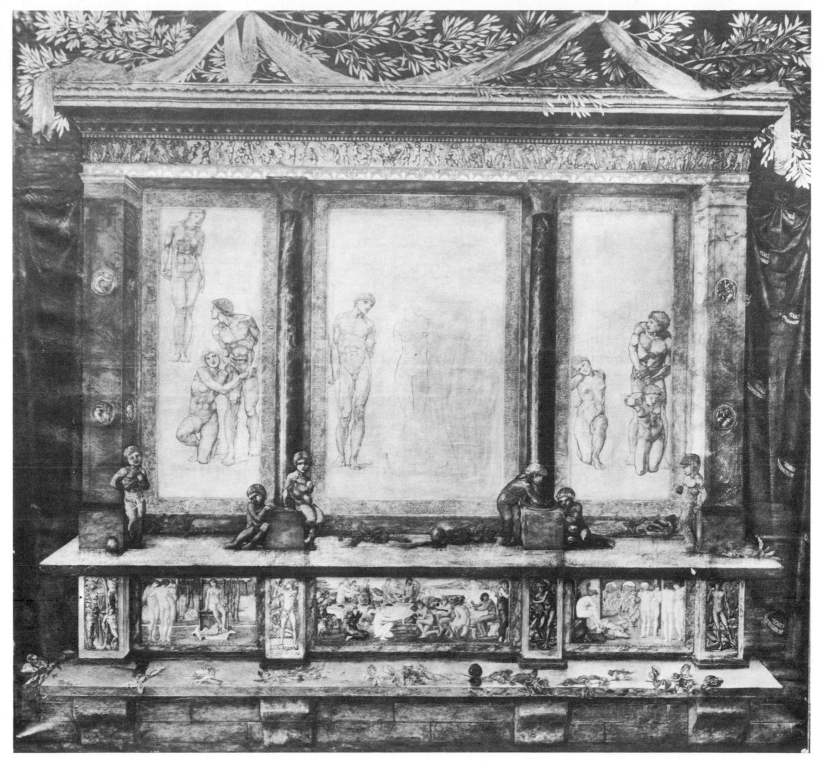

and the figures stand or lie at awkward angles—features which are particularly noticeable in the first 'Briar Rose' series, begun about 1868. And so in September 1871 he decided, suddenly, to go to Italy. He gave his reasons to his American friend, Charles Eliot Norton of Harvard:

> . . . for what with overwork, and the increasing feelings of its eccentricity as every year I found myself more alone in it, the miserable feeling of being a mistake was growing; and towards the last though I worked harder and harder it brought me no comfort—but now I am well. . . . And really I think I don't care one bit for the way they are received—though I want some people to like them. I have 60 pictures, oil and water, in my studio & every day I would gladly begin a new one.

He visited Genoa, Florence, Pisa, San Gemignano, Siena, Orvieto and Rome. With

144. 'Troy' polyptych, begun 1870, oil on canvas, $107\frac{1}{2} \times 116$; Birmingham City Museum & Art Gallery
This painting within a painting was almost certainly based upon the altarpiece by Mantegna in the Church of San Zeno, Verona, which Jones had visited in 1862. Painted in the grand style, it was to have been his *chef d'oeuvre*, but although many important paintings grew out of it, it remained unfinished.

Rome he was disappointed, finding it 'pompous and empty', but he was overjoyed to find the paintings in the Sistine Chapel not in such a deteriorated state as he had been led to expect. So, as Georgiana Burne-Jones tells us, 'he bought the best opera glass he could find, folded his railway rug thickly, and, lying on his back, read the ceiling from beginning to end, peering into every corner and revelling in its execution.'

On his return he wrote, 'So that now I care most for Michael Angelo, Luca Signorelli, Mantegna, Giotto, Orcagna, Botticelli, Andrea del Sarto, Paolo Uccello and Piero della Francesca.' He also said: 'this time, for some reason artistic excellence *alone* had little charm for me—so that I never wanted even to look at Titian and saw the Raphaels at Rome for the first time as unaffected by them as I can see the cartoons in London.'

With Michaelangelo so high in Burne-Jones's esteem it is not surprising that Ruskin distressed him when he read to him his highly critical lecture on Tintoretto and Michaelangelo, prior to its delivery at Oxford in 1870. Ruskin's attack is on the artists of the High Renaissance who, he felt, had debased the purity and piety of the quattrocentists. He is able to accept 'John Bellini' who 'precedes the change, meets, and resists it victoriously to his death', but 'Then Raphael, Michaelangelo, and Titian together bring about the deadly change, playing into each other's hands—Michaelangelo being the chief captain in evil, Titian in natural force.' Outlining the former's faults he continues:

> Now the changes brought about by Michael Angelo . . . are in the four points these:
> First. Bad workmanship. The greater part that [he] did is hastily and incompletely done; and all that [he] did on a large scale in colour is in the best qualities of it perished.
> Second. Violence of transitional action. The figures flying—falling striking or biting, scenes of judgement—battle—martyrdom—massacre; anything that is in the acme of instantaneous interest and violent gesture. . . .
> Third. Physical instead of mental interest. The body, and its anatomy made the entire subject of interest, the face shadowed . . . unfinished as in twilight; or entirely foreshortened, back shortened and despised, among labyrinths of limbs and mountains of sides and shoulders.
> Fourth. Evil chosen rather than good. On the face itself instead of joy or virtue, at the best, sadness, probably pride, often sensuality, and always by preference, vice or agony as the subject of thought.

Ruskin took a moral tone, much as Buchanan had in his tirade on Rossetti, seeing the simplicity and naïve religious fervour of the primitives as the only genuine virtues. His *coup de grâce* was not aimed at Michaelangelo himself but at those who admired him: 'But it is one of the chief misfortunes affecting Michael Angelo's reputation that his ostentatious display of strength and science has a natural attraction for comparatively weak and pedantic persons.' A peevish attitude, and one wonders how Burne-Jones received it when Ruskin read it to him face to face. What Ruskin really objected to was the paganising force which took hold of Michaelangelo. The great power of humanism predominates in his interpretation of biblical events, man is shown on a par with God himself, his suffering is raised to Olympian heights of pathos. In his objection, Ruskin showed himself to be one of the older generation which had arisen with the Gothic revival; Christianity went hand-in-hand with medieval art, which included the early Renaissance. For that generation the simple Christian ethic was inseparably tied to art; they were moralisers with a heavy social conscience. Burne-Jones and Morris had first formulated their ideas under the influence of Ruskin. Gradually, Burne-Jones moved from this type of thought into more purely aesthetic regions, while Morris, going part of the same way, retained a strong sense of the duty of art and crafts, and became a committed socialist in the 1880s.

But the relationship between artist and critic was not to end there: for sentimental reasons neither wished to terminate their longstanding friendship. Avoiding such controversial topics as Michaelangelo, Ruskin gave one of his *Art in England* series of lectures in 1883, entitled *The Mythic Schools of Painting—Burne-Jones and Watts*. In it he defended

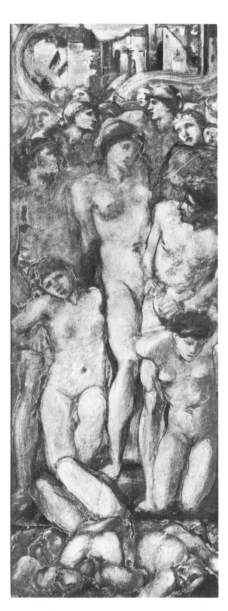

145. 'Helen at Troy', 1871, gouache, $40\frac{3}{4} \times 14\frac{1}{2}$; Birmingham City Museum & Art Gallery

This unfinished work, which was part of the 'Troy' polyptych, reveals the artist's method at this date. According to T. M. Rooke, a red ground was first laid on the paper, over which the painting was done mainly in Chinese white and raw umber. The warm ground colour shines through the pale modelling of the figures.

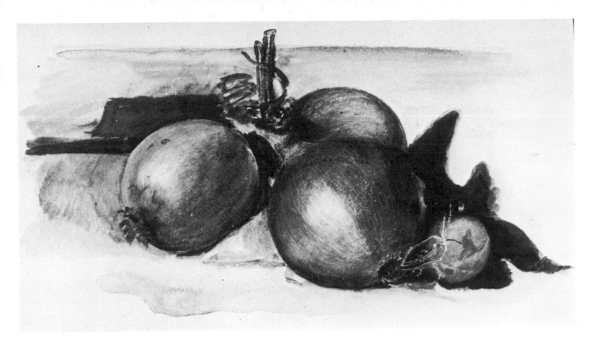

146. Still life, c. 1874, watercolour and gouache, $7\frac{1}{8} \times 12\frac{5}{8}$; Birmingham City Museum & Art Gallery. A very rare subject for Burne-Jones, studies of such objects were made in association with the 'Troy' polyptych.

the significance of myths as archetypes against the contemporary writers who liked to dismiss them as outmoded and primitive, without relevance for the nineteenth century. He proceeded to make two salient points that show that, had he wished, he would have been a fine apologist for the art of his friend:

'His outline is the purest and quitest that is possible to the pencil', and 'Again, though Mr Jones has a sense of colour, in its kind perfect, he is essentially a chiaroscurist, diametrically opposed to Rossetti, who could conceive in colour only.'

A paganising force entered the arts as a reaction against the Gothic revivalist Christianity. Stories of the Greek and Roman heroes became more frequent, instead of using the biblical stories as vehicles of the artists' vision they drew upon Ovid, Virgil and Homer. Associated with this was an admiration for the High Renaissance artists, particularly Michaelangelo, Leonardo, Raphael, and Botticelli. The two spokesmen for the new movement were Walter Pater and John Addington Symonds, as Ruskin had been for the earlier group. Of Michaelangelo, Symonds says in his *Italian Renaissance* (1875–86):

> Michael Angelo is the prophet and Sibylline seer; to him the Renaissance discloses the travail of her spirit; him she embues with power; he wrests her secret, voyaging, like an ideal Columbus, the vast abyss of thought alone.

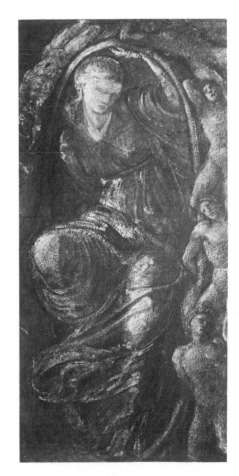

He describes the Sistine Chapel ceiling in a way that could equally be an interpretation of Burne-Jones's later works:

> To speak of these form-poems would be quite impossible. Buonarroti seems to have intended to prove by them that the human body has a language, inexhaustible in symbolism—every limb, every feature, and every attitude being a word full of significance to those who comprehend, just as music is a language. . . . The grace of colouring realised in some of these youthful and athletic forms, is such as no copy can represent. Every posture of beauty and of strength, simple or strained, that it is possible for men to assume, has been depicted here. Yet the whole is governed by a strict sense of sobriety.

Then follows a comparison between Michaelangelo and Pheidias, whose work typified the taste of this generation:

> The human form in the work of Pheidias wore a joyous and sedate serenity; in that of Michael Angelo it is turbid with a strange and awful sense of inbreathed agitation. Through the figure-language of the one was spoken the pagan creed, bright, un-

147. 'The Wheel of Fortune', c. 1870, blue gouache heightened with white, $19 \times 9\frac{1}{2}$, Carlisle Museum & Art Gallery
From the collection of G. F. Watts, with whose work it has a great deal in common.

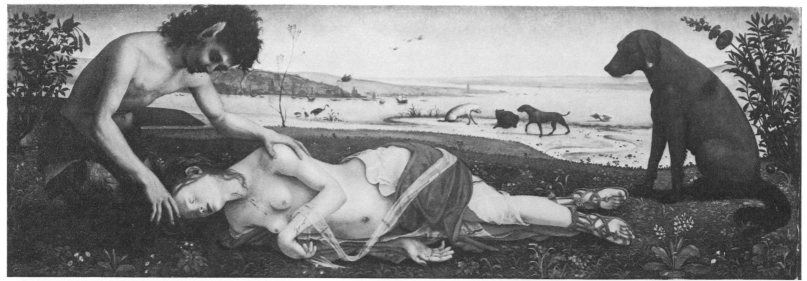

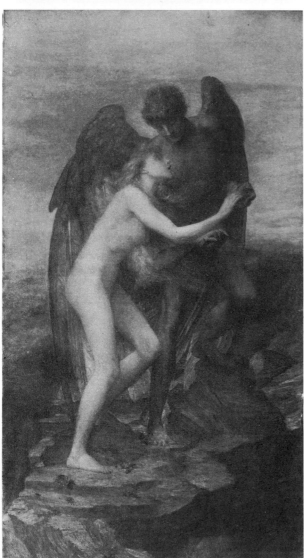

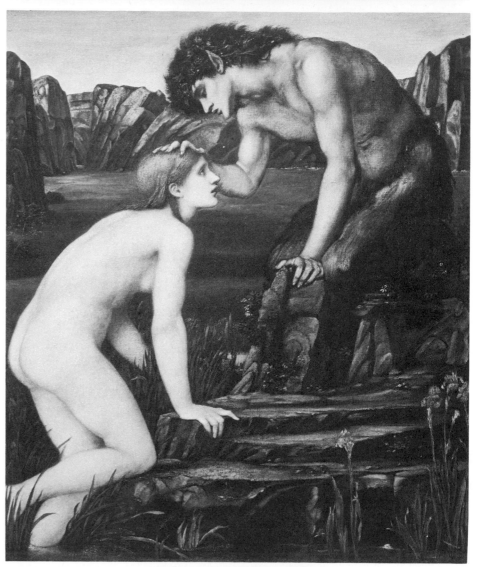

148. 'The Death of Procris' by Piero di Cosimo, late-fifteenth century, oil on panel, $25\frac{1}{2} \times 72$; The National Gallery, London

Burne-Jones based his design 'Pan and Psyche' on this picture in 1864 when making the illustrations for *The Earthly Paradise*.

149. 'Love and Life' by G. F. Watts, *c.* 1884–85, oil on canvas, $87\frac{1}{2} \times 48$, Tate Gallery, London.

This painting leans heavily on Burne-Jones's 'Pan and Psyche'.

150. 'Pan and Psyche', 1869–74, oil on canvas, $25\frac{5}{8} \times 21\frac{3}{8}$, The Fogg Art Gallery, Cambridge, Massachusetts

The design first appeared as a wood engraving illustrating the Cupid and Psyche story in Morris's *Earthly Paradise*.

perturbed, and superficial. The sculpture of the Parthenon accomplished the trans-figuration of the natural man. In the other, man awakes to a new life of contest, disillusionment, hope, dread, and heavenly striving.

The High Renaissance saw a reintroduction of pagan themes, they figure in the work of Raphael and Leonardo as often as those of Christianity. Walter Pater noticed that there was a paganising treatment of the Christian themes in the work of Leonardo ('Essay on Leonardo' in *The Renaissance*, 1869):

> And so it comes to pass that though he handles sacred subjects continuously, he is the most profane of painters; the given person or subject, Saint John in the desert, or the Virgin on the knees of Saint Anne, is often merely the pretext for a kind of work which carries one altogether beyond the range of its conventional associations.

'I love Da Vinci and Michaelangelo most of all.' So wrote Burne-Jones to his friend Charles Eliot Norton in 1871. Leonardo's chimeric enigmas, softly cradled in sfumato, his disturbing figures half-male, half-female, prepared the way for Burne-Jones's pre-possessing androgynes. Like the inventions of Leonardo's fantasy, they too conceal as much as they suggest. The questions they pose are as disconcerting as they induce an equal introspection in the viewer. Out of Leonardo's puzzling psychology came the impetus for the seductive mermaid in 'The Depths of the Sea', the becalmed distance of 'Vespertina Quies', and 'King Cophetua and the Beggar Maid', and the serpentine figures in 'The Feast of Peleus'.

The Hellenism that we see in such works of Burne-Jones's as 'The Mirror of Venus' and 'The Beguiling of Merlin' is thus typical of the emerging Aesthetic Movement in the first half of the seventies. So too are the Michaelangesque figures which appear in his stained-glass designs and Perseus series, at this time.

Having found his 1871 visit to Italy so beneficial, Burne-Jones decided, in the spring of 1873, to return. This time he was accompanied by Morris; they went first to Florence to pay a call on Spencer Stanhope who was living there. Thence they travelled to Siena where Fairfax Murray was staying. Even this beautiful city failed to excite Morris, who was becoming more depressed and difficult as time went on and who returned after visiting Siena, leaving his friend to enjoy the country alone. From Siena Burne-Jones passed on to Volterra, Gemignano, Bologna, and Ravenna. But he grew ill. In fact, he had

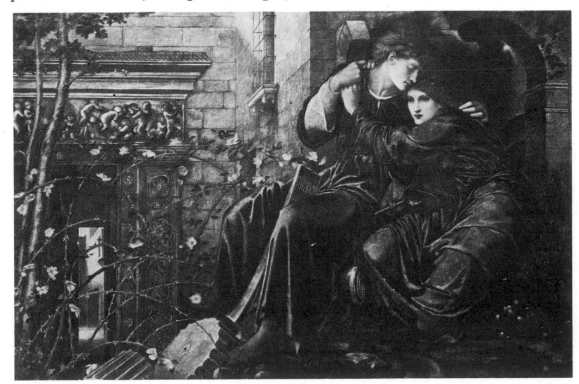

151. 'Love Among the Ruins', 1870–73, gouache, $38\frac{3}{4} \times 60\frac{1}{2}$; private collection
The title suggests Watts, but Burne-Jones has interpreted the theme in a most un-Wattsian way. There is nothing of the heavy allegory of Watts, instead a simple depiction of a pair of lovers who have become aware of the ephemerality of love and youth. This painting was damaged at a photographer's in 1893, stimulating the artist to make a second version in oils. Later, however, he was able to restore the original to its former glory. The oil version is in the Wightwick Manor collection, near Wolverhampton.

to curtail the trip, not going to Umbria as he had intended. Having been weak for most of his tour, he brought back little work.

Returning to London he was confronted in his studio with the sixty or so works which he had begun, the most important being the highly complex polyptych, 'The Story of Troy', an ambitious painting begun in 1870. It comprised a central triptych, 'Helen carried off by Paris', 'The Judgement of Paris' and 'Helen captive at the burning of Troy'. Below these were three predella pictures of 'Venus Concordia', 'The Feast of Peleus' and 'Venus Discordia'. All six of these paintings were incorporated into an illusionary frame painted in perspective, upon which were four decorative panels showing 'The Wheel of Fortune', 'Fame overthrowing Fortune', 'Oblivion conquering Fame', and 'Love subduing Oblivion'. At either end of this frame were figure medallions. To prevent the work being cut up for the sake of the individual subjects, festoons of branches were painted across the top, a series of putti was situated at the base of the three main episodes, flowers were strewn across the shelf at the base and a frieze of more putti laid across the top. The whole complex is an extraordinary extravaganza. It is inconceivable that it should ever have been hung as a framed picture, and it must, therefore, have been the artist's intention to let it into a wall as a decorative panel. After 1873 the whole thing was taken to a studio at Watt's house where it was intended for Burne-Jones to work alongside Watts—brothers in art—but this did not take place and the painting remained untouched. It provided the impetus for a number of paintings for, though the originals remained unfinished, large versions of all of the predella paintings were made over the next twenty years. Only 'A Feast of Peleus' and three versions of 'The Wheel of Fortune' finally reached completion; yet there remains at least one version of each of the predellas on a large scale, unfinished.

As 'The Story of Troy' stands today, it is mostly the work of studio assistants: 'Venus

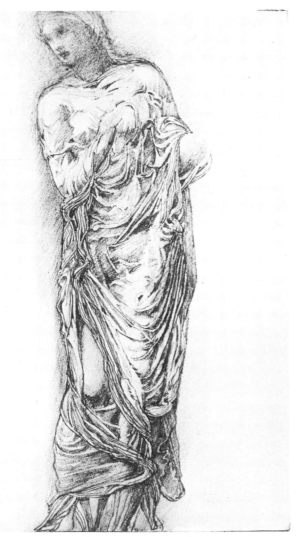

152. Pencil study for 'Merlin and Vivien' from a sketchbook *c.* 1874; Fitzwilliam Museum, Cambridge
One of an entire book devoted to drapery studies for the figure of Vivien, it shows his method of using wet draperies on the model, in the manner of the ancient Greeks.

153. 'The Annunciation' by Charles Fairfax Murray (?) after Burne-Jones, *c.* 1872, oil on canvas, 47 × 38; Museo de Arte, Ponce, Puerto Rico
A copy of the design for stained glass at Castle Howard, Yorkshire. Murray was Burne-Jones's assistant from 1866, but there is a possibility that T. M. Rooke may have worked this oil since he joined the studio in 1869.

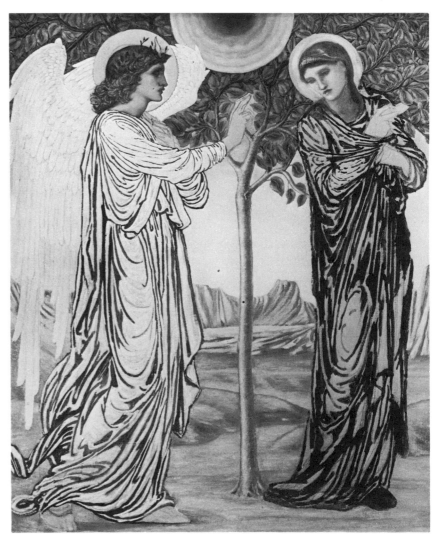

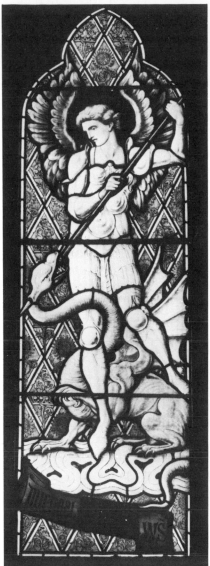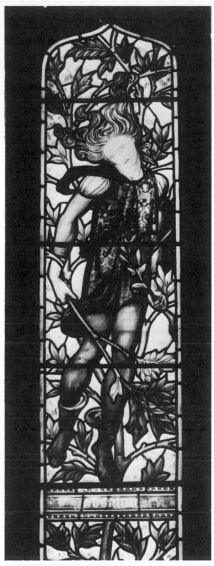

154. 'St Michael Killing the Dragon'. Window in the Chancel, north side, of St Michael's Church, Rocester, Staffordshire. Designed and executed by William de Morgan in 1872. De Morgan designed stained glass for Powell's during the 1860s, and from 1869 to 1872 had his own glass-making workshop at 40, Fitzroy Square, London.

155. 'Absalom'. Window on the south side of St John the Evangelist Church, Knotty Ash, Lancashire, 1872.

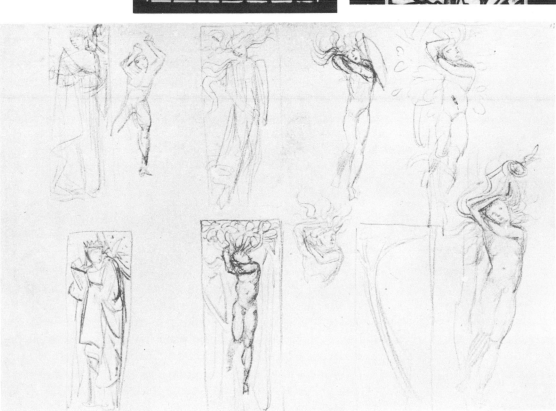

156. Page from a sketchbook of 1872, showing the emergence of the 'Absalom' panel at St John the Evangelist Church, Lancashire; Fitzwilliam Museum, Cambridge.

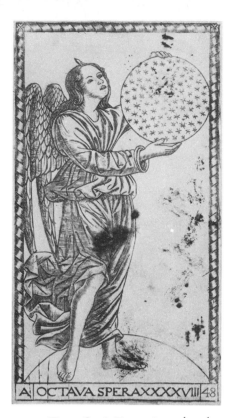

157. Tarot Card. Engraving, $7\frac{1}{2} \times 3\frac{1}{2}$, The British Museum, London
At the date (*c.* 1865) when Burne-Jones first encountered this engraving it was attributed to Mantegna. The influence of these Tarot cards is evident in 'The Days of Creation', 'Astrologia', and the windows in Cheddleton Church.

158. 'The Fifth Day of Creation', 1870–76, gouache, $47\frac{1}{4} \times 14\frac{1}{4}$. The Fogg Art Gallery, Cambridge, Massachusetts.

159. 'The Sixth Day of Creation', 1870–76, gouache, $47\frac{1}{4} \times 14\frac{1}{4}$. The Fogg Art Gallery, Cambridge, Massachusetts.

Discordia' and 'Concordia' were painted by T. M. Rooke in the winter of 1871–72; 'The Feast of Peleus' was reduced and copied in 1873 by an American artist, Francis Laythrop, who also worked for Morris and Company, and in the studio of Spencer Stanhope. Much of the other unfinished work associated with the project was executed by assistants, all of the immense 'Feast of Peleus' is studio work, in which a number of hands can be traced. Burne-Jones's system was to execute highly detailed pencil versions from which the assistant worked, transferring them on to the canvas in terre-verde, or burnt sienna. When all the underpainting was finished Burne-Jones would then overpaint in colour. Here lies the reason why so much of his work is unfinished—for by hiring a large number of assistants, a great amount of work could be prepared, but it was a much slower process for Burne-Jones to finish each picture off.

It was, during the 1870 decade, Burne-Jones's ambition to create a workshop in the manner of the Renaissance painters. He had in mind a group of gifted pupils who could carry out the ideas of the master up to his standard without requiring a great deal of supervision, so building up a huge body of work. Apart from Murray, Rooke and Laythrop who have been mentioned, it is known that a Matthew Webb spent some time in the studio from 1877, J. M. Strudwick almost certainly did—and it is probable that Louis Davis had some connection, and perhaps others who cannot at present be identified.

The impact of the two Italian tours had a profound effect on his outlook as an artist; after a period of despondency which lasted until February 1874, his confidence grew. But during those years his friends commented on his low spirits, and we find him writing to Watts, whom he treated as a father figure:

> I suppose I have done something but I look in vain for it—and about every fifth day I fall into despair as usual. Yesterday it culminated and I walked about like an exposed imposter feeling as contemptible as the most of them could feel and if it were not for old pictures that make one forget self for a time I don't know how I should ever get to work again . . . and when I think of the confidence and conceit and blindness of ten years ago I don't know whether most to lament that I was ever like that or that I ever woke out of such a baseless dream—.

His depression was the cause of so many unfinished canvasses. Uncertain of the direction his art should take he quickly became discontent with a work before it had gone very far. For this reason the great work, 'The Story of Troy', remained incomplete; he had outgrown the idea. His confrontation with the mainstream of High Renaissance art had caused him to reject its early Renaissance form in favour of pursuing new ideas.

After a period in the early 1870s of either repeating designs which already existed in the form of book illustrations or stained glass, or of working on a small scale, Burne-Jones began to find confidence and mastery in his new style. His fecundity of invention had provided innumerable ideas to be worked on, and now he was able to carry them through to completion. Many significant later works had their origin in these years. Besides those deriving from the 'Troy' complex, there were 'The Car of Love' (worked on until it was left unfinished at his death), 'The Golden Stairs' (worked 1876–80), 'The Sirens' (unfinished at his death), and 'Merlin and Vivien' (redesigned in 1873). With this period of invention, combined with the experience gained by designing for stained glass and *The Earthly Paradise* illustrations, the majority of the ideas for the later years had been created.

Of the paintings finished during the period 1870–78 the most important were 'Merlin and Vivien', 'Laus Veneris', based upon the watercolour of 1861, 'Love among the Ruins' (1870–73) and 'The Days of Creation' (1872–78), which was a development of a stained-glass design made in 1870. These are the great works of his middle period.

'Merlin and Vivien' like 'Phyllis and Demophoön' (1869–70) deals with a relationship between two figures, male and female in a highly dramatic situation. They are revealed as participants in the eternal struggle between the sexes. Burne-Jones shows himself intrigued by the strength of this, the most vital relationship in existence. Acknowledging the power of love, he represents the individuals involved in their struggle for supremacy. In the former he shows a woman as the seductress and the conqueror, whilst 'Phyllis' depicts a

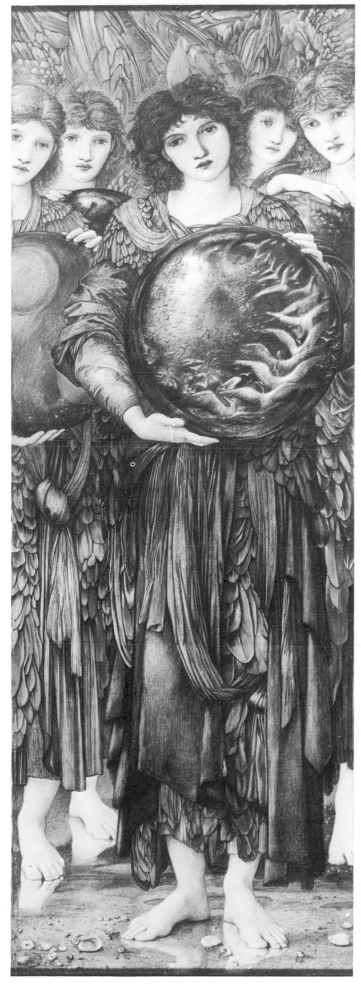

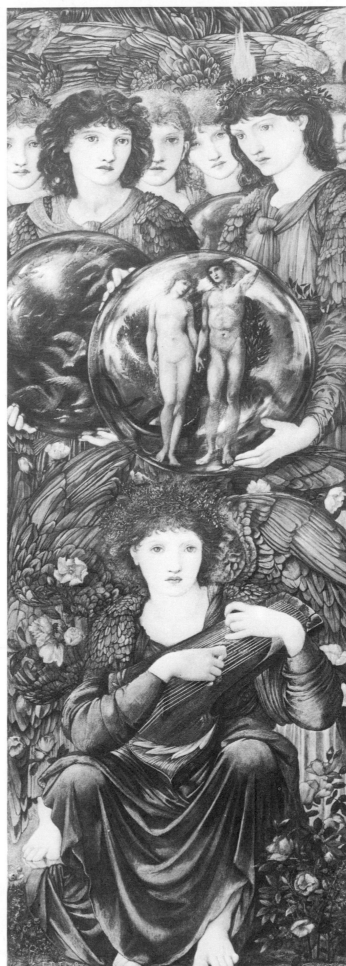

160. 'The Artist in his Studio', comic drawing, *c.* 1872

An illustration of the reason for the artist's despair on his return from Italy when he faced at least sixty unfinished canvases. From *Memorials*.

161. 'St Luke', cartoon for a window at Jesus College Chapel, Cambridge, east side of the south transept, 1872

The most overtly Michelangelesque designs were made at this time when Burne-Jones had returned from Italy having studied at length the ceiling of the Sistine Chapel. Cartoon, crayon and coloured chalk, $48 \times 20\frac{1}{2}$, Tate Gallery, London.

162. 'Destruction of Sodom', design for a window in Calcutta Cathedral, India, made in 1874. Crayon and coloured chalk, the Cecil Higgins Art Gallery, Bedford.

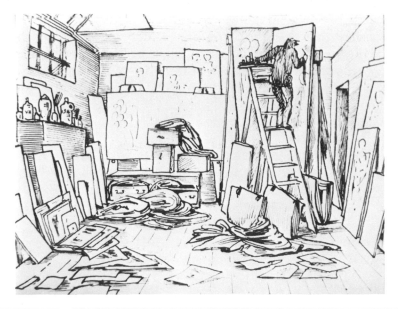

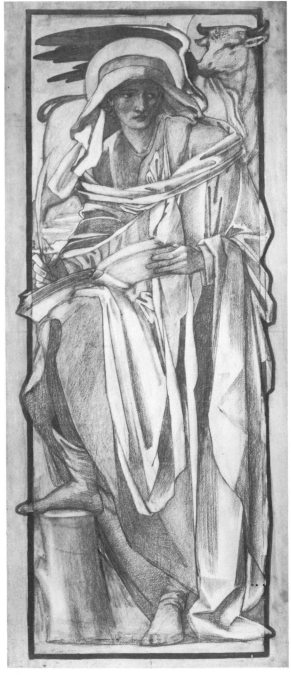

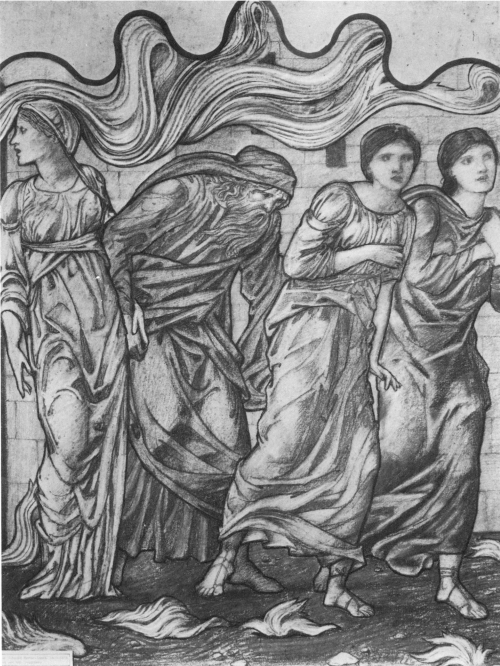

woman who sadly realises the feeling of rejection. Notable about both pictures is the helplessness of the protagonists; one senses that, as in the Greek dramas, the figures are merely acting a predestined part. Man is the puppet of Fortune. In a comparison of the two works 'Merlin and Vivien' represents a considerable advance over the earlier work. 'Phyllis and Demophoön' is set simply in a bare but hilly landscape, Phyllis's hair and drapery are used as linear accessories which accentuate the mood by their controlled, rhythmic flow; in 'Merlin and Vivien' this quality is developed to considerable degree. Landscape is eliminated, there is no depth, each part of the canvas being of equal importance. The tree writhes its commentary on the tension between the two figures, and the draperies continue the movement across their bodies. The picture is emphatically linear, line being as much a part of the work as the figures themselves. Burne-Jones, realising that a situation cannot be recreated simply by copying the physical world, has utilised the very qualities of the visual medium to do it for him. Equally he is able, through using the medium in this way, to convey the power of his personal emotional interpretation of the event, the clash between the sexes. In a similar way the cruciform composition shows an advance over that of 'Phyllis and Demophoön'. There is a dynamic impact between the vertical form of Vivien and the horizontal figure of Merlin, and the two together represent a brilliant use of the rectangular shape of the canvas. A further point impresses itself, there is an interesting reversal of the roles of male and female; Vivien is shown standing, occupying the main vertical plane usually a symbol of the active male, whilst Merlin lies passive, relaxed, his power ebbing away.

'Phyllis and Demophoön' also demonstrates Burne-Jones's method of translating ideas into visual form. He relies upon the greater part of the canvas to create a sympathetic emotional ambiance for the primary theme, which is generated from a series of focal centres. These are the points which make specific reference to the type of emotion that operates within the painting; in 'Merlin and Vivien', as in most of his work, they are firstly the faces, then the hands and feet.

'The Days of Creation' was first designed as a stained-glass cartoon in 1870 for the Parish Church at Middleton Cheney, Northamptonshire. It consisted of six small lights above Shadrach, Meshach, and Abednigo in the fiery furnace. Burne-Jones had first designed a Creation window for Waltham Abbey in 1860 which comprised seven small circles. The following year the firm produced another (designed chiefly by Philip Webb) for Selsley Church. In 1863 Burne-Jones made a series of watercolours on the subject for the Dalziel brothers, intended for their *Illustrated Bible Gallery*. Behind the stained-glass designs, therefore, lay some experience in treating the theme, but in the latest version he introduced something entirely new. The images of the Creation show the descent from the earlier attempts, but his innovation was to have them held in crystal balls by a series of angels. The artist has presented us with, not literal scenes of creation, but a series of visions which inform us of the miraculous events that occurred in the remote past. His interpretation is further complicated since the six panels do not have one angel each but the second contains the first, the third the second and first, and so on until all seven angels appear in the sixth panel (two being introduced in the final one). This means that we are not expected to receive the six panels at one glance or take them in as a whole, but to move from each one, viewing it as complete in itself, witnessing the creation of each day as a separate event. As the artist first presented the series they were side by side in a classical type of Renaissance frame, which surely was at variance with his intention to make the sequence appear as a continuous organic experience. The optimum hanging conditions would allow for a good distance between each panel, thus enabling the spectator to witness the panels as separate events which reach a climax in the sixth day, thus introducing him to the important factor of time, which, after all, is contained in them. Jenny Morris, William's daughter, posed for some of the angels, but others are generalised Botticellian types.

It was the artist's practice to use his friends as models for faces, or perhaps to use a face of someone he saw in the street, and to use professional models for the bodies. W. J. Stillman, the husband of a pupil of Rossetti, sat for Merlin in 'Merlin and Vivien', Mrs Drummond (sister of W. A. S. Benson), sat for Medusa, Frances Horner was used for one of the sea nymphs in 'Perseus and the Sea Nymphs'. At this time two favourite professional

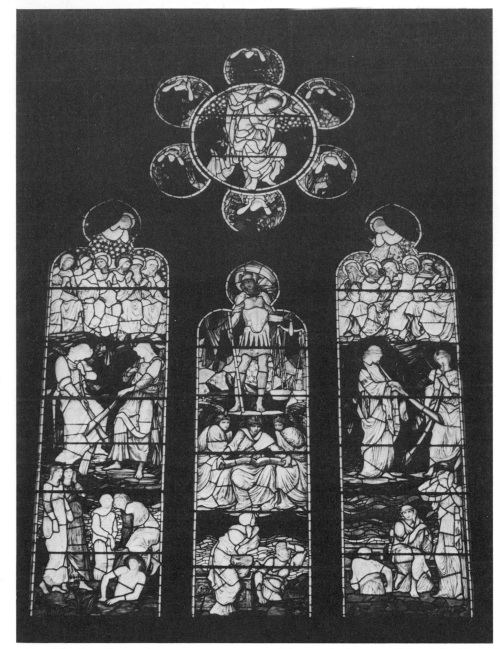

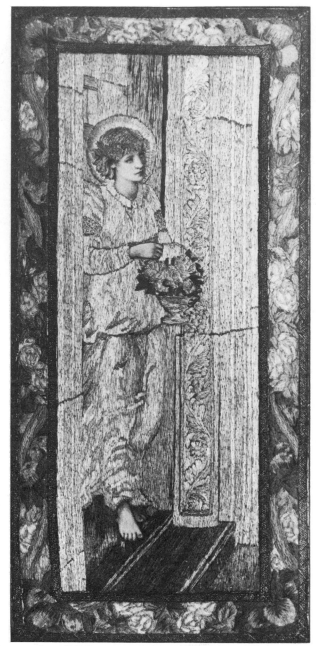

163. 'The Last Judgement', east window, St Michael and All Angels Church, Easthampstead, Berkshire, 1874–75.

164. 'The Angel Carrying Roses to Theophilus', *c.* 1878, embroidery, 10 × 4¾; private collection, England
The figure was taken from the artist's 'Theophilus and the Angel'. Burne-Jones painted the face, hands, and feet, and the embroidery was worked by Frances Horner.

models were often used, both Italian, Alessandro di Marco and Antonia Caiva. They were used together in 'Love among the Ruins', and nude, they figure frequently in the work of the seventies, Antonia particularly in 'The Golden Stairs' in which all the figures were modelled from her.

In 'Laus Veneris' Burne-Jones once again chose an erotic theme. This time there is an air of malaise within the painting. In the densely packed space the queen is portrayed in her claustrophobic chamber being entertained with music by her attendants. Outside, seen through a rectangular window, some knights ride by, and already they seem captives to the women within. Lest there should be any doubt in the viewer's mind, the artist has painted scenes on the walls of the chamber which reflect the central story, on the right the passing of Venus and in the upper-left corner a siren luring her victim. The colour is like that of a sumptuous illuminated manuscript from the Middle Ages. Reds, orange, purple and blue predominate and impart a sense of resplendent luxury—but with one exception, the rectangle containing the knights is modelled in cold blues—seemingly symbolic of their hopeless situation. The painting represents a peak in Burne-Jones's use of colour, nothing before it was as dramatically rich. He used darker tones in the eighties, and silvery ones in the nineties. As mentioned in Chapter Four, an earlier version of this painting was made in watercolour in 1861 that relates to Swinburne's poem of the same title. Swinburne prefaced his poem with part of the Venusberg legend as related by Maistre Antoine Gaget

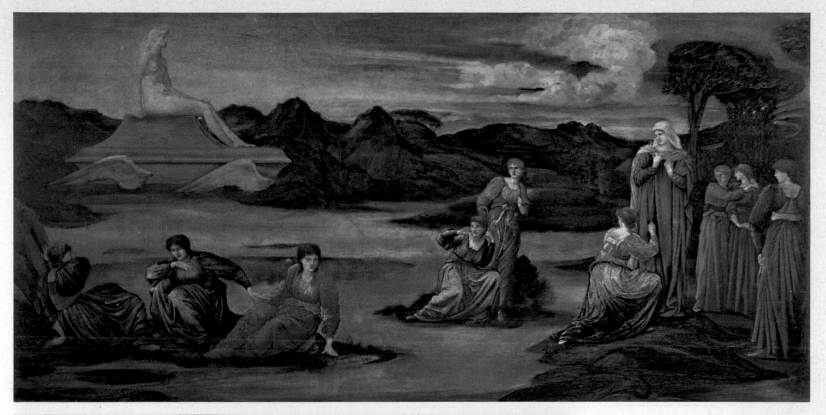

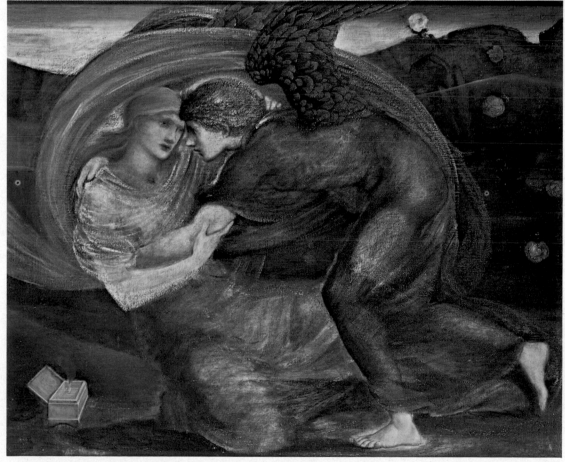

26. 'The Passing of Venus', *c.* 1875, oil on panel; the Junior Common Room, Exeter College, Oxford. The design was elaborated into the tapestry of the same name in 1898, an oil version of which is in the Tate Gallery, London.

27. 'Cupid Delivering Psyche', *c.* 1871, oil on canvas, 30½ × 36½; Sheffield Art Gallery. Gouache versions of this design, which first appeared as an illustration for *The Earthly Paradise*, are at Fulham Library and The Cecil Higgins Gallery, Bedford. Both date from 1867.

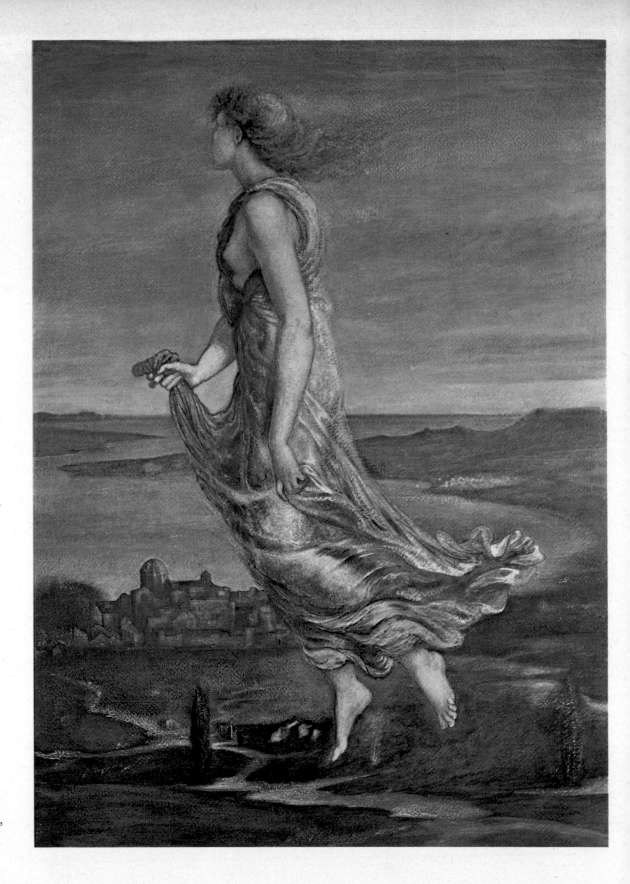

28. 'Hesperus, The Evening Star',
1870, gouache, 31 × 22; private
collection, England.

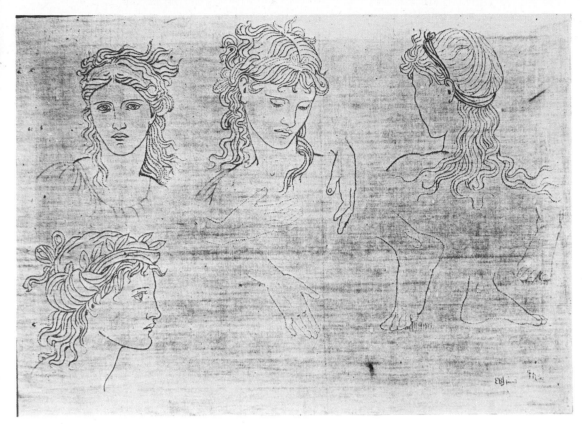

165. Studies of Faces, Hands and Feet, *c.* 1876, brown crewel on canvas, 23 × 18; private collection, England
An experiment in embroidery, Burne-Jones drew directly on to the canvas and Frances Horner embroidered over them.

(1530). The same legend, via Ticck's Romances (late medieval) had been the source of Morris's 'The Hill of Venus' in *The Earthly Paradise*, for which Burnc-Jones had made a sequence of illustrations. Attracted by the story which stresses the polarity between sensualism and piety, the three artists treated it each in his own way. Morris related it with quiet lyricism without undue sensuality, bringing the story to a close with Walter's return to Christianity; Swinburne is the most carnal:

> Asleep or waking is it? for her neck,
> Kissed over close, wears yet a purple speck
> Wherein the pained blood falters and goes out;
> Soft, and stung softly—fairer for the fleck
> ....
> There loverlike with lips and limbs that meet
> They lie, they pluck sweet fruit of life and eat;
> But me that hot and hungry days devour,
> And in my mouth no fruit of theirs is sweet.

In the verse:

> Knights gather, riding sharp for cold; I know
> The ways and woods are strangled with the snow;
> And with short song the maidens spin and sit
> Until Christ's birthright, lily-like, arow.

Burne-Jones came very close to Swinburne's description with his cold-blue setting for the hapless knights, but on the whole his painting is less forcefully erotic. It has the characteristic, pervading sadness which Jones attached to affairs of the heart.

The inspiration drawn from later Italian painting was as basic to the art of this period as Gothic-medieval had been in his earlier production. With Burne-Jones it was not an eclectic form of historicism, he was too much an individual for that. Where he borrowed from earlier painters he thoroughly integrated their devices into his personal style. There is always a style that is carried through in any single painting, which is totally Burne-

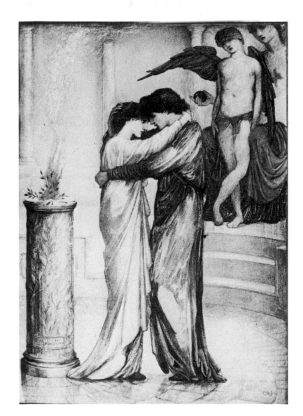

166. 'The Altar of Hymen', 1874, gouache touched with gold, 15 × 10¼; private collection

Originally the design was an illustration to the Pygmalion story in *The Earthly Paradise*. In this form it was made as a wedding present for William Graham's daughter, Amy, on her marriage to Kenneth Muir-Mackenzie.

Jones, no matter from where the original stimulus came. Botticelli inspired the figures and facial types of 'The Hesperides', Annibale Carracci's 'Christ in Glory' (Pitti, Florence) the pose of the king in 'The Wheel of Fortune', and Michaelangelo the torsos of the figures. Piero di Cosimo's 'Death of Procris' (National Gallery) was the source of 'Pan and Psyche' and 'Bacchus playing to Silenus' (National Gallery) has a close resemblance to 'The Garden of Pan'. Mantegna's influence persisted from the mid-sixties until the mid-eighties; originally Jones discovered him through his etchings in the British Museum. The most important features that came from Mantegna were a type of composition, the draperies, the disposition of the hands holding them, and the tight, sculpturally conceived curls of the male figures. It was in the designs for stained glass that his borrowings were more obvious, but they never became pastiches, and the majority are as successful as the paintings. Most striking, the examples of Michaelangelo's influence are to be found in Jesus College Chapel, Cambridge, in the form of Sibyls and the four Evangelists. They are massively conceived, occupying the whole area of their compartments and such is their strength that they appear to bulge out of the frame. Reflecting the Sistine Chapel figures, they adopt ingenious contraposto. Also found in Jesus College Chapel is a predella window showing 'The Sacrifice of Abraham' which is almost a recreation of Andrea del Sarto's painting of the subject. But Burne-Jones's ingenuity was endless. It had to be, because he would often be commissioned to do three or more versions of the same subject. For this reason he was obliged to call upon earlier designs by other artists to provide a source of variation. It became even more necessary after 1875, when he became the sole stained-glass designers for the firm, drawing upon a wide range of artists from Byzantine and early and late Renaissance sources.

March 1875 saw the completion of the dissolution of the old company of Morris, Marshal, Faulkner and Company. Reasons for this are impossible to find. Presumably the seven artists originally the partners, drifted in different directions and the set-up became unworkable. Feelings were strained between Morris and Rossetti, the reorganisation bringing any communication to a halt between them. Three of the partners, Marshal, Rossetti, and Madox Brown, claimed their right to their full share of the value of the business and they became estranged from the others because of this, but one can understand their conduct especially that of Madox Brown, who was never very well off and could not afford to be magnanimous. From this point on Burne-Jones had the burden of being the only figure designer for the firm; before the dissolution there had been in fact a gradual decline in the number of designs supplied by the other members. In his account-book in 1872 there is a sudden increase in the number of cartoons recorded, and with this multiplication he employed Fairfax Murray to draw the cartoons from his own smaller-scaled drawings. These cartoons made by Murray are sepia brush-drawings with little shading and bold lines and are stiffer than those made by Burne-Jones himself.

The majority of small designs became the property of Morris and Co. for subsequent re-use, but the more important ones were returned to his studio to be coloured and then, hopefully, sold. A complex design specifically made for a particular church was impossible to adapt for second use and was impressive enough when coloured to be attractive in its own right. 'The Last Judgement' made for Easthampstead and 'The Rivers of Paradise' for Allerton, both dating from 1875, are fine examples. They represent the beginnings of Burne-Jones's practice of employing a large window as a continuous picture that unites all the separate parts. This type of window found full expression at Allerton (1880s), 'The Nativity' at Hawarden (1898), 'St Paul preaching at Athens' at Morton, Lincolnshire (1891). That the Easthampstead 'Last Judgement' is transitional is shown by the symmetry of the window, the two side-lights are almost mirror images of one another, yet they show a distinct asymmetry which creates a refreshing poise and points to the later developments. In spite of the strong Michaelangelesque influence, there are many features that recall earlier windows; the building up of the design on three separate layers harks back to the Gothic tiers of saints in the sixties, and the relationship between the figures is simple, each one having a complete silhouette.

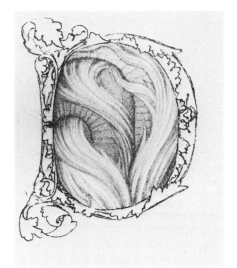

Embroidery was another field in which Burne-Jones was actively involved. The earliest examples date from Morris's move into Red House in 1860, when he made a series of figures from *Morte d'Arthur*. Embroidery also featured in the firm's prospectus. He was called on to supply designs for a series of Chaucer's heroines in 1861, these being adapted for Ruskin in 1863. In the early seventies the firm received a commission from Sir Lowthian Bell to supply designs for an embroidered frieze to be hung round the dining room of his house, Rounton Grange, which was in the process of construction from Philip Webb's plan. The subject chosen was Chaucer's *Romance of the Rose*, and the scheme was begun in 1874. Sir Lowthian's wife and daughter embroidered the frieze, finishing it in 1880. Morris and Burne-Jones co-operated in its design—the latter was responsible for the figures whilst Morris designed the briar background and prepared the working drawings.

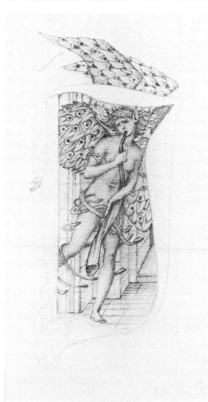

Art needlework was becoming popular amongst certain 'aesthetic' ladies at this time, and Burne-Jones, Thomas Armstrong, Henry Holiday and Lord Leighton, among others, became interested in it. Gertrude Jekyll worked many of their designs, and Burne-Jones found a fine executant in his friend Frances Graham, William's daughter. May Morris displayed great skill in this craft, later taking over that branch of the firm. Frances Graham and Burne-Jones worked closely together experimenting with the medium, he drawing on the cloth and she embroidering over his marks. In this way she became able to execute exactly what he demanded, producing some lovely fabric pictures. Most notable is 'L'amor che Muove' (Mells Church), which is an immense piece of work. Other, smaller pieces, were taken from his designs for paintings and stained glass, in these the embroideress left the hands and faces to be painted by the artist. The resultant needleworks are quite consciously placed within the English tradition of embroidered pictures that Burne-Jones had encountered in the William Graham collection. An unusual product of their co-operation was a pair of shoes in blue cloth with a white lily embroidered on it, made by Frances for her sister.

The Royal School of Art Needlework was founded in 1872 by Princess Christiana of Schleswig Holstein for 'the twofold purpose of supplying suitable employment for gentle-women and restoring ornamental needlework to the high place it once held among the decorative arts'. Various artists were asked to supply the school with designs, including William Morris, Walter Crane, and Burne-Jones. The latter's contribution were two large designs for portières, 'Musica' and 'Poesia', the latter representing the pedestalled muses surrounded by her attendants. Each was worked in outline with brown crewel on linen, and they proved to be so popular that a number of copies were carried out. Likewise,

167-68. Two designs for initial letters in Virgil's *Aeneid*, 1874

Morris and Burne-Jones intended to produce a translation in lavish form illustrated throughout. Eventually, however, Morris's translation was published without decoration, and the illuminated manuscript remained unfinished. It was later taken up by Fairfax Murray and others and is now in the Camarillo Monastery in California.

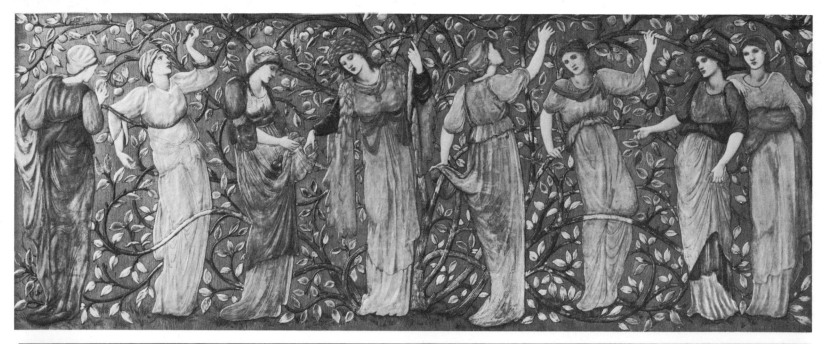

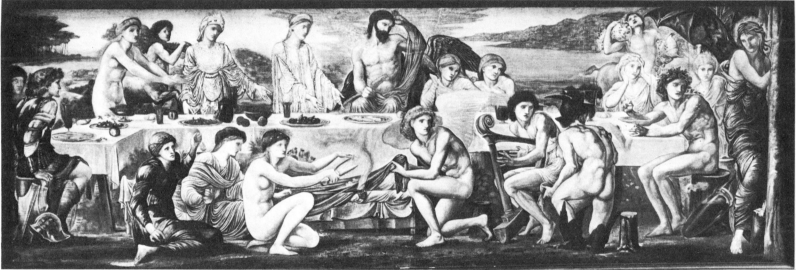

169. 'The Apple Gatherers', 1876, gesso on wood, 29 × 72, executed by assistants from designs by Burne-Jones. Tate Gallery, London.

170. 'The Feast of Peleus', *c.* 1878, oil, $58\frac{7}{8}$ × 172. Victoria & Albert Museum, London
A complex studio work in which one can detect the work of several assistants. It is an enlargement of part of the predella of the 'Troy' polyptych.

a series of six panels illustrating scenes from The Song of Solomon were to have been outline embroideries. Designed in 1876, possibly a little later than the foregoing Music and Poetry embroideries, they were more complex designs with more fluency in the rhythms of the outlines. Only one of the designs, full size, has come to light, the 'Sponsa di Libano'. This may well have been the only one executed; it would have been an immense task to have embroidered all six designs.

The artist liked 'Sponsa' so much that in 1891 he recast it as a large watercolour (128 in. × 61 in.). The six small designs and the one large one were all owned by Frances Horner, so presumably she was to have embroidered them, but—perhaps because of the immense amount of labour involved—they do not seem to have been carried out.

It has often been commented how Burne-Jones's style of art stresses the two-dimensional nature of the medium and how natural was his movement from painting to the decorative arts. It is not surprising, therefore, that he made many attempts to adorn expanses of wall space, never in true fresco but always on canvas, which was later applied to the location. Georgiana Burne-Jones says that, 'What he always sought for was to design on a large scale for special places and paint his pictures in situ. "I want big things to do and vast spaces, and for common people to see them and say Oh!—only Oh!".'

This was not to be; nothing of the kind came from his brush, of the three schemes of decoration he began, only one reached the final stage and that with the help of two assistants. All three had their origin in book illustration, a logical step to the artist's mind since mural painting as Burne-Jones understood it was book illustration on a large scale—a

118

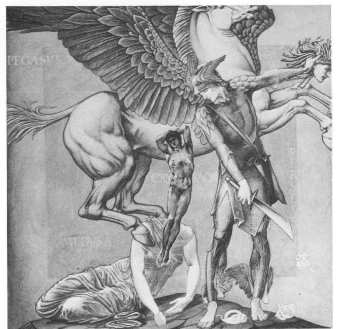

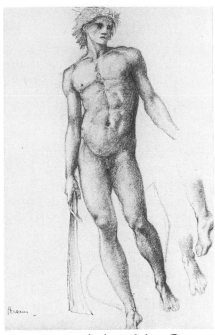

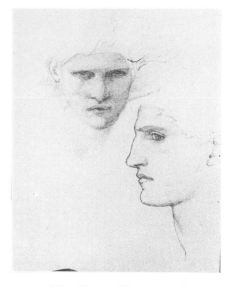

171. 'The Birth of Pegasus and Chrysaor', *c.* 1877, gouache on canvas, 48½ × 46; Southampton Art Gallery
This is one of the trial series, the final series in oil—never fully made into a scheme of decoration—are now in The Staatsgalerie, Stuttgart, Germany.

172. Perseus, pencil drawing from a sketchbook, *c.* 1875; Birmingham City Museum & Art Gallery.

173. Head studies of Medusa and Perseus from a sketchbook, *c.* 1878, pencil; Birmingham City Museum & Art Gallery
The model for Medusa was Mrs Drummond, sister of W. A. S. Benson, and the model for Perseus was a gypsy named Smith.

series of related images that recount a story. The first was commissioned by George Howard for his townhouse at 1 Palace Green, Kensington. Howard, who was to become the ninth Earl of Carlisle, was a painter of merit in his own right, working in a detailed Pre-Raphaelite style; the greater part of his work was landscape. Morris and Burne-Jones were frequentors of his cosmopolitan circle of friends and fellow painters, who included Alphonse Legros, Giovanni Costa and Guiseppe Mazzini. All of them stayed at his castle in Cumberland. As a wealthy man, Howard was able to commission large quantities of furniture, carpets, and other of their products, and he furnished 1 Palace Green, Kensington, in the firm's taste. At that time he also commissioned Morris and Burne-Jones to decorate his dining room with the story of Cupid and Psyche. The twelve designs were salvaged from the rejected *Earthly Paradise* illustrations. Beginning with twelve small preparatory watercolours, to decide the colour scheme, Burne-Jones set about painting the fine-scale murals. Months passed, and still the series remained at a preliminary stage, until finally, George Howard, impatient that his dining room remained incomplete, called in Walter Crane to continue. He worked from the artist's drawings and described his part in their development:

> The frieze was to be painted in flat oil colour on canvas enriched with raised details guilded somewhat after the manner of Pinturrichio. The canvases—in various stages, some blank, some just commenced, some, in parts, considerably advanced—were all sent to my studio at Beaumont Lodge, and I started on the work, having the prints from the woodcuts above mentioned to go by. One or two of the subjects, such as 'Zephyrus and Psyche', 'Cupid finding Psyche asleep', and 'Cupid recovering Psyche from the effects of the Opened Casket' had been treated by Burne-Jones in water-

174. Scale-drawing of the Perseus decoration *in situ*, *c.* 1875, gouache, 16 × 52; Tate Gallery, London
Arthur Balfour commissioned a series of decorations to his music room on his first visit to Burne-Jones's studio in 1875. He left the choice of subject to the artist who chose, as in his frieze for George Howard, to base them on *The Earthly Paradise* illustrations. In this case it was the story of Perseus. From left to right the incidents are 'The Finding of Medusa', 'The Birth of Pegasus and Chrysaor', and 'The Death of Medusa'.

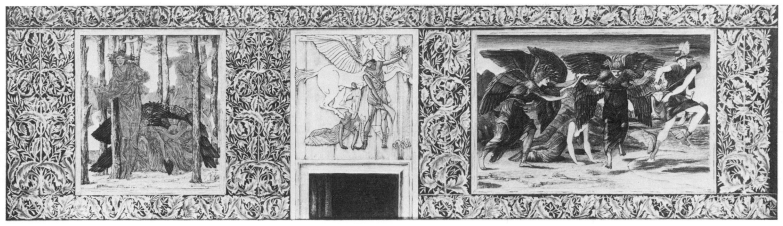

colour as completed pictures, but in the frieze these formed groups, and became parts of larger compositions containing several incidents in the story.

A few of the series were entirely Burne-Jones's work and the majority bear witness to Crane's intervention. Morris's part in the scheme was to paint patterns that surrounded the frieze and to complete the decoration of the room. Explaining the story immediately below the frieze were extracts from *The Earthly Paradise* also from Morris's brush. The dining room from start to finish took fifteen years, from 1872 until 1887.

In 1875 A. J. Balfour, on a visit to the Grange expressed a desire to have his music room decorated by Burne-Jones. The Perseus legend was decided upon and so began a series of paintings that occupied Burne-Jones at intervals until his death. Once again the scheme sprang from the projected *Earthly Paradise* illustrations. There are many points of similarity between the Perseus and Cupid and Psyche schemes; both were to have had Morris's type of decorative setting and both were to have embossed details. Perseus represents an advance, however, over the earlier work. At first, as in the Psyche frieze, the artist wished to make the narrative comprehensive by including as many scenes as possible, ten at first. As he developed the idea he became more interested in the decorative role they had to play, reduced the number to eight and simplified each design into single actions. The first is primitive in this way as it still contains two scenes: 'The Rock of Doom' and 'The Doom Fulfilled'. They were originally part of one panel but, though they risk appearing repetitive, they were both retained and used separately because they include an excuse to paint a female nude. Initially, Jones experimented in the method of representation of Perseus's armour; emphasising the purely decorative role of the painting he tried cutting thin metal sheets to the shape of the armour and applying them to the wooden panels to allow a certain relief, and then finishing off in the traditional manner with oil paint. It proved difficult, and being adversely criticised when 'The Grey Graiae' was exhibited in this form in the Grosvenor Gallery, he abandoned the idea. Some of the panels, notably 'The Grey Graiae' and 'Pegasus and Chrysaor' have done away with a figurative background, and the artist has outlined the central figures against an abstract ground; in others he has simplified the landscape into bare massive hills which have the same function—to create a decorative, rather than a naturalistic or illusionary, impression. Burne-Jones was working on the series for so long that some of the later versions lost this primary decorative role and reverted to easel paintings once again with detailed landscapes. Like the Psyche murals, the Perseus series was to have had quotations telling the story, not from the Morris's poems but from a Latin source.

A third series of murals was commissioned by R. H. Benson which, once again had its origin in book illustrations, this time in three subjects from Spenser's *Faerie Queene*. The illustrations had been made in the early seventies, some going so far as to be drawn upon the woodblock but, like the earlier enterprises, got no further. Similarly, the project remained at the pre-painting stage, large full-scale pencil drawings were prepared and preliminary oil sketches of the colour scheme. Had the project materialised it would have fulfilled the wish he had made in 1870:

> This year I have 4 subjects which above all others I desire to paint and count my chief designs, for some years to come.
> The Chariot of Love—to be painted life size,
> The Vision of Britomart—in 3 pictures also life size,
> The Sirens—small life size.
> and a picture of the world—with Pan and Echo and sylvan gods, and a forest full of centaurs and a wild background of woods, mountains and rivers—upon these four subjects all my leisure time will be spent.

These notes demonstrate how, had he been given the opportunity, Burne-Jones would —like his counterpart in France, Puvis de Chavannes—have become a devoted mural painter, but there was no large-scale patronage, and his dream of painting large spaces, like Watt's similar dream, had to be suppressed. However, he was able to modify his 'Vision of

Britomart' into the Benson commission, but, unhappily, it too proved abortive. In fact all four designs mentioned in the quotation above were eventually frustrated, 'The Chariot of Love' remained unfinished in spite of being taken up again in the nineties, similarly 'The Sirens'. Coming nearest to fulfilment, the Pan picture materialised as 'The Garden of Pan' (1886–87) but the centaurs etc., which derive from Piero di Cosimo, were excluded.

When Morris moved from Queen's Square in 1872 because the firm needed more space, he found a new home in Turnham Green. He described it as 'a very little house with a pretty garden, and I think it will suit Janey and the children; it is some half hour's walk from the Grange'. So began a habit of breakfasting with the Burne-Jones's every Sunday and spending the rest of the morning in the studio. Morris was making a translation of *The Aeneid* of Virgil and reading a portion each Sunday, and together they evolved the idea of an illuminated manuscript of his text. It was nothing new to either of them—both had studied medieval manuscripts in the Bodleian while they were at Oxford, and Morris had experimented with it then. Together they took up the activity again in 1870 with an illuminated set of verses by Morris set amongst foliated decoration. Miniature figure subjects were designed by Burne-Jones and Fairfax Murray and executed by Murray. Thereafter followed two scripts of *The Rubaiyat* of Omar Khayyam, one with miniatures by Murray (1872) and another in which they are by Burne-Jones. These are six delightful, idyllic love scenes. Bright in colour, they are like jewels amongst the more neutral tones of Morris's borders. Two subjects for full-sized paintings make their first appearance in these manuscripts, 'Love among the Ruins' occurs as the fourth miniature in the Omar Khayyam, and 'Merlin and Vivien' illustrates the poem 'Love and Death' in the book of Morris's verse. But by far the most advanced, showing how Burne-Jones had progressed as a designer, were his drawings for *The Aeneid*. In their skilful use of decorated letters, their asymmetry, their brilliantly controlled but unpredictable line, they anticipate the art nouveau illustrators of the late nineties. At the same time the strength of his bizarre images intensifies the text and creates an almost surreal mood. Unfortunately, this too

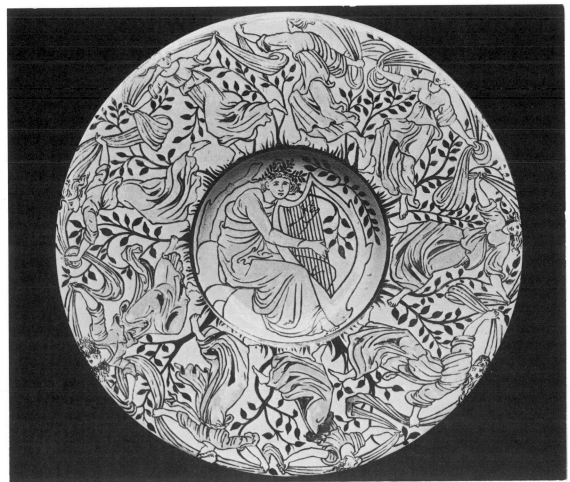

175. 'The Orpheus Plate' by William de Morgan, figures designed by Burne-Jones, *c.* 1875, $11\frac{7}{8}$ diameter. Victoria & Albert Museum, London.

121

figures in the list of abandoned work, and the book, as it stands today, is the combined work of a number of people, as the following note made by two of them at the turn of the century shows:

> Begun Winter 1874-5 and with the exception of Books II–VI inclusive, was written to the foot of page 177, almost at the end of Book VI, half page miniature, of Venus and Aeneas, after Burne-Jones, was painted on the opening page and the text on the same page was written, with the red 'bole' ready for guilding, on a grey-purple ground, also twenty two decorated initials in the margin of various pages between page 45 and 72 inclusive. The work was abandoned and unfinished and the manuscript was sold to Fairfax Murray and completed by Graily Hewitt. Fairfax Murray painted half page miniatures in the margins of the other pages, all from Burne-Jones's designs. Mrs Powell drew foliated borders and decoration based on [Kelmscott] Chaucer borders.

That the enterprise was begun enthusiastically enough is shown by Burne-Jones's letter to C. E. Norton:

'Every Sunday morning you may think of Morris and me together—he reads a book to me and I make drawings for a big Virgil he is writing—it is to be wonderful and put an end to printing.'

But by May 1875, Morris was calling in Murray to help, and not long later it was given up.

Concurrently with the hand-made books of 1871-72, the two artists were planning an illustrated edition of Morris's verse play 'Love is Enough'. Experimental blocks were cut from designs for borders by Morris with illustrations by Burne-Jones which were to have been used with conventional commercial letterpress. History repeated itself, however, and the idea was abandoned, later in 1874 the text appeared unadorned. It is easy to understand why, for there is a distinct incongruity between the initial letters decorated by Morris and the lifeless print. The time had not yet come when Morris could solve the problems of book design; he was as yet unable to realise that the answer lay not so much in his ability to create ornamental pages, but in a responsibility for the entire visual effect, including as a most important element, the type. He was not ready to do this until the foundation of the Kelmscott Press in 1891.

From its inauguration in 1768 the Royal Academy had established itself as the supreme arbiter of British art. Such was its power in the nineteenth century that there was no alternative centre that could provide hanging space of any significance and there was no other spokesman outside its walls who voiced an opinion that could rival it. It represented institutionalised art, respectable art that posed no threat to the comfortable views of the cultured classes. If an artist did not conform to its definition of art then he was not given an opportunity to exhibit there, and for someone who wished to be taken seriously there was nowhere else of importance. The Academy had an intolerable stranglehold on the muse and looked like exterminating her altogether. The Pre-Raphaelite revolt in 1848 attempted to release her and inject some integrity, but after a *succès de scandale* it proved ineffectual, and the foundations of the Academy looked as firm as ever. The ridiculous and insensitive cramming of paintings on exhibition, resulting in the 'skying' of many, continued; the favoured hacks were still given pride of place.

Although the founders of the Grosvenor Gallery in 1877 went to great lengths to deny any competition with the Academy, in effect it made a dissent from its dictatorial power. The insensitivity of the Academy's hanging committee was one of the chief causes of its emergence, and characteristically this group of artists insisted on adequate space for each painting and an appropriate decorative setting. In spite of showing works by Leighton, president of the Academy the next year, Alma Tadema, and Poynter—all active academicians—the Grosvenor was in effect a secession from the Royal Academy and it was primarily because they realised this that these three joined, attempting to overlay the impression of its breaking away from establishment ideas.

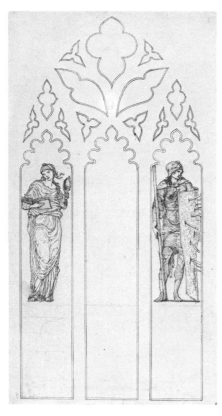

176. Scale-drawing of a window at St Patrick's Church, Dublin, for which, in 1875, Burne-Jones designed the two new figures shown here: Prudence and Fortitude. $18 \times 25\frac{7}{8}$; Birmingham City Museum & Art Gallery.

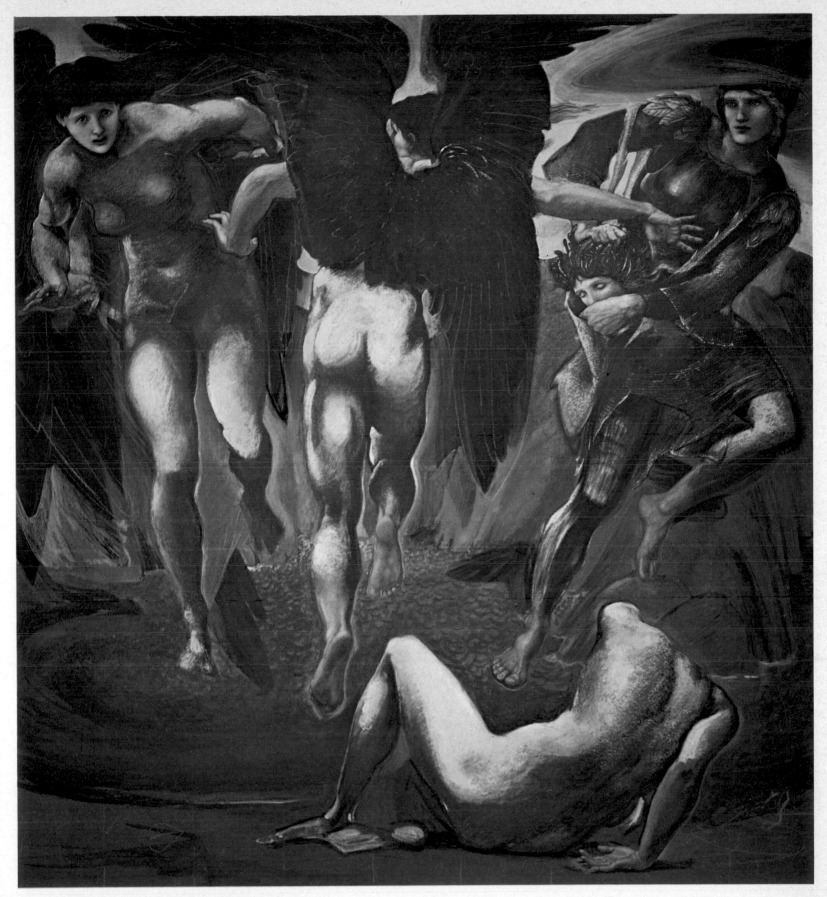

29. 'The Escape of Perseus', 1875-88, gouache on
canvas, $59\frac{1}{2} \times 53\frac{1}{2}$; Southampton Art Gallery. One of
a series of ten cartoons, from which the final eight
were prepared, the two not used in the decorative
scheme being 'Atlas Turned to Stone' and 'The Birth
of Pegasus and Chrysaor from the Blood of Medusa'
(plates 171-3).

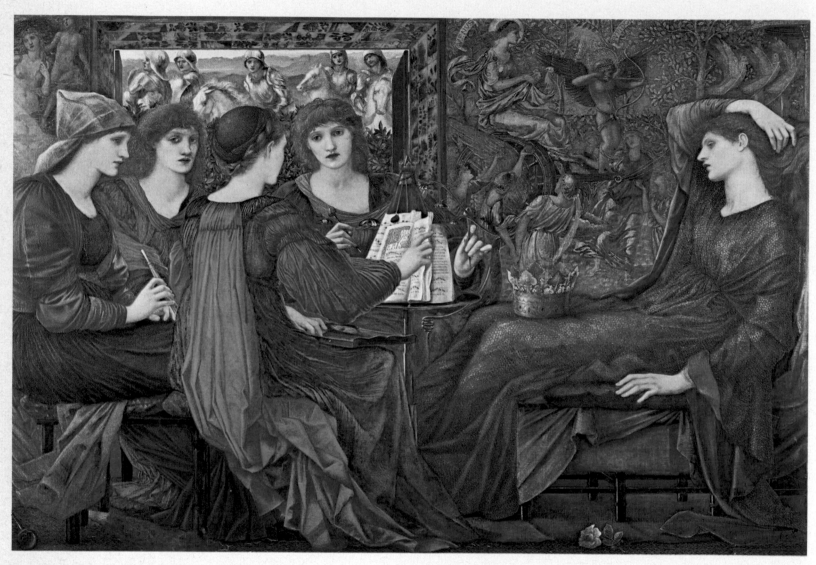

30. 'Laus Veneris', 1873-75 (and worked on later),
oil, 47 × 71; The Laing Art Gallery, Newcastle-
upon-Tyne.

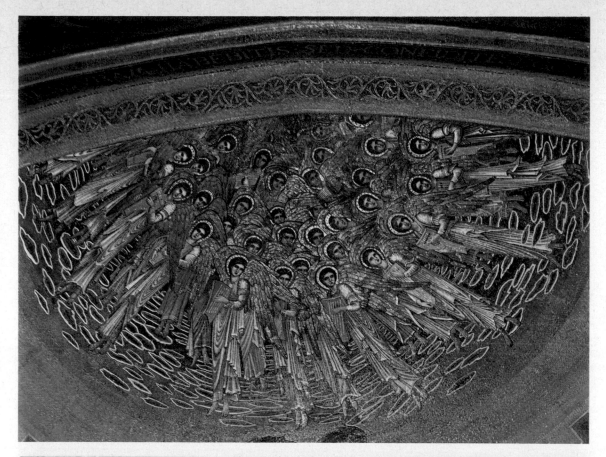

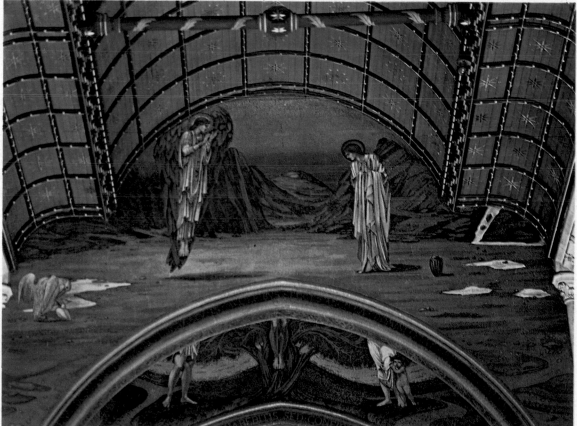

31 and *32*. Two views of the mosaics in St Paul's
American Church in Rome: The ceiling of the apse;
and the spandrels above the Chancel showing 'The
Annunciation'. At first a Nativity was designed for
this space; beyond can be seen part of an allegorical
crucifixion, 'The Tree of Life'.

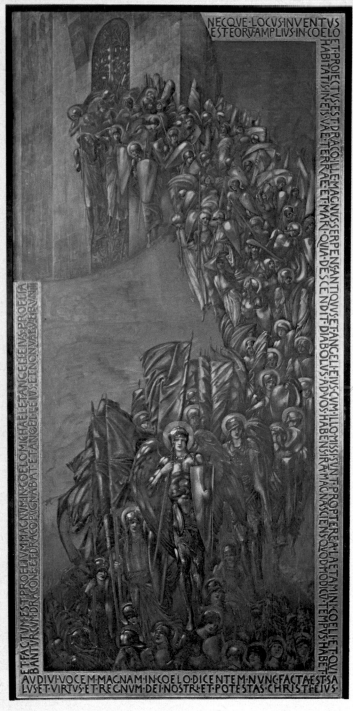

33. 'The Fall of Lucifer', 1894,
gouache and gold, 96 × 46½; Robert
Walker Collection, Paris. This work
originated as part of the scheme for
the American Church in Rome; it was
not carried out, but Burne-Jones was
unable to reject the idea and so made
it into this painting.

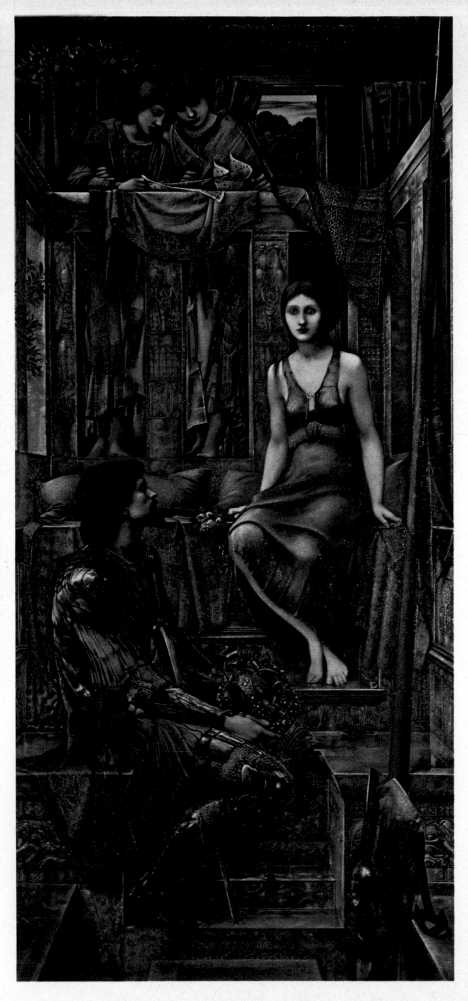

34. 'King Cophetua and The Beggar
Maid', 1884, oil on canvas, 115½ × 53½;
Tate Gallery, London.

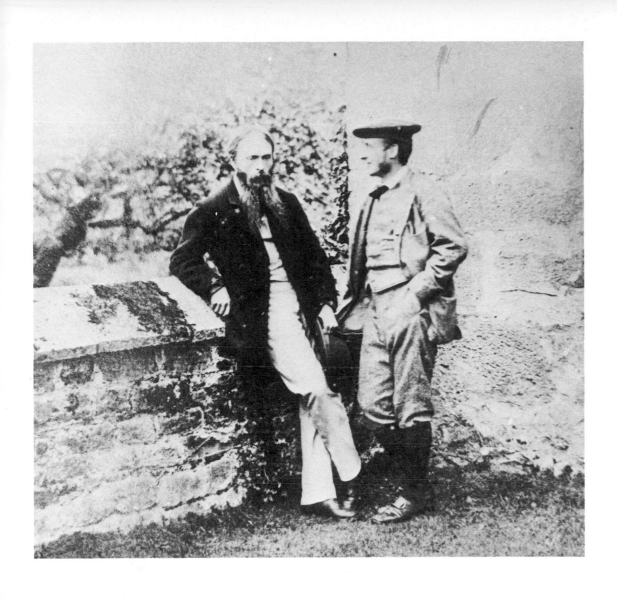

177. Burne-Jones and George Howard
at Naworth Castle, 1874, probably
taken by Benjamin Scott of Carlisle.

Chapter Seven

Acclaim

Situated off Bond Street, the Grosvenor Gallery became the show place of the Aesthetic Movement. It was designed by an architect named Sams, who created a facade in the Palladian style which actually included an authentic doorway designed by Palladio, originally part of the Church of Santa Lucia in Venice. Very consciously non-Gothic, the Italianate style invaded the interior decor; green marble was brought from Genoa, the staircase had pedestals for statues, the wall panels were divided by Ionic pilasters, the blue ceiling was powdered with stars, and the chairs and tables were of old Italian design. The walls were entirely covered with deep crimson damask.

Sir Coutts Lindsay, who financed the whole scheme, was assisted by Charles Hallé, an artist who had studied in Paris under Mottez and who had known Ingres, and later by J. Comyns Carr, a critic and writer on the arts. Together they drew up an enlightened set of rules: few pictures in relation to wall space, sympathetic pictures were to be hung together, no picture to be hung where it could not be seen, all work hung in a good light and the artists were to receive an invitation to exhibit work of their own choice. All points were notably in opposition to the conditions prevailing at the Royal Academy.

The first exhibition contained 'Merlin and Vivien', 'The Days of Creation', 'Mirror of Venus', 'Spes', 'Fides', 'Temperantia', 'St George' and 'A Sybil' by Burne-Jones, and works by Watts ('Mrs Percy Wyndham'), Whistler ('Harmony in Black'), Thomas Armstrong ('Sea Piece'). Millais exhibited six works ('Countess Grosvenor', 'Lady Beatrice Grosvenor' etc.), Leighton ('A Study', 'An Italian Girl', 'H. E. Gordon'), Walter Crane (a watercolour landscape). Later shows included Poynter, Legros, Alma Tadema, Holman Hunt, Alfred Stevens, and an important group of amateur and younger generation artists who stood little chance with the Academy, together with work by dilettante aristocrats. The opening was a grand occasion as an eye-witness recounts:

'The Gallery was opened with great éclat. The Prince and Princess of Wales were invited to dine, which they graciously consented to do, and all that London held of talent and distinguished birth were summoned to meet them. We dined in a restaurant underneath the Picture Gallery, and afterwards a large reception was held upstairs.'

Charles Hallé recalls how difficult it was to manage all the protocol connected with such an illustrious crowd:

'It was a great success, but gave us a deal of trouble in settling who was to take who. The matter was entrusted to Arthur Sullivan and me, and we spent days poring over peerages and finding out dates of creation of the various titles of nobility, so that no one should take the wrong person in to dinner or go in before his turn.'

Until its closure eleven years later, the gallery maintained its high social following:

'The Grosvenor Gallery was such a success that, at one time, it was considered a great compliment to be invited to exhibit in it. The glamour of Fashion was over it, and the

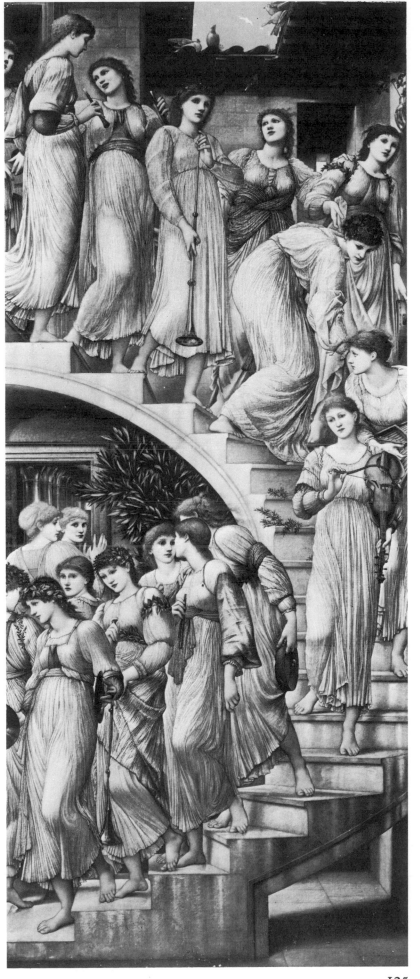

178. 'The Golden Stairs', 1872–80, oil on canvas, 106 × 46; Tate Gallery, London

At first, this picture was known as 'The King's Wedding'. The model for the bodies of the girls was an Italian, Antonia Caiva. Together with 'Troy' and 'The Car of Love' the painting was the first of his large-scale canvases.

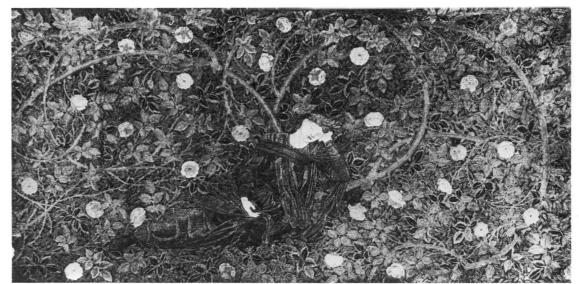

great help that Lady Lindsay was able to give, by holding Sunday receptions there, made it one of the most fashionable resorts of the London seasons.'

This was important to Burne-Jones because, after the success of the first exhibition, he began to venture into society and indeed, much to his discomfort, became something of a fashionable portrait painter, but basically it was to a few families that his real patronage belonged, which, added to the pre-existing ones, was adequate for his needs. His technique in disposing of his work to his new patrons was exactly the same as before, on a personal level and conducted primarily from his studio. Thus his circle of friends changed considerably from 1877, rising higher on the social scale.

His fame as an artist spread to a much wider public, including the continent, as in 1878 he exhibited with some success his 'Merlin and Vivien' at the Paris Exposition Universelle. At home he had an unexpected effect upon certain sections of the community:

'Fashion, always ready to adopt anything new, set all the town wild to copy the dress and attitudes of his wonderful nymphs. As Schwenck Gilbert wrote in his amusing play of 'Patience': "Greenery yallery Grosvenor Gallery" costumes were the mode.' (Louise Jopling).

Not everything associated with the first exhibition was quite so successful. Ruskin, 'oppressed by sensations of giddiness and dizziness', visited the gallery after an extended season amongst the glories of Venice and Carpaccio. On seeing Whistler's 'Nocturne in Black and Gold—The Falling Rocket', he became outraged at its lack of finish and abstraction. As the author of *Academy Notes*, a guide to paintings on exhibit in each Royal Academy Summer Exhibition, his loyalty lay with that institution and so was prejudiced against the Grosvenor Gallery, and as a Gothicist he was pledged to unambiguously figurative work. How strange that the defender of Turner should attack a painter who was the only one to approach him in thirty years! Ruskin acted by publishing an attack in *Fors Clavigera* of July 2, 1877:

'For Mr. Whistler's sake, no less than for the protection of the purchaser, Sir Coutts Lindsay ought not to have admitted works into the gallery in which the ill-educated conceit of the artist so nearly approached the aspect of wilful imposture. I have seen and heard much of cockney impudence before now, but never expected to hear a coxcomb ask two hundred guineas for flinging a pot of paint in the public's face.'

With this diatribe Ruskin punctuated the conflict between the old and the conservative and the new and progressive. In Paris and London alike the feud raged; it had begun earlier in France with the Salon des Refusés in 1863 when Manet and the Impressionists broke away from the Salon. With the founding of the Grosvenor Gallery a similar secession was inaugurated. This was without the earth-shattering results of the French movement but had a similar concern for the life of the art object itself. Whistler, of course, was bringing the French attitude to English soil, but in Burne-Jones and some other of the 'Aesthetic' painters we find a parallel development of the abstract and decorative elements, though in a very different form. Whistler responded to the article by suing Ruskin for

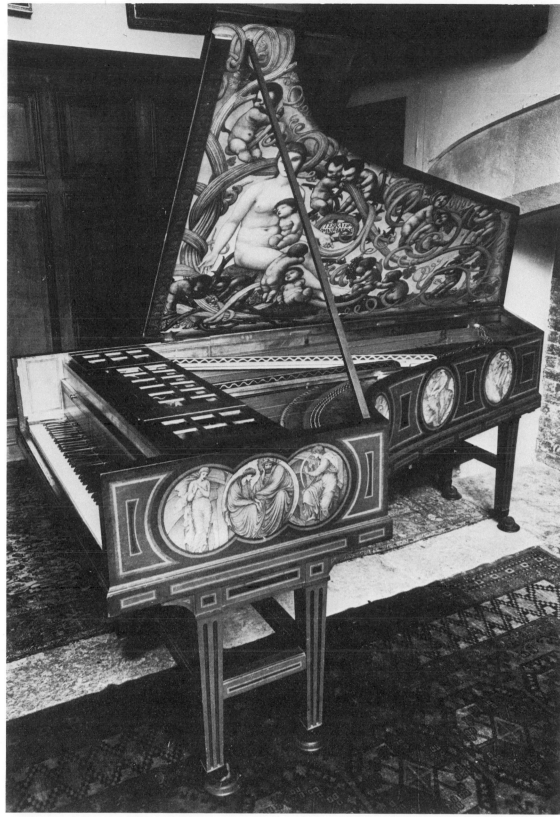

180. The Graham piano, 1880; private collection, England
The pencil designs of the Orpheus story are dated 1875, but the piano was not completed until 1880. It is the most elaborate of the pianos that Burne-Jones was involved with.

181-82. Two details of the Graham piano, both oil on wood: 'Across the Flames' and 'The Regained Lost'.

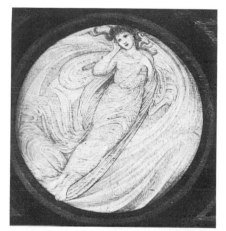

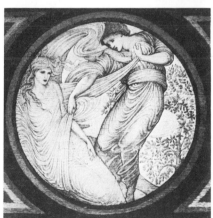

damages of £1000. The case was tried in November 1878 and Burne-Jones was called in as a very unwilling witness on behalf of Ruskin, who was unable to attend because of illness. He was in a difficult position; really he did not feel that Whistler fell short as an artist but was obliged, because of his long-standing friendship with Ruskin, to support him. When asked in court his opinion he suggested that the works were unfinished, but was hardly an effective witness on Ruskin's behalf when he said, on being asked if the picture showed any artistry:

'Yes, there must have been great labour to produce such work, and great skill also, but I think he has evaded the chief difficulty of painting, and has not tested his powers by carrying it out.'

W. P. Frith, the painter of 'Ramsgate Sands' and 'Derby Day' was much more suited to defend Ruskin's view than Burne-Jones; he was incapable of understanding Whistler's view and agreed with all that the Royal Academy stood for. How heavily the episode lay on Burne-Jones's conscience is shown in a letter he wrote to Frances Horner some eight years later:

'Do you remember I let myself be put in a pillory to help him at Whistler's trial . . . and even thought him wrong and Whistler right in a way.'

And it indicates something of the dilemma into which he was pitched:

'. . . and yet I was right. He had lifted all England by his life and given himself and wasted himself: it would have been a shame not to have been on his side.'

When the affair ended Whistler was awarded a farthing damages, which he insisted on receiving. He wore the victorious coin on his watch chain.

Portrait painting as such had little attraction for Burne-Jones and any that he undertook were generally of close friends. His views on the subject were singular and in character:

'The only expression allowable in great portraiture is the expression of character and

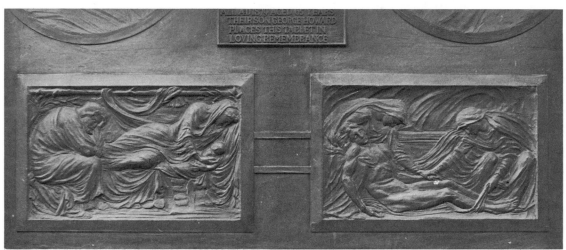

183. 'The Nativity' and 'The Entombment', metal plaques executed by Sir Edgar Boehm after designs by Burne-Jones; at Lanercost Prior, Cumberland, 1879.

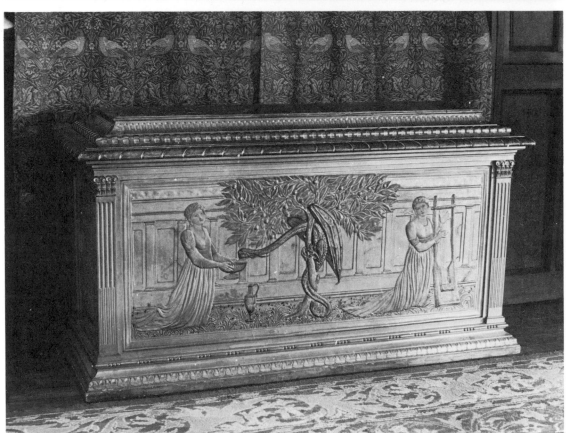

184. Cassone with a design by Burne-Jones, 'Feeding the Dragon in the Garden of Hesperides', executed in gesso by an assistant, probably by T. M. Rooke in 1882. On loan to Wightwick Manor, near Wolverhampton, from Birmingham City Museum & Art Gallery.

moral quality, not anything temporary, fleeting accidental. . . . The moment you give what people call expression you destroy the typical character and degrade them into portraits which stand for nothing.'

By this he means the physiognomy, together with any passing expression of temporary mood in the sitter, bear little relationship to the real qualities of that person. Appearance is skin deep but a portrait should be much more—a reflection of inner life and character, the essence of that person. It is obvious, therefore, that he could only paint those people whom he knew intimately, and always they are depicted in complete repose. At the same time as in any great portrait, each one reflects much of the artist himself. Until 1877 the majority of his portraits were of his family or of his intimates but from that time, as the circle of his friends began to include people who requested portraits, they became more frequent. They were mostly three-quarter length, rarely full-length, the sitter in a relaxed position with his arms limply placed at his side or on his lap. Never is there any gesture, all is calm and quiet. Colour plays an important part in conveying the character of the sitter. Katie Lewis painted as a child lies on an orange couch and wears a dark blue dress, Caroline Fitzgerald wear a dark green velvet dress and holds an open book amidst a background of grey-green canvas, and his most superb portrait, that of his daughter Margaret, is in tones of blue with a second portrait within a convex mirror that hangs immediately behind her. It was a habit of his to present his friends with informal but highly finished pencil portraits which have the gentle repose of the oils, yet are more intimate and tender in tone.

Music-making frequently figures in the art of Burne-Jones; innumerable figures play rebecs, psalteries, dulcimers, portable organs, and shawms; many others are still, as though listening to music. He himself was passionately fond of music and encouraged Georgie to exercise her ability in singing. It is not surprising therefore, to find him decorating a piano just before his marriage in 1862, and at about the same time he executed another for his friend G. P. Boyce. The decoration of these two upright pianos consists of easel paintings which occupy the front panels. As decoration they are naïve and could easily be hung separately as pictures. This cannot be said for the grand pianos he was involved with from the late seventies, which, except for panels painted in the studio and then mounted on organs belonging to George Howard and William Graham, were his next real contribution to the decoration of instruments. The first of the pianos was commissioned by William Graham and it proved to be a very ambitious undertaking. On a base of green-stained wood he covered all the surfaces of the piano with ornament; the whole of the uppermost surface is covered with sprays of leaves, a scroll of poetry, and a muse appearing to a reclining poet, in an ingenious, if not wholly successful, composition. Inside the lid Mother Earth sits naked surrounded by numerous impish babies, evidence of her fecundity, who play amid a swirling knot of tendrils. By using a grapevine he was able to overcome the difficulties inherent in the awkward shape of the piano, allowing it to invade otherwise empty areas. This more successful design is typical of the artist's whimsy as it comes as a surprise, set as it is amongst more serious subjects. Around the narrow strip at the sides is a series of medallions which recount the story of Orpheus. These show Burne-Jones at his greatest; the story crescendos through the first seven designs to reach a climax in the 'Regained Lost' which shows the pathetic struggle as Euridice gradually slips back into oblivion. Three medallions illustrate her final moments. Like his painting 'Merlin and Vivien', they are conceived in terms of line which is at once an expression of mood and a symbol of pathos as it blinds them, helpless, to their plight. In the final of the three, Euridice has become frozen like a corpse as she sinks back to Hades, shrouded in drapery; Orpheus frantically snatches at her garment, attempting to prevent the will of the Gods. The final scene, however, 'The Death of Orpheus', is quieter, more solemn and simpler as a design in keeping with its subject.

The next pianos with which he was associated did not include scenes of a story but were pure decoration. In these he worked with Kate Faulkner, who specialised in gesso work.

I have been wanting for years to reform pianos, since they are as it were the very altar of homes, and a second hearth to people, and so hideous to behold mostly that with a

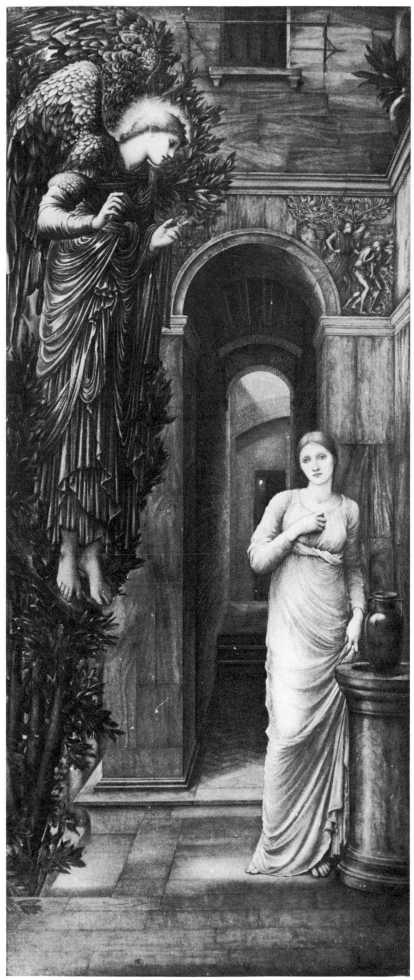

185. 'The Annunciation', 1876–79, oil on canvas, 98 × 44, The Lady Lever Art Gallery, Port Sunlight, Cheshire

Originally owned by George Howard who hung it at 1 Palace Green, Kensington. 'The Expulsion' painted as a frieze on the building is based upon a stained-glass design of 1877 for Lamerton in Devon. Apparently a completely new treatment of the subject, it is in fact a development of the early 'Flower of God' as the sketches in the previous illustration show.

186. Pencil sketches for the design of 'The Annunciation', from a sketchbook, 1876, Fitzwilliam Museum, Cambridge.

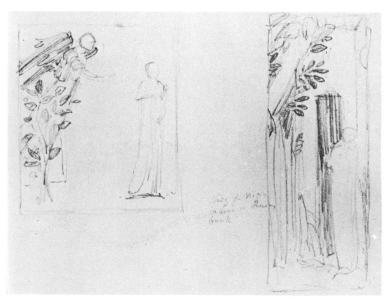

fiery rosewood piece of uglyness it is hardly worthwhile to mend things, since one such blot would and does destroy a whole house of beautiful things. But people wont pay much to have it beautified. I have a little mended the mere shape of the grand piano, and luckily the change adds no extra cost and with an oak piano of the amended form people can do very well. But I feel as if one might start a new industry only it is important that people shall not be frightened at the outset, and think that nothing can be done under 2 or 3 hundred pounds. I cant say how much the Graham piano would cost to reproduce—a horrible big sum—but I should like Broadwood to be venturesome and have a few made on speculation—some only stained—not *always* green—sometimes other colours—and then a few here and there with an ornament well designed and painted—and at least one covered with ornament, and presently we should see if people would have them or not.

So. Mr. Mackenzie's letter pretty closely says what I meant; he is ready to give £50 for ornament on his piano and I thought no one could do it so well or better than you and told him so, and any help Morris or I could be to you, you know is most gladly yours. It might be a good thing just to look at the few specimens in S. Kensington (I would go with you), and then spend a day with us at Northend so as to watch the ways of our piano so ideas would come.

Although Burne-Jones saw these gesso-ornamented pianos as a compromise, as this letter to Kate Faulkner of 1880 shows, in fact they succeed as decorative objects by remaining simple, taking their overall colour from the wood with a pattern of foliage or flowers in gilded gesso over the whole surface. This combined with his 'cleaning up' of the piano shape converts it into a pleasing piece of furniture.

There were a few other adventures into furniture designing but little of merit resulted: *Hesperides* cassone, which was covered with gesso and painted in relief, *Pandora's Box,* similar, but on a smaller scale, and a decorative panel which was a repeat of a panel from the *Hesperides* cassone, designed to be hung over the fireplace at Ashley Cottage, Walton on Thames, owned by Lady Lewis, and various other slight pieces. They were executed by assistants and were not highly regarded by the artist as works of art.

An opportunity came in 1881 for him to fulfil his wish to have large areas to cover with designs, in a commission from the Protestant Episcopal Church whose members in Rome wished to have a permanent place of worship. Dr R. J. Nevin, who supervised the raising of the money, called on G. E. Street to plan the church, which he did in Italian Gothic style. Burne-Jones was requested to design mosaics for the apse and the choir. The enterprise caused much disturbance to the artist since, not only was he unable to visit the site, having to work removed from the mosaic, but at one time money ran out and the scheme had to lay dormant for several years.

He chose a late Byzantine style based on the mosaics found in Venice and Ravenna. Christ in Majesty he chose as a focal point of the apse which dominates the church in typical Byzantine fashion, attended by the archangels on either side, angels in the firmament below, and saints below them on earth. Situated in the spandrels of the arches above the choir is, firstly an Annunciation in an arid rocky landscape and, secondly, a bloodless Crucifixion, 'The Tree of Life', that is attended by Adam and Eve and their two babies. The whole scheme emphasises salvation and there is none of the sense of persecution and judgement associated with many Byzantine mosaics; the scale and colour are drawn from that period but the impression is gentler and less heiratic.

Much trouble arose from the Compagnia di Venezia-Murano, the Italian firm who were making the mosaics, because they were unable to follow their instructions. When they sent the first trial angel Burne-Jones was almost in despair, as the company seemed at first unable to work in a style to which it was unaccustomed. Luckily T. M. Rooke was on one of his summer trips in Venice and was able to supervise, after receiving the following letter from Burne-Jones:

O Rookie—scold them, pitch into them, bully them, curse and refrain not—otherwise I must, late as it is give it all up. You see they dont copy my outline, they dont keep

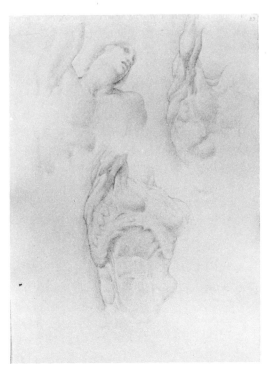
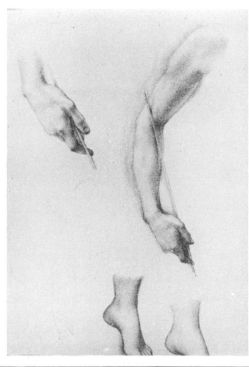

187. Pencil studies for the upper male figure in 'The Wheel of Fortune' from a sketchbook, *c.* 1878, Fitzwilliam Museum, Cambridge.

188. Pencil studies of the king's arm in 'The Wheel of Fortune' from a sketchbook, *c.* 1878, Birmingham City Museum & Art Gallery

The king appears to have been derived from a king in Annibale Caracci's 'Christ in Glory' in the Galleria Pitti, Florence.

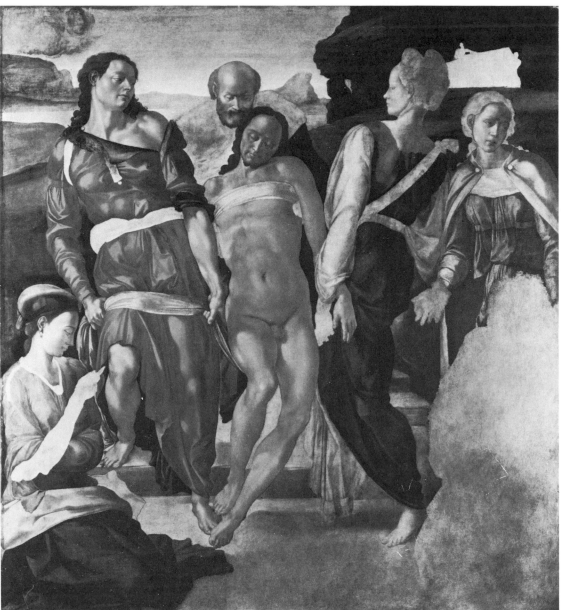

189. 'The Deposition' by Michelangelo, unfinished, oil on panel; The National Gallery, London

The fleshly torsos of Michelangelo made an enormous impression on Burne-Jones's work of the 1870s, as can be seen by comparing this entombment with 'The Wheel of Fortune'.

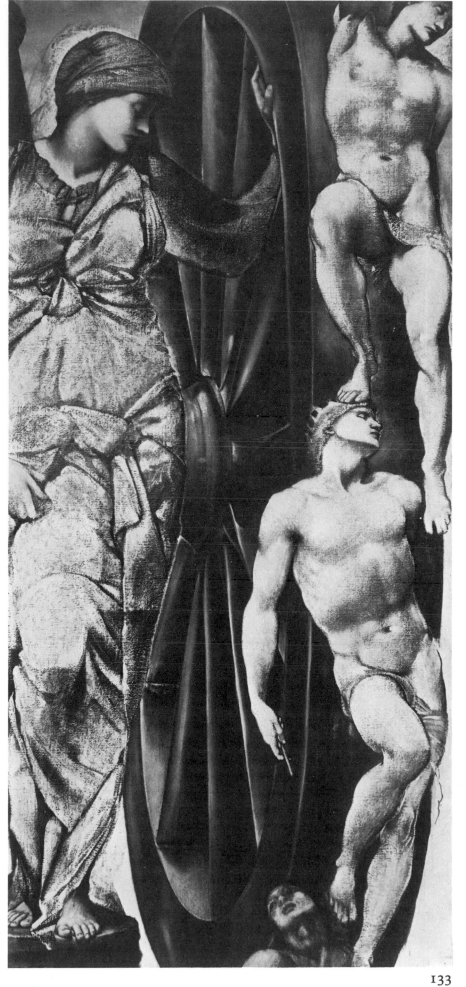

190. 'The Wheel of Fortune', *c.* 1882, gouache, $6\frac{1}{4} \times 29$; The National Museum of Wales, Cardiff

A favourite design of Burne-Jones, which exists in a number of versions in the National Gallery of Victoria, Australia, Watts Gallery, Compton, Surrey, and elsewhere.

133

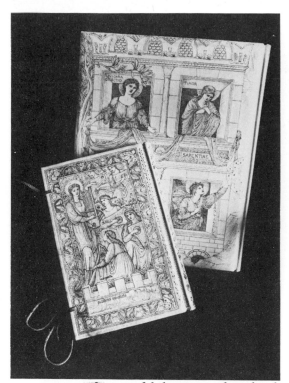

191. Book of Common Prayer and the Apocrypha, bound in vellum with pen and ink drawings, c. 1880; private collection, England
Presented by Burne-Jones to Frances Horner.

to my colours told them, so what the devil can I do? The hair is dark against pale faces, they have made yellow hair against Red Indian faces—what can I do more than mark the tesserae, and what less can they do than not read my instructions? I wonder if it would have been better if I had sent no instructions at all. I wonder if it has only bewildered them. . . . But it is heartrending work—they are close to the best mosaic in the world and they can turn out this—have I bewildered them? . . . O for God's sake let them forget all I said about the tesserae being a part, if this is the result—but why should the tesserae in the face be seven times as big as those of the wings—and why oh why, all over it? . . . All these things are possible, since the pavement of the South Kensington Museum gives these things—any trumpery work gives them. It must be done or I will destroy my cartoons and hand back the money.

So it went on and was not finished at the artist's death, T. M. Rooke taking over the work at that time. Morris gave some help in selecting the colours and general arrangement from the selection of samples from the company which they had sent to Burne-Jones. One of the archangels, absent from the side of Christ, was Lucifer; originally part of the mosaic, he was to have been included with a procession of his followers passing down to Hell, but this was not carried out and the design became converted into a painting known as 'The Fall of Lucifer' finished in 1894. The rather clumsy series of saints executed after the artist's death includes portraits of those concerned with the erection of the new church, Burne-Jones as St John Chrysostom, Lady Burne-Jones as St Barbara and Margaret Burne-Jones (Mrs Mackail) as St Dorothea. What should have been a fulfillment of Burne-Jones's principal ambition proved to be well short of the masterpiece he wished it to be. Nevertheless, 'The Tree of Life' is not without merit, being close to the intentions of the artist, who described it:

'He is blessing Adam and Eve, and while His hands are stretched in blessing He is in the attitude of the Cross. There is the corn behind Adam to show that he must labour. On the left is Eve with her children, and behind her is the white lily, which means the Annunciation and the promise.'

Unlike 'The Annunciation' on the spandrel before it, 'The Tree of Life' occupies the architectural space well, with the trees spreading across to relate the figures to each other. Designed in 1892, later than the others, it is a stronger, more impressive design.

The Byzantine influence showing itself here for the first time announces a new style which predominated in the work of the later eighties and the nineties—a tendency to further elongation of the figures and a more formal presentation of the draperies they wear.

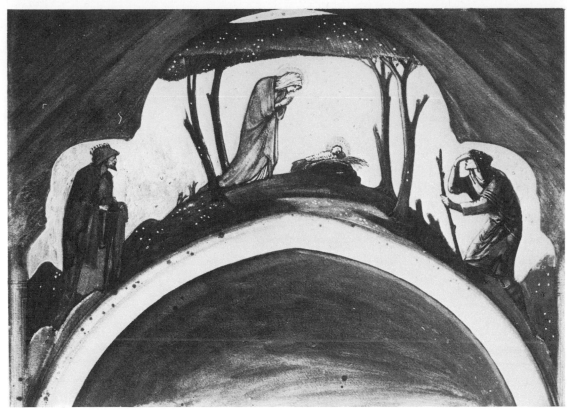

At the same time his admiration for Botticelli results in some work, 'Sponsa di Libano' (1891), for instance, having more animated draperies and a delicate Botticellian poise in the models. In 1884 he was quick to begin subscribing to the Berlin Photographic Company's reproductions of Botticelli's designs to Dante's *Divine Comedy*. The interest, however, was only a resurgence of a longstanding passion for Botticelli, whose influence can be detected from his first acquaintance in 1859.

Ruskin, writing to William Morris in April 1883, received this reply to his enquiry regarding the production of stained glass:

> We *paint* on glass; first the lines of drapery, features & the like with an opaque colour which when the glass is held up to the light is simply so much obscurity; with thinner washes and scumbles of the same colour we shade objects as much as we deem necessary, but always using this shading to explain form and not as shadow proper.
> 2nd. Finding that it was difficult to get flesh coloured glass with tone enough for the flesh of figures, we use thin washes of reddish enamel colour to stain white glass for flesh colour and sometimes though rarely, for other pale orange fruits. N.B. this part of our practice is the only point in which we differ from medieval glass painters.
> 3rd. We use a yellow stain on white glass (or on blue to make greens) this is chiefly done by means of silver, is quite transparent and forms part of the glass after firing; it may therefore be considered rather a diffusion of colour in the glass than a painting on it. The body of the glass is of two kinds. First what is technically called pot-metal in which colouring matter is fused with the glass & is essentially part of it: and 2ndly what is called flashed glass, in which white body is covered with a coloured skin: this is done by the workman taking on the end of his hollow rod first a large lump of white metal then a small dip of coloured metal, he then trundles the lot, making a disk like a small piece of crown glass. This kind of glass however is not much used for the red coloured by copper called technically 'ruby glass', this owing to its make is often curiously striped and waved; this glass is I must tell you, perilous to fire the painted colours upon as the kiln generally changes it more or less, sometimes darkening it almost to blackness, sometimes carrying the colour away: to avoid the risk we are sometimes obliged to paint the necessary lines on a piece of thin white glass & lead up the two together: this, which is called plating, I have sometimes done with two pieces of coloured glass to get some peculiar tint: one must be careful not to overdo

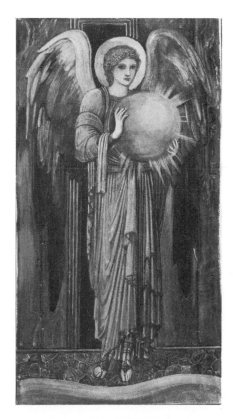

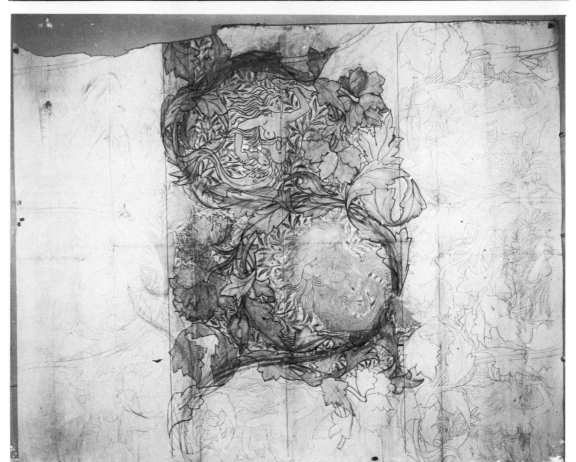

194. 'Helen', *c.* 1880, oil on canvas, 12 × 28½; Carlisle Museum & Art Gallery
Possibly a decorative panel dedicated to Helen Mary Gaskel.

195. 'Mermaid Wallpaper', *c.* 1880, pencil, ink and watercolour; William Morris Gallery, Walthamstow
Little is known about this design, presumably for wallpaper. Very probably it is a collaboration between Burne-Jones and Morris, who would have drawn the floral parts. The uppermost mermaid is a re-working of Burne-Jones's painting 'The Sea Nymph' (1878–81). The wallpaper may well have been intended to decorate the room at Rottingdean which Burne-Jones finished as a tavern and which he called 'The Merry Mermaid'.

the process however, or you will get a piece of glass at once cumbrous and liable to accident.

I should mention that all the glass is very thick and that in some of the pot metals, notably the blues, the difference between one part of a sheet and another is very great. This variety is useful to us in getting a jewel-like quality which is the chief charm of painted glass—when we *can* get it. You will understand that we rely almost entirely for our colour on the *colour of the glass*; and the more the design will enable us to break up the pieces, and the more mosaic-like it is, the better we like it.

The latter remark seems at variance with the cartoons Burne-Jones was supplying to the company, but it must be remembered that the artist supplied a drawing and that the lead lines were put on in the workshop. The glass-makers were at liberty to create the pattern of lead lines where it most suited them. Morris is here speaking as a Gothicist true to the principles of Charles Winston. It was possible with Burne-Jones's designs to treat them in a true mosaic fashion by making the lead lines thin and the glass pieces tiny

136

and numerous. This was the tendency in the late glass.

Burne-Jones made fewer designs for glass each year during the eighties, but many of them are large pictorial windows such as 'The Marriage at Cana' (Biarritz), 'The Building of the Temple' (Boston, Mass.), 'Christ entering Jerusalem' (St Peter's, Vere Street, London), and 'Crossing the Jordan' (St Giles, Edinburgh). The figures generally are simpler in outline without the contraposto of the middle period and the draperies become less animated. In 1883–84 Morris became a member of the Social Democratic Federation and gradually the socialist activities encroached upon the time he spent with the firm. Burne-Jones was alarmed at his friend's political activities, which were perhaps a little embarrassing to him since his choice of friends was amongst the well-to-do, and he did not like J. H. Dearle, who took over when Morris was away. Dearle did not have Morris's refined sense of colour. As a disciple of Morris he was capable of executing his master's ideas, but only in a prosaic pedestrian fashion, the glass he was responsible for is usually very dense, almost blotting out daylight. Morris's absence from the firm may account for a series of designs of the Norse Gods by Burne-Jones being executed by a French glass firm in Tours. These make an interesting comparison with the company's methods; the little leading that is used follows Burne-Jones's outlines, large areas of glass of a single pastel colour bear the design which is painted in brown enamel and the overall tone is neutral.

Tapestry weaving had begun to interest Morris in 1878 when he discussed it with Thomas Wardle, manufacturer of decorative products, who insisted that the only great tapestries are ones with figures. Outlining the necessary features of a good tapestry designer he wrote:

'1. General feeling for art, especially for its decorative side

2. He must be a good colourist

3. He must be able to draw well; i.e., he must be able to draw the human figure, especially hands and feet

4. Of course he must know how to use the stitch of the work.'

Quite obviously Burne-Jones fulfilled all these requirements and so it comes as a surprise to find the first design was made by Walter Crane, who adapted a book illustration,

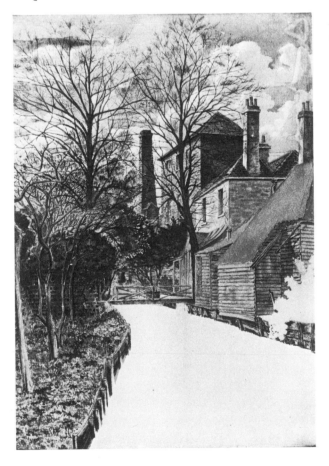 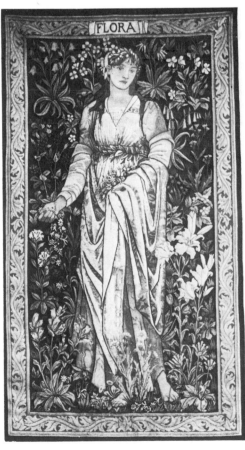

196. 'Merton Abbey', unfinished watercolour by Walter Crane; private collection, London
Morris and Company moved here in 1881.

197. 'Flora' tapestry designed by Burne-Jones in 1885. The background was added from drawings by Morris. The Junior Common Room, Exeter College, Oxford.

137

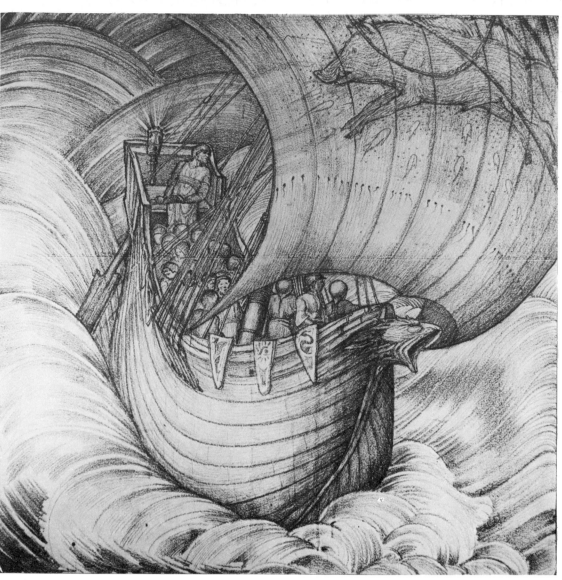

198. 'Voyage to Vinland the Good', cartoon for one of a series of six windows for a private house, 'Vinland', Rhode Island, 1884. Black crayon, $30\frac{1}{4} \times 30\frac{3}{8}$, Carlisle Museum & Art Gallery.

'The Goose Girl' for tapestry in 1881. All the subsequent figure tapestries, however, were designed by Burne-Jones until 1894. At first they were single figures set amid an ornamental foliage background—'Flora and Pomona' (1885), and sometimes they were adapted stained-glass designs—'St Agnes', 'St Cecilia' and 'St George' (1887) 'Peace' (1889). Becoming more skillful they began work on larger, more complex compositions, 'The Adoration of the Magi' was designed in 1887 and completed in 1890, followed by the elaborate Morte d'Arthur series begun in 1893. Needless to say the type of art Burne-Jones had made his own, which had arisen through years of designing for stained glass and embroideries, was equally suited to tapestry. The technique used in the large-scale tapestries was much the same as the one employed in the production of large stained glass. After the usual preliminary studies, a small but complete design was prepared and then photographed. The next step was to enlarge it to the full-sized cartoon, thus saving the time and effort of the designer. The photographs, some of them as much as eight-feet high and six-feet wide, a few even larger, became the final cartoons after Burne-Jones had gone over them clarifying details. This process had the advantage of being cheaper than employing a copyist who was also likely to diverge from the original design.

A similarity in presentation between the decorative work and the fine art enabled Burne-Jones to adapt many of his designs into pure paintings. 'The Passing of Venus', first conceived as a painting in 1881, was later adapted into a design for a large tapestry; 'Pilgrim at the Gate of Idleness' began as an embroidery in the 'Romance of the Rose' series and, with many other scenes from that group, was converted into a painting; 'Peace' was first used for stained glass, (English Church, Berlin, 1886) and later as a tapestry design, whilst 'Launcelot at the Chapel of the Holy Grail' occurs as a painting (1883), as

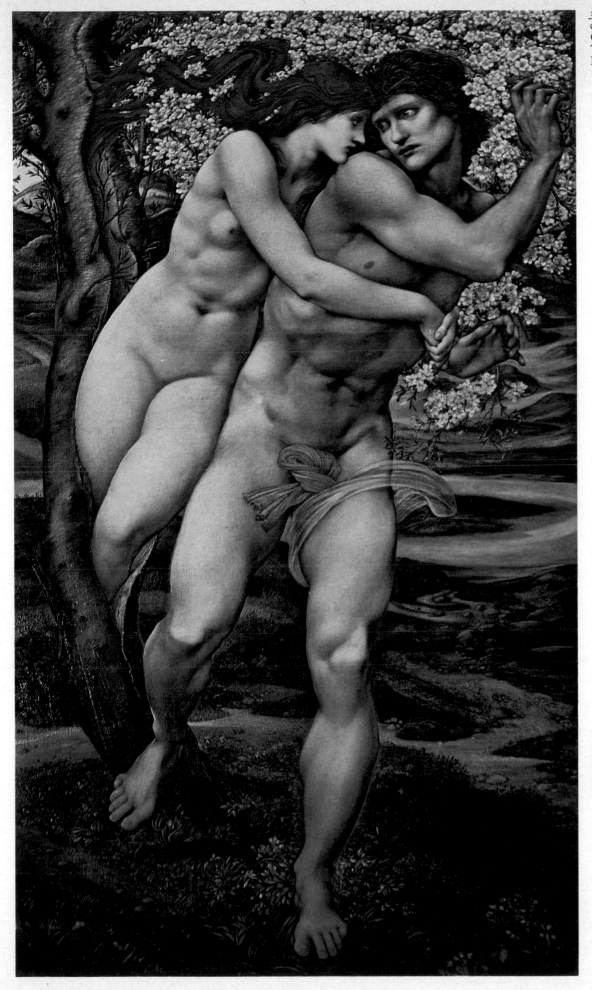

35. 'Tree of Forgiveness', oil on
canvas, 75 × 42; Lady Lever Art
Gallery, Port Sunlight, Cheshire.
This is a large version of 'Phyllis and
Demophoon', the gouache painted in
1870.

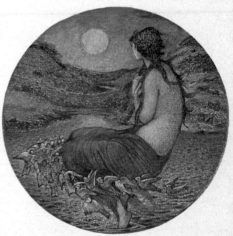

36. 'The Mirror of Venus', c. 1885,
gouache, six inches in diameter;
British Museum, London. An original
design for 'The Flower Book' although
not related to the oil painting of the
same name which is in the Calouste
Gulbenkian Collection, Lisbon.

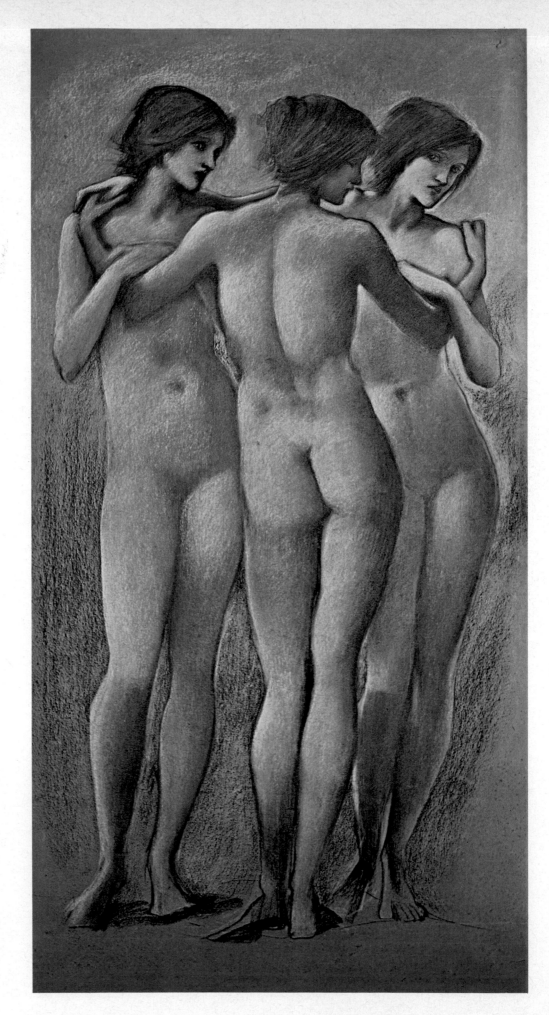

40. 'The Three Graces', *c.* 1885, pastel, 53½ × 27½; Carlisle Art Gallery. Given to Carlisle by Sir William Rothenstein, it is a study for 'Venus Concordia' (Plymouth Art Gallery, unfinished) which was first designed in 1870 for the predellas in the Troy Polyptych.

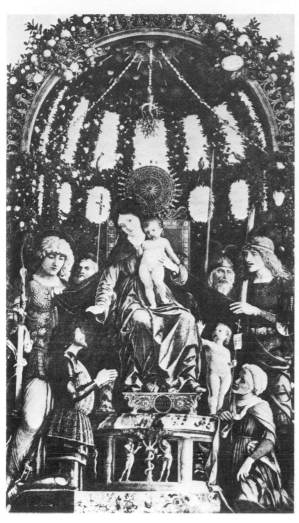

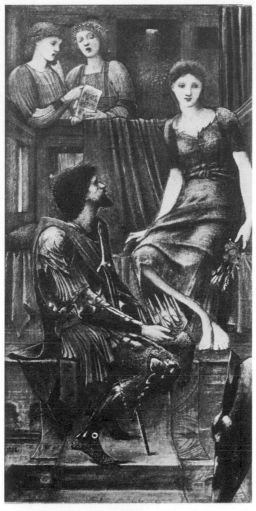

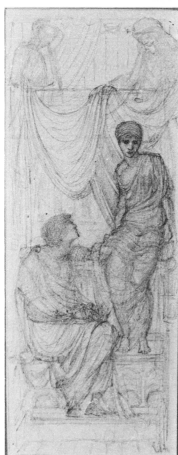

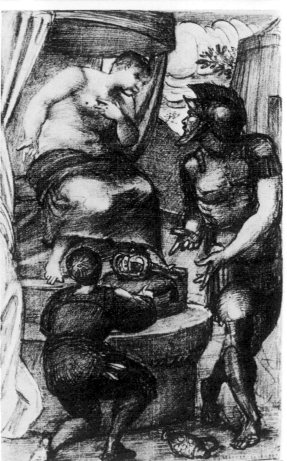

199. 'Madonna della Vittoria' by Mantegna. The germ of the idea for Cophetua is contained in this painting. The relationship between madonna and knight is similar to that between beggar maid and king, and the saint looking down at the knight is comparable with the two singing boys. The perspective which demands that the picture should be seen from below is the same in both works.

200. Design for 'King Cophetua and the Beggar Maid', completed in 1885, gouache; private collection, London.

201. Design for 'King Cophetua and the Beggar Maid', c. 1883, pencil, $13\frac{1}{4} \times 5$; National Museum of Wales, Cardiff

An early conception showing the boys on either side of the composition.

202. 'Cophetua as though painted by Rubens', c. 1885, pencil, from a decorated letter; British Museum, London

Rubens was Burne-Jones's *bête noir* and he frequently made him the butt of his satirical drawings.

a tapestry, woven in 1894, and was utilised by J. H. Dearle at Haslemere as a memorial window to Tennyson in 1899.

With the quite considerable success that Burne-Jones achieved through the Grosvenor Gallery, he was able to afford, in 1881, a house by the sea as a retreat from the pressures of life and work in the metropolis. He found a house in Rottingdean which was then an undeveloped village on the seaward side of the South Downs of Sussex. The surroundings attracted him for their sweeping hills that cut clean into the sky like a razor's edge, the picturesque windmill with its bold silhouette, and the village itself that clustered around the church in the valley. All these things inspired him and figure in his drawings and sketchbooks, but most of all his imagination was fired by the sea; as he looked out from the cliffs into the limitless blue or grey he imagined distant lands that gave free play to his creative powers, and so, too, did the world beneath the sea. He peopled this submarine world with mermen, mermaids and their children who became victims of his sense of humour; but there was one important exception. 'The Depths of the Sea' was painted in the spring of 1886 and was exceptional in a number of ways. It was the only painting of his to be exhibited at the Royal Academy; it has a macabre touch unusual for him. Basically it is a familiar theme of two figures struggling, like 'Phyllis and Demophoön' and 'Merlin and Vivien', but it contains a more overt reference to the power of the seductress; in pulling her victim beneath the surface the mermaid physically destroys him.

Burne-Jones was reluctant to accept the title 'Associate of the Royal Academy' which had been proposed by Briton Riviere, the animal painter, and passed by a large majority. His fear of the Academy was of long standing. Initially it had arisen through his lacking in self-esteem but latterly it had developed into a realisation of his having little in common with the institution. Only the one painting by him hung on their walls during the period he was an A.R.A. On his resignation in 1893 he wrote to Sir Laurence Alma Tadema:

'It was best to do it—we have got stuck fast—and nobody was ever born to whom freedom is more necessary than it is to this friend of yours. I hope you are not vexed—I am not myself one least bit. I think they are quite right, and I think I am quite right, and there it is, and we shall live happy ever afterwards. You see, dear friend I am particularly made by nature not to like Academies. I went to one when I was a little boy, and didn't like it then, and thought I was free for ever when I grew up, when suddenly one day I had to go to an Academy again—and now I've run away.'

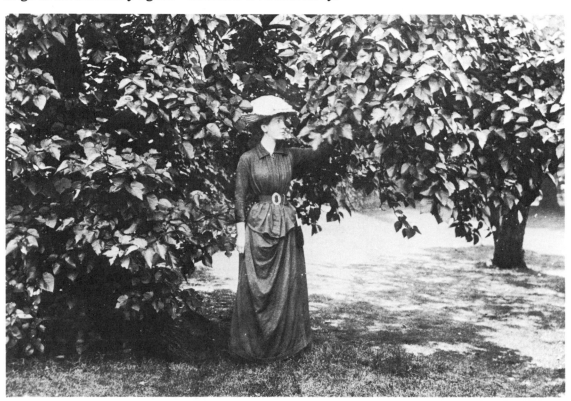

203. Margaret Burne-Jones, the artist's daughter, standing against the mulberry tree in the garden at the Grange, *c.* 1885. Private collection, England.

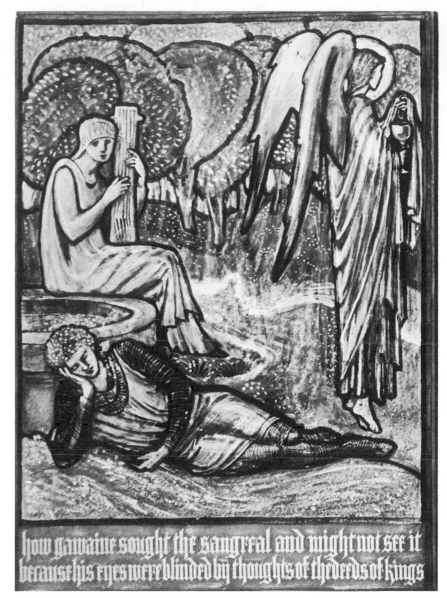

how gawaine sought the sangreal and might not see it
because his eyes were blinded by thoughts of the deeds of kings

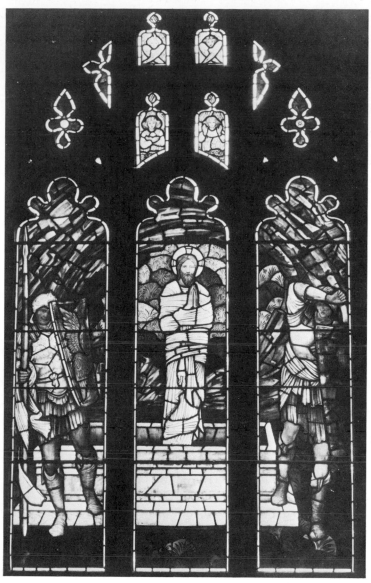

In his attitude to the Royal Academy he was true to the ideals of the first Pre-Raphaelite Brotherhood who refused to confrom to banal concepts of painting. As a thinker as well as an artist he felt uncomfortable among such a conservative group of painters. At the same time he realised that his loyalties lay with the Grosvenor, who treated his pictures sympathetically. It was a cunning move by the Academy to bring to heel a rebellious gallery by taking away their chief painters, but it failed, and the Grosvenor closed for very different reasons in 1888.

'King Cophetua and the Beggar Maid' was exhibited at the Grosvenor Gallery in 1884. It became synonymous with the artist, and was reproduced time and time again. It represents a king who has, after searching far and wide, found his ideal, a beautiful soulful maiden who hovers between life and the spirit world. Like a mirage, she seems likely to dissolve should we approach her. Cophetua appreciates this and sits, gently absorbed by her presence; it is a moment of magic when time is stopped and the world is transmuted into an eternal stillness.

Like many of his works, its first conception as revealed in the sketchbooks was dynamic. The king having found her, reaches up to take the maid, almost violating her essential purity. This idea was quickly succeeded by something akin to the final painting but the details of composition varied from it for some time. It was based upon Mantegna's 'Madonna della Vittoria' (Louvre) which consists of a Virgin and Child attended by four saints, two on either side, a donor in armour, who kneels at the foot of the pedestal upon which she sits. The onlooker identifies with the donor because the perspective is such that it requires him to interpret the scene as though it was seen from below. The resultant

204. Cartoon for one of a series of four windows depicting scenes from the story of the Holy Grail. Designed by Burne-Jones in 1885 for a window in his house at Rottingdean, Sussex. That this was an important series is evidenced by the fact of there being a number of sketches for it in the 'secret' book of designs. Sepia gouache, $20\frac{3}{4} \times 18$, William Morris Gallery, Walthamstow.

205. 'Resurrection', window in the north aisle of All Hallows Church, Allerton, Lancashire, 1885–86
The sequence of aisle windows at Allerton represents an important development in Burne-Jones's ability to spread a single design across an entire window, which introduced certain asymmetry. The peaceful figure of Christ is in contrast with the jagged rocky setting and the restless poses of the two sentries, which are further emphasised by the unusually angular leading. These features became increasingly prevalent in the firm's later work and point the way to the twentieth-century Expressionist designers of glass, such as Douglas Strachan.

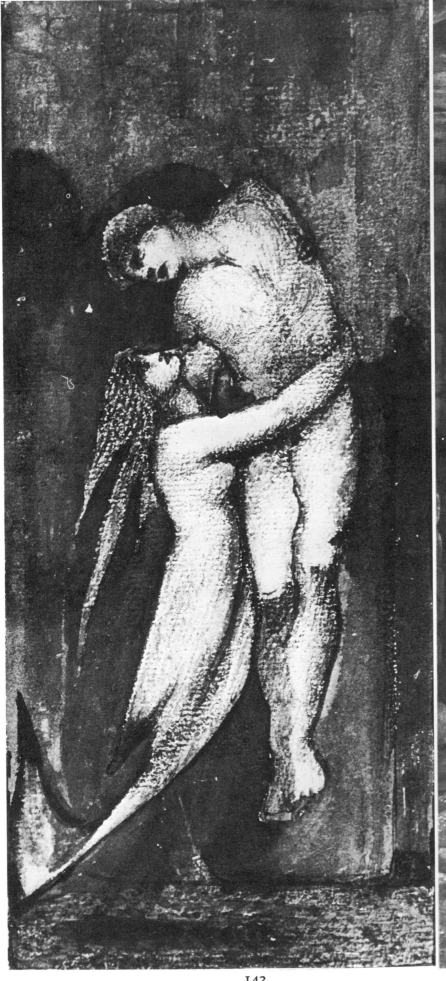

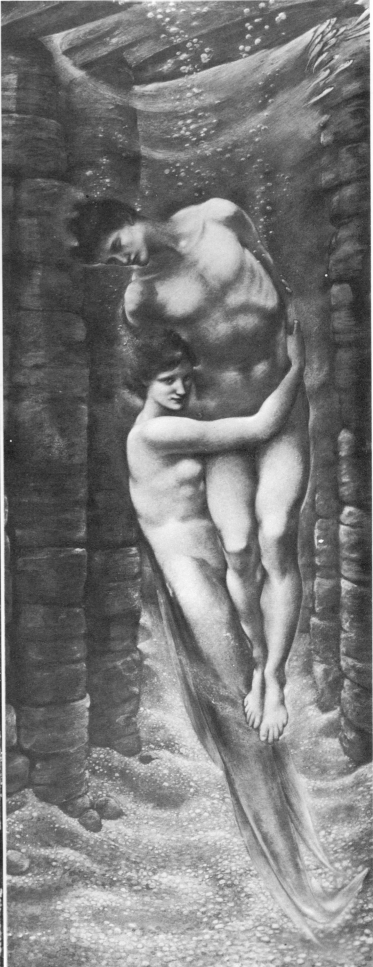

142

feeling of awe was desired by Burne-Jones, who recreated exactly this viewpoint for his painting. The relationship between donor and Virgin and the king and the beggar maid is very similar, but in order to present an even more awe-inspiring distance between the maid and the viewer, instead of having attendant figures at her side they are taken to the top of the design and look down on her. At first, keeping close to the Mantegna, Burne-Jones had four boys, two on either side, and only later took two away, leaving a more pleasing asymmetrical design. In fact, the embryo of Burne-Jones's design lies in the relationship between Mantegna's Virgin, the donor and the kneeling female figure on the right; but Burne-Jones's design is more interesting than that of Mantegna, showing a greater refinement of balance between the figures.

He had treated the story earlier in a panel designed for the front of a cabinet which, like Holman Hunt's illustration in the Tennyson of 1857, keeps close to Tennyson's version of the story:

> Her arms across her breast she laid;
> She was more fair than words can say:
> Bare-footed came the beggar maid
> Before the king Cophetua
> In robe and crown the king stept down,
> To meet and greet her on her way;
> 'It is no wonder' said the Lords,
> 'She is more beautiful than day.'
>
> As shines the moon in clouded skies,
> She in poor attire was seen:
> One praised her ancles, one her eyes,
> One her dark hair and lovesome mien.

206. Study for 'The Depths of the Sea', *c*. 1886, watercolour, 8¾ × 4, The Ashmolean Museum, Oxford.

207. 'The Depths of the Sea', 1887, gouache, 77 × 30, The Fogg Art Gallery, Cambridge, Massachusetts
The only painting to be exhibited by Burne-Jones at the Royal Academy was the painting of which this is a copy. He exhibited it there in 1886 and it went immediately to Australia. The expression of the mermaid recalls, and is as ambiguous as, Leonardo's 'Mona Lisa'.

208. 'The Sleeping Beauty', 1886-88, gouache on canvas, 38 × 58. Private collection, London
A variant painting, with minor changes, of the Sleeping Beauty theme. It is simpler and more monumental than the final version. The picture was given to the artist's daughter in 1888.

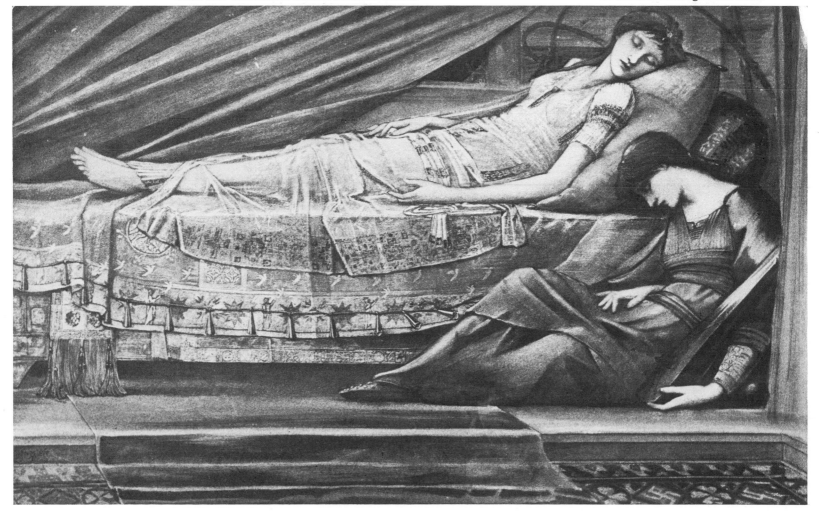

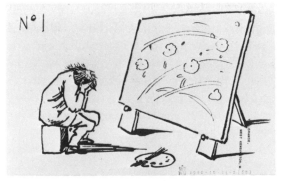

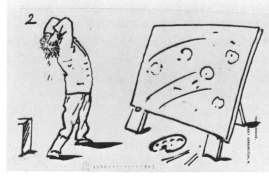

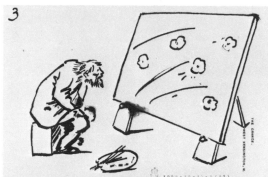

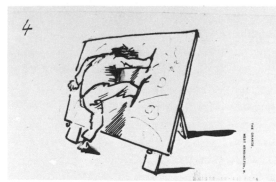

209–13. 'The artist attempting to join the world of art with disastrous results, 1883, pen and ink; The British Museum, London

These comic drawings, contained in a letter to the artist's small friend, Katie Lewis, reveal much about Jones's state of mind at the time. They display his despair with the world and his wish to escape from it. It is significant that the work he shows himself attempting to enter is 'The Briar Rose', which deals with a world brought magically to a halt. It was a logical step from this situation to portray himself as Arthur asleep in Avalon.

So sweet a face, such angel grace,
In all that land had never been:
Cophetua sware a royal oath:
'This beggar maid shall be my queen.'

And like Holman Hunt's, Burne-Jones's early version has the king descending from his throne to the maid which has the quality of his bestowing a favour upon her, totally unlike the more famous version in which the king has become as nothing before beauty and sits at her feet—a reversal of their roles. This theme, renunciation of material wealth for an ideal of beauty, had great significance for artists of the period, who, apprehensive of the erosion of spiritual values by worldly considerations, saw the danger to society and the individual which lay in his total pursuit of wealth. On a higher level they saw scientific materialism destroying the imaginative power. So accentuating the power of the mind, i.e. the creation of beauty, which did not accept the world as it appears, they gave it full play to interpret, transfigure or even reject external appearance. Morris's verse play 'Love is Enough' deals with a king who gives up his kingdom for love; 'Pygmalion and the Image' is a variation of the theme in which the sculptor, disillusioned with his contemporaries falls in love with a figure he has fashioned—an even more direct symbol. In the light of this imagery it is easy to understand the attraction of the Holy Grail stories. A group of knights, whose life was spent in the pursuit of a spiritual mystery, regarded the temporal world as a necessary discipline preparing them for the final mystical fulfilment.

Socialism, as interpreted by Morris, was a natural offshoot of this type of thought; impatient with painting as a means of teaching the message, he turned to politics to bring about a reform. Art was too subtle a means of converting society, so he took to polemics and the platform. In 1883 he joined the Social Democratic Federation. Although it caused some concern to Burne-Jones it is not inconceivable that during their many conversations they touched upon the subject and that 'Cophetua', with its implied negation of social barriers, was inspired by his friend's exploits. Certainly he makes a joking reference to Morris's views in his account book when he charged the firm for a cartoon of a Viking ship voyaging to America and wrote beneath 'making for other people's property'. This was in 1883, the year he was working on 'Cophetua'.

In its development the painting was typical of the method Burne-Jones used from the 1870s; beginning with a rough exploratory sketch, he gradually clarified the design until it became a coherent entity. At this stage and at a few points later, watercolour versions were made on a small scale to give an idea of colour and total effect. When he was satisfied with this there followed a characteristic series of drawings that isolated each detail of the design. Experimenting with every conceivable variation within the possibility of the design, he crystallised the exact image that he sought. Eliminating any possibility of chance from the painting he made certain that every inch of the canvas expressed exactly what he wished. Even in these preliminary drawings he was in complete control of the pencil or crayon. Whereas many artists treated the study as a form of discovering the accident of the hand's mark-making, Burne-Jones made sure that the marks were precisely as his creative sensibilities wanted. His images may have been drawn from the external world but they had to be specific in their role as symbols of his particular vision. How sensitive he was to the importance of his drawings is shown in the following extract:

> . . . I never use it [pencil] to sketch with, I use it as a finishing instrument. But it's always touch and go whether I can manage it even now. Sometimes knots will come in it and I never can get them out, I mean little black specks. There's no drawing I consider perfect. I often let one pass only because of expression, or facts I want in it, but unless—if I've once india rubbered it, it doesn't make a good drawing. I look on a perfectly successful drawing as one built up on a groundwork of clear lines till its finished. Its the same kind of thing in red chalk. It mustn't be taken out. Rubbing with the finger's all right. In fact you dont succeed with any process until you find out how you may knock it about and in what you must be careful. Slowly built up texture in oil painting gives you the best chance of changing without damage when its necessary.

Consequently a painting by Burne-Jones is a collection of chiselled images welded into a total composition—'a reflection of a reflection of something purely imaginary' as the artist put it. For this reason he frequently made the accessories in his paintings himself, not so much as a model to give the correct light and shade but so that they bore less resemblance to any real objects found in everyday life. He designed armour, swords, chariots, a model town, the costume his models wore, the instruments they held, and the chairs they sat in; he went so far as to design a ship, completely rigged with sails, for his painting 'The Sirens'. However, he was not exceptional in this, Leighton, Henry Holiday, and Watts all made models of parts of their composition but, unlike Burne-Jones, it was to obtain the correct chiaroscuro effect. Holman Hunt and Watts went so far as to make a sculptured version of some of their paintings.

The two later versions of 'The Annunciation' (1876–79, 1876–87) would seem, at first sight, to have little in common with 'The Flower of God' (1862–63) with its illuminated-manuscript orientation. In fact, as a sketchbook of about 1872 reveals, a series of drawings rearranged the early composition, and the later versions arose directly from it. A comparison between the three paintings shows how the artist has progressed in the intervening fifteen years. During the early sixties he was interested in texture and colour used within a basically Gothic idiom. Deep perspective acts as a counterpoise to the relationship between angel and Virgin; although perspective recession is used in the later version it is presented frontally, so are the figures, the lines are calmer and there is a simpler and more refined design. Scale, so important in creating the right attitude in the onlooker, is more intimate

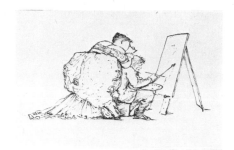

214. 'The Price of Success', pen and ink, The British Museum, London After his success at the Grosvenor Gallery it became the custom for the fashionable to visit Burne-Jones's studio. While he welcomed this as it supplied patronage, it must at times have been trying.

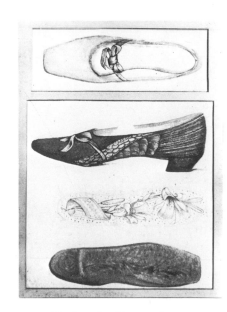

215. Designs for Shoes, 1877, watercolour; private collection, England.

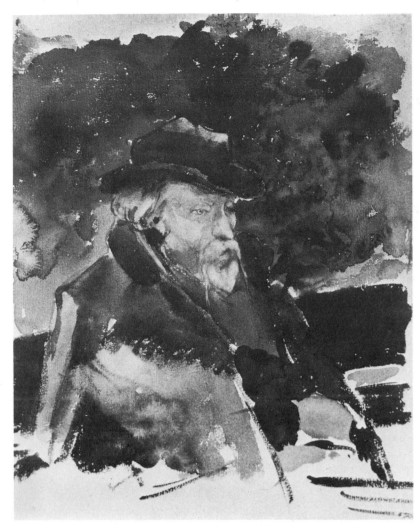

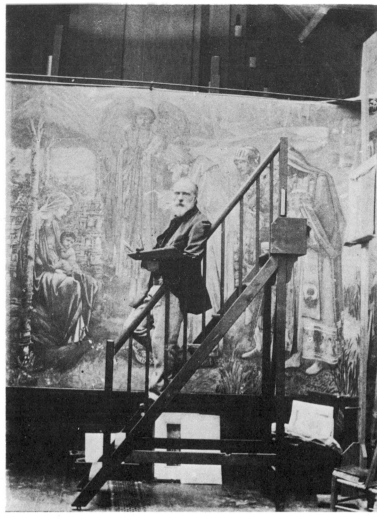

216. Burne-Jones by Jules Bastien Lepage, *c.* 1882, watercolour, Birmingham City Museum & Art Gallery.

217. Burne-Jones at work on 'The Star of Bethlehem' *c.* 1889. From a contemporary photograph. The painting was commissioned by the Corporation of Birmingham, who asked for a large watercolour version of the tapestry.

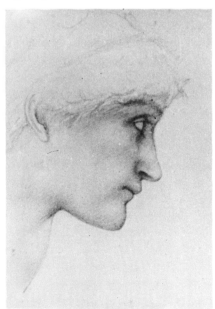

218. Study for 'Danae', *c.* 1887, pencil, 9 × 6 approx.; Glasgow Art Gallery
The model was Marie Stillman.

in the first work whereas the immensity (98 in. × 44 in.) of its later counterpart overawes us. An Italianate elegance has replaced the Gothic intimacy.

Many other later works exist in two versions, the final oil and a full-sized watercolour replica; the reason for this is given by his son:

> It was my father's almost invariable custom, after he had roughly sketched out the plan of the picture, and at the same time that he was making studies from the model for various details—hands, feet, drapery etc.—to draw out upon brown paper, the same size as the intended canvas, an elaborate scheme in colour for the picture he was about to paint. This preliminary design or cartoon was usually drawn in pastel or watercolour, often in a mixture of the two, a medium which he found convenient for rapidly giving a general idea of the effect which he wished to produce.

Because of the rapidity with which these working drawings were made, they are often fresher and lighter than the final oils; sometimes, because the technique that he used encouraged a tendency to labour his designs, the finished paintings lose some of their impact. This quality of freshness is found too in the informal drawings he made for friends when he was incapacitated by illness. His bouts of illness increased as he grew older, and these small drawings could be made in the sick bed. Of this order are his drawings inspired by the names of flowers, later published by his wife in a limited edition under the title of *The Flower Book*. They began in 1882, most of them being executed at Rottingdean. Never do the drawings represent flowers but are fantasies woven around the traditional flower names. To the medieval mind each flower in some way revealed part of the mystery of the universe, so it was to Burne-Jones's imagination. He asked a friend to collect any that might interest him:

'Pray send me as many names as ever you can for alack it is not one in ten that I can

146

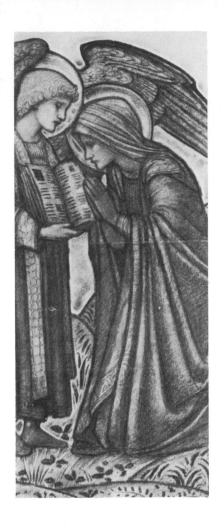

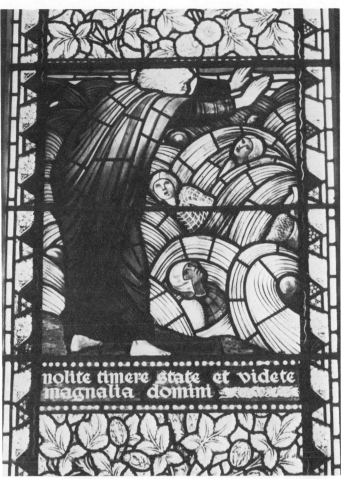

nolite timere state et videte magnalia domini

219. 'St Frances', cartoon for right-hand panel of a three-light window in the north aisle of St James Church, Weybridge, Surrey, 1887. Black crayon, $31\frac{1}{2} \times 13\frac{3}{4}$, the Piccadilly Gallery, London.

220. 'Egyptians Drowning in the Red Sea', part of the east window at Kirkcaldy Old Parish Church, Fife, Scotland, 1885.

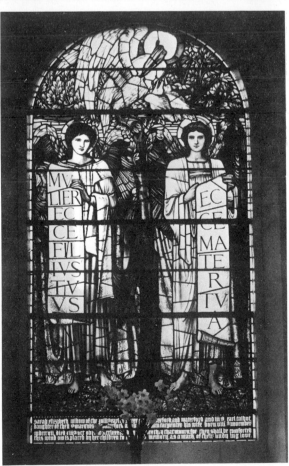

221. Pelican and two Angels, window on the north side of the Chapel at Ingestre Hall, Staffordshire, 1889.

use. Of course I could make pictures to all, but I want the name and the picture to be one soul together, and indissoluble, as if they could not exist apart; so many lovely names and nothing to be done with them.'

They show a curious relationship with some of his paintings; many are re-interpretations of his familiar themes—'Golden Shower' shows Danae inside the tower, 'Love in a tangle' is 'Fair Rosamond', 'Grave of the Sea' is a variant of 'Depths of the Sea', 'Flower of God' is an Annunciation, 'Traveller's Joy' represents the Magi, 'Golden Cup' and 'Honours Prize' are subjects from the Grail legend, and 'Wall Tryst' shows Thisbe looking at the chink. His concentrated and sometimes esoteric vision produced in these non-public, even secret, set of designs an intimate sequence of highly personal pictures, a credo in miniature, in which he re-examined the themes and images he held most important.

Burne-Jones continued to exhibit at the Grosvenor Gallery until 1887; in spite of what he considered a harsh setting for his pictures—the red plush—he exhibited all his major works there during the period from 1877. The reasons for its closure were a change in policy arising from the estrangement of Sir Coutts and Lady Lindsay and from a curtailment of Sir Coutts's income. Lady Lindsay had attracted fashionable gatherings at the gallery and without her good taste things began to decline; in the words of Charles Hallé:

'Difficulties, which began in 1884, when, in consequence of domestic differences, Sir Coutts's private means were considerably curtailed made it necessary for him to turn the gallery to better financial account. The 'man of business' was called into council, and instead of Lady Lindsay we had Mr Joseph Pyke, the jeweller from next door to give prestige and social éclat to our artistic venture. It did not take long to bring the whole thing down like a pack of cards.'

Comyns Carr and Charles Hallé decided to begin a gallery of their own. They commissioned E. R. Robson, recommended by Philip Webb, to design a building for a site in Regent Street, and the New Gallery was ready for opening in May 1888. Burne-Jones was on the committee and, with Watts and Alma Tadema, was the chief exhibitor there, having a retrospective show in 1894 followed by a memorial show on his death in 1898. From 1887 the New Gallery took on the main responsibility for exhibiting his work.

Chapter Eight

Avalon

Because of the premonition that he would die before his fifty-seventh birthday, Burne-Jones hurried to complete the 'Briar Rose' series in 1889, and it was in fact finished early in 1890. Thomas Agnew and Sons of Old Bond Street, London purchased the paintings and exhibited them in their gallery in April of that year. Burne-Jones exhibited no other paintings in 1891 owing to his preoccupation with the series, but a collection of studies and designs was exhibited at the New Gallery. Agnew's sold the paintings to Alexander Henderson; before he bore them off to his mansion in Buscot Park to become a decorative frieze around the drawing room, they were again exhibited at Whitechapel in April 1891. To enable the poorer classes to have a glimpse of fairyland the entrance was free. The series proved so popular that a tour of the provinces and America was considered but not put into practice.

Burne-Jones selected the episode from the fairy tale *Sleeping Beauty*, which Perrault recounts in his *Contes du Temps Passé* of 1742, but it was familiar to children throughout the nineteenth century by way of nursery books. The story, too familiar to recount in detail here, tells how a beautiful princess and all living things around her are bewitched into a long sleep and how a brave and gallant prince cuts through the magic thorns to wake her with a kiss. Tennyson treated the legend in his poem *Day Dream* of 1842 and included it in the illustrated Tennyson of 1857 for which Rossetti was preparing designs when Burne-Jones first entered his studio. The four paintings have more in common with Tennyson's symbolism than with Perrault or the children's tale. He is not interested in the narrative *per se* but in a fragment. Within the framework of the legend both Tennyson and Burne-Jones isolate the passage towards the end, in which the world succumbs to a passionate sleep. Tennyson includes 'The Revival' to emphasise the significance of the awakening; 'A touch, a kiss! the charm was snapt.' Burne-Jones avoids this to explore a poignant and psychologically more complex moment when the prince breaks through the thicket. What confronts him, he feels momentarily powerless to change, struck as he is by the heavy stillness.

The design of the first series, 'The Briar Wood' is an ingenious expression of its subject. The prince, standing full height, creates a vertical form which is in opposition to the knights, who are arranged horizontally. His determination to break the spell is thus represented both literally, because he is the only being awake, and symbolically, because he is the only part of the composition to extend from the bottom to the top of the painting. But throughout the scene the briar rose has grown, and its tangled coils coalesce into a formidable barrier, whilst at the same time, the rhythms it creates act as a foil to the heavy stupor of the unsuccessful knights.

Tennyson describes precisely the same moment in the following way:

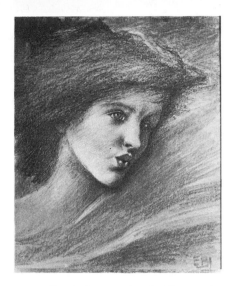

A fairy Prince, with joyful eyes,
And lighter footed than the fox.

The bodies and the bones of those
That strove in other days to pass,
Are wither'd in the thorny close,
Or scatter'd blanching on the grass.
He gazes on the silent dead:

Creating a sense of unity and wishing to retain a powerful impression of languor, Burne-Jones avoided the gruesome aspects contained in the poem. He also differed from the poet's 'joyful eyes' and painted a melancholy prince. Verses were written by William Morris to be printed in the catalogue and read in front of the painting; they are weak as verse but as adjuncts to the paintings they intensify the response and increase the involvement of the viewer.

The fateful slumber floats and flows
About the tangle of the rose;
But lo! the fated hand and heart
To rend the slumbrous curse apart!

Industry frozen by magic sleep is the subject of the next two paintings. Firstly, 'The Council Room' sweeps the eye along a lateral plane in a sequence of sleeping courtiers, each of intrinsic interest, yet firmly part of the overall design. Similarly, the maidens of 'The Garden Court' maintain a continuous lateral flow. At the same time they are individually beautiful and, as units in a larger pattern, arrest the eye and suggest intricate subsidiary rhythms in their arrangement with one another. Morris's verses for these two scenes are as follows:

The threat of war, the hope of peace,
The Kingdom's peril and increase
Sleep on, and bide the latter day,
When fate shall take her chain away.

The maiden pleasance of the land
Knoweth no stir of voice or hand.
No cup the sleeping waters fill,
The restless shuttle lieth still.

222. Study for a zephyr in 'Sponsa de Libano', 1891, red paper, white, and black chalk, $13\frac{3}{8} \times 10\frac{7}{8}$, The Lady Lever Art Gallery, Port Sunlight, Cheshire
The painting is in the Walker Art Gallery, Liverpool.

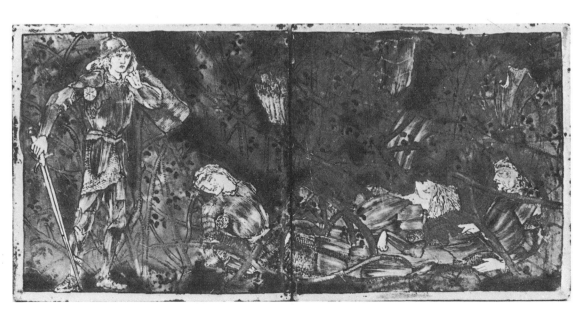

223. 'The Prince Entering the Rose Thicket', 1862, tile, 6×12; William Morris Gallery, Walthamstow
Painted by Kate or Lucy Faulkner. The design remained fundamentally the same when Burne-Jones used it in the 1880s in the 'Briar Rose' series.

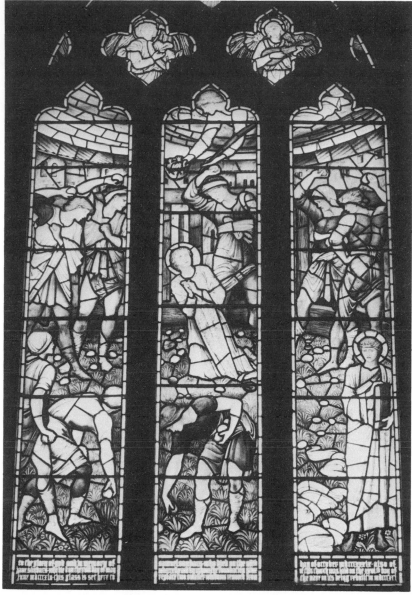

224. 'Stoning of St Stephen', north transept window, St Paul's Church, Morton, near Gainsborough, Lincolnshire, 1891
A startlingly effective design in the master's late style, unfortunately let down by the stock musical angels in the tracery lights.

In the fourth of the series, Sleeping Beauty lies unconscious of her imminent awakening. She is the culmination of the rhythm created by the chain of heavy sleepers—the knights, the courtiers and the maidens. At the same time, the drapery strewn across the balustrade behind her, relates her recumbent form to that of the prince at the opposite end of the series. The folds at the left side are collected into a vertical knot that echoes the prince's position, but gradually, across the canvas, the folds modulate until the right edge of the hanging follows the line of the princess's body. With consummate art Burne-Jones has thus made a disguised reference to the magic vitalising kiss, yet it remains secondary to the total impression of inertia.

Morris's verse accompanying the scene clearly indicates that the idea within the painting is not one of the awakening but the moment before:

> There lies the hoarded love, the key
> To all the treasures that shall be;
> Come fated hand the gift to take,
> And smite this sleeping world awake,

and Burne-Jones, when asked why he had not shown the awakening, replied, 'I want it to stop with the princess asleep and to tell no more, to leave all the afterwards to the invention and imagination of people, and tell them no more'—an indication of his preoccupation with the theme of sleep, a preoccupation which relates to his own withdrawal

151

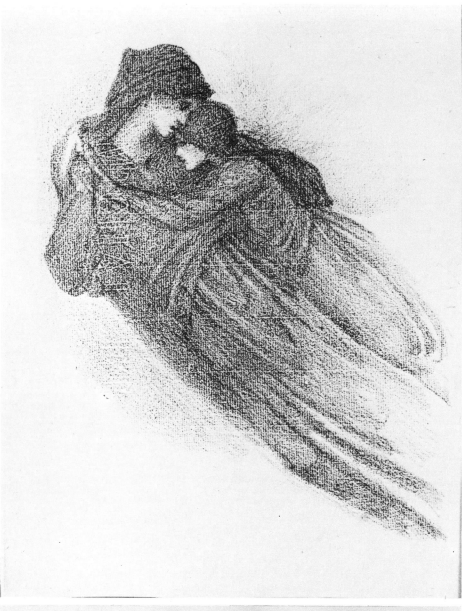

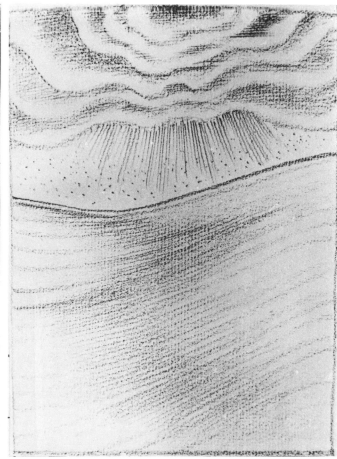

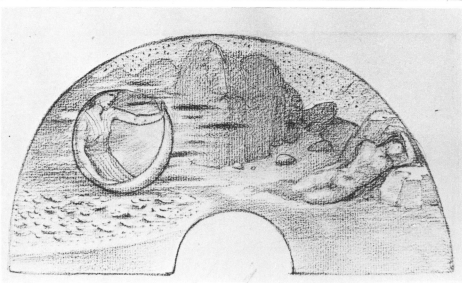

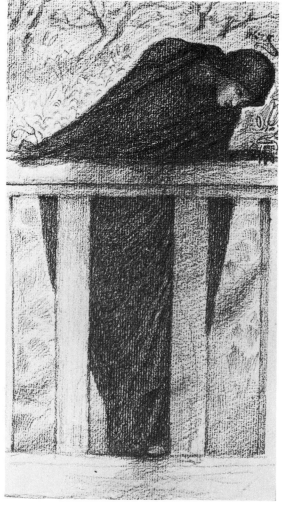

225-28. Drawings from the 'secret' book of designs, begun in 1885, now in The British Museum.

225. 'Paolo and Francesca' (?), black crayon.

226. 'Sky and Waves'.

227. Design for a Fan.

228. 'The Blessed Damozel'.

from contemporary problems. In his last works sleep, symbolising escape, occurs repeatedly reaching its zenith in 'Arthur in Avalon'.

The opinion of the press on the 'Briar Rose' was generally enthusiastic. On April 25 *The Times* commented:

'. . . the subject chosen is one admirably suited to his art . . . . We are accustomed to to this evidence of loving care in Mr. Burne-Jones's pictures but it has never been shown before on so large a scale and with such exuberance of fancy as in these four pictures. The world of dreams and fairies has surely never been so prodigally illustrated.'

The Athenaeum critic admired the treatment of light and recognised it as a 'superb series' but his colleague of *The Speaker* had reservations, finding the treatment of textures likely to bore and the colour perhaps predictable:

'He indicates but one material, though in some cases we wish he would make it less felt or baize-like, something a little diaphanous would here and there be such a relief. And this brings us to the artist's abiding fault. His colour is superb; his management of crimsons, blues and purples of oriental voluptuousness and splendour and yet a "soft lustre" suffuses it all. But it lacks brilliancy, depth, light variety, a sense of monotony characterises all this artist's paintings giving them almost the appearance of tapestries.'

The latter criticism is, in reality, sympathetic to the artist's aims, for it emphasises Burne-Jones's dislike of deep perspective. For him a painting was decorated surface and an object separate from the natural world. 'I love my pictures as a goldsmith does his jewels. I should like every inch of surface to be so fine that if all but a scrap from one of them were burned or lost, the man who found it might say whatever this may have represented it is a work of art, beautiful in surface and quality of colour.'

An earlier series comprising three paintings, in which there is no equivalent to 'The Garden Court', was made during the period from the end of the sixties to 1873. Superficially, the design is identical, figure for figure, but the treatment and atmosphere are radically different. The prince in the earlier version appears hesitant and apprehensive, seeking protection from his shield. His stance and expression present him as youthfully naïve in contrast to the maturity of the later figure. Differences of this kind occur between the two princesses; in the 1870 version she lies uneasily upon her couch, her neck and shoulders thrust at an awkward angle, whereas the repose of the later princess is evident from her relaxed position and the way she sinks into her pillow. Lying among a chaos of briars, the knights too contribute to the uneasy atmosphere, their bodies drawn into jagged shapes unlike the smooth collapsed forms of those of the later painting.

From this comparison we may begin to see how Burne-Jones had evolved his mature style from that of the early seventies. The earlier version is by an artist exploring the means of his art. He paints it primarily to tell a story. The resulting visual experience is less controlled and more expressionist that the later version, and he was obviously unsatisfied, as many studies and designs were made in the interim period between the two complete sets. The final version succeeds in the fulfilment of his idea because by this time he had completely mastered the skills of colour, line, and form. The impression of languor is created by means of effective use of linear rhythms, draughtsmanship, and controlled design and colour. By this time he had discovered that an idea in terms of pictorial art must be expressed through these elements. The difference between the two versions lies in his ability to portray his vision in terms of them. Consequently the atmosphere arises not by portraying a number of people asleep but through slowly undulating line, subdued colour, ability to create a unifying light, and mastery of anatomical form. These elements then translate the subject, which we are able to recognise from its reference to the natural world, into something quite separate, a work of art.

Although the conception of 'The Sirens' dates from the first half of the seventies, and indeed was never completed, the bulk of work upon it took place between 1891 and 1898. Once again, the moment chosen is that before an action—in this case catastrophic. In common with the 'Briar Rose' and 'Avalon' it shows a concern with silence and stillness, not as absolute qualities but ones which the viewer is made to realise are about to be shattered. It is not clear in 'The Sirens' who is about to be destroyed, but the implication of destruction is conveyed through the eerie light and uneasy glances exchanged between

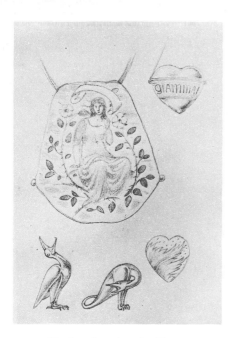

229. Design for a bag for Frances Horner and designs for jewellery, from the 'secret' book of designs, begun in 1885, now in The British Museum.

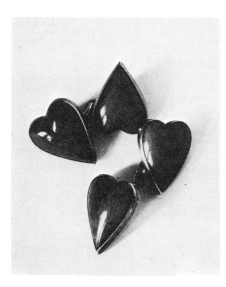

230. Cuff-links in silver and semi-precious green stones, which take the form of a pair of hearts bound together by a silver chain. Designed by Burne-Jones for his own use, 1890, private collection, London.

the sailors and the sirens. Brilliantly organising the composition, Burne-Jones has suggested that the ship will move into the predominantly empty foreground—at once indicating and increasing the sense of peril. In a letter to Frederick Leyland of 1891 he describes the painting:

'It is a sort of Siren-land—I don't know when or where—not Greek sirens but any sirens anywhere, that lead men on to destruction. There will be a shore full of them, looking out from rocks, and crannies in the rocks, at a boat full of armed men, and the time will be sunset. The men shall look at the women and the women at the men but what happens afterwards is more than I care to tell.'

Of another work, 'Venus Concordia', also begun in the early seventies and left very incomplete after further attention during the nineties, he says:

'Love's asleep you see, and only Beauty's going on till he wakes up. They're waiting for him to wake up and then they can begin.'

Once again he makes reference to a moment before an act of great consequence. The central idea underlying all these paintings is that of mankind on the brink of some momentous event. We gather from the artist's comments here quoted that this is synonymous with the sexual experience. The more specific reference to 'The Sirens' indicates that this time is very definitely pre-sexual; he does not stress a state of innocence but an instant when the victims have just become aware of the approaching event. Burne-Jones, in his letter to Leyland, emphasises the universality of his theme and also reveals the disillusion inherent in it. The same disillusion is portrayed in the sequel to 'Venus Concordia', 'Venus Discordia', in which he shows the angry result of Cupid's awakening.

Completing the sequence of pregnant moments is the artist's magnum opus, 'The Sleep of King Arthur in Avalon'. After receiving mortal wounds, Arthur is borne off by three queens to Avalon. There, the legend has it, he would lie, waiting for a summons calling him to rise and once again perform his acts of faith in the world. Here the moment is prolonged and there is no immediate indication of its conclusion. Silence is as much the subject of the painting as Arthur himself. Whereas the lateral movement in 'The Briar Rose' suggests the impending union, its absence in 'Avalon', and the sequence of dislocated verticals (the queens and the architecture), are vehicles for expressing the unresolved moment, whilst at the same time they intensify the stillness. The artist has mirrored in his structure the substance of his narrative. The only area where he has permitted any concentration of rhythms is at the centre where they form a cocoon around the sleeping king. This area also has the brightest colour in a painting, whose tone is generally subdued, in keeping with its funereal subject.

Originally, in 1881, George Howard commissioned the painting to hang in his library at Naworth Castle. When he understood how important it had become to the artist he relinquished his claim. In its stead he accepted a large relief panel 'Flodden Field', executed by Edgar Boehm R.A. from a design by Burne-Jones, to hang in its place. Because of its size, a studio was taken specially for 'Avalon' in the Campden Hill Road, but only a little progress was made until it was again moved to his studio at Rottingdean. Later, in September 1897, when he needed to be able to stand well back to see the total effect, it was again moved to a studio rented exclusively for it. The design underwent many changes. When it was first planned it was in the form of a triptych. On either side 'Hill Fairies' watched, naked, for the signs that would indicate the time for Arthur to awake. They were fleshly, Michaelangelesque figures, out of sympathy with the later conception. Consequently, he removed them, reducing the reference to this part of the story to the three girls standing at the outer limits of the composition. Also dropped from the final plan was the idea of showing a battle raging not far from the cloister where Arthur lies. In enlarging the architecture which is so important in creating the solemn atmosphere, a rocky partition dividing the central portion from the outside world had to be removed; in doing so the overall design became much simpler and more effective. He also experimented with a composition containing all the queens and attendants standing, but these tended to dwarf the king, and he rearranged them into their former pattern.

The vicissitudes in the history of the painting over a period of seventeen years indicate how important the artist held it to be. When not actually engaged upon painting it—it was

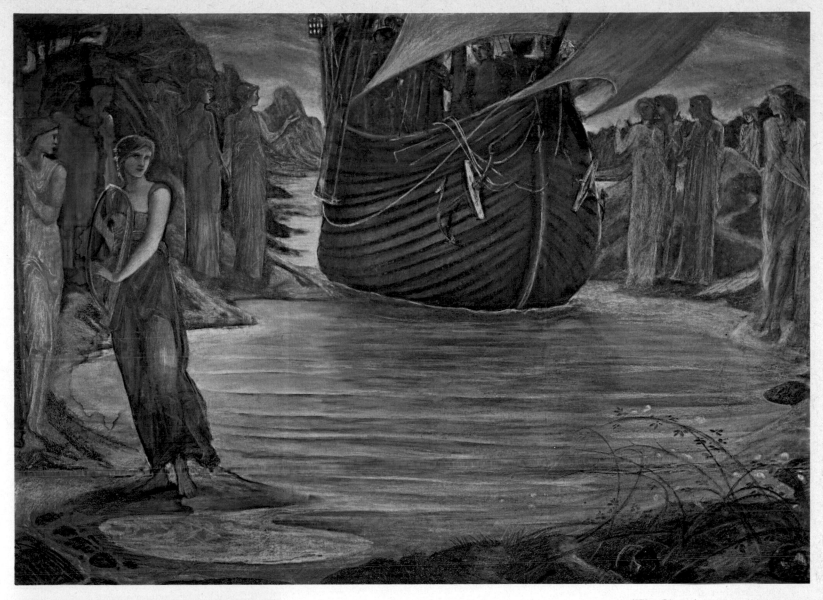

41. 'The Sirens', c. 1875 (and worked on later), pastel, 67 × 92½; private Collection, Spain. A full-scale study for the unfinished oil is in the Ringling Collection, Sarasota, Florida; another large study is in the National Gallery of South Africa, Cape Town.

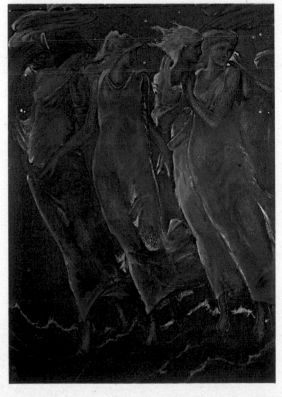

42. 'Nymphs of the Stars', 1896, gouache and gold, 13 × 10; the National Museum of Wales, Cardiff.

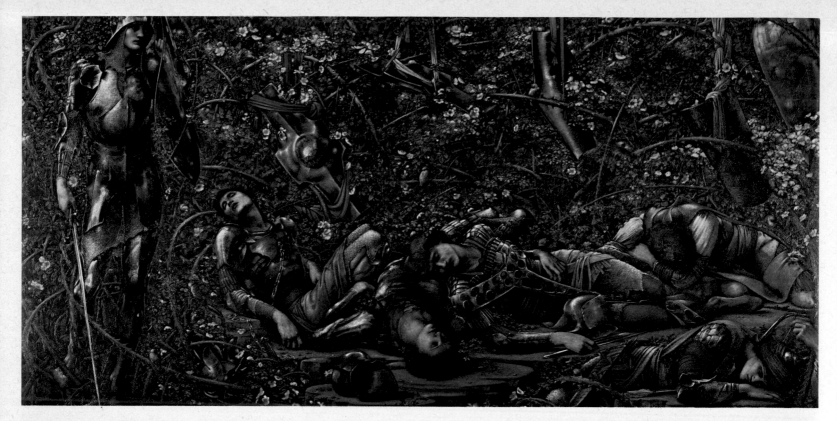

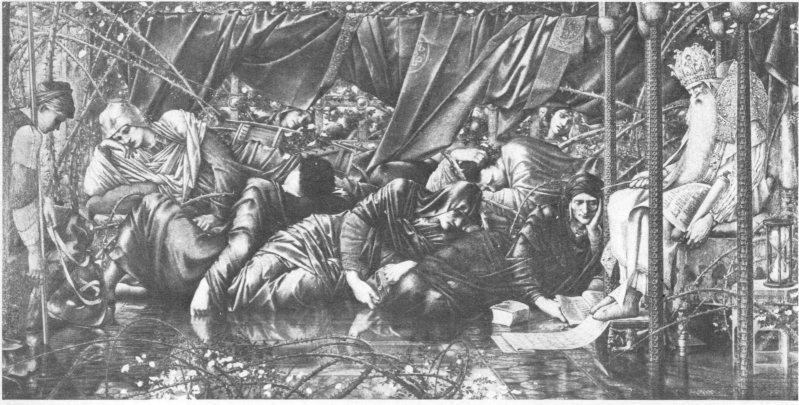

43. 'The Briar Rose' Series, 1: 'The Prince Enters
the Briar Wood', 1870-90, oil on canvas, 48 × 98;
Faringdon Collection Trust, Buscot Park,
Faringdon, Berkshire.

43a. 'The Briar Rose: The Council Chamber',
1871-90, oil on canvas, 48 ×94; Faringdon Collection
Trust, Buscot Park, Faringdon, Berkshire.

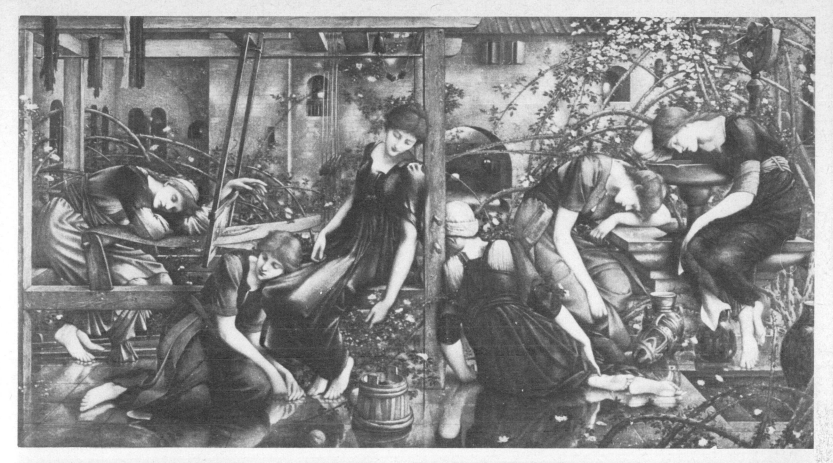

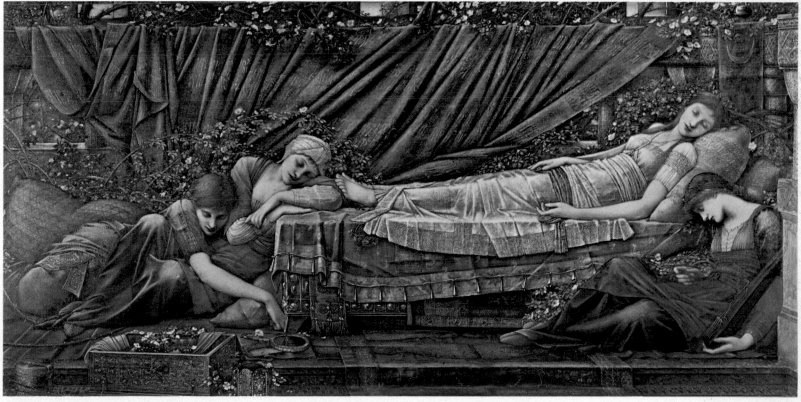

43b. 'The Briar Rose: The Rose Bower', 1870-90, oil on canvas, 48×94; Faringdon Collection Trust, Buscot Park, Faringdon, Berkshire. There is a second version, mostly by assistants, in the Bristol Art Gallery.

44. 'The Briar Rose' Series 4: 'The Sleeping Beauty', 1870-90, oil on canvas, 48 × 90; The Faringdon Collection Trust, Buscot Park, Faringdon, Berkshire.

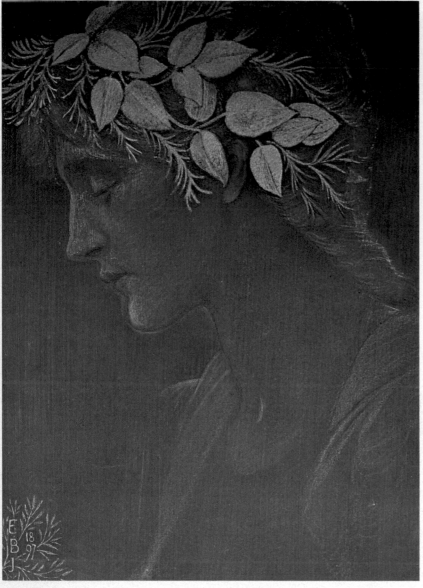

45. 'Girl's Head', 1897, gouache and gold paint on purple paper, 13½ × 9½, Fulham Library, London.

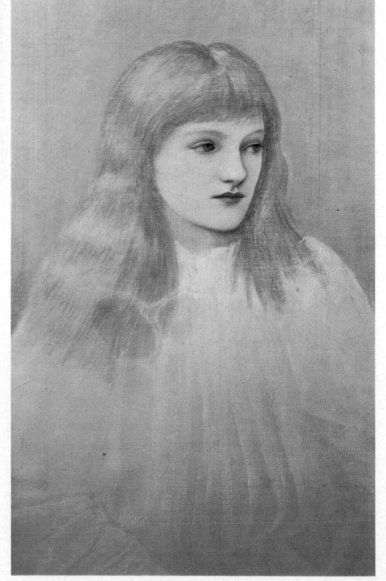

46. 'Portrait of Cecily Horner, *c.* 1895, oil on canvas; private collection, England. The art of portraiture is not considered Burne-Jones's forte, but this superb example is as great as any of the period.

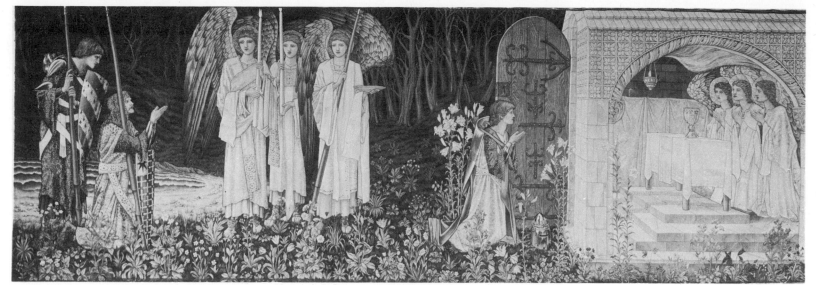

left for long periods during the eighties—Burne-Jones made numerous studies of details and design variants. After 1890, when his large works were not selling and it would have been more profitable had he concentrated on smaller things, he became even more determined to finish it. As much as three days a week were set aside for work on it. At this time, both he and Morris began to anticipate death. Morris is quoted as having said to his friend, 'The best way of lengthening out the rest of our days now, old chap, is to finish off old things.' There was an air of approaching finality at this time which invaded the painting whose theme is sleep in death. The similarity between 'Arthur' and the artist is obvious, and the painting is autobiographical in nature. Both have battled against an alien world, both cherished an ideal and remained true to it; Arthur lies attended by beautiful young women, a situation which aptly mirrors Burne-Jones's delight in such company. His identification with the sixth-century hero went as far as unconsciously adopting Arthur's position when he himself slept, and he frequently referred to the painting as a place—'I am at Avalon, not yet in Avalon.' Another letter quotes the address as Avalon. In his final and greatest work, Burne-Jones has transcended the barriers between Art and Life, and Life and Death. In dying when he did, during the painting's final stages, he moved from Life into Art; he became immortal.

In the eighties and nineties painting and the theatre almost began to overlap in the work of Leighton, Tadema, and Burne-Jones; the large canvases they produced, with life-sized figures, created an environment into which the viewer felt as if he could actually pass, into the world of painting. Approaching one of these large works, one experiences such a powerful impression of its sheer size, that it becomes a total experience in such a way that it easily becomes possible to see that such artists were anticipating the cinema, even the wide-screen panoramas. Co-operation between these artists and the theatre was inevitable; Alma Tadema designed costume and scenery for Sir Henry Irving's productions of *Cymbeline* and *Coriolanus* which were followed later by Beerbohm Tree's *Hypatia* and *Julius Caesar*. Burne-Jones contributed the designs for costumes and settings for Comyns Carr's *King Arthur* produced at the Lyceum under Sir Henry Irving in the Autumn of 1894. Irving commissioned this work originally from a Mr Wills, who produced such an unsatisfactory play that Irving asked Carr, who was then manager of the Lyceum, to write a new one. On being asked to contribute to the production, Burne-Jones willingly agreed and set to work designing armour, dresses, furniture, and settings. He took great delight in the scene-painters' activities, admiring the large scale; it was almost as if he had moved into one of his own paintings. Sadly, the settings were all destroyed in a fire on their return from a tour of America, and nothing remains today, so that the list and short descriptions he made in a small sketchbook are invaluable in reconstructing his designs:

1st. prologue—excalibur Arthur & Merlin coming down—a limitless meer, a high rock & path down which they come—rocks & rocks

231. 'The Achievement of Sir Galahad, accompanied by Sir Bors and Sir Perceval', tapestry, 1894, private collection
The flowers were designed by J. H. Dearle.

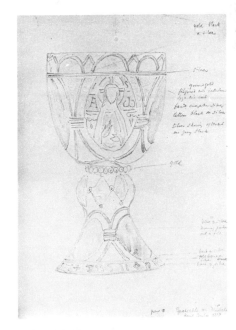

232. Chalice, with details of colours and metals used in its construction. Pencil drawing from a sketchbook, c. 1890. Birmingham City Museum & Art Gallery
This type of chalice is used in the 'Achievement' tapestry.

1st. scene—chamber in Arthur's court—closed interior—no outlook—Audience chamber & Guinevere bower—an upper chamber—a window at back through which Elaine can look down & see knights assembling to go on graal—principal feature is window which Elaine may throw open chamber by entrance on both sides

Last scene—great hall at Camelot—a broad high opening & knights riding by as in Laus Veneris—a big dais & throne—knights filing past while the king persuades Launcelot to stay—open air outside is essential—door on stage right—no door on left

Act 2—Queen's Maying

Act 3—Chamber above river—little chapel to left as you look at stage for her body. The rest of the stage is a heavy roofed loggia—with a parapet & view of the winding river

In the middle of the loggia are steps up which the knights come bearing the body

Act 4—poison scene—with guarded window at back which changes to last scene of 1st. Act.

Sir Arthur Sullivan wrote music to accompany the play and was so inspired by the production that he asked Comyns Carr to adapt it into a libretto for an opera. However, he was prevented from continuing with the idea by his failing health.

After all the preparation, Burne-Jones was disappointed and described his feelings in a letter to his friend Mary Gaskell:

The armour is good—they have taken pains with it—made in Paris & well understood—I wish we were not barbarians here. The dresses were well enough if the actors had known how to wear them—one scene I made very pretty—of the wood in Maytime—that has gone to nothing—fir trees which I hate instead of beeches & birches which I love—why?—never mind.

The architecture will do—& the furniture—but mostly the armour is good—and Perceval looked the one romantic thing in it—it is enough for its purpose the whole thing.

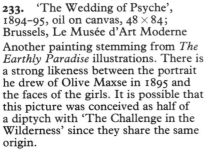

233. 'The Wedding of Psyche', 1894-95, oil on canvas, 48 × 84; Brussels, Le Musée d'Art Moderne
Another painting stemming from *The Earthly Paradise* illustrations. There is a strong likeness between the portrait he drew of Olive Maxse in 1895 and the faces of the girls. It is possible that this picture was conceived as half of a diptych with 'The Challenge in the Wilderness' since they share the same origin.

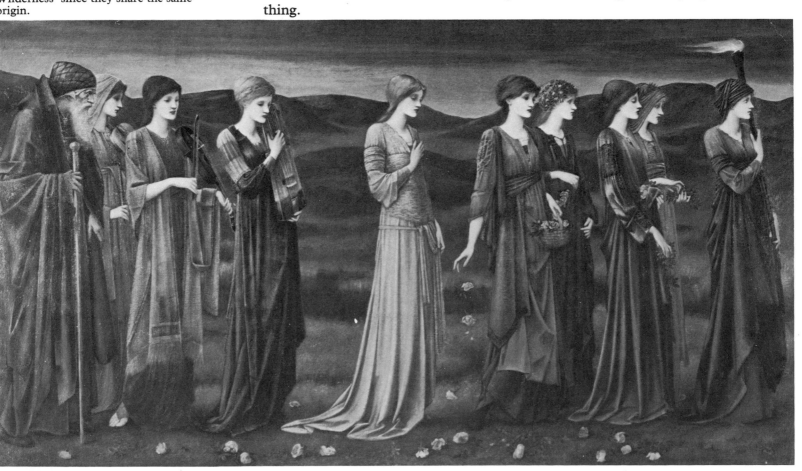

Merlin I designed carefully—they have set aside my designs and made him filthy & horrible—like a witch in Macbeth—from his voice I suspect him of being one of the witches—I hate the stage, dont tell—but I do—dont tell but I do but dont tell.

Perceval looks beautiful—some of them are terrible grays but I didnt design their faces did I? Such a careless artist did that—carried away perhaps by a morbid love of variety. . . .

Morgan le Fay is simply dreadful, you remember she is half divine in the ancient story—as Merlin is—here they are scandel mongering gossips. . . . The banners with the chalice on them looks nice.

This unique opportunity for working for the theatre, in which fantasy (however inadequately) became reality must have given him an exciting fulfilment, especially because he was working on the tapestries and 'Arthur in Avalon' at the same time. Always real to his mind, the figures reassuringly took on a material form to create a totality of experience.

In his last paintings Burne-Jones had finally achieved a high standard of professionalism. Once he had overcome his limitations, when his craft had become as developed as his intellect, then his mastery was assured. Every element of a painting was isolated from its context, carefully considered, and then either included or altered to fit into the artist's plan. For he was fully aware of both the nature and the role of his art:

'In my life, having found what is essential to it, I must keep to that only, penetrate and live deep down in it.'

The personal significance of his art, its necessity to his life, he fully understood. For him the creative act was consciously an introspective analysis:

'I mean by a picture a beautiful romantic dream of something that never was, never will be—in a light better than any light that ever shone—in a land no one can define, or remember, only desire (and then I wake up with the waking of Brynhild).'

This does not mean that his art is self-indulgent—a therapy for a man born out of his time. He believed that it was the duty of the artist to explore his inner life, deriving from the personal vision a concept of beauty to uplift and ennoble his fellow men. The act of creation was a religious and mystical experience:

'To me this weary, toiling, groaning world is none other than "Our Lady of Sorrows". . . . Art—the power of bringing God into the world . . . is giving back her child that was crucified to "Our Lady of Sorrows".'

An inherent problem in this type of painting is in converting the personal vision into one of universal significance without being esoteric. Burne-Jones overcame this by using

234. Detail of the Leyland Tomb in the Brompton Cemetery. F. R. Leyland died in 1893; for many years he had been an important patron of Rossetti and Burne-Jones. His collection included 'Phyllis and Demophöon', 'Day', 'Night', 'The Four Seasons', 'The Wine of Circe', and 'Mirror of Venus'.

235. Stage-set for the third act of the play 'King Arthur'. From a photograph in the possession of the Museum of British Theatre, London
The production was mounted at the Lydeum Theatre in January 1895. Henry Irving, a close friend of Burne-Jones, played the title role. Ellen Terry played Guinevere, and Forbes Robertson played Sir Launcelot.

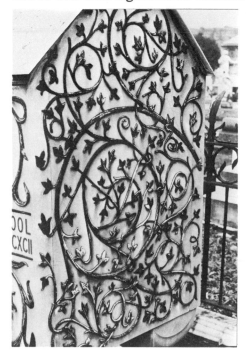

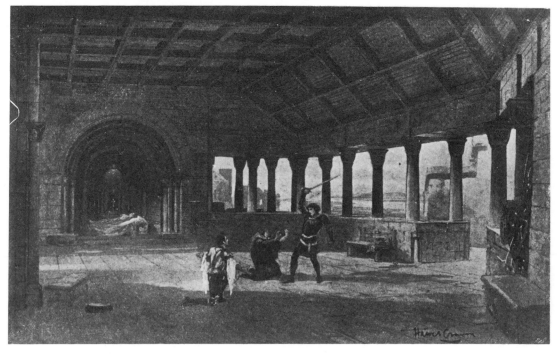

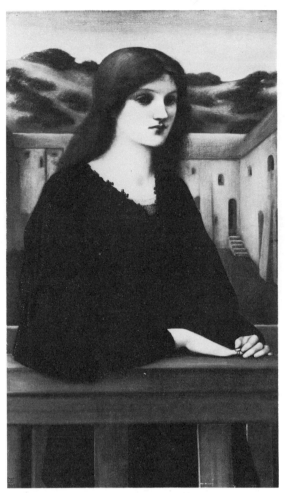

236. 'Vespertina Quies', 1893, oil on canvas, 42½ × 24½, Tate Gallery, London

Bessie Keene was the model. Maud Beddington, a young artist admirer, has described how Jones set about painting this picture: 'He began by drawing the figure in raw umber. I think that was done before I came. Then he modelled the face in white and raw umber, lightly putting a little red on the lips, nostrils, and eyes—the blue of the frock and all the strong colours were painted in sweeping strokes of full colour. He used a mixture of spike oil and turpentine as a medium. He used flat brushes to keep his canvas smooth. . . .' Clearly, both this picture and 'Depths of the Sea' owe a debt to Leonardo da Vinci for their ambiguous facial expressions.

archetypal situations and not leaning too heavily on the narrative source. No knowledge of the story is required for the paintings to be meaningful. They convey everything in terms of themselves, unlike the majority of narrative paintings of the period. All the elements combine into a unifying mood which is the real substance of the painting. Nature is used as a vehicle to convey an emotional state. It is used because of its universality as a language of images.

A further problem arose in deciding the amount of naturalism needed:

'One of the hardest things in the world is to determine how much realism is allowable in any particular picture. It is of so many different kinds too. For instance, I want a shield or a crown or a pair of wings or what not, to look real. Well, I make what I want or a model of it, and then make studies from that. So that what eventually gets on to the canvas is a reflection of a reflection of something purely imaginary.'

An accident of history placed Burne-Jones in the Pre-Raphaelite school. In fact, his aims are very different. As a pupil of Rossetti, the least Pre-Raphaelite of the group, he was unlikely to conform to their strictures. Such accurate observation of the multiplicity of nature never attracted him, even in early life. For a short time he enthusiastically drew natural objects in detail in the tradition, but from the mid-sixties he began eliminating those he considered irrelevant to concentrate upon an ideal type. Unlike Holman Hunt, he is not interested in an analysis of nature's physical appearance. The transition of emphasis from observation to interpretation parallels the development of Mannerism out of the Renaissance. John Shearman, in discussing the evolution of Mannerism, could equally be describing Burne-Jones's dissimilarities with the Brotherhood when he says:

'An insistently cultured grace and accomplishment is accompanied by the kindred qualities of abstraction from natural behaviour and appearances, bizarre fantasy, complexity and invention.'

Burne-Jones was perhaps thinking of Pre-Raphaelite realism when he wrote:

'Direct transcription from nature? I suppose that by the time the photographic artist can give us all the colours as correctly as the shapes, people will begin to find out that the

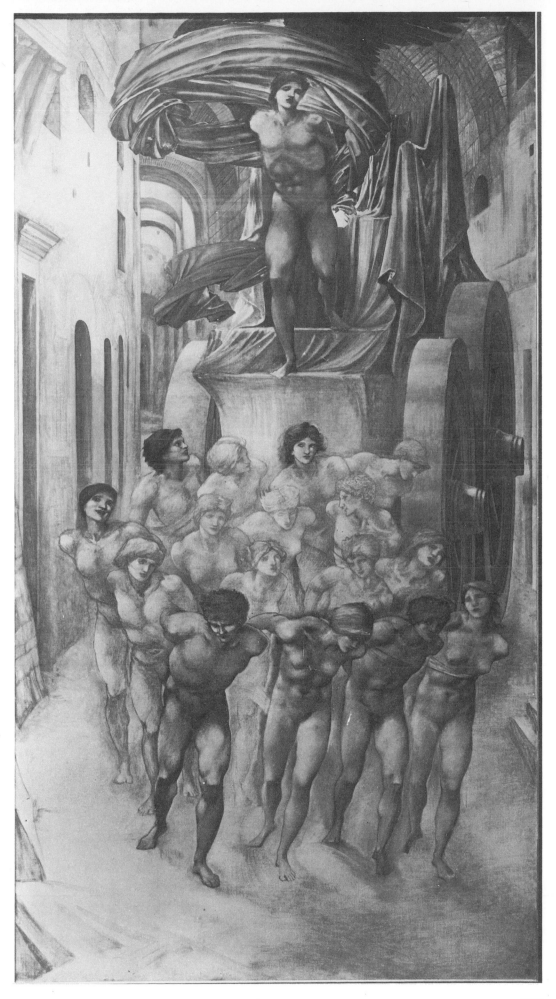

237. 'The Car of Love', begun in 1870, oil on canvas, *c.* 15ft by 6ft; Victoria & Albert Museum, London

A large design for this picture is in the Auckland Art Gallery, New Zealand. The streets down which the chariot rolls were based upon those in Siena, which the artist encountered on his stay there in 1871.

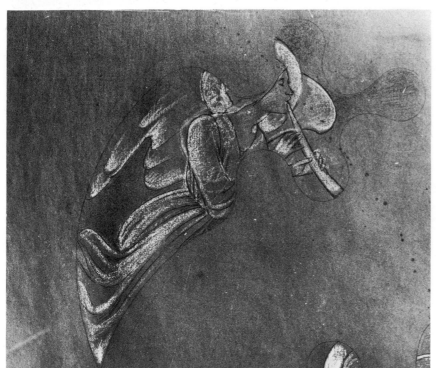

238. Angel Playing Shawm, detail of a cartoon for a tracery light in the Albion Congregational Church, 1893. Pencil and black, white and blue chalks on brown paper, (full size of cartoon) $47\frac{3}{4} \times 32\frac{3}{4}$, The Whitworth Art Gallery Manchester.

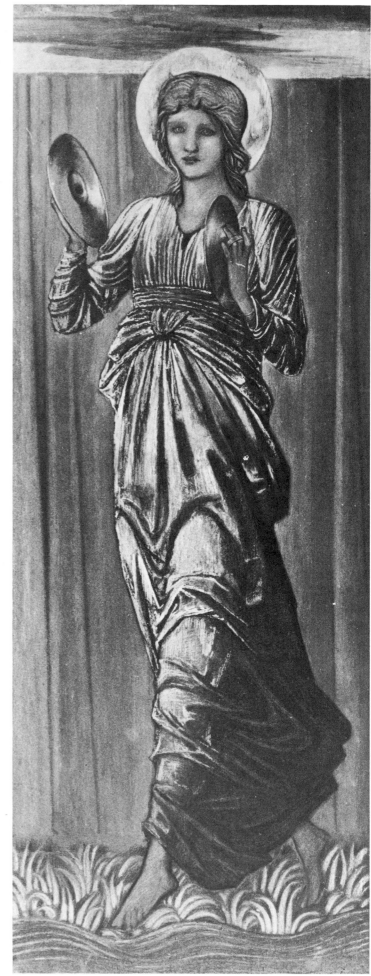

239. 'Miriam', cartoon for a panel in the north transept of Albion Congregational Church, Ashton-under-Lyme, Lancashire, 1895. Chalks, 62×23, Northampton Central Museum & Art Gallery

The same figure appears as 'Aurora' (Queensland Art Gallery, Brisbane, Australia; unfinished version, private collection, England). Occasionally Burne-Jones would work up a cartoon, such as this one, with the addition of the curtain background, white highlights and touches of gold, to make it more desirable to the art market.

realism they talk about isn't art at all but science.' This is another indication that he was not at all interested in the material world for its own sake and wished to leave that kind of literal observation to the scientists.

He has often been accused of not keeping close enough to natural substance, of taking liberties with anatomical details, especially in the women he painted. But in art of the kind he chose it would appear ridiculous to paint any other than that which represented his ideal. His women figures should not be judged by their relation to reality, but by their successful integration into the work of art itself, their contribution towards the mood, and their vitality as Art.

Beautiful women had played an important part in the art of his earlier years—the *femme fatale* first appeared in 'The Beguiling of Merlin' in 1857—but as he grew older they more frequently figured in both his art and his life. In the nineties his friendships became increasingly important as the memory of his own youth grew dim.

'There are two kinds of women I like, the very good—the golden haired, and the exceedingly mischievous—the sirens with oat coloured hair. Perfect snips they are.'

His relationships with young women were of a tender, platonic nature, encouraging them in their youthful whims, and with gentle humour he often gave avuncular advice. A letter to Olive Maxse indicates the tone of his friendship:

'A certain kind of silly rubbish has always helped me, deep down, as we are all face to face with enough solemnity—we can guess that much of each other with certainty even if we know nothing—so I shall be silly till you want me to be sad and then you shall have all the sadness that is in me.'

When Olive told the artist that her fellow students at the Académie Julian in Paris detected a similarity between her features and a Burne-Jones drawing, he replied, obviously pleased:

'Those students at Julian's conceived a high ideal of me if they think they are at all like any heads I paint—I hope it's a little true—for I think you beautiful—and an old artist may tell a young girl that without hurt or blame—and when you come back I shall claim my privilege of drawing from you.'

Besides Olive Maxse and her sister, Burne-Jones was on familiar terms with Judith Blunt, Cicely and Frances Horner, Katherine Lewis, Amy Gaskell and Frances Stanhope, to name only a few; but above all he loved his daughter Margaret whose enchantingly beautiful face he used as a model for 'The Sleeping Beauty'. In surrounding himself with female beauty he created a situation in his life which exactly corresponded with his portrayal of Arthur as he sleeps in Avalon.

Throughout his life he had made exaggerated claims for his own antiquity, particularly as each birthday approached, but it was now becoming a reality. He saw in the liveliness of young women the optimism of his own youth, which through experience he knew would prove ephemeral. In drawing and painting them, therefore, he sought to capture it. His solution was to intensify the transience by not only portraying the youth and beauty of his models, but also by gently animating the features as though catching them whilst their attention was aroused for a moment. In doing this, he emphasises the element of time, turning our attention back to the elusiveness of youth.

The drawings gradually changed from being studies for larger works to become complete in themselves. Nominally they remained studies for particular works, 'The Sirens', 'The Car of Love', 'The Hill Fairies' etc., but it is obvious from their completeness that they are something in addition. These late drawings show the benefit of a lifetime's experience in the handling of media. Textures produced by charcoal, crayon, pencil, and pastel are all recognised and used for their intrinsic characteristics. His technique varies with each one, but they all show an acute sensitivity to the positioning of a line or mass within the framework of paper. Whatever his subject, his first consideration is how to express it in terms of the medium.

The Kelmscott Press began printing its first trial pages in January 1891. It represents a fulfilment of Morris's and Burne-Jones's hitherto frustrated attempts at book production dating from their days at Oxford. Burne-Jones's first important commission from Archi-

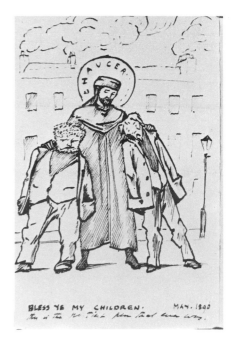

240. 'Bless Ye My Children', May 1896, pen and ink, from a photograph (present whereabouts unknown). Chaucer holds figures of Burne-Jones and Morris. Made to celebrate the completion of the Kelmscott Press *Chaucer*.

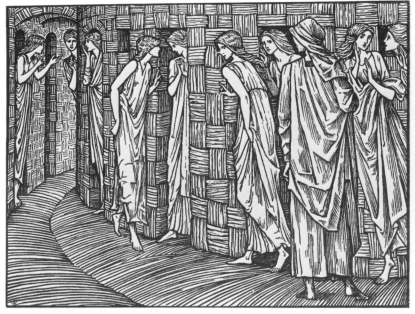

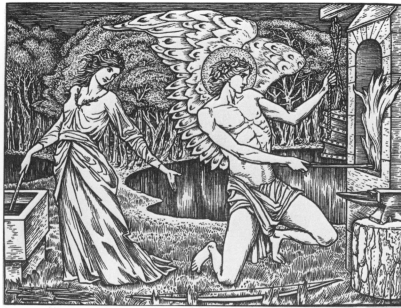

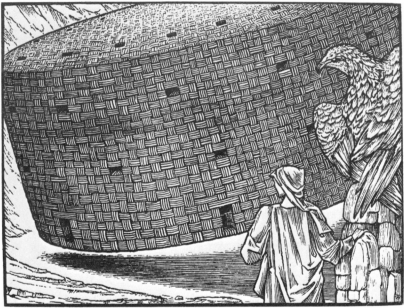

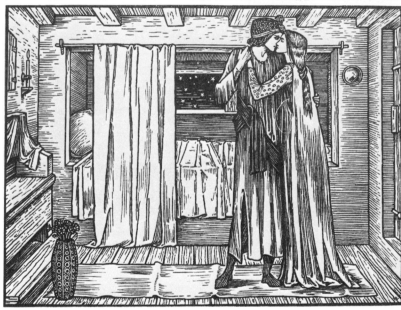

241-44. Four illustrations from the Kelmscott Press *Chaucer*, 1895, wood engravings cut by W. H. Hooper. (a) 'Cupid and Delight', illustration to 'The Assemblie of Fowles', the design is a reinterpretation of the early picture, 'The Forge Of Cupid'; (b) 'Troilus and Creseyde'; (c) and (d) 'The House of Fame'.

bald Maclaren in 1854, had consisted of book illustration for his *Fairy Family*, but like the subsequent *Earthly Paradise*, *Fors Clavigera*, and *Virgil* designs, for various reasons, it did not reach the printing stage. This renewed interest began in November 1888, when Morris helped Emery Walker prepare his lecture on printing to be given to the Arts and Crafts Society. He was inspired to begin designing type, and in 1888 and 1889 his *House of Wolfings* and *The Roots of the Mountains* were printed at the Chiswick Press in a type which he designed, based upon an old Basel fount. At the same time he had begun again to collect medieval books; two of these, Leonard of Arezzo's *History of Florence*, printed at Venice by Jacobus Rubens in 1476 and Jenson's *Pliny*, also printed in that year, proved the inspiration for the first type he invented for the Kelmscott Press. Having mastered their form by studying enlarged photographs of pages from them, he designed the Golden type. Later, he designed the Troy type, which, although based upon a medieval precursor, owes less to it than the Golden type. By enlarging it he arrived at the third of his important types, the Chaucer. Morris was not only responsible for the type, but the design and decorative borders, and capitals, the layout of the page, and the general presentation of the book.

The first Kelmscott Press book to use an illustration by Burne-Jones was *A Dream of John Ball and A King's Lesson*, dated 13th May and issued 24th September 1892. However, the drawing 'When Adam delved and Eve Span' was not designed especially for the Kelmscott Press edition, it had been used in an earlier edition of 1888, appearing as a line block. *The Golden Legend* by Jacopus de Voragine was in fact the first to have original

162

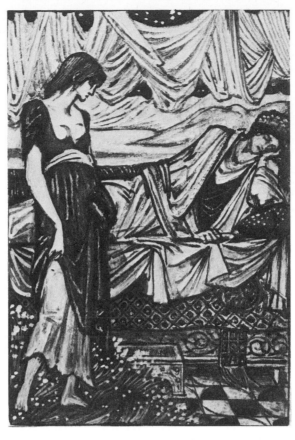

245. 'Azais and Pharamond', 1897, watercolour, $8\frac{1}{4} \times 5\frac{1}{2}$; William Morris Gallery, Walthamstow
A preliminary sketch for the illustration to Morris's *Love is Enough*, the Kelmscott Press edition.

designs by Burne-Jones. The two illustrations were not engraved until August 1892, eighteen months after the founding of the Press; they are both contained in the first only of three volumes. Beside this imbalance there is other evidence to show that the book was not as successful as those that were to follow. The illustrations pay more attention to drawing of details than to a two-dimensional texture and the handling of the masses within the overall pattern gives a fragmented impression. There were most probably six illustrations planned for *The Golden Legend*, but in his enthusiasm to complete it Morris did not wait for the artist to prepare them. Burne-Jones often held up the book in hand, presumably through pressure of other work, as the following extracts from letters of Sir Sidney Cockerell—secretary to the Press—show:

'Oct. 4th 1894, Sir E. Burne-Jones has not yet furnished us with the illustrations for Jason.

'Oct. 30th 1894, The book is nearly all printed but Sir E. Burne-Jones has not yet supplied the illustrations.

'Feb. 8th 1895, Sir Percival is to have a picture by Sir E. Burne-Jones and though it is nearly printed, this will delay it.'

When Burne-Jones was satisfied with a design he passed it to Catterson Smith, who worked over it in black ink and chinese white, condensing it, under the supervision of the master, into a firmly linear structure which was suitable for converting into a wood block. After Burne-Jones had once again inspected this ink drawing, W. H. Hooper would finally cut the design into the block, proofs were taken from it, and once again these were subjected to Burne-Jones's scrutiny. A complex process, but one which ensured maximum expression of the artist's aims and occupied a minimum amount of his time.

The later illustrations show a growth in mastery of the medium which finds its perfect expression in the three important late books, *The Works of Chaucer*, *The Story of Sigurd the Volsung*, and *Love is Enough*. Although Morris considered *Sigurd* his most accomplished book, which it certainly is from the bibiophile point of view, the crowning achievement, as far as Burne-Jones is concerned, is the *Chaucer*, the most important since it contains eighty-seven designs by him. Each Sunday for two and a half years from 1893–95 he spent working on it. This would account for the delay in making drawings for the other books, as *Chaucer* meant more to him than almost anything else.

In a letter of December 1894, to Charles Eliot Norton, Burne-Jones's willingness to submit to the discipline of book illustration, Morris style, is apparent:

> And so you don't like Chaucer—that is very sad—for I am beside myself with delight over it. I am making the designs as much to fit the ornament and the printing as they are made to fit the little pictures—and I love to be snugly cased in the borders and buttressed up by the vast initials—and once or twice when I have no letter under me, I feel tottery and weak; if you drag me out of my encasings it will be like tearing a statue out of its niche and putting it into a museum—indeed when the book is done, if we live to finish it, it will be like a pocket cathedral—so full of design and I think Morris the greatest master of ornament in the world—and to have the highest taste in all things. . . .

Morris, in turn, reciprocated the admiration and would not allow any of the drawings to be printed outside the context for which they were designed. They did have an idea that perhaps some of the drawings could be made on a large scale and sold cheaply to enable poorer people to have access to good prints, but for reasons outlined above it was inevitable that the scheme should not come to fruition. Morris outlined his ideas on book design in a short essay *A Note by William Morris On His Aims in Founding the Kelmscott Press*. He says:

> I began printing books with the hope of producing some which would have a definite claim to beauty, while at the same time they should be easy to read and should not dazzle the eye or trouble the intellect of the reader by eccentricity of form in the letters. . . . I found I had to consider chiefly the following things: the paper, the form of the type, the relative spacing of the letters, the words and the lines; and lastly the position of the printed matter on the page. . . . It was only natural that I, a decorator by profession, should attempt to ornament my books suitably: about this matter, I will only say that I have always tried to keep in mind the necessity for making my decoration a part of the page of type. I may add that in designing the magnificent

246 & 247. 'David Lamenting', 'David Consoled', formerly in the east window of St Cuthbert's Church, Newcastle upon Tyne. The Laing Art Gallery, Newcastle upon Tyne
They were painted at the time of Morris's death, in 1896, and Burne-Jones poured his feelings into them.

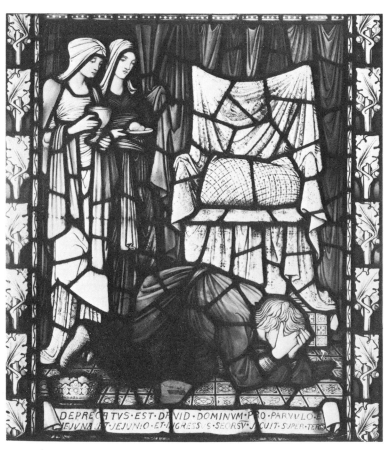

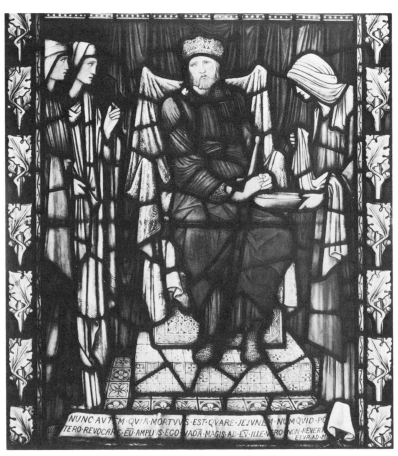

and inimitable woodcuts which have adorned several of my books, and will above all adorn the Chaucer which is now drawing near completion, my friend Sir Edward Burne-Jones had never lost sight of this important point, so that his work will not only give us a series of most beautiful and imaginative pictures, but form the most harmonious decoration possible to the printed book.

Burne-Jones was able to move into the discipline because his art was very much in a two-dimensional idiom already. His profound instinct for the capabilities of line and texture were ideally suited to the kind of illustration required by Morris. Whilst basing his imagery on natural form, the abstract nature of his art is given full play: at the same time it utilises with great virtuosity the possibilities of a black and white medium. Within the flat area his development of line and texture is somewhat akin to that of music. Often he creates a grid of trellised verticals (trees or pillars), against which in counterpoint, he makes dancing, erratic or smoothly flowing rhythms (flames, draperies, wings), The balance between black, white, and the intermediate greys is equally controlled, and they combine with his line to impart a uniformity quite in sympathy with Morris's surrounding decoration.

Of the eighty-seven designs in the *Chaucer*, twelve are related to earlier ones. Bearing in mind the differing media, nothing shows more clearly Burne-Jones's evolution from his early 'Gothic' to his later 'aesthetic' style than a comparison between the early work and the designs based on it. The illustration showing Chaucer lying, dreaming of the Good Women, was originally a watercolour dating from 1865. The dark mood and 'flemish' draperies are replaced by elegance and a fluid, linear arabesque; the earlier design figures a few martyrs, placed simply, in a row, behind Alceste and Cupid, whilst in the illustration the martyrs are used to make a complex, asymmetrical pattern in counterpoint with a massive, bare landscape. For many of the illustrations the artist places his characters in bizarre situations, in haunting, unpopulated landscapes where they appear hopelessly isolated. Often, particularly in 'Troilus and Cresseda', the last to be completed, the world is physically crumbling or in the process of fantastic change. In an attempt to escape from this alien place the maidens give way to a frenzied dance. Others, immobile, accept the judgement of Fate. All these features, together with the plants that twist and writhe in a hostile world, imbued with an unearthly calm, anticipate the work of the Surrealists. They,

248. 'Love and the Pilgrim', 1896–97, oil on canvas, 62 × 120, Tate Gallery, London
Burne-Jones dedicated this painting to Swinburne.

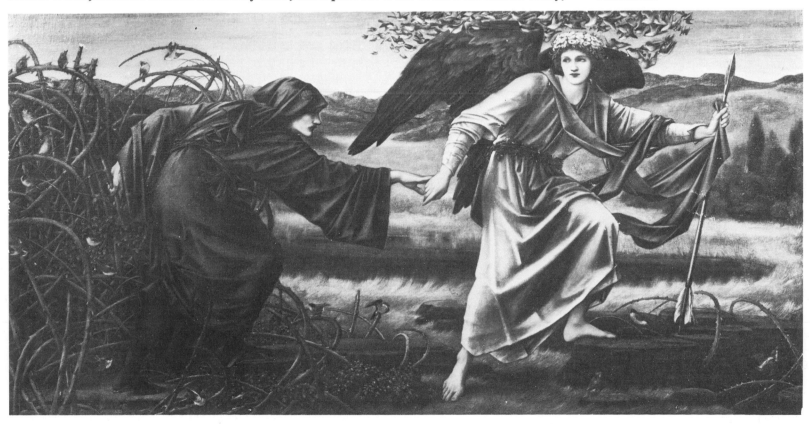

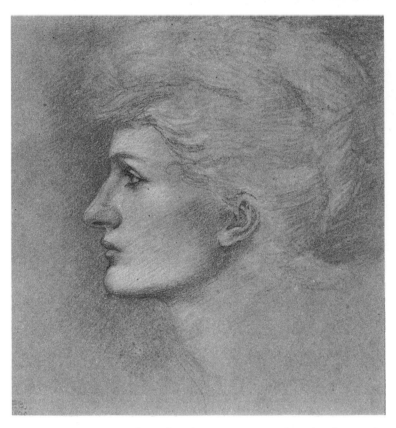

249. Portrait of Kate Dolan, 1896, coloured chalks, 18 × 11¾; private collection.

too, drew upon the imagination, to exaggerate the fantastic aspects of nature.

Once again a scheme to produce Morris's *Cupid and Psyche* illustrated with the woodcuts made for it in the sixties, was foiled. In January 1897 trial pages of text with a single illustration were set up at the Kelmscott Press and it was intended to issue an edition with all fifty-two designs. Morris had died in 1896 and when the Press had fulfilled all its outstanding commitments, early in 1898, it closed down. Then it was arranged that the book should be printed at the Chiswick Press and published by Longmans, Green and Company, but this was prevented by Burne-Jones's death in June 1898. For the same reason a similar edition of *The Ring Given to Venus* using the illustrations, slightly altered from the same source, was finally interrupted.

These excursions into projects originating in their youth frequently occupied Morris and Burne-Jones together during the period from 1890. They had been on less intimate terms for a time when Morris was actively engaged upon propagating his form of socialism, during the eighties; Burne-Jones was unable to accept his friend's views. Together, they returned to those books about which they were enthusiastic as young men—Malory's *Morte d'Arthur* and Chaucer. As we have seen, one result was the Kelmscott *Chaucer*, another was *The Quest of The Holy Grail* tapestries. Morris and Company had received a commission from the Australian mining millionaire, W. K. D'Arcy, to furnish his house, Stanmore Hall, near Uxbridge. It had a large dining room and Morris persuaded him to make use of tapestry to cover the walls. On undertaking to decorate the room in this way, Morris asked Burne-Jones to draw cartoons for a series based on the Holy Grail legend. The set consisted of five large panels, a smaller one of a ship, and a dado of verdure with the knights' shields hanging from the trees. The five scenes were as follows:

The Knights of the Round Table summoned to the Quest by a strange Damsel.
The Arming and Departure of the Knights.
The Failure of Sir Lancelot.
The Failure of Sir Gawaine.
The Achievement by Sir Galahad Accompanied by Sir Bors, and Sir Perceval.

They took a number of years to execute, the first was completed in 1894. Three panels were repeated for Laurence Hodson in 1895–96; the set was repeated for D'Arcy's

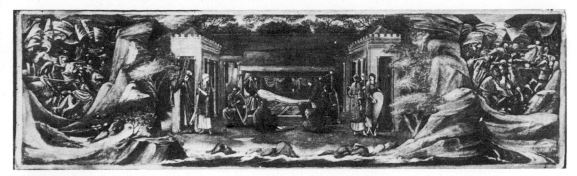

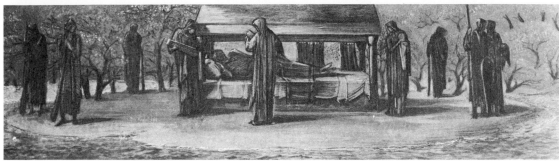

250. Modello for 'Arthur in Avalon' from a photograph, 1894

A further development in the evolution of the design was the inclusion of battle scenes in the wings, but it was soon rejected on the grounds of its causing the work to lose its grandeur and sense of repose.

251. Modello for 'Arthur in Avalon', *c.* 1890, pastel, 21 × 75; The National Museum of Wales, Cardiff

At first the idea was to stress the nature of Avalon as an island. Compared with the final version, this sketch has greater solemnity and is more elemental.

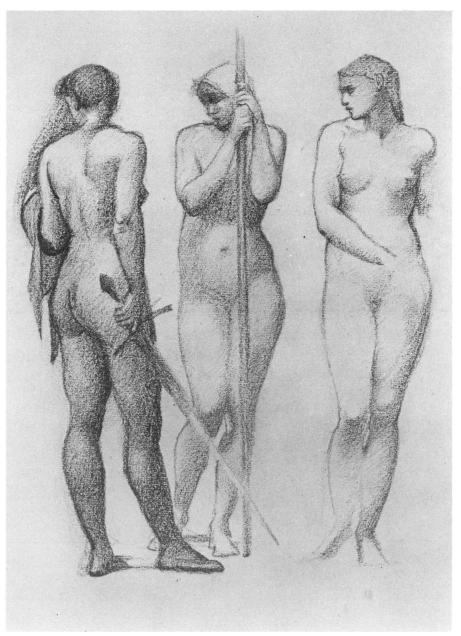

252. Nude studies for the attendant figures in 'Arthur in Avalon', *c.* 1890, 13 × 9½; Museo de Arte, Ponce, Puerto Rico.

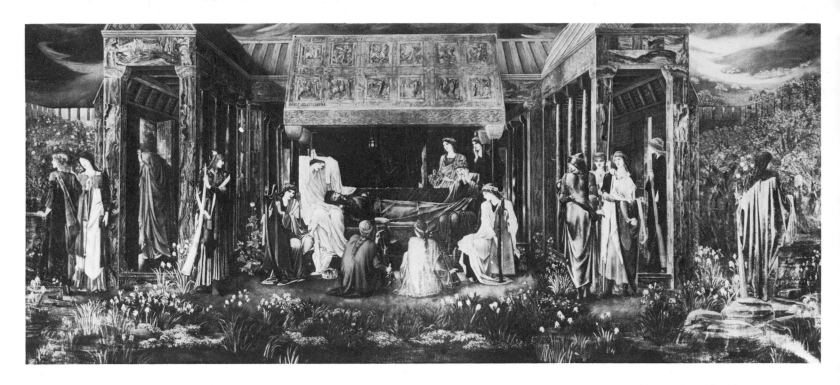

253. 'Arthur in Avalon', 1881–98, oil on canvas, 111 × 254; Museo de Arte, Ponce, Puerto Rico

Burne-Jones's masterpiece. The master has finally succeeded in joining the world of his imagination. The scenes above the bier are from the Quest of the Holy Grail.

mining partner, George McCulloch in 1898. After this, D'Arcy bought the cartoons to prevent any more versions being made; years later his widow sold them back to the firm and a further two subjects were woven in 1927 for H. Beecham of Lympne Castle.

J. H. Dearle was responsible for the profusion of foreground flowers, except for the symbolic white lilies, which have burst into flower where Lancelot kneels. It seems that Burne-Jones was less able to create the flatness on a large scale, which he deemed necessary, since in comparison the tapestries are less flat than the small-scale illustrations to Chaucer. They do succeed as tapestries because of the emphatic frontality and reduction of perspective. The trees are once again used as a means of conveying the peculiarly intense atmosphere, especially in 'The Failure of Sir Lancelot', where they create a sense of magic unreality. The design of this scene, it is interesting to note, is very similar to Rossetti's version in the Oxford mural series of 1857, although in reverse, and Burne-Jones must have found it more interesting than the others, as he converted the design into a painting in 1896.

St Philip's Cathedral, Birmingham, is fortunate in possessing the most important stained glass (1897) made in the final period of Burne-Jones's life. In the west window is a design showing the Angel of Judgement blowing her trumpet; it consists of three units, the people on earth, the angel who links them with Christ in Glory surrounded by angels. There is great clarity in this tripartite design, made effective once again by the distinct two-dimensionality. Colour also contributes a major part to its success; Christ in yellow robes is surrounded by angels in red ones. The Angel of Judgement is part of this circle, but as she is placed on a diagonal axis she is initially the most prominent part of the window. Her figure leads both up to the Glory of Christ and down to the people below. Her red robes are set dramatically against the brown area which represents the world in the chaos of destruction. Arguably the focal point of the composition, her feet have a most arresting silhouette and are the nexus of the top and bottom parts. The populace at the base of the design turn their gaze towards the angel; their colour is less prominent than the upper figures, and the direction of the lines of drapery is upwards, leading to the angel and Christ. Salvation is the theme of the window; symbolically, the colours, blazing reds and yellows, proclaim this, and the lines, smoothly flowing, create a mood of relative calm. The aspect of destruction is deliberately played down; the crumbling world is very much a brown setting for the figures, and there is almost a total absence of aggressive linear movement. It is interesting to compare the Last Judgement window at Easthampstead, designed in 1874, with the one at Birmingham. This was one of the earliest windows to attempt to spread a picture across the lancets. The impression is balanced, but fragment-

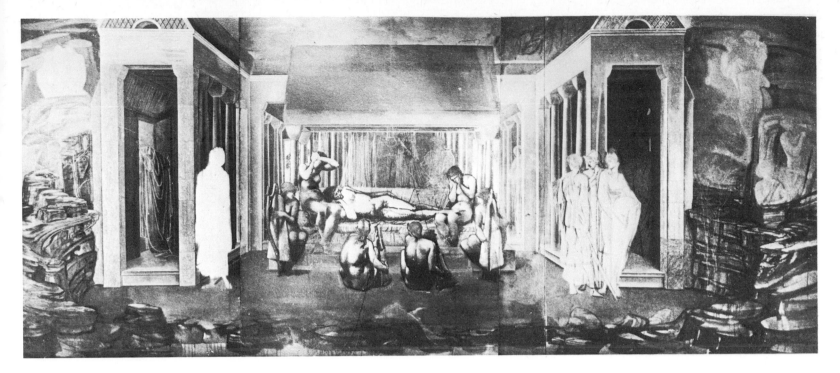

ary, and judgement is emphasised rather than salvation. The figures on earth are much smaller than those in heaven and they are more obviously suffering; the Archangel Michael as judge plays an important part in the design whilst Christ, as Dies Domini, plays a lesser part in the uppermost light. The most significant difference, however, is that of scale. At Easthampstead the figures are small and numerous, being dwarfed by the size of the windows, but at Birmingham they dominate the setting and the onlooker.

At Hawarden in Flintshire is a four-light window portraying the Nativity. It was designed in the autumn of 1897 and erected the following year by Gladstone's children, who presented the window to the church in commemoration of their father's 'long and splendid life'. Like the window in Birmingham Cathedral, Burne-Jones was responsible for the colour since they both date from after Morris's death and he felt the commissions too important to be left to the workshop. Production of the window involved paying visits to Merton Abbey, a painful reminder of the absence of Morris. The resulting window is a sweet and gentle thing with a row of child angels kneeling before the reclining figure of the Virgin; at the sides are adoring Magi and Shepherds. Completing the group of surrounding figures is a row of angels beyond the mother and child; they link with the others into a rectangular design which extends across the four windows. In a way similar to that of the Birmingham window the figures are all positioned at the same distance from the onlooker, and the window is interpreted as a vertical plane. Another feature it has in common with the Last Judgement at Birmingham is that the focal point is a diagonal figure placed in a central position, in a composition that is primarily upright.

These late windows demonstrate how Burne-Jones was able to utilise the medium of stained glass to its maximum effect. He treated it in these, his most successful of the period, as narrative in terms of colour and flatness. The story is explained simply and without recourse to a detailed knowledge of biblical detail; in simplifying the design he allows colour to take priority, and this he ensures by artful juxtaposition. There are signs of a re-interpretation of the role of stained-glass in certain of the very last windows Burne-Jones created (Albion Congregational Church, Ashton under Lyne 1895, Hawarden Parish Church 1898). Whereas, the earlier examples relate to the architectural setting in a distinctly planar fashion and by the generally central placing of the figures, these windows dissolve the flatness by creating an illusionary area beyond. The effect is brought about by increasing the size of the tracery angels so that they are larger than the light they occupy and by allowing the frame to cut into the figures in a startling manner. When viewing the window, the worshipper experiences angels floating past, as though Paradise was a short distance away, or at least a miraculous manifestation of angels was taking place.

169

254. Photograph of 'Arthur in Avalon' in progress by Frederick Hollyer
After abandoning the idea of including a battle, Burne-Jones tried making the work into a triptych. He painted two panels of hill fairies to go on either side of the main scene. This too was abandoned, and in this photograph one can see him experimenting by including the hill fairies in the wings where the battle once raged. At this stage the rocks are retained, but later they were painted out at the request of Helen Mary Gaskell, and flowers substituted. Much of the painting to be seen is by the hands of assistants. It is interesting to note the different stages of completion of the various parts of the canvas, revealing something of the evolution of the final painting.

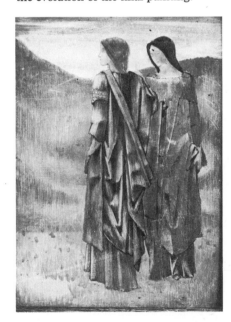

255. Two of Arthur's attendants from the painting 'Arthur in Avalon'. This unfinished gouache was on the easel in Burne-Jones's studio on the the day he died and was the last work to engage his attention. Private collection, London.

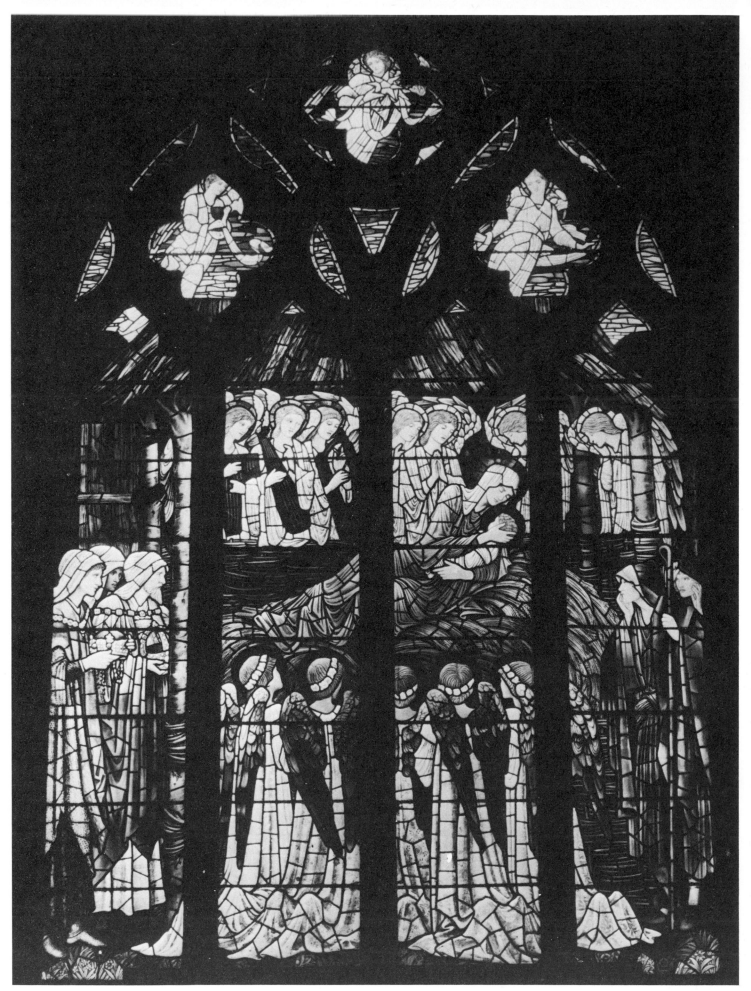

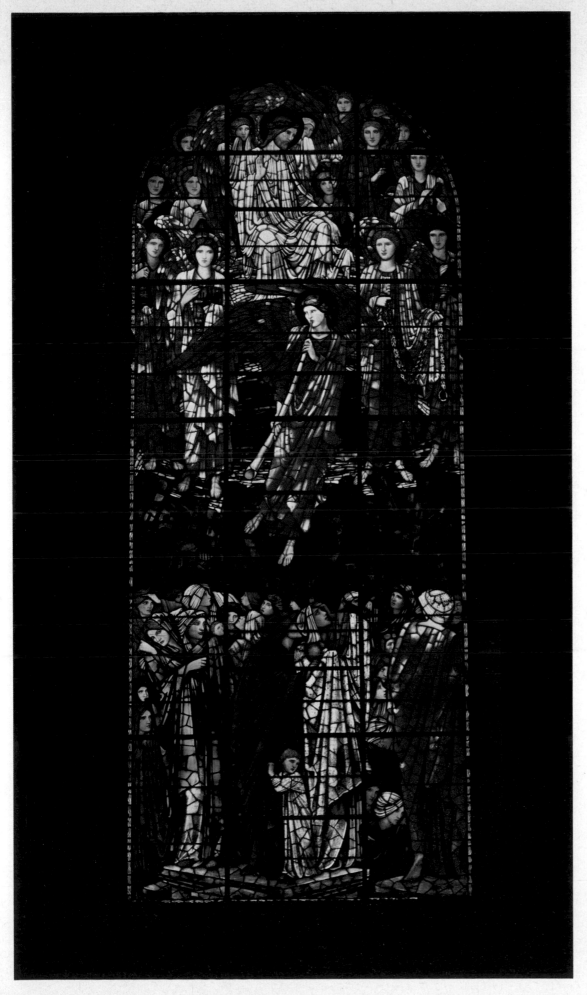

47. 'Last Judgement', West Window, St Philip's Cathedral, Birmingham, 1896. This, the artist's most successful window, is a large single space, arising from the classical form of the building. Significantly, his greatest design is not encumbered by the mullions and traceries of a gothic window. It allowed the picture-making tendency, implicit in his later designs, full expression, without descending to the three-dimensional banalities of the Munich School and their English counterparts.

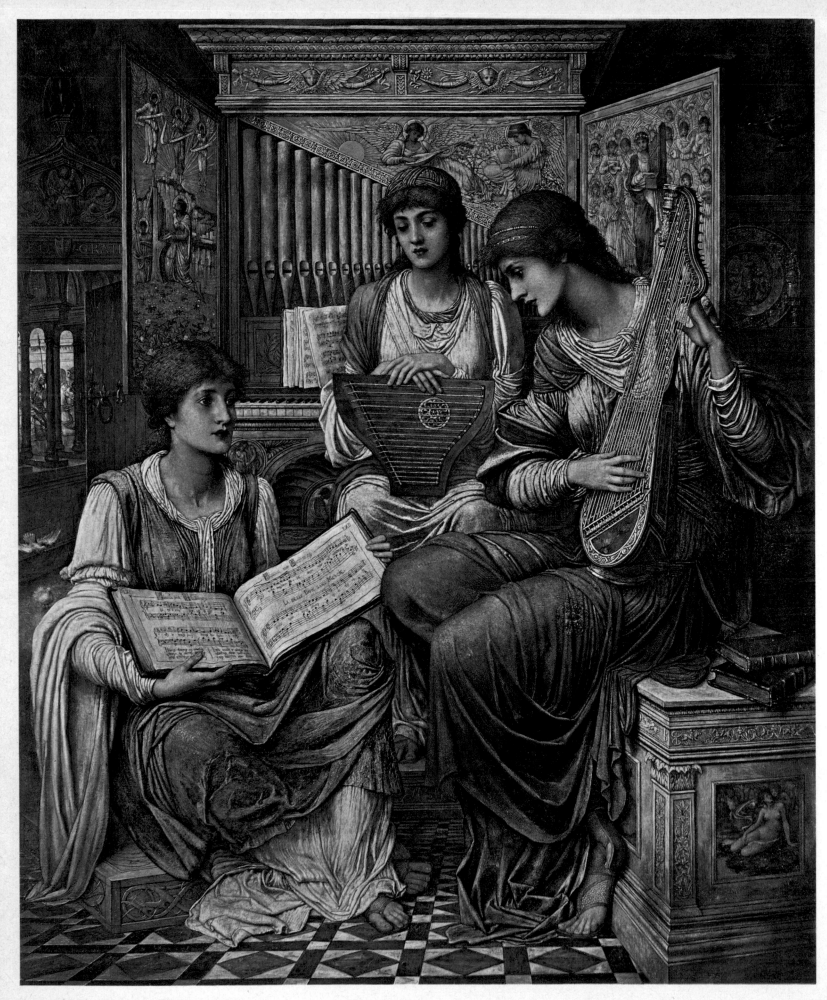

50. 'The Gentle Music of a Bygone Day', by
J. M. Strudwick, oil on canvas, 31 × 24; private
collection.

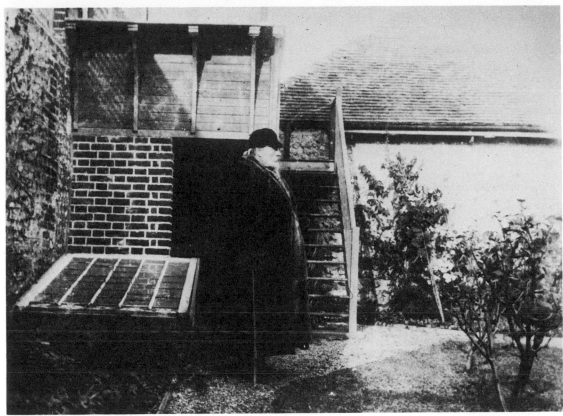

Such a mystical, transcendental interpretation of the glass is in keeping with 'Arthur in Avalon', the gold drawings, and the late book-illustrations. Because of this the windows of the nineties are as successful in their way as any of those of the sixties.

At the same time as Burne-Jones was making new designs, the firm was producing windows from cartoons of earlier periods and J. H. Dearle was making cartoons himself very much in the Burne-Jones manner. Manchester College Chapel, Oxford, has a window, 'The Days of Creation', installed in 1895 by Morris and Company, which was designed in 1870 and used a little later at Tamworth and Middleton Cheney. In the two earlier versions the figures are small, but they fully occupy their part of the tracery, appearing in sequence across the top of the main lancets. When they were redesigned for Manchester College they were greatly enlarged to become the main feature of the south window. The scaling up has made the figures weaker, and they no longer relate to the surrounding window frame, appearing dislocated; their strength in being exactly the right scale for the window is completely lost. Not only this, but their dilute colour of red set against pale green foliage, weakens the total impression. This is not an isolated example of the firm's decline after Morris's death or when Burne-Jones did not personally supervise, as many windows were made throughout the country up to 1940 using his designs. In these windows and those executed by J. H. Dearle, the colours used are generally much darker and opaque, and the design is frequently poor in the relation between figure and setting.

During these final years Burne-Jones was not wholly occupied with large schemes, decorative or otherwise; he was often ill and was, of necessity, required to work on much smaller projects. This was no hardship, for he was naturally drawn to intimate expression, as has been seen in the long involvement in book illustration and manuscript illumination. But those made in the years before his death took on a different nature. A letter to Mrs Amy Gaskell (1893) introduces a new element in his work:

'For lack of better things I worked upon a little golden figure on vellum,—never did one before, and it's not easy the first time, and if you make a false touch it can't be got out . . . . It is a funny drawing, and if you hold it slanting the gold looks amusing.'

Gold had been used in his work from the sixties in keeping with his decorative approach to painting; the late gold exercises grow out of this experience. They display the artist's sensitivity to texture and colour, and he uses them almost for their own sake, allowing the abstract qualities as much a part as the figurative. Some of them were actually executed in

171

silver by Catterson Smith in 1896. As in many of the *Chaucer* illustrations the balance and play of line is the vehicle of expression, but to this is added the sumptuousness of coloured paper, often purple, and the metallic lustre of a gold medium. The effect is one of Byzantine elegance; although secular, they operate on an hieratic level. Here may be found the key to the entire output of Burne-Jones. While at an early age he decided against entering the Church, he always treated the world and his experience of it, in his art, from a spiritual point of view resulting in a sacred treatment of temporal themes.

Chapter Nine

Influence

Success at the Grosvenor Gallery in 1877 was followed by a spreading reputation abroad. The year after the opening, Burne-Jones exhibited 'Merlin and Vivien' at the Universal Exhibition in Paris in the English Fine Arts Section, where it received applause from the French critics. In 1882 he and Leighton were invited to contribute to the exhibition of international contemporary art which was held in Paris. Subsequently, many of his major works were shown there between 1889 and his death, among them 'King Cophetua', 'Fortune', 'Love Among the Ruins' and part of the Perseus series. Together with the numerous studies shown during that time, these works had considerable influence on the younger generation of painters who became the Symbolists, and painters such as Puvis de Chavannes and Moreau recognised a kindred spirit working in England.

Similarly, Puvis was aiming to explore a monumental stillness in some works, a primeval calm that is central to our experience. This trance-like state that parallels the role prayer has in the Christian ritual obsessed both artists and they recognised and admired it in each other's paintings. It was Puvis who invited Burne-Jones to exhibit in the Champs de Mars in 1891, and he sent 'Fortune'. Decidedly pagan, this painting emphasises the essential similarities and dissimilarities between their outlooks; there is the same introvertant inertia, but Puvis was much more a traditional, admittedly mystical Christian without Burne-Jones's pessimism. Puvis's colour is quieter, he is more painterly, massive and less linear. But for all this the two artists could appreciate their community of ideas.

It was very different, however, with the younger generation of Symbolists. Building their art on the basis of a similar subjectivity, they went to extremes of mental and emotional situations. Whilst the violence of Burne-Jones, when it occurs, is represented as a generalised meeting of opposing forces, the Symbolists exploited hysterical gesture, facial expression, and horrific scenes to disturb their audience. Often there is a more basic divergence between the British master and his French admirers: Burne-Jones's art became more and more concerned with the medium as the expressive element of painting. The figurative image brought the observer's attention to a particular area upon which he wished to comment, and then the medium took over the interpretive role. Painters such as Osbert, Point, Schwabe, Klinger, and Kalmacoff thought that by portraying bizarre scenes, unusual combinations of objects, extremes of facial expression, they were able to symbolise subconscious events. This is symbolism at a most superficial level and can never be more than illustration, for a painting can powerfully render these subconscious nuances not by a faithful copying of external conditions, but through intrinsic qualities in the art object itself. Then the painting becomes a symbol in the true sense, a symbol of a human experience. Odilon Redon, Gustave Moreau, and Puvis de Chavannes used this technique with telling effect; Redon's lithographs and drawings, like their equivalents by Burne-Jones and Rossetti, suggest the subconscious world by an effective use of texture from which the forms emerge and into which they dissolve. Whilst Fernand Khnopff's paintings

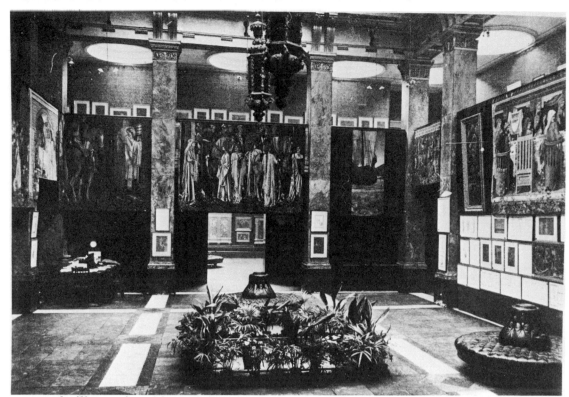

are mostly illustrative, his drawings have the same illusionary qualities; he was the only member of the Symbolist group known by Burne-Jones. A Belgian of partly English parentage, he was frequently in England and occasionally exhibited at the Grosvenor Gallery. His description of 'King Cophetua' gives an interesting insight into the way Symbolists saw the older painter's work:

> Before the pallid beggar maid, still shivering in her little grey gown, sits the king, clad in brilliant black armour, who having surrendered to her his throne of might, has taken a lower place on the steps of the dais. He holds on his knees a finely modelled crown of dark metal lighted up with red rubies and coral, and his face, in clear cut profile, is raised in silent contemplation. The scene is incredibly sumptuous; costly stuffs glisten and gleam, luxurious pillows of purple brocade shine in front of the chased golden panelling, and the polished metal reflects the beggar maid's exquisite feet, their ivory whiteness enhanced by contrast with the scarlet anenomes that lie here and there. Two chorister boys perched above sing softly, and in the distance, between the hanging curtains, is seen a dream, so to speak, of an Autumn landscape, its tender sky already dark. In the exquisite setting the two figures remain motionless, isolated in their absorbed reverie.

Khnopff was an exhibitor at the Salons de la Rose Croix, a series of exhibitions from 1892–97 which took place in Paris. They were organised by an eccentric critic and novelist, Josephin Pèladan, and were the gathering place for the extreme forms of Symbolism. The fifth of the rules he drew out for the invited contributors reveals their chief preoccupations:
'The Order favours first the Catholic Ideal and Mysticism. After Legend, Myth, Allegory and Dream, the Paraphrase of great poetry and finally all Lyricism, the Order prefers work which has a mural-like character, as being of superior essence.'
Given such ideas it is not surprising that the manifesto also stated: 'we will go to London to invite Burne-Jones, Watts and the five other Pre-Raphaelites'. In fact he wrote to Burne-Jones, who commented on the letter to Watts:

> I dont know about the Salon of the Rose-Cross—a funny high falutin sort of pamphlet has reached me—a letter asking me to exhibit there, but I feel suspicious of it—it was so silly a piece of mouthing that I was ashamed of it—& I had a letter from Paris a day or 2 back warning me in a friendly way against the thing which letter I have

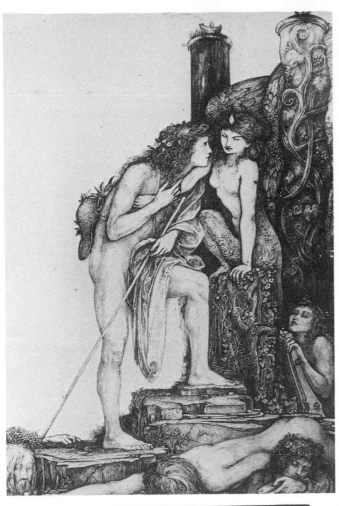

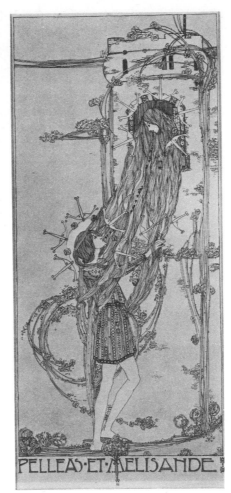

PELLEAS·ET·MELISANDE.

259. 'Oedipus and the Sphinx' by Charles Ricketts, 1891, pen and ink, $9\frac{1}{8} \times 8\frac{1}{8}$, Carlisle Museum & Art Gallery.

262. 'Oberon', woodcut frontispiece by Charles Ricketts, from Drayton's *Nymphidia*, published by The Vale Press.

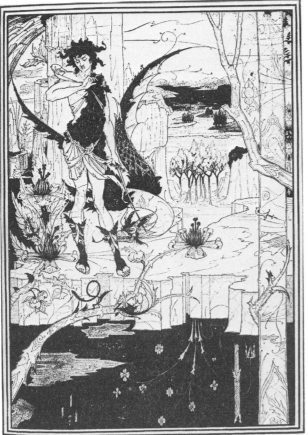

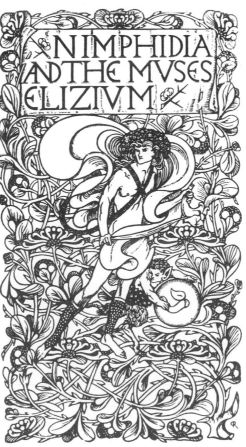

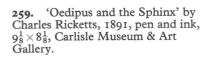

260. 'Pelléas et Melisande' by Jessie M. King, *c.* 1898, pen and ink, 11×5; Fine Art Society, London.

261. 'Siegfreid Act II' by Aubrey Beardsley, *c.* 1890. India ink and wash, $15\frac{3}{4} \times 11\frac{1}{4}$. Beardsley gave this drawing to Burne-Jones. Now in the Victoria & Albert Museum, London Illustration from *The Studio*, 1893.

175

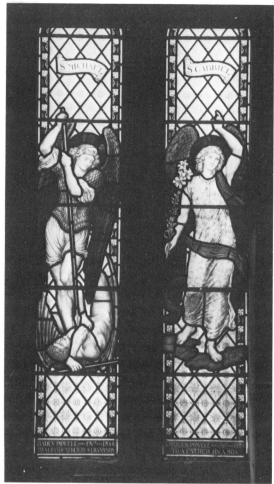

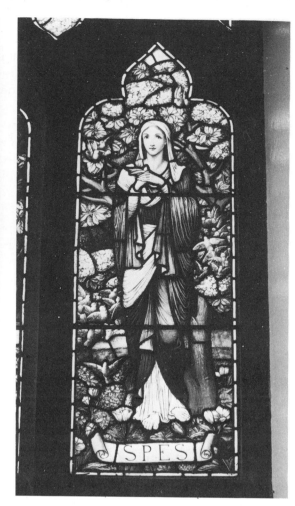

263. 'St Michael, St Gabriel', window in the north aisle of All Saints Church, Langton Green, Kent, designed by Henry Holiday, 1885, executed by Powell's.

264. 'Spes', stained-glass window designed by J. M. Strudwick, c. 1905, Christ Church, Hampstead, London.

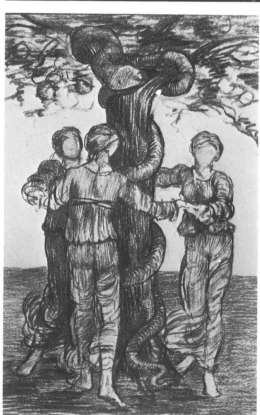

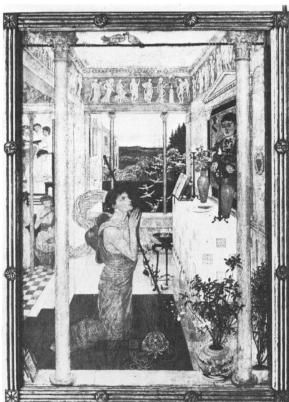

265. 'The Garden of Hesperides' by Spencer Stanhope, c. 1873, charcoal, $9\frac{1}{2} \times 6$, Hartnoll & Eyre, London Heavily influenced by Burne-Jones's version of the story.

266. 'The Altar of Love' by Walter Crane, 1870, oil, $30\frac{3}{8} \times 21\frac{3}{4}$, William Morris Gallery, Walthamstow.

hunted for this morning, high & low, to send to you—but it has gone . . . at any rate I shall not [exhibit] at once . . . but will make further enquiries & tell thee my dear— the pamphlet was disgracefully silly, but I was in the mood you are in, at first, to help in anything that upholds the ideals I care for. I shall know more of this in a week, for I will write again to Paris. Do you know Puvis de Chavannes? Who has lifted the same banner.

The news he received from Paris must have warned him off because he did not contribute any work. It was typical of his caution to distrust the eccentric Péladan and also not to offend the establishment that had awarded him a Knighthood of the Légion d'Honneur in 1889. He would, however, have found a sympathetic setting for his work in these exhibitions; practically all their themes he had anticipated years before: like them, he saw art as a religious activity; like them, he accepted myths as archetypal with contemporary relevance. He, too, applied a paganising force to Christianity and vice-versa, for him the personal had a universal significance; he saw the artist as a medium through which divine revelation passed and the art object as the symbol and materialisation of it. Yet his embarrassment was founded upon a genuine cause, he was not eccentric, his art was mature, meditated, refined and elegant; he deliberately excluded the grotesque and the horrific, quite aware of their significance, but was willing to leave them in less formal work and in personal communications to his friends, and he was rarely rhetorical. He had little in common with their naïve, macabre imagery, their rather adolescent hysteria and perversity. That is not to say that all who exhibited at the Rose-Croix had these faults, much of the work was of a high quality, but it is true of a great many and this was their reputation.

France was not the only country where he was held in high regard; he was given honours in Munich (1893), Antwerp (1894), Dresden (1895), and again in Munich (1897). His works were exhibited throughout Europe until the outbreak of the First World War and influenced a great many artists. Even the young Picasso was affected when he saw an exhibition of drawings in Barcelona which included studies for the 'Briar Rose' series; his 'Woman Ironing' of 1904 has the pose and isolation of one of these. Burne-Jones and Rossetti were held in such high esteem that they are mentioned in Kandinsky's *Concerning the Spiritual in Art*, where they are used as examples of artists who looked for the abstract or non corporeal as the subject of painting. Kandinsky contrasts them with the Impressionists, arguing that the latter synthesised concrete paintings involved with the suburban world, whilst the Pre-Raphaelites attempted to portray the mysteries of the spirit. As a man of the new age, Kandinsky saw that great contemporary art should combine both qualities.

The Grand Duke of Hesse purchased, at the beginning of the century, Burne-Jones's 'St George' and had it installed as the centrepiece of his celebrated Art Nouveau room and, as such, it had considerable influence. However, this reworking of a stained-glass design of the mid-sixties, which exists in at least three versions, is hardly the most important source of proto-Art Nouveau. Elements which were taken up by Art Nouveau painters existed in his work from the early seventies: densely packed space, flowing, pulsating linear rhythm, his treatment of leaves and girls' hair, all this strongly anticipates the movement. His designs for the *Aeneid*, the 'Orpheus piano' and certain stained-glass designs, had they been done thirty years later would have been considered a pure manifestation of Art Nouveau. Such works had direct influence on artists such as Toorop, Thorn Prikker, Klimpt and Mucha, owing to the availability of his design through the reproductions made by Frederick Hollyer and Caswall Smith. Hollyer had co-operated with Burne-Jones from before 1875 in producing reproductions of high quality, so much so that today many a collector has had a disappointment with what he thought to be an original. Hollyer advertised at home and abroad and had considerable success in selling his photographs of works by Watts, Rossetti, and Burne-Jones.

A second and later cause for the dissemination of his influence was the Kelmscott Press. Books are easily distributed, more easily than paintings, yet are equally useful as exhibition objects. In 1894 Octave Maus wrote on behalf of the *Libre Esthétique* in Brussels (of which Fernand Khnopff was a member), requesting to have examples of books from the Press.

Among the books sent was a specimen page from the *Chaucer* with a design by Burne-Jones. Morris's books were studied far and wide, in America, Sweden, Austria, France, and Italy, and a whole generation produced books close to them in style with illustrations founded upon Burne-Jones's.

Art Nouveau and Symbolist painting became dangerously dependent on literature as a source. Many of the artists were intimately associated with writers or had an exaggerated regard for Baudelaire, Mallarmé or Lautréamont. They benefited from their imagery, but all too often their paintings stopped short at the level of book illustration, by not allowing the visual to be entirely free of its original source, or if the picture was independent of its source it did not exploit the potentialities of the medium. For this reason it is easy to separate the Symbolist work of Gauguin, Munch, and Klimpt from the rest; they create parallel mysteries in terms of paint, they do not remain close to natural forms but take creative liberties to invent a truly visual aesthetic experience. In the most successful of Burne-Jones's work, 'Merlin and Vivien', the Orpheus design, and in many of his late drawings, he operated in this way, not using their painterly method but as a linear designer.

A man of vision, determination, and belief in his own ultimate power inevitably attracts attention of minor artists or the rising generation. So it was with Burne-Jones. From the time he began working in Rossetti's studio he stimulated admiration in his fellows as a man of singular power:

'Jones is doing designs which quite put one to shame, so full are they of everything—Aurora Leighs of art. He will take the lead in no time.' (Rossetti 1856)

'. . . Jones by name—a real genius! Really a genius!' (Watts, 1859)

'Edward Jones, whose work you would like amazingly. . . . It might have been done by Giotto, only Giotto could not have done it near so well.' (James Smetham on *The Prioress's Tale* Cabinet, 1860).

'He is perhaps the most remarkable of all the younger men of the profession for talent, and will, undeniably, in a few years fill the high position . . . at present he holds in the professional world.' (Holman Hunt, 1861)

'Jones is a great genius.' (du Maurier, 1863) and Ruskin's enthusiasm was boundless.

In the early sixties Burne-Jones's influence can be felt in the work of his friends, Simeon Solomon, Henry Holiday, even Albert Moore. Later with his propensity for studio assistants, a number of satellite artists arose round the master. Among these was Fairfax Murray, whose original works show as much of Rossetti as Burne-Jones. Never a draughtsman of calibre, he had a good sense of colour which is best in his decorative work. In common with Burne-Jones he was an Italophile, living in Italy for some time and building up a famous collection of Italian paintings. T. M. Rooke's work, when incorporating the figure, is frequently derivative, especially in his stained-glass and other decorative designs. Many of his paintings of incidents of the Old Testament are dated and their meaning, familiar to the Victorians, has no longer any direction for this century. Yet he learned a solid technique from his master; his work had good colour and some details of flowers, landscapes or sumptuous fabrics have redeeming qualities. His forte was, however, in watercolour, his subjects mostly architectural; in these his meticulous approach and conscientious observation resulted in pleasing records of Italian churches and cathedrals which he executed for Ruskin each summer from the mid-seventies until 1886. He was also, when called upon, able to make adequate portraits; there is a particularly good one of William Graham. Nothing like Burne-Jones's portraits, they make no attempt at interpretation of the subject but are literal, with the aim of being a good likeness. More than most artists, Burne-Jones suffered from his epigonic followers. Without understanding his strength they took his mannerisms and created, or attempted to create, an art of them. The result was an ineffectual group of paintings that many people take to be the essential Burne-Jones.

J. M. Strudwick was closely associated with Burne-Jones's studio for a few years in the seventies and came greatly under his influence. His work is delicate, almost saccharine, in its sentiment, he has a chromatic sense related to his master, but it is more obvious and colourful. The abundance of drapery he uses is without the structural role that one finds in Burne-Jones, and his draughtsmanship, although assured, lacks the subtlety of observa-

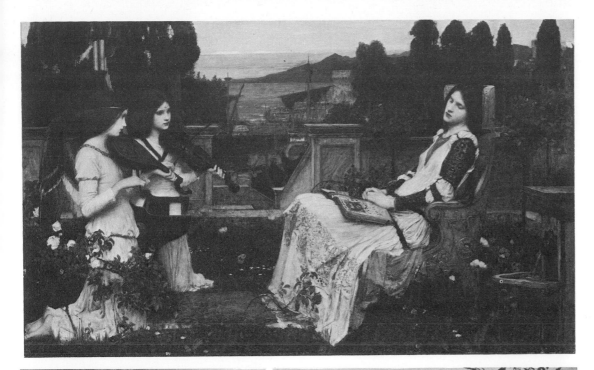

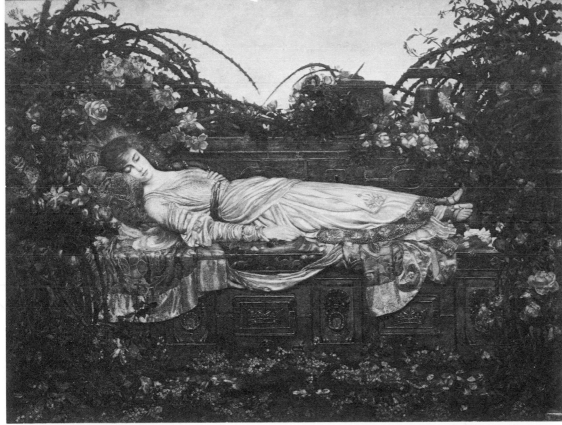

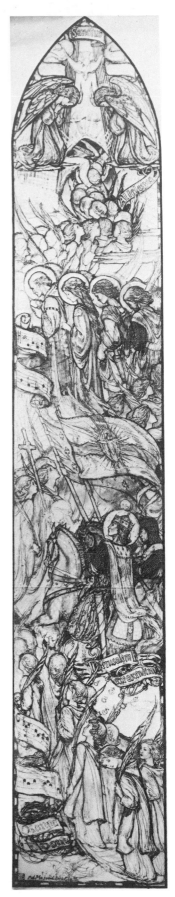

267. 'Saint Cecilia' by J. W. Waterhouse, 1895, oil on canvas, $48\frac{1}{2} \times 78\frac{1}{2}$; private collection.

268. 'The Sleeping Beauty' by Archibald Wakely, 1901, oil on canvas, $47\frac{1}{2} \times 63$. The Maas Gallery, London
The artist had the opportunity to study Burne-Jones's versions at the New Gallery in 1898–99. Although the figure of the princess shows work close to Burne-Jones's technique, the floral parts are much more painterly, with a higher impasto.

269. 'Gates of Heaven', cartoon for a window, used at Colmonell Church, Ayrshire, Scotland, c. 1907. Designed by Louis Davis, executed by Powell's. $104\frac{3}{8} \times 20\frac{1}{4}$, Leva Gallery, London.

179

tion that enlivens the older painter's work. There is a similar concern with the decorative role of painting, every inch being covered with an incident of some kind. Surfaces within the painting, boxes, walls, furniture and instruments are decorated with scenes that are sympathetic to a central theme, a technique he received from the Flemish artists via Burne-Jones. Strudwick is at his best in simple designs with few figures, such as 'Summer Songs' (exhibited 1901), 'The Gentle Music of a Bygone Day' and 'Peonia' (1878), in these his bright colour and gentle mood unite into a charming picture. When working on a larger scale, as in 'The Ramparts of God's House' and 'A Golden Thread' (1885, Tate) his mannerisms become disturbing, his sentiments anaemic and 'Victorian', and his composition lacks cohesion.

Like Strudwick, Evelyn de Morgan followed Burne-Jones's style closely, but her art is much stronger than Strudwick's, although without his charm. It is a hard and mannerist art clearly based upon another artist's experience; she combines the styles of her uncle, Spencer Stanhope, Burne-Jones and occasionally Botticelli. Her Wattsian allegories 'The Soul's Prison House', 'The Sleeping Earth and Waking Moon', 'Lux in Tenebris', 'The Garden of Opportunity', 'The Gilded Cage' and 'Knowledge Strangling Ignorance' like his, are difficult to interpret and have not the archetypal independence of Burne-Jones's. 'Flora' is her masterpiece, and in this she benefits from Botticelli's dancing lines with which she clothes a model of Burne-Jones type, setting her amidst exotic fruit and foliage in an evening landscape. Watt's influence on Evelyn de Morgan came via her uncle who had studied under him at Little Holland House. It was there that Burne-Jones first met Stanhope, and after working together on 'the jovial campaign' at Oxford they became fast friends, often working together in the same studio. They held each other's work in high regard, Burne-Jones thinking 'His colour was beyond any the finest in Europe; an extraordinary turn for landscape he had too . . .'. 'Love Among the Ruins' was painted in his studio and Stanhope's 'Beauty and the Beast' was exhibited at his friend's studio before it went on to the Academy. The influence of Burne-Jones began early in his output; in 1863 they were painting together from a landscape around Cobham in Surrey, where Stanhope had a house built from Philip Webb's plans. The studies made by Burne-Jones were used as a background for 'The Merciful K⁻ᵍht'. Also during this stay he worked on his Annunciation, 'The Flower of God'. Stanhope's 'I Have Trodden the Winepress Alone' of the mid-sixties shows how strong an impression 'The Merciful Knight' had had on him. Both have figures contained in a cubic foreground space that occupies most of the picture and through which is seen a distant landscape. In his later work, he is the only painter who chose a type of expression derived from Burne-Jones, that is assimilated into an independent style. He does not approach his friend's breadth, but in his own way he shows a strong feeling for design, a firm draughtsmanship derived from his period of tuition with Watts, and powerful colour which he inherited from his study of the earlier Pre-Raphaelites, Hughes, Holman Hunt, and Millais. His most famous decorative scheme can be found in Marlborough College Chapel where a series of twelve panels is installed on both sides of the chancel; they represent six ministrations of angels on earth from the Old Testament, and six from the New. Although varying in their success all are strong figure studies with bold silhouettes against the subordinate landscape and in fact are superior to the contemporary 'Cupid and Psyche' scheme in George Howard's dining room.

Figure studies by George Howard are rare and inadequate as he had difficulty in drawing from the model. A painting based upon a Norse fairy tale, with three diaphanously draped girls hailing a rowing boat, shows a strong influence from Burne-Jones, which is hardly surprising given their intimate friendship. At times George Howard took his difficulties to Burne-Jones who would help him with them, explaining methods of design and giving him the benefit of his experience.

Philip Burne-Jones, the artist's son, had a talent for portraiture and landscape, and like George Howard, infrequently ventured into imaginative or figure work. Working mostly in gouache or watercolour, once again like Howard, his style could never be confused with his father's though it approaches it in 'Ezekiel in the Valley of Dry Bones', which was exhibited at the New Gallery in 1888.

During the year 1885-86 Burne-Jones filled the post of President of the Royal Society

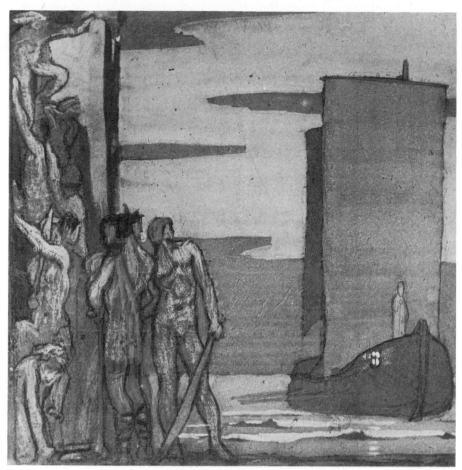

270. 'The Landing of St Patrick in Ireland' by Cayley Robinson, *c.* 1895, tempura, $8\frac{7}{8} \times 8\frac{3}{4}$; Carlisle Museum & Art Gallery. A larger version is in the William Morris Gallery, Walthamstow, and both are studies for the work in National Gallery of Ireland, Dublin.

271. 'Sleeping Beauty' by Paul Nash, 1910, watercolour, $7\frac{1}{8} \times 6\frac{1}{4}$; Carlisle Museum & Art Gallery

Both Burne-Jones and Rossetti provided inspiration for this early work by Nash.

272. 'Clytie' by Evelyn Pickering (de Morgan), 1886–87, oil on canvas, 41×17; Hartnoll & Eyre, London.

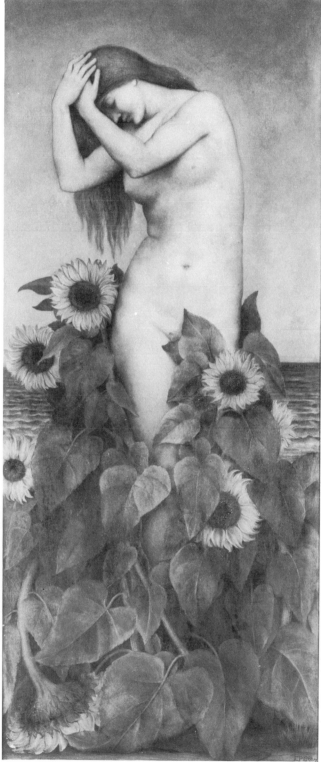

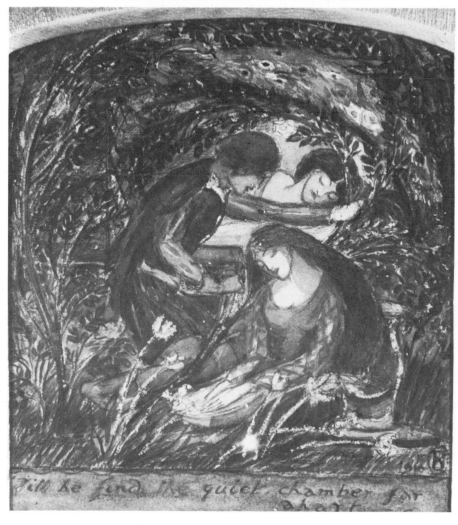

Till he find the quiet chamber for a time

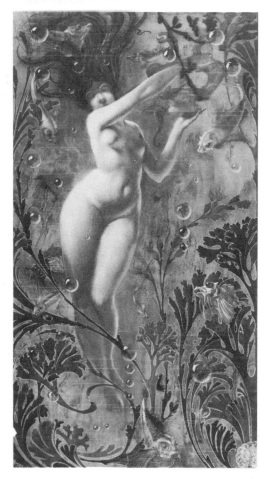

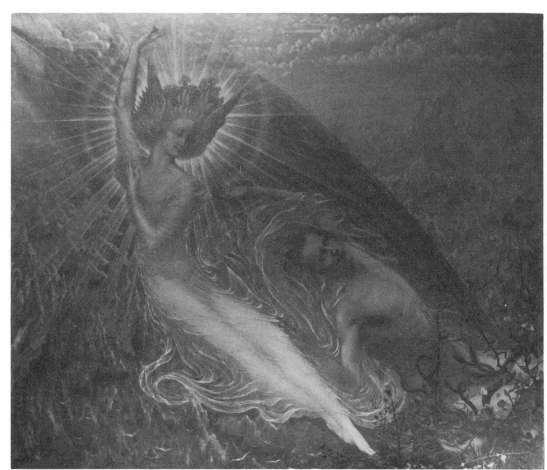

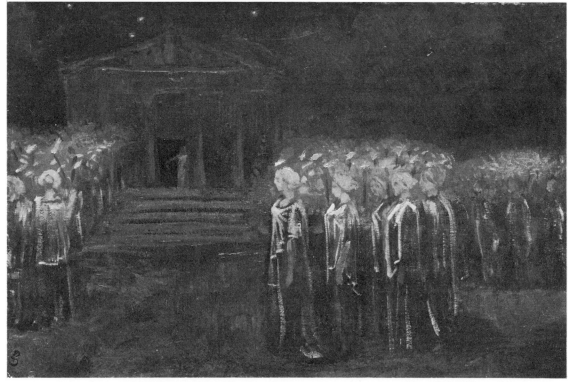

273. 'Ondine' by Louis Lessieux, 1902, gouache, $39 \times 20\frac{1}{2}$. The Piccadilly Gallery, London.

274. 'L'Ange des Splendeurs' by Jean Delville, 1894, oil on canvas, $50 \times 57\frac{1}{2}$. Collection of Anne-Marie Grillson-Crouet, Belgium.

275. 'Mystères d'Eleusis' by Paul Serusier, oil on canvas, $19\frac{3}{4} \times 28\frac{3}{4}$. The Piccadilly Gallery, London.

of Birmingham Artists and at the same time took some interest in the Art School. Because of his close connection with his native city, a number of proselyte artists are associated with it, the most obvious being Sidney H. Meteyard (1868–1947). He was long associated with the Birmingham College of Arts and Crafts and was secretary of the Society. His works are reminiscent of Burne-Jones in colour, imagery, and atmosphere, yet they are more corporeal and less languorous, and his interpretations of the themes is quite different. The latter is marked in his illustrations to *The Golden Legend* by Longfellow which have none of the structural unity of figure with its surroundings or the drama to be found in Burne-Jones's book illustrations. The same can be said for his designs in stained glass and for murals, superficially they recall his work but are quieter, gentler and more pictorial. A. J. Gaskin (1862–1928) together with C. M. Gere (1869–1957), who was chiefly a landscape artist, were commissioned by William Morris to provide designs for the Kelmscott Press. The designs they made were tempered by the existing examples by Burne-Jones, but none the less equal to them. Gaskin's paintings are most inspired by the Italian primitives and the earlier Pre-Raphaelites, but occasionally one can detect the influence of Burne-Jones. Similarly, with J. E. Southall (1861–1945) there are passing references to Burne-Jones's work. Like his two students Gaskin and Gere, he was interested in tempera and had pioneered a modern method of using it. However, his distinctive colour, convincing draughtsmanship, and strong designs are entirely his own. In the best of his work there is a great force of isolation that carried Burne-Jones's inertia a stage nearer the Surrealists— in 'Ariadne in Naxos' for example, each item, though unified into the overall design, fragments it; Ariadne, the ship, the parrot, and the vases all have separate lives, yet by their rigidity within the structure they are welded into a coherent pattern. The reason for the hypnotic character of the painting is the unity and clarity of its light; natural forms are subjected to unreal illumination and there are virtually no shadows. This fundamental feature he shares with the creator of 'King Cophetua', 'The Wedding of Psyche' and 'Love and the Pilgrim'.

The Birmingham School of Art trained a whole generation of students in the Burne-Jones style at the turn of the century; in this it was not exceptional. Throughout the country, following the example of the Morris movement, art schools and classes of the applied arts took an interest in all fields of art and design. Naturally, they based their idiom on Morris's chief designer. Burne-Jones's angels appear on embroidered altar clothes, curtains, murals, stained glass, metal work and all the other types of decorative art, one only has to glance at contemporary copies of *The Studio* to see how general the influence was.

It is inconceivable to think of British nineteenth-century stained glass without Morris and Burne-Jones, it was they who, after the initial outburst of Gothic revival glass, made a recognisable style that was truly original and modern whilst relying on the best technology inherited from the past. Towards the end of the century their design became a common-place amongst stained-glass producers. Henry Holiday (1839–1927) took over as designer for Powell's Whitefriars Glass Works when Burne-Jones gave it up in 1861 to concentrate on Morris and Company. His designs, though obviously derived from Burne-Jones, are vigorous, less flattened, and more picturesque. His drawing is assured, but his sentiment is less subtly portrayed. Powell's colour, though different, less dense than Morris and Company, is equal to it, often it is a matter of personal preference in deciding which company created the better glass. Holiday and Walter Crane had similar socialist ideas, applying their art, which can easily be confused, to political ends. What differentiates their work is the academic character of Holiday's drawing. Both used the same Hellenistic draperies to clothe their Burne-Jones-type models, but there is a more convincing anatomy beneath those of Henry Holiday. Crane designed both tapestry and stained glass for Morris and Company, he adapted his book illustration 'The Goose Girl' for tapestry which was followed by two stained-glass designs in 1886 for 'Clare Lawn', East Sheen and designs for a series of panels for the windows of the library in 'Vinland', a house in Newport, Rhode Island. All of them comprised figures of girls representing the appropriate abstractions. During the eighties Morris and Company had a link with The Century Guild, a group of designers working under the leadership of the architect, A. H. Mackmurdo,

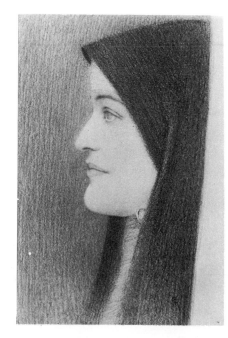

276. 'The Veil' by Fernand Khnopff, c. 1890, pencil, $15\frac{3}{4} \times 8\frac{5}{8}$. Collection of Anne-Marie Grillion-Crowet, Belgium.

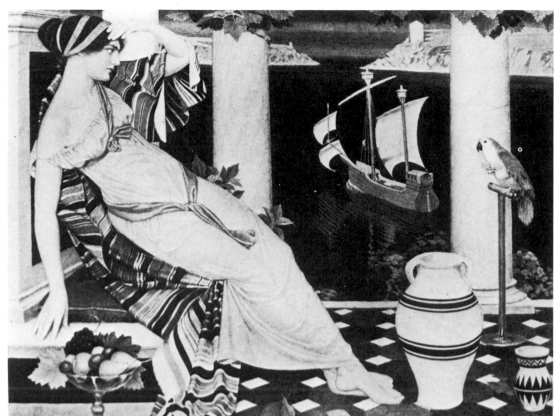

277. 'Ariadne in Naxos' by Joseph Southall, *c.* 1915, oil; present whereabouts unknown.

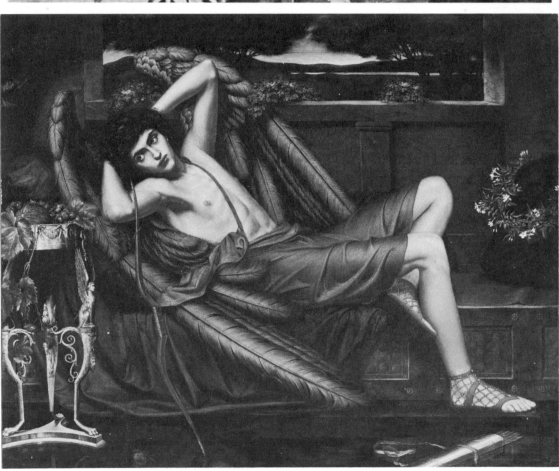

278. 'Icarus' by Sydney Meteyard, *c.* 1900, oil on canvas, $34 \times 41\frac{1}{2}$, The Piccadilly Gallery, London.

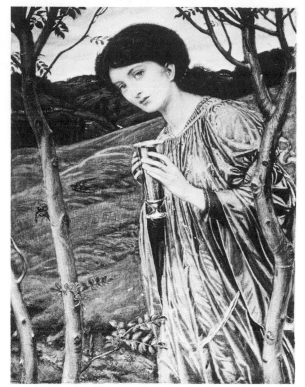

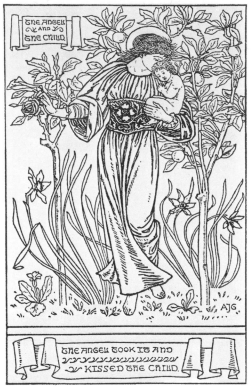

whose celebrated dining chair of 1882 and title page of his book, *Wren's City Churches*, of the following year owe their swirling proto-Art Nouveau lines to Burne-Jones designs of the early seventies. Much of what the guild sold was from their own design, but they also included certain items of Morris and Company's products. Selwyn Image (1849–1930), an ordained priest who relinquished his orders in 1873, poet, painter and designer for the guild, was an eclectic whose sources included eighteenth-century landscape, Italian primitives, Burne-Jones, and plant life. Heaton, Butler and Bayne manufactured his characteristic stained glass, more rugged in design than Burne-Jones's but showing none the less an obvious debt to him in its style and imagery. Whilst his glass is as two-dimensional in appearance, his figures are more planar and stiff, lacking the flow of Burne-Jones's.

The late Byzantine style inspired its own particular following: a similar etiolation occurs in the stained glass of the Belgian, Baron Arild Rosencranz (as at Wickhambreux Parish Church 1896) and in J. D. Batten's tempera decorations in a Lichfield Church.

Among the artists of the 'decadent nineties' Burne-Jones has his place. The refined sensitivity of Beardsley, Ricketts, and Alfred Gilbert had its origin with him. These English equivalents of the Symbolists inherited his ability to combine sensuality with economy of line, to fuse content with design, and to contain expression within the abstract elements. Alfred Gilbert (1854–1934) was a linear sculptor, his art takes the implications of such designs as 'The Pelican' (1880) or the illustration for the *Aeneid* (1874–75) into the third dimension. A tightly controlled fluency permeates his sculpture similar to that in the work of his friend, Burne-Jones. They knew and respected one another's work, exhibiting together at the Grosvenor Gallery. Gilbert describes their second meeting:

As a fervent admirer of the only work of Burne-Jones I was acquainted with at that time, 'Love Among the Ruins', I was prepared to content myself with smaller achievements. Instead, I found myself in the presence of his greatest work and one of all time, 'King Cophetua and the Beggar-Maid'. It roused mingled feelings of wonder and joy, and I felt such a rush of enthusiasm and sympathy with the artist and his aims, as still recurs when I think about his works.

We passed on to new and other pictures in progress. The 'Briar Rose' series, as yet incomplete, was a revelation of the power of human genius to assert itself as a teaching factor of the potentiality of imagination over material effort. From that moment I became a humble proselyte to the aims of two of the greatest artists of modern times—Turner and Burne-Jones.

What many consider to be Gilbert's masterpiece, the memorial to the Duke of Clarence in Windsor Chapel, includes a portrait of Burne-Jones as St George and has much that is reminiscent of his art. Fleshly, relaxed figures are encumbered by wilfully linear tendrils, figurative images are used in such an austere decorative function that they verge into the abstract; both artists were virtuosi, able to perform amazing decorative arabesques that were integrally a part of their art forms.

With Beardsley it was different, at first he took on the guise of a proselyte, creating dilutions of Burne-Jones's work, anaemic saints and madonnas, with nothing of his strength. Beardsley had introduced himself in the summer of 1891 and was received with the usual cordiality that the master bestowed on potential followers. He encouraged the young artist and in return he received a drawing—an illustration to Wagner's *Siegfreid*. At that time Burne-Jones was occupied with designs for the Kelmscott Press and showed Beardsley his method of converting rough drawings into hard economic lines with the use of tracing paper—a technique that Beardsley later utilised with great skill. From 1892 until 1894 Beardsley was engaged upon an illustrated *Morte d'Arthur* commissioned by J. M. Dent, the publisher. Beginning in a markedly decorative style with all the paraphernalia associated with Burne-Jones, there is a gradual lessening of the influence as the book progresses. Although quite distinctly borrowed, the figures were never exactly like the originals, having a slightly grotesque character. His subsequent development moved farther into the bizarre and erotic, revealing the influence of Japanese art, the Rococo and Whistler. This was the art that Burne-Jones grew to despise:

'The drawings were as stupid as they could be, empty of any great quality & detestable. I was looking at some the other day, and they were more lustful than any I've seen—not that I've seen many such. There was a woman with breasts each larger than her head, which was quite tiny and features insignificant, so that she looked like a mere lustful animal.'

Beardsley's pornographic qualities were alien to Burne-Jones's mind, not because he did not think the erotic important, we have seen the contrary, but because it was vulgarly and obviously presented. Burne-Jones was too much of an artist to be content with describing sexual activity, sensuality is absorbed into the structure of the painting itself; the theme and the treatment of the theme are inseparably bound. For this reason Beardsley must always remain a highly talented adolescent. Rickett's graphics have, in common with Beardsley's, this *fin de siècle*, elegant manifestation of a personal hedonism. A skilled craftsmanship is used to explore a singular and often secretive imagination. A debt to Rossetti is evident in his earlier designs, and in later years to Burne-Jones and Gustave Moreau. The illustrations he made together with Charles Shannon for their Vale Press derive not only imagery and decorative technique from Burne-Jones but also the articulation of the marks within the rectangle. Like him, Ricketts used the edge of the design to strengthen it by cutting into the images. The picture space he no longer regarded as a quasi real unit but as a fragment, an abstract synthetic area that created its own reality, which in doing so revealed the artist's mind. By taking these elements of Burne-Jones's art a little further, giving a primordial role to imaginative and abstract elements, Ricketts and Beardsley began to anticipate the pure abstraction in the years to come.

Appendix 1

Select List of stained-glass windows designed by Burne-Jones

DATE	SUBJECT	LOCATION	NOTES
1857	Good Shepherd	King Street Congregational Church, Maidstone, Kent.	
1857	Call of St Peter	Powell & Co., Wealdstone, Middlesex.	
1858	Adam and Eve Tower of Babel King Solomon and the Queen of Sheba	Bredfield College, Berkshire.	
1859	Legend of St Frideswide	Christ Church Cathedral, Oxford.	
1860	Creation Tree of Jesse	Waltham Abbey, Essex.	All the above windows executed 1857–60 by Messrs. Powell, Whitefriars Glass Factory.
1860	Annunciation	St Columba Church, Topcliffe, Yorkshire.	Executed by Lavers & Barraud.
1861	Song of Solomon (Story in 12 lights)	St Helen's Church, Darley Dale, Derbyshire.	
1861 1862	Christ Blessing Children Resurrection Christ in Majesty Adam/Eve St Peter/St Paul	All Saints Church, Selsley, Gloucestershire.	From 1861 all windows designed by Burne-Jones executed by Morris, Marshall, Faulkner & Co. After the re-formation of this company in 1874 as Morris & Co., Burne-Jones became virtually its sole designer of stained glass.
1862	Seven Angels Playing Bells Virgin and Child Flight into Egypt Baptism of Christ John Baptist	Church of St Michael, Brighton, Sussex.	

It was the practice of the Morris firm to re-use original cartoons—often very many times. The locations listed here refer specifically to windows designed by Burne-Jones, and only to the original use of a cartoon.

DATE	SUBJECT	LOCATION	NOTES
1862–63	Tomb of Tristram and Iseult Madness of Sir Tristram Wedding of Sir Tristram	Cartwright Memorial Art Gallery, Bradford Yorkshire.	

DATE	SUBJECT	LOCATION
1862–63	A large and complex east window comprising 3 main lights in 2 tiers, 4 narrow lights in 2 tiers and 8 trefoils—all the figures designed by Burne-Jones. Deliverance of St Peter from Prison Martyrdom of St Stephen Elijah Calling Fire from Heaven Battle of Beth-horon	St Michael's Church, Lyndhurst, Hampshire.
1863	Magdalene Washing Christ's Feet	St Ladoca Church, Ladock, Cornwall.
1863–64	Editha Judgement Window	St Editha Church, Amington, Warwickshire.
1864	Chaucer	Victoria & Albert Museum, London.
1864	St Nicholas St George St Michael	St Nicholas Church, Beaudesert, Warwickshire.
1864	Chaucer's Good Women	Combination Room, Peterhouse College, Cambridge.
1865	Four Rivers of Paradise	St Edward the Confessor Church, Cheddleton, Staffordshire.
1865	David/Melchidedec Ezekiel/Isaiah John/Peter Nicholas/Stephen Boniface/Richard Angels with Children	St John's Church, Torquay, Devon.
1865	Most of the figures in the large east window	All Saints Church, Cambridge, Cambridgeshire.
1866	Faith/Hope/Charity	St Edburg Church, Bicester, Oxfordshire.
1866–67	6 Garland Weavers	Green Dining Room, Victoria & Albert Museum, London.
1868	St Ursula Christ Blessing Children	St John's Church, Tue Brook, Liverpool, Lancashire.
1869	Peter/Paul Cherub/Seraph Cecily/Catherine All of these in east window, together with figures designed by Morris.	Our Lady of Bloxham Church, Bloxham, Oxfordshire.
1869	3 Trumpeting Angels	St Edward the Confessor Church, Cheddleton, Staffordshire.
1870	Shadrach/Meshach/Abednego Days of Creation	All Saints Church, Middleton Cheney, Northamptonshire.
1872	Nativity Miriam	St Michael and All Angels Church, Waterford, Hertfordshire.
1872	Vyner Memorial window	Christ Church Cathedral, Oxford, Oxfordshire.
1872	Crucifixion	Jesus Chapel, Troutbeck, Cumberland.

DATE	SUBJECT	LOCATION
1872	Absalom	St John the Evangelist Church, Knotty Ash, Lancashire.
1872	Adam/Eve	St John the Divine Church, Frankby, Wirral, Cheshire.
1872–73	Magdalen Washing Christ's Feet Sacrifice of Noah Sacrifice of Abraham Envy/Folly/Despair	St Chad's Church, Rochdale, Lancashire.
1872–77	In the nave and transepts a large and important collection including the Michelangelesque 'Sibyls'	Jesus College Chapel, Cambridge, Cambridgeshire.
1874	St Catherine	Christ Church Cathedral, Oxford, Oxfordshire.
1874	4 subjects of Virtuous women	Paisley Abbey, Renfrewshire, Scotland.
1874	Ascension	The original version in the parish church at Brown Edge, Staffordshire is badly damaged. The same cartoon was used in 1878 for the east window at Christ Church, Tunbridge Wells, Kent.
1874	An important Collection, including the excellent 'Reception of Souls into Paradise'.	Calcutta Cathedral, India.
1874–75	Last Judgement	St Michael and All Angels Church, Easthampstead, Berkshire.
1874–75	Rivers of Paradise	All Hallows Church, Allerton, Lancashire.
1875	St Michael and the Dragon	St Michael's Church, Geneseo, New York U.S.A.
1876	Baptism/John Baptist Calling of St Peter/St Peter St Paul at Athens/St Paul Vision of St John/John Evangelist 4 small subjects of the Holy Family	Paisley Abbey, Renfrewshire, Scotland.
1877	*Noli me tangere* Angels at the Sepulchre	St Michael and All Angels Church, Easthampstead, Berkshire.
1878	Angeli Laudantes Angeli Ministrantes	Salisbury Cathedral, Wiltshire.
1878	St Catherine (3 lights with predellas)	Christ Church Cathedral, Oxford.
1880	Large east window in 15 compartments of single figures with central light of Pelican	St Martin's Church, Brampton, Cumberland.
1880	Christ and the Woman of Sumaria	St Peter's Church, Vere Street, London W1.
1880	Christ Disputing with the Doctors	All Hallows Church, Allerton, Lancashire.
1882	Marriage in Cana	English Church, Biarritz, France.
1882	Building of the Temple	Holy Trinity Church, Boston, Massachusetts, U.S.A.

DATE	SUBJECT	LOCATION
1882	Annunciation to the Shepherds	All Hallows Church, Allerton, Lancashire.
1883	Parable of St Maurice	St Michael and All Angels Church, Easthampstead, Berkshire.
1883	Entry of Christ into Jerusalem	St Peter's Church, Vere Street, London W1.
1885	Adoration of the Magi	St Michael and All Angels Church, Easthampstead, Berkshire.
1885	Ascension	St Philip's Cathedral, Birmingham, Warwickshire.
1885–86	Resurrection Nativity House of Simon Baptism	All Hallows Church, Allerton, Lancashire.
1886	Passage of the Jordan	St Giles Church, Allerton, Lancashire.
1886	St Michael St George Peace/Justice	English Church, Berlin, Germany.
1887	St Frances (3 panels)	St James Church, Weybridge, Surrey.
1887	Resurrection	St Philip's Cathedral, Birmingham, Warwickshire.
1889	Pelican and 2 Angels	Ingestre Hall Chapel, Staffordshire.
1890	Annunciation to the Shepherds	Lanercost Priory, Cumberland.
1891	Stoning of St Stephen Paul Preaching at Athens	St Paul's Church, Morton, near Gainsborough, Lincolnshire.
1892	Moses and the Burning Bush The Burial of Moses	St Brycedale Church, Kircaldy, Fife, Scotland.
1893–95	Large windows each of 10 panels of single figures for north and south transepts. Especially important tracery lights.	Albion Congregational Church, Ashton-under-Lyme, Lancashire.
1894–97	St Margaret St Mary Virgin Jacob's Dream Tree of Jesse	St Margaret's Church, Rottingdean, Sussex.
1896	David Lamenting David Consoled	Laing Art Gallery, Newcastle.
1896–97	Last Judgement	St Philip's Cathedral, Birmingham, Warwickshire.
1897	Christ the Sower Christ Stilling the Waves	St Martin's Church, Brighouse, Yorkshire.
1898	Nativity	St David's Church, Hawarden, Flintshire, Wales.

Appendix 2

Public Collections Containing Works by Burne-Jones

THE BRITISH ISLES

ABERDEEN Art Gallery and Industrial Museum: three drawings.

BEDFORD The Cecil Higgins Art Gallery: studies and the gouache 'Cupid Delivering Psyche', 1867.

BEMBRIDGE The Ruskin Gallery, Bembridge School: stained-glass cartoon, drawings, and studies.

BIRKENHEAD The Williamson Art Gallery and Museum: a triptych, 1872-76, mostly by an assistant; 'Pyramus and Thisbe'.

BIRMINGHAM City Museum & Art Gallery: The most important collection anywhere. With the Middlemore Loan, includes the Troy Polyptych; 'The Cupid and Psyche Frieze' from 1 Palace Green, London; 'Phyllis and Demophöon'; 'The Hesperides'; a small 'Feast of Peleus'; 'The Merciful Knight'; 'The Wizard'; and a large collection of unfinished works, studies, sketchbooks, and cartoons.

BRADFORD City Museum & Art Gallery, Cartwright Hall: a small collection of drawings and the Tristram series of stained-glass windows.

BRIGHTON The Art Gallery: two drawings and two late stained-glass cartoons.

BRISTOL City Art Gallery: two studio works, 'The Return' from the St George series, and a version of the 'Garden Court' from the late 'Briar Rose' series, and a cartoon for glass, 1876.

CAMBRIDGE Fitzwilliam Museum: a good collection of early drawings and cartoons, 'The Wedding of Buondelmonte', 1860 and 'Going to Battle', 1858—both pen and inks; the important series of drawings to 'The Aeneid'; eighty-seven drawings for the Kelmscott *Chaucer*; various late studies; large coloured cartoons for 'Angeli Laudantes and Ministrantes' at Salisbury Cathedral; and a seminal collection of documentary material.

CARDIFF The National Museum of Wales: a small but high-quality collection of studies; large cartoons for 'The Wheel of Fortune', 'Merlin and Vivien' and 'Arthur in Avalon'; the superb 'Nymphs of the Stars' and 'Nymphs of the Moon'; and two unfinished oils, 'Portrait of Lady Windsor' and 'Venus Discordia'.

CARLISLE Museum & Art Gallery, Tullic House: The Bottomley Bequest contains the 1861 gouache 'Girl and Goldfish' and various studies. There is also a collection of cartoons; the pastel 'The Three Graces'; and an early version of 'The Wheel of Fortune'.

COMPTON Surrey, The Watts Gallery: 'Fortune, Fame, Oblivion, Love', four small oil studies from the predellas of the Troy Polyptych; a gouache study for the Queen in 'Laus Veneris'; and a few other good studies.

DUBLIN The National Gallery of Ireland: a stained-glass cartoon, and studies.

DUBLIN The Municipal Gallery of Modern Art: two stained-glass cartoons.

EDINBURGH The National Gallery of Scotland: a cartoon for stained glass at Amington, 1864.

FARINGDON Faringdon Collection Trust, Buscot Park, Berkshire: the final and most important 'Briar Rose' series.

GLASGOW Art Gallery: the large oil 'Danae and the Tower of Brass', 1888; a small oil of an angel, 1881; and three drawings for stained glass.

LECHLADE Gloucestershire, Kelmscott Manor: cartoons for the 'Signs of the Zodiac' in the Green Dining Room, Victoria & Albert Museum.

LEEDS Art Gallery: a few studies.

LEICESTER Art Museum & Gallery: a Wattsian oil, 'Christ and the Twelve Apostles'.

LETCHWORTH Museum & Art Gallery: 'St

Valentine', cartoon for Christ's Hospital, Ilford, 1891.

LIVERPOOL   The Walker Art Gallery: 'Sponsa de Libano', 1891, large and excellent; an angel gouache, 1878.

LONDON   Borough of Hammersmith Public Libraries, Fulham Branch: The Cecil French Bequest contains 'Morgan le Fay', 1862; 'The Garland', one of a set of six paintings based upon the stained glass in the Victoria & Albert Museum, 1866; 'Cupid Delivering Psyche', 1867; and 'The Wheel of Fortune', 1872–86, all gouache; and a fine collection of studies.

LONDON   Borough of Waltham Forest, William Morris Gallery: Many cartoons for glass; tiles, and stained-glass panels. The drawings cover a wide period and include a nude composition design for 'Love disguised as Reason'. There are two important works, 'The Lament', 1866, and 'St George and the Dragon', 1868.

LONDON   The British Museum; a number of important studies; 'The Secret Book of Designs', 1885–98; two gouaches: 'Cupid's First Sight of Psyche', 1865, and 'The Annunciation', a small version of the 1876–79 painting; the original Flower Book watercolours, and the highly finished pencil designs for the St George series, c. 1865.

LONDON   Courtauld Institute Galleries: a few studies.

LONDON   St Clement's Church, Notting Dale: the cartoon for 'Christ and the Woman of Samaria', stained-glass window at St Peter's, Vere Street, London, 1880.

LONDON   Tate Gallery: 'The Golden Stairs' and 'King Cophetua' are the best known, but there are many important works which are rarely hung, such as 'Clerk Saunders', 'Girls Picking Apples', 'Fair Rosamond and Queen Eleanor', 'Love and the Pilgrim', 'Clara Von Bork', 'Sidonia Von Bork', 'Vespertina Quies', 'The Nativity' triptych, 'The Passing of Venus', and 'The Magic Circle'. The collection is strong in early drawings, and there is a good selection from the other periods.

LONDON   Victoria & Albert Museum: two excellent gouaches, 'The Beguiling of Merlin', 1861, and 'Dorigan of Bretagne', 1871; a good collection of drawings and sketchbooks; many interesting, late unfinished works; 'Pilgrim in the Garden of Vices'; 'The Car of Love'; a very large 'Feast of Peleus'; painted furniture: 'Prioress's Tale' Cabinet, 'Good and Bad Animals' Cabinet; and a large plaque commemorating the death of Laura Lyttleton, 1886.

MANCHESTER   The City Art Gallery: 'Sibylla Delphica', 1877; 'The Sleeping Beauty', 1871; 'Cupid and Psyche', 1867, and various studies.

MANCHESTER   The Whitworth Art Gallery; various studies and cartoons and highly finished drawings in pencil of 'Venus Concordia' and 'Venus Discordia'.

NEWCASTLE UPON TYNE   The Laing Art Gallery: a small collection of early drawings and two stained-glass panels rescued from St Cuthbert's Church.

NEWCASTLE UPON TYNE   The Stone Gallery: a pencil study for 'Apple Blossoms'.

NORTHAMPTON   Central Museum & Art Gallery: four late drawings.

NORWICH   Castle Museum: 'The Annunciation', gouache replica of the painting at Port Sunlight; also a version of 'The Star of Bethlehem' tapestry.

OXFORD   The Ashmolean Museum of Art and Archaeology: an early oil version of 'Danae'; good studies of the early and late periods; the drawings for the 'Cupid and Psyche' illustrations; and two excellent sketchbooks.

OXFORD   Christ Church Art Gallery: two cartoons for the 'St Catherine Window' at Christ Church Cathedral, Oxford.

OXFORD   Exeter College, The Junior Common Room: 'The Passing of Venus' and a few studies; also the 'Flora' and 'Pomona' tapestries.

OXFORD   Lady Margaret Hall: cartoon for stained glass, 'Stella Mututina'; and, in the Chapel, the 'Nativity' triptych.

PLYMOUTH   City Museum & Art Gallery: 'Venus Concordia', an unfinished oil.

PORT SUNLIGHT   Cheshire, The Lady Lever Art Gallery: 'Merlin and Vivien' oil; 'Phyllis and Demophöon' oil; 'Dies Domini' pastel; many late drawings of good quality.

SHEFFIELD   *Graves Art Gallery*: The ten cartoons for 'The Perseus Series', and the oil 'Launcelot at the Chapel of the Holy Grail'.

WIGHTWICK MANOR   near Wolverhampton: the late oil version of 'Love Among the Ruins'; four sketchbooks, and various studies.

YORK   City Art Gallery: 'Two Sleeping Girls', pastel, c. 1873.

AMERICA

CALIFORNIA   Los Angeles, County Museum of Art: 'The Ascension', cartoon for glass at Ruskington, Lincolnshire, 1874, and a sketchbook.

CALIFORNIA   San Diego, Fine Arts Gallery: three drawings, including a superb study for 'The Sirens', 1895.

CONNECTICUT   Hartford, The Wadsworth Atheneum: 'St George', oil, 1877, based upon a design for glass at Peterhouse College, Cambridge.

CONNECTICUT   New Haven, Yale University Art Gallery: various studies and 'Cupid and Psyche' gouache, c. 1866.

DELAWARE   Wilmington, The Society of Fine Arts: 'The Council Chambre', oil, a repeat of the third 'Briar Rose' painting 1872–92;

'The Prioress's Tale', gouache, a repeat of the cabinet painting 1865-98; 'Hymenaeus', oil, 1875; and a 'Head of Nimue' gouache, *c.* 1873 from the painting at the Lady Lever Gallery.

FLORIDA Sarasota, The John and Mable Ringling Museum: 'The Sirens', oil, 1870-98, unfinished.

ILLINOIS Chicago, The Art Institute: gouache study for 'The Doom Fulfilled' of the Perseus series, 1876; a gouache version of 'Cupid's Hunting Fields', *c.* 1885; two cartoons of 'Timothy' and 'Samuel' for glass in Christ Church Cathedral, Oxford, 1872; and a sketchbook of the 1875 period.

INDIANA Indianapolis, Museum of Art: a cartoon, 'Visiting the Sick', for glass at Fochabers, Scotland.

KANSAS Kansas City, Nelson Gallery: gouache of an angel *c.* 1880, based on a window in Oxford Cathedral.

KENTUCKY Louisville, The A. R. Hite Institute: 'Head of a Girl', pencil.

MASSACHUSETTS Boston, The Museum of Fine Arts: 'Cinderella', 1863, and 'Chant d'Amour', 1865, two major early works in gouache; 'Hope', oil, 1896; and a few drawings. The museum also owns seven volumes of reproductions of the artist's work.

MASSACHUSETTS Cambridge, The Fogg Art Gallery, Harvard University: The most important American collection—'The Blessed Damozel', 1860; 'Venus Epithalamia', 1871; 'Day', 'Night', 1869-70; 'The Depths of the Sea', 1887, all gouache; the oils, 'Flamma Vestalis', *c.* 1878; 'Pan and Psyche', 1869-74; 'Danae and the Brazen Tower', 1872; and an impressive collection of studies and sketchbooks. The collection's major work is the series of paintings 'The Days of Creation', 1872-76.

MICHIGAN Ann Arbor, University Museum of Art: pencil study of Andromeda.

MINNESOTA Minneapolis, Institute of Arts: sketchbook.

NEW JERSEY Newark, The Museum: 'The Princess Chained to a Tree', oil, 1866, one of the 'St George' series.

NEW YORK New York City, The Metropolitan Museum of Art: 'Chant d'Amour', oil, 1868-73; some decorative panels on doors; and 'The Backgammon Player's' Cabinet, 1861.

PENNSYLVANIA Philadelphia, Museum of Art: a most important drawing of lilies, 1865.

VIRGINIA Norfolk, Museum of Arts and Sciences: a few interesting drawings for 'The Hours', 'Romaunt de la Rose', etc.

PUERTO RICO

PONCE Museo de Arte: 'Arthur in Avalon' 1881-98, the major work with various studies for it.

AUSTRALIA AND NEW ZEALAND

ADELAIDE The National Gallery of South Australia: various drawings and a large unfinished oil of 'The Rock of Doom' and 'The Doom Fulfilled' on one canvas; also a 'Star of Bethlehem' tapestry.

AUCKLAND City Art Gallery: 'The Fountain of Youth' and 'The Car of Love', pencil.

BRISBANE Queensland Art Gallery: 'Aurora', oil, 1896.

MELBOURNE National Gallery of Victoria: a few drawings and a fine version of 'The Wheel of Fortune', oil.

PERTH Western Australian Art Gallery: some drawings.

WANGANIU The Sargeant Gallery: 'The Fountains of Youth', pencil, and 'Thisbe', an unfinished oil.

CANADA

NEW BRUNSWICK Sackville, Owens Museum, Mount Allison University: two studies for the 'Briar Rose' series in gouache.

TORONTO University Department of Fine Art: 'Mercury and Love', a work mostly by T. M. Rooke; and a fine portrait of 'Miss Fitzgerald', 1884.

VANCOUVER The Centennial Museum: 'Fides', 1867.

SOUTH AFRICA

CAPE TOWN National Gallery of South Africa: 'The Wood Nymph', oil, 1883; 'Love Disguised as Reason', gouache, 1870; a cartoon for 'The Sirens'; and two stained-glass designs.

BELGIUM

BRUSSELS Le Musée d'Art Moderne: 'The Wedding of Psyche', oil, 1894-95.

FRANCE

PARIS Le Musée National d'Art Moderne: 'The King's Daughter', gouache; the first of the 'St George' series; and some excellent studies of heads for 'Fortune'.

PORTUGAL

LISBON The Calouste Gulbenkian Gallery: two superb oils; 'The Bath of Venus', 1873-88, and 'The Mirror of Venus', 1873-77.

GERMANY

KARLSRUHE The Staatsgalerie: stained-glass windows from Stonehouse, Kent.

STUTTGART The Staatsgalerie: the unique 'Perseus' series, Burne-Jones's most important contribution to the art of mural painting.

Select Bibliography

BURNE-JONES

G. B. J. (Georgiana Burne-Jones), *Memorials of Edward Burne-Jones*, in two vols., Macmillan, London, 1904. The most important source book, sympathetic and well written, basically biographical.

Malcolm Bell, *Sir Edward Burne-Jones: A Record and Review*, George Bell, London, 1892. A comprehensive review, erroneous in detail.

Fortunée de Lisle, *Burne-Jones*, Methuen, London, 1904.

Julia Cartwright, *The Life and Work of Sir E. Burne-Jones, Bart (Art Annual* 1894), published by *The Art Journal*.

Aymer Vallance, *The Decorative Art of Sir Edward Burne-Jones, Baronet (Art Annual* 1900), published by *The Art Journal*.

T. Martin Wood, *Drawings of Sir Edward Burne-Jones*, Newnes, London, 1907.

Malcolm Bell, *Sir Edward Burne-Jones* (Newnes Art Library), Newnes, London, 1907.

Arsene Alexandre, Sir Edward Burne-Jones (Newnes Art Library, Second Series), Newnes, London, 1907.

J. Comyns Carr, *Coasting Bohemia*, Macmillan, London, 1914. Perhaps the best essay on Burne-Jones is contained in this collections of writings by Carr.

O. von Schleinitz, *Burne-Jones* (the Kunstler-Monographien series) Verlhagen ung Klassing, Bielefeld and Leipzig, 1901.

W. Graham Roberton, *Time Was*, Hamish Hamilton, London, 1931.

Frances Horner, *Time Remembered*, Heinemann, London, 1933.

WILLIAM MORRIS

J. W. Mackail, *The Life of William Morris*, Longmans, Green & Co, London, 1899.

Written at the instigation of Burne-Jones.

Paul Thompson, *The Work of William Morris*, Heinemann, London, 1967.

Philip Henderson, *William Morris, His Life Work and Friends*, Thames and Hudson, London, 1967.

D. G. ROSSETTI

Virginia Surtees, *The Paintings and Drawings of Dante Gabriel Rossetti, a catalogue raisonné*, Clarendon Press, Oxford, 1971.

David Larg, *Trial by Virgins*, Peter Davies, London, 1933.

Oswald Doughty, *A Victorian Romantic: Dante Gabriel Rossetti*, Frederick Muller, London, 1949.

THE PRE-RAPHAELITES

John Dixon Hunt, *The Pre-Raphaelite Imagination 1848–1900*, Routledge and Kegan Paul, London, 1968. An erudite exploration of the artists' imagery.

Robin Ironside and John Gere, *Pre-Raphaelite Painters*, Phaidon, London, 1948.

Renato Barilli, *I Preraffaelliti*, Fratelli Fabri, Milan, 1967. A pleasant collection of paintings and designs.

Percy Bate, *The English Pre-Raphaelite Painters, Their Associates and Successors*, Bell, London, 1910. An unusually broad review for its date.

GENERAL

Linda Nochlin, *Realism*, Penguin Books, London, 1971.

John Milner, *Symbolists and Decadents*, Studio Vista, London, 1971.

Nikolaus Pevsner, *Pioneers of Modern Design*,

Faber, London, 1936. Reprint Penguin, London, 1968.

Robert Schmutzler, *Art Nouveau*, Thames and Hudson, London, 1962.

John W. Dodds, *The Age of Paradox : A*

Biography of England, 1841–51, Gollancz, London, 1953.

William E. Fredeman, *Preraphaelitism, a Bibliocritical Study*, Harvard University Press, 1965.

Index

Index

Prepared by Brenda Hall, M.A.
Registered Indexer of the Society of Indexers

NOTE:
References in normal type (e.g. 23) are to page numbers.

References in italic type (e.g. *23*) are to the black and white illustrations
or to material contained in the captions for those illustrations.

References in bold type (e.g. **23**) are to the colour plates or to
material contained in the captions for the colour plates.